THE FLEET AIR ARM HANDBOOK
1939–1945

DAVID WRAGG

SUTTON PUBLISHING

First published in the United Kingdom in 2001 by
Sutton Publishing Limited · Phoenix Mill
Thrupp · Stroud · Gloucestershire · GL5 2BU

This paperback edition first published in 2003

British Library Cataloguing in Publication Data
A catalogue record for this book is available from the British Library

ISBN 0 7509 3430 1

Typesetting and origination by
Sutton Publishing Limited.
Printed and bound in England by
J.H. Haynes & Co. Ltd, Sparkford.

To the memory of
Lt (SD) S.H. 'Harry' Wragg RN
1918–2001

CONTENTS

INTRODUCTION

When I wrote the introduction to the original hardback edition of this book, I lamented the fact that the Royal Navy had just two operational aircraft carriers, and that the need for work on one of them meant that at one stage the service was down to just one ship, HMS *Illustrious*. Since then, history has repeated itself, except for the fact that the one ship was HMS *Ark Royal*, despatched to the gulf with just a frigate and a destroyer as an escort, rather than the four or, ideally, six ships that such a valuable asset warrants. During World War Two, HMS *Courageous* was lost with just such inadequate protection.

The Royal Navy has been promised two new large aircraft carriers, bigger than any it has had so far, but this boost has to be set against plans to retire the Sea Harriers in 2006, leaving any task force without air defence for up to six years while F-35 deliveries are awaited. Given the strains on the defence budget, and a Treasury without any appreciation of the true costs of failing to provide adequate defences, one can only hope that the new ships and aircraft do arrive, and do not suffer the same fate as the ill-fated CVA01 project.

In World War Two, the Royal Navy was able to hold its own in the attack from the outset thanks to the skill and courage of the aircrew flying the lumbering Fairey Swordfish, but fighter protection of the Fleet was inadequate until high performance fighters arrived.

All of this has echoes of the situation that bedevilled British naval aviation between the two world wars. The result was that the Royal Navy in 1939 had new ships on order that were to be outstanding, but he development and procurement of aircraft for the Royal Navy had been badly neglected.

Worse, RAF control meant that the opportunity for the Royal Navy to have a generation of senior officers familiar with the use of air power at sea was lost. How much more effective might the Fleet Air Arm have been at the outset of the Second World War had the situation been otherwise? HMS *Courageous* might not have been lost, and we almost certainly would not have lost HMS *Glorious*. It is also unlikely that HMS *Hermes*, *Prince of Wales* and *Repulse* would have been lost either.

Naval aviators are sailors who fly, not aviators who go to sea. They need to develop the instinct to use aviation in a maritime context. This applies even when operations from the carrier are likely to be over land and against shore-based targets, for they must be happy at sea and willing to cope with the cramped conditions of warship life. They must be advocates of the carrier, able to use the two-thirds of the world's surface that is covered by water, arriving ready for operations, and not needing to establish an airfield, its defences and its facilities. For these reasons, naval aviators are not part of some homogenous defence force, but a cadre of very special people. In countries that have attempted to establish defence forces in preference to distinct navies, armies and air forces, it has only worked with very small defence forces in which everything is a branch of the army, and has never worked well with larger countries, as the Canadian experience has shown.

It would be good to be able to look at the Fleet Air Arm between 1939 and 1945, and say that the lessons have been learnt, and that we have power projection and a defence posture with a strong deterrent effect. Perhaps we could say this in 1961, when

HMS *Victorious* was able to forestall a threatened Iraqi invasion of Kuwait, even providing fighter control for RAF fighters when they did arrive, preventing what could have been an earlier Gulf War. At the time, we had five aircraft carriers and two commando carrriers. Today, the entire Fleet Air Arm fighter strength could fit on the smallest of those carriers. Yet the present British Government sees the the armed services as providing a strong expeditionary force! How is it that the United States, with 300 million people, can afford to keep eleven large aircraft carriers, each twice the size of the largest carriers ever operated by the Royal Navy, and one in reserve, while with 60 million people, we struggle to keep two operational, with a third in reserve, and each capable of carrying just twenty aircraft?

David Wragg
Edinburgh
July 2003

ACKNOWLEDGEMENTS

In researching and compiling any such book as this, an author is heavily dependent on the help and assistance of many others. In particular, I am indebted for the provision of photographs and other material to Lord Kilbracken, who, as John Godley, flew as an RNVR pilot, eventually reaching the rank of Lieutenant-Commander, during the war; to Douglas Macdonald of the Fleet Air Arm Officers' Association for putting me in touch with Lord Kilbracken and others; to Mrs Marjorie Schupke, for photographs of her brother, Sub Lt Gordon Maynard, RNVR, who lost his life in action while flying with 1836 Squadron off HMS *Victorious*; to my father, Lt S.H. 'Harry' Wragg, RN, for his collection of wartime photographs and other material.

Inevitably, official and semi-official sources have also been invaluable. Like many other researchers, I am grateful to Jerry Shore, Curator and Archivist of the Fleet Air Arm Museum, and his enthusiastic team, for help and advice, and a warm welcome. I must also thank Ian Carter of the IWM; Mike Schwarz of Vought Aircraft; Laura Barrett-Oliver of Northrop Grumman and Lawrence Feliu of the Northrop Grumman History Centre for their help; as well as Dawn Stitzel of the United States Naval Institute.

No work on something as vast as our wartime Fleet Air Arm can cover every inch of ground, and for those whose appetite is whetted by this book, I would draw their attention to the bibliography at the back. There are accounts of the air war at sea from every perspective, including the all-important personal accounts, as well as volumes of sheer factual matter, essential for the serious student and the modeller alike.

CHAPTER 1

HISTORICAL BACKGROUND

In peacetime, it may be frankly admitted, seaplanes available for picnics, shooting parties, or as substitutes for captain's galleys when lying at anchor far from shore, would be fun.

Captain, RN, *c.* 1930.

The United States Navy takes the credit for the first flight from a warship, but the Royal Navy invented the aircraft carrier. The origins of the aircraft carrier lay in the realisation that aviation was important to the fleet for reconnaissance, the protection of merchant shipping and for attack. This was coupled with recognition of the poor performance of both the seaplane carrier and of their aircraft, hindered by the drag of their floats and unable to make an effective bomber, or have the speed and rate of climb to become an effective fighter. Seaplane carriers lacked the speed to keep up with the fleet or the capacity for an adequate number of aircraft, largely because they were converted merchant vessels.

By the outbreak of war, British naval officers had been experimenting with aircraft for some four years. Despite a certain coolness towards aviation among many senior officers, aircraft had even taken part in exercises. However, the new form of warfare had its adherents among many in the Royal Navy and Royal Marines. In between the enthusiasts and the traditionalists, many of whom would have agreed whole heartedly with one British Army officer who had complained that

aircraft spoiled an exercise, there were those who saw the aeroplane as having a limited role as the eyes of the fleet.

More far-sighted views must have prevailed, however, for as early as Christmas Day 1914, seven seaplanes left the seaplane carriers, HMS *Engadine, Riviera* and *Empress* to bomb the German airship hangars at Nordholz, near Cuxhaven.

Many solutions were tried before the first aircraft carrier appeared. One of these was to launch aircraft from lighters towed at speed by destroyers. This at least got landplane fighters into the air, but as with the catapult-launched fighters of the Second World War, the aircraft had to be ditched after completing its sortie.

In an attempt to obtain a ship that could keep up with the fleet, the Cunard liner *Campania*, at 18,000 tons much larger and faster than the existing seaplane carriers, was requisitioned. When she joined the fleet in 1915, HMS *Campania* had a 200-ft wooden flight deck built over her forecastle. Fairey's new seaplane, also named the Campania, was able to take off using wheeled trolleys placed under the floats and could be recovered after landing in the sea. The following year, the take off platform was lengthened after the ship's fore-funnel had been divided. The ship and aircraft were an improvement over anything that had gone before, but both were still too slow, the Fairey Campania only had a cruising speed of 80 mph and a ceiling of 2,000 ft. The aircraft's great strength was its three-hour endurance, so that it had potential for reconnaissance, but not as a fighter.

Birth of the Aircraft Carrier

However, HMS *Campania* was a step forward. A larger and faster ship combined with landplanes was the obvious solution. No one had any idea of what the end result would be like, but the decision was taken to convert one of three battlecruisers. These were seen as ideal for conversion, larger than cruisers and faster than battleships, lacking the latter's heavy protective armour.

While still under construction, the decision was taken to modify the 22,000-ton HMS *Furious*, by removing her forward turret and building a flight deck forward. The single aft turret was retained at first. However, had she been completed as originally planned, HMS *Furious* would have been an embarrassment, having 18-in guns rather than the 15-in guns of her two sisters; when they were fired, her lightly built hull rippled! The aft 18-in gun turret was also removed and replaced with a deck for landing on. This was seen as necessary after Sqdn Cdr (the RNAS equivalent of Lieutenant Commander) Dunning had proved that landing on a ship underway at sea was possible, but, unfortunately, he drowned when attempting to repeat the performance a few days later. The decking continued on either side of her funnel and bridge so that aircraft could be manhandled from the landing-on deck to the flying-off deck. Modified in this way, *Furious* launched the first successful attack from an aircraft

carrier on 19 July 1918, when seven Sopwith Camels attacked the airship sheds at Tondern in northern Germany, destroying the airships *L.54* and *L.60*.

Furious was far from being a satisfactory carrier by later standards. She had arrester wires that ran fore and aft to catch hooks on the undercarriage spreader bar. For aircraft failing to catch the wires, there was a large net as a last resort. The landing-on deck was sometimes used to carry a reconnaissance airship. Ideas on carrier design were still fluid at this stage and *Furious* was to be rebuilt, modified and then modernised, as time went on.

A second aircraft carrier was completed before the end of the war. HMS *Argus* was an Italian liner under construction, but was requisitioned and completed as an aircraft carrier. Smaller and slightly slower than *Furious*, *Argus* weighed 15,775 tons and had a maximum speed of 20 knots; she joined the fleet in September 1918, just two months before the Armistice. Even with the landing-on deck, experience with *Furious* had shown that turbulence from the superstructure was a problem, so the new carrier did not have any superstructure. The bridge and wheelhouse were mounted on the starboard side on a lift that had to be put down during flying operations, making manoeuvring difficult. Instead of funnels, boiler room smoke was expelled through ducts at the stern, making landing difficult and unpleasant.

Peacetime saw a demand for naval air power. Allied participation in the Russian Civil War, initially to keep Russia in the war against the Central Powers, and then in support of the White Russians, saw aircraft from the seaplane tender, HMS *Vindictive*, bombing the Red Fleet in Kronstadt Harbour on 18 August 1919.

Another effect of the First World War was the collapse of Turkish rule throughout

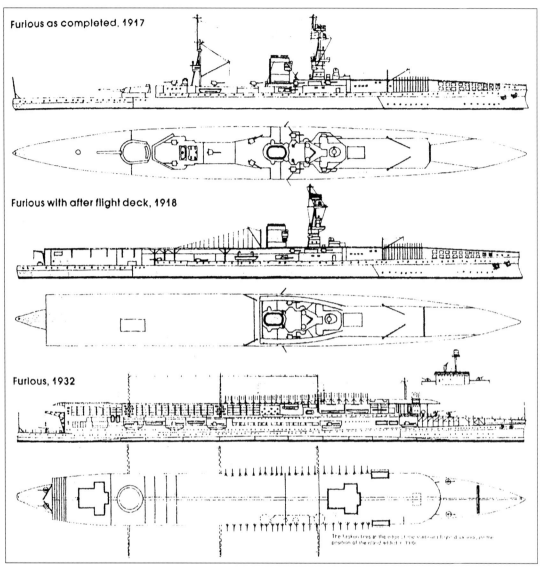

Furious as completed, 1917

Furious with after flight deck, 1918

Furious, 1932

The evolution of the aircraft carrier, showing the series of changes to the battlecruiser *Furious*, culminating in the addition of an island before the outbreak of war.

much of the Middle East and then revolution within Turkey itself. In 1920 Turkish nationalists fought Greek forces in european Turkey and then came face to face with British occupation forces in Constantinople, now Istanbul, and Chanak. The seaplane carrier HMS *Ark Royal*, was dispatched from Egypt with five Fairey IIID seaplanes.

The ship evacuated Army units in Chanak and then its aircraft flew spotter patrols, until HMS *Argus* arrived with Nieuport Nightjars and additional Fairey IIIDs.

It was clear that in solving many of the problems inherent in the early conversions of *Furious*, fresh problems had been created with *Argus*. The third aircraft carrier was

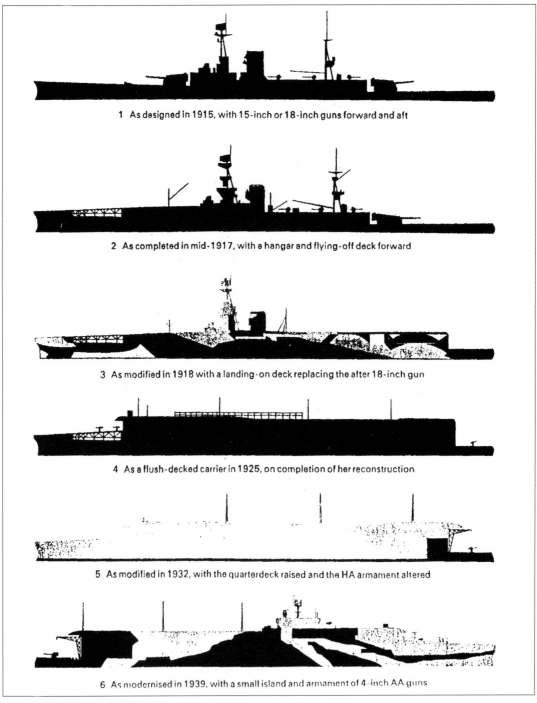

1 As designed in 1915, with 15-inch or 18-inch guns forward and aft

2 As completed in mid-1917, with a hangar and flying-off deck forward

3 As modified in 1918 with a landing-on deck replacing the after 18-inch gun

4 As a flush-decked carrier in 1925, on completion of her reconstruction

5 As modified in 1932, with the quarterdeck raised and the HA armament altered

6 As modernised in 1939, with a small island and armament of 4-inch AA guns

The evolution of the aircraft carrier, showing *Furious* in silhouette.

Slow and dated by 1939, the converted battleship *Eagle* nevertheless provided sterling service during the early years of the war, until lost on the famous Malta convoy, Operation Pedestal. (*FAAM Carrier E/165*)

also to be a conversion. HMS *Eagle*, 22,600 tons, commissioned in February 1924, was based on the Chilean battleship, *Almirante Cochrane*, incomplete as work had been suspended on the outbreak of war. This was the first ship to conform to modern ideas on the appearance and layout of an aircraft carrier, with the now familiar starboard side 'island'. She also introduced the cambered 'round down', in a further attempt to minimise turbulence.

The fourth carrier, HMS *Hermes*, was the first to be designed from the keel up. Although laid down in January 1918, displacing just 10,850 tons, her construction was delayed while decisions were taken on the ideal layout for an aircraft carrier. With her hull plated up to flight deck level, her starboard island and single large funnel, *Hermes* appeared to be the classic aircraft carrier.

The starboard island was set to become the standard, although the Japanese were also to experiment with port side islands. It has been suggested that the starboard island was chosen for traditional reasons, because before the advent of the ship's wheel, vessels were steered by a large oar on the starboard, or 'steerboard' side. However, there was another reason. Experience had shown that pilots in trouble tended, for reasons that are still not fully understood, to veer to port and a starboard position for the island was the safest. The Japanese *Akagi* and *Hiryu*, had port side islands so that they could operate in pairs with ships with starboard islands, allowing aircraft to operate on different approach patterns without congestion. Reports suggest that they had double the number of serious flight deck accidents as a result.

THE STRUGGLE FOR CONTROL OF NAVAL AVIATION

Other changes had been taking place that had seriously affected the development of naval aviation. At the height of the First World War, the British Government had commissioned the South African General and statesman, Smuts, to produce a report on the future of military aviation. Before the war, for a short period, the RFC had contained all service aviation, operating through Naval and Army wings. However, during the war years, there had been overlap between the role of the Royal Naval Air Service and the Royal Flying Corps. Smuts favoured a single air service, free of Naval and Army influences. Thus it was that, on 1 April 1918, the RNAS and RFC were merged into the new Royal Air Force.

The importance of naval aviation by this time can be seen from the fact that on 1 April 1918, 2,500 aircraft and 55,000 officers and men were transferred from the Royal Navy into the new Royal Air Force. This compares with a total strength for the Royal Navy and Royal Marines of 43,700 today.

The decision was made without the benefit of hindsight and possibly also without a true understanding of the different requirements of Naval and Army aviation, or organic and strategic air power, and largely because so few would foresee the potential of air power. It created a strong, strategic air service, but it denied the Royal Navy and the British Army the air power they needed and failed to force senior officers in both services to understand air power.

Aircrew and maintainers aboard the aircraft carriers and seaplane carriers or tenders, all became members of the Royal Air Force, co-existing alongside the general service officers and ratings that formed the ships' companies of the carriers. The only exception to this arrangement was personnel concerned with the operation of seaplanes and flying boats, which were operated from battleships and cruisers, who remained naval aviators. These craft provided a reconnaissance and spotter role for the guns of the fleet. Aboard the carriers, however, there was a demarcation line between the seafarers and the aviators. This was emphasised to a greater extent by the system under which RAF stations in the Mediterranean and Far East included flights that could operate from aircraft carriers in those areas. In practical terms, units were under Admiralty control while afloat and Air Ministry control while ashore.

In the immediate postwar period, the RAF suffered a large reduction in strength, dropping quickly to just twelve squadrons. This was partly due to the desire to create a new service, free from the rivalries between former RFC and former RNAS personnel, but it also reflected a lack of awareness of the potential and importance of air power. Reconstruction and expansion was inhibited by the austerity measures of the Depression years. Struggling to find a role, the RAF discovered the concept of air control, helping and to some extent relieving ground forces of much of the work needed to maintain order in Mesopotamia, in what is now Iraq. This was accorded a higher priority than maritime aviation.

Following the recommendations of the Balfour Committee of 1923, which examined Royal Navy and Royal Air Force co-operation, the Fleet Air Arm of the Royal Air Force was formed, with five squadrons belonging to what was then known as RAF Coastal Area, becoming Coastal Command in 1936.

CREATING THE CARRIER FLEET

International efforts to guarantee peace and disarmament after the First World War resulted in several initiatives, including the creation of the League of Nations in 1920. The Washington Naval Treaty of 1922 attempted to restrict the size of warships, with an upper limit of 27,000 tons on new construction and limits on armaments, as well as on the total tonnage allowed to each of the signatories for each type of warship and for their overall fleets. The upper tonnage for a cruiser, for example, was set at 10,000 tons. The Royal Navy and United States Navy were both allocated a maximum aircraft carrier tonnage of 135,000 tons, out of a maximum fleet tonnage of 525,000 tons each.

The high proportion of the total tonnage taken by aircraft carriers suggested that at least some foresaw the significance of this new arrival on the naval scene. More significantly, the Treaty provided an indirect and possibly unintentional, stimulus to aircraft carrier construction by its limits on the size of the battlecruiser fleets, requiring Britain, the United States and Japan to cut their battlecruiser tonnage. Each of these three nations converted two battlecruisers into aircraft carriers; the United States and Japan each had two incomplete ships to convert, the Royal Navy took the two sister ships of HMS *Furious*, the 15-in gun HMS *Courageous* and *Glorious*.

By this time, HMS *Furious* had undergone extensive reconstruction, having rejoined

A pre-war shot of *Furious* at speed, taken from an aircraft that has just taken off from her. (*via S.H. Wragg*)

The most modern carrier on the outbreak of war was *Ark Royal*, whose three lifts and twin catapults can be seen clearly in this aerial shot. (*via S.H. Wragg*)

the fleet in 1925 as a flush-decked aircraft carrier, with a separate take-off deck leading from the hangar deck. Her two sisters reflected changing ideas on aircraft carrier design, having a separate take-off deck from the hangar, but with the more conventional starboard island. Both ships had a displacement of 22,500 tons and a maximum speed of around 30 knots. *Courageous* entered service in May 1928 and was joined by her sister in March 1930. During their short lives, the take-off decks fell into disuse as aircraft sizes grew and they were fitted with accelerators to assist aircraft take off.

The British wanted to see the maximum size for aircraft carriers reduced from the 27,000 tons of the Washington Treaty to 22,000 tons. This was a strange decision, since many of the participants at the London Naval Conference of 1930 had been in favour of raising the limits. It was clear that Japan would not agree to be bound by these, even before she renounced the treaty conditions in 1934. The British approach meant that her next aircraft carrier, and only the second to be laid down as such, had to be limited to 22,000 tons displacement. The designers of the new HMS *Ark Royal* went to considerable lengths to ensure that the ship made good use of the available tonnage. Weight was reduced by welding, reducing the armour, except for some around the hangar and by extending the flight deck beyond the hull fore and aft to provide the maximum length. The hull was plated up to flight deck level at both the bow and the stern. She was fitted with two accelerators, and, unusually in a British carrier, three lifts. She was designed to accommodate seventy-two aircraft, although for operations, sixty was more realistic and this number was reduced as the size of aircraft increased. The *Ark Royal* had a good turn of speed, being capable of 32 knots.

By the time the new carrier joined the fleet in November 1938, the first ships of a new class were under construction; a new fast, armoured carrier. Four of the new carriers were ordered in 1936, intended as replacements for the *Argus, Furious, Eagle* and *Hermes*. Two more were ordered in 1937. It was soon realised that the new ships would not be replacements, but instead they would be additions to the fleet, which would need every ship as war loomed closer.

The new carriers had an armoured flight deck and hangar deck, providing an armoured box capable of withstanding heavy punishment. Unusually they had triple screws. Despite the heavier

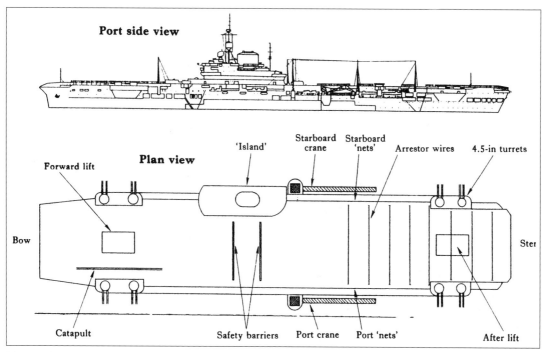

The evolution of the aircraft carrier, showing *Illustrious*, the most modern carrier of her day.

displacement of 23,000 tons, their aircraft capacity was well below that of the *Ark Royal*. The six new ships, HMS *Illustrious, Victorious, Formidable, Indomitable, Implacable* and *Indefatigable*, differed in many important features and are described more fully in chapter twelve. In addition to having accelerators, the barrier landing system was introduced to the Royal Navy, so that aircraft missing the arrester wires were stopped before reaching the deck forward, which could seldom be kept empty as aircraft returned from their missions.

A seventh ship, the maintenance carrier HMS *Unicorn*, had just two screws and increased headroom in her hangars. She was the forerunner of light fleet carriers of the future.

On 30 July 1937, The Minister for the Coordination of Defence, Sir Thomas Inskip, recommended to the government that the Fleet Air Arm be handed over to the

Admiralty. This became known as the 'Inskip Award'. Nevertheless, the Admiralty did not formally take control until 24 May 1939. In 1938 the Admiralty had been authorised by Parliament to implement a 300 per cent increase in Fleet Air Arm personnel.

The new ships and the expansion of the fleet may have looked as if the Royal Navy was finally equipping its Fleet Air Arm for war, but the reality was different. There were few naval aviators and maintenance personnel, hardly any naval air stations and large numbers of these were to be built from scratch, with some, in unsuitable sites for the bombers and fighters of the RAF, transferred to naval control, and there were no high performance naval aircraft. For offensive purposes, the Fairey Swordfish biplane was to be the mainstay of the fleet, and for defensive purposes, there were two aircraft, the monoplane Blackburn Roc and the Gloster Sea Gladiator, another biplane.

CHAPTER 2

ENGAGING THE ENEMY MORE CLOSELY

The Swordfish relies on her Peggy,
The modified Taurus ain't sound.
So the Swordfish flies off on her missions
And the Albacore stays on the ground.

Bring back, bring back,
Oh bring back my Stringbag to me . . .

The Fleet Air Arm Song Book

Historians make much of the so-called 'phoney war', the period between the outbreak of war and the invasion of Denmark and Norway, and then France and the Low Countries, that marked the real beginning of hostilities. However, for the Royal Navy, there was no phoney war. The Royal Navy was not simply at action stations, but engaged in operations from the outset, and this continued beyond the surrender of Japan, as it fell to British warships to take the surrender of Japanese forces in Hong Kong, Singapore and Malaya. The Fleet Air Arm was involved from beginning to end.

In home waters, the Fleet Air Arm's shore-based aircraft provided cover for convoys from the beginning of the war in Europe on 3 September 1939, until German surrender on 8 May 1945. At times Fleet Air Arm squadrons were placed under RAF Coastal Command control to ensure better integration. The FAA complemented the work of the RAF, with the latter using larger twin-engined, and in due course, four-engined long range aircraft, while the FAA operated over shorter ranges in the North Sea and the English Channel.

According to the Imperial War Museum the Fleet Air Arm entered the Second World War with 232 aircraft and 360 qualified pilots, with another 332 under training. The Royal Navy had seven aircraft carriers, of which four, HMS *Argus, Eagle, Furious* and *Hermes,* had officially been due to retire, but had been kept in service as war clouds gathered over Europe. This meant that, while the first of the Illustrious-class carriers was awaited, the best ships were the converted battlecruisers, HMS *Courageous* and *Glorious,* and the new *Ark Royal.* However, not one of these three ships was to survive the first two years of war. There was also the seaplane carrier, HMS *Pegasus,* mainly used for training aircrew for the catapult flights aboard cruisers and battleships.

There were few Royal Naval Air Stations at the outset. HMS *Daedalus* at Lee-on-Solent, on the Hampshire coast was one of them. Not only was Lee convenient for the ships of the fleet based at Portsmouth, it also had a slipway for seaplanes and amphibians. Meanwhile, Yeovilton was under construction and the Fleet Air Arm had lodging facilities at RAF bases. Initially, the RN could not increase its aircrew strength without RAF cooperation, as basic and intermediate training was entirely in the hands of the RAF. Ground crew were also trained by the RAF.

EARLY LOSSES

In contrast to the First World War, the Royal Navy was quick to instigate a convoy system to protect Britain's vital supplies from Germany's substantial and growing U-boat fleet and surface raiders. The initial approach was to deploy ships on anti-submarine sweeps, an operation that could be compared with looking for the proverbial needle in a haystack. It was on one of these sweeps that the carrier, HMS *Courageous* was lost, on 17 September 1939, a fortnight after the war had started. Poorly protected, with

First of many carrier casualties in the war was *Courageous*, lost to enemy submarine action within a fortnight of the war starting.

just two escorting destroyers, the ship's Swordfish aircraft had spent the day on anti-submarine patrols over the Western Approaches, to the south-west of Ireland. The last aircraft had landed on for the night, when *U-29* fired a salvo of three torpedoes at the ship, of which two hit her, sinking her in just twenty minutes with the loss of 500 men.

The loss of such a major fleet unit so early in the war was only partly compensated for by the loss of the German pocket battleship, or *panzerschiff, Admiral Graf Spee*, in the Battle of the River Plate, scuttled in Montevideo Roads on 17 December 1939. The German ship proved to be insufficiently armoured to withstand shellfire from the British heavy cruiser *Exeter* and her two supporting light cruisers during the battle on 13 December. The Fleet Air Arm was, of course, limited to a reconnaissance role for this operation, with catapult-launched aircraft of 700 Squadron playing their usual part. However, even the catapult flights had less effective aircraft than might have been possible, since they compared unfavourably with the performance of their opposite numbers serving with the German Navy.

When Germany invaded Denmark and Norway on 9 April 1940, it was clear that Denmark was a lost cause as German forces swept over the border, while a landing force sailed into the harbour at Copenhagen. Norway was a different matter, however. The size of the country and the inhospitable terrain – high mountains interspersed with fjords with deep snow still on the ground – meant that German forces could be challenged. Despite landings by air and sea, German forces could not seize enough of the country quickly, while the loss of the heavy cruiser *Blücher* at Oslo, with the German headquarters' staff, gave the King and the Norwegian Government time to flee the city and organise resistance. Britain and France quickly assembled an

initial expeditionary force of 13,000 men, supported by air and naval forces, although it was estimated that an Army of 50,000 would be needed to liberate the country.

Difficult terrain and the shortage of good air bases ashore meant that the Norwegian campaign was ideal for the aircraft carrier, had the Royal Navy been equipped with high performance aircraft. Initially, aircraft were provided by HMS *Furious*, which also acted as an aircraft transport. However, she did not have any fighters and the Fleet Air Arm, at that time, had nothing heavier than a 500-lb bomb. During the campaign, six Supermarine Walruses from 701 Squadron were based ashore at Harstad.

At first, all went well. Successful actions by destroyers and the battleship *Warspite* were matched on 10 April when twenty Blackburn Sea Skuas, of 800 and 803 Squadrons operating from Hatston, on Orkney, sunk the cruiser *Konigsberg* at Bergen: the first sinking of a major operational warship by aircraft. These aircraft had been left behind in March, when *Ark Royal* had been sent to the Mediterranean.

Ark Royal and *Glorious* were hastily recalled and sent to operate off Norway. *Ark Royal* sent Swordfish of 810, 820 and 821 Squadrons to attack targets ashore, bombing the airfield at Vaernes, as well as maintaining anti-shipping and anti-submarine patrols. Nevertheless, despite these successes and the basing ashore of RAF Hurricane and Gladiator fighters, the battle ashore went against the Allies. Eventually, after the invasion of France and the Low Countries, it was decided to evacuate Norway to reinforce France, now under heavy attack by fast moving German forces.

The evacuation was covered and then assisted by *Ark Royal* and *Glorious*. Ashore, the RAF had been told to destroy their aircraft and join the evacuation, but conscious of the need to save as many aircraft as possible, especially the Hurricanes, it was decided to fly these to the carriers. Despite her shorter deck, *Glorious* was chosen for Hurricanes because her larger lifts meant that the aircraft, which did not have folding wings, could be struck down into her hangars without having their wings removed, which would take time. The alternative was to leave the aircraft to obstruct the flight deck, which could prevent further operations by the ship's aircraft. A brave decision, since the Hurricanes did not have arrester hooks and their pilots were not carrier-trained, instead they used sandbags to weight down the tail wheels, and successfully landed on the carrier, proving that high performance fighters were capable of carrier operations.

Short of fuel, *Glorious* sailed from Norway on 8 June, steaming at a stately 17 knots, considered fast enough to protect her from submarine attack. Aircraft were struck down into the hangar and patrols were not flown, while torpedoes and other munitions were also removed. The ship lacked radar, but a watch was not maintained from the crow's nest. At 16:00, the two German battle-cruisers, *Scharnhorst* and *Gneisenau*, among the few enemy ships to be fitted with radar, opened fire at 28,000 yds with their 11-in guns. The carrier was outgunned. Frantic attempts were made to range her aircraft on the deck, and five Swordfish were on the deck by 16:15 when the first German shells scored their first hit, destroying the aircraft. Further shells then penetrated the flight deck and exploded among the Hurricanes on the hangar deck, detonating fuel and ammunition still in the aircraft. In an instant, the hangar deck was an inferno. Although the ship increased speed to 27 knots, by 17:00, when a salvo destroyed the bridge, she was a pillar of smoke. Her escorting destroyers, *Ardent* and *Acasta*, were lost making a valiant torpedo attack on the

German propaganda had *Ark Royal* sunk many times – exactly how they explained the real sinking must have been interesting! (*via S.H. Wragg*)

Scharnhorst, with one of *Acasta*'s torpedoes damaging the battlecruiser, although this was not known at the time.

Glorious finally sank at 18:00. Some believe that as many as 900 of her ship's company and embarked RAF aircrew of 1,500 may have survived the sinking, but of those who did escape the sinking, just thirty-nine survived the two days in cold water, without food or drink, before they were rescued.

In an act of retaliation, on 12 June, Skuas of *Ark Royal*'s 800 and 803 Squadrons were sent to attack *Scharnhorst* and *Gneisenau* in the harbour at Trondheim. The aircraft came under heavy attack from defending fighters as well as intense AA fire, so that eight of the fifteen aircraft were lost and their crews either killed or taken prisoner.

This is *Glorious* during the withdrawal from Norway with recently-landed RAF Hurricanes on her flight deck. The next day, she was sunk.

This operation, likened to the Charge of the Light Brigade by one of the participants, did not inflict any damage, as the only bomb to hit *Scharnhorst* failed to explode.

THE FORGOTTEN VICTORY

A number of Fleet Air Arm squadrons provided cover for the evacuation of the British expeditionary Force from Dunkirk, helping to ensure that the vulnerable vessels bringing back the troops were not exposed to German warships. Much has been said about the absence of fighter aircraft over the beaches while troops were waiting to be taken off, but the limited range of the fighters meant that any sustained defensive sweeps would have been difficult for the RAF to mount, as it had already withdrawn its Advanced Air Striking Force from France, and impossible for the Fleet Air Arm, as it had no high performance fighters.

A shortage of aircraft enabled the Fleet Air Arm to second pilots to the RAF for the Battle of Britain. Fifty-six naval airmen flew with RAF Fighter Command during the Battle of Britain, including Sub Lt (later Lt Cdr) Dickie Cork, who was wingman to the great fighter ace, Douglas Bader.

Meanwhile, the squadrons in the carriers were involved in disarming the part of the Vichy French fleet based in North and West Africa. On 3 July 1940, aircraft from *Ark Royal* augmented the guns of the Mediterranean Fleet's battleships at Mers El-Kebir, helping to blow up the old battleship *Bretagne* and cripple the battlecruiser *Dunkerque* and the battleship *Provence*, both of which had to be run aground to save them from sinking. Some ships managed to escape to Toulon, including six destroyers and the battlecruiser *Strasbourg*. Five days later, aircraft from HMS *Hermes* supported two heavy cruisers attacking Dakar in West Africa, damaging the battleship *Richelieu*.

MUSSOLINI GIVES THE LIE TO A FAMOUS GOEBBELS FANTASY

Mussolini's airmen try hard to do what Goebbels so often claimed the Nazis had done—sunk the aircraft-carrier Ark Royal. This picture shows how far the Italian bombs fell from their mark—but no doubt Mussolini will sink the vessel just the same—in his propaganda.

A newspaper cutting shows *Ark Royal* under attack, suggesting that Mussolini will claim that his forces have sunk the ship! (*via S.H. Wragg*)

Security restrictions meant that even British accounts often had to rely upon artists' impressions, such as this showing *Ark Royal* under heavy enemy aerial attack while the fleet sought to assist a crippled submarine. (*via S.H. Wragg*)

After the fall of France, the Fleet Air Arm had the unpleasant task of helping to neutralise the Vichy French Fleet, so recently Allies, in North and East Africa. This Swordfish seaplane successfully landed on *Ark Royal* after the arrester wires had been removed, with news that the French had rejected a British ultimatum. (*via S.H. Wragg*)

Ark Royal under heavy aerial attack – at one stage those on the escorts thought that she had been sunk! (*via S.H. Wragg*)

There was little enthusiasm for an attack on a Navy that had so recently been an ally, but it was recognised that these major fleet units would have been invaluable to the Germans. At this stage of the war it was not clear whether Vichy France would attempt to remain neutral or become an ally of the Germans.

During the Abyssinian crisis in the late 1930s, when Italy attempted to colonise the country now known as Ethiopia, the League of Nations had considered intervention. HMS *Glorious* was the aircraft carrier with the Mediterranean Fleet at the time and it was one of her officers who conceived the idea of an attack on the Italian fleet and its base at Taranto, in southern Italy. These plans were revived after Italy had entered the Second World War on the side of Germany, a few days before the fall of France in June 1940.

The original plan was for two aircraft carriers to be used for the operation, HMS *Illustrious* and *Eagle*, attacking on 21 October 1940, the anniversary of Nelson's great victory at Trafalgar. However, a serious hangar fire aboard *Illustrious* meant that she could not be ready for 21 October. While the fire had cost the ship just two of her aircraft, the rest had been doused with water and had to be completely stripped down before any operation. More seriously, *Eagle* had been attacked by Italian aircraft, which had damaged her aviation fuel system, forcing her to remain at Alexandria for repairs.

These changes meant that the date of the operation had to be put back to the next full moon, the night of 11–12 November, using just *Illustrious*, and instead of using thirty aircraft, a total of twenty-four was assembled, mainly from the ship's 815 and 819 Squadrons, but reinforced by aircraft from *Eagle*'s 813 and 824 Squadrons. For the attack these squadrons had the Swordfish. Extra fuel tanks were fitted to the aircraft, taking the

Revenge! An Italian Savoia Marchetti SM79 *Sparviero* (Hawk) downed by aircraft from *Ark Royal*. (*via S.H. Wragg*)

observers' cockpits and forcing the observers, with their bulky 'Bigsworth' boards (on which charts and maps were displayed during flight) into the less spacious confines of the telegraphist air gunner cockpits.

Using a convoy of reinforcements to Greece as a cover, *Illustrious* left Alexandria on 6 November with a cruiser and destroyer escort. Secrecy was further maintained by successful CAP flown by 806 Squadron, operating Fairey Fulmar I fighters. The squadron's total tally of twenty enemy aircraft during its spell aboard *Illustrious* in the Mediterranean included Italian reconnaissance aircraft shot down en route to Taranto.

The operation seemed fated at first. One Swordfish had to ditch in the sea on the day before the attack, due to engine failure and the following day, another aircraft suffered the same problem. It was discovered that one of the ship's aviation fuel tanks was contaminated by sea water, so all of the aircraft had to have their fuel systems

drained and then refuelled. Another aircraft suffered a failure shortly before the operation started, reducing the number available to just twenty-one.

The raid was led by Lt Cdr Kenneth Williamson, with Lt Norman 'Blood' Scarlett-Streatfield as his observer; it consisted of two waves, the first with twelve aircraft and the second with nine. Finding their way from the flying-off point to Taranto was simplified, despite cloud, once the port's anti-aircraft defences opened up to shoot at a patrolling RAF Short Sunderland flying-boat. The first two aircraft of the first wave were flare droppers, followed closely by Swordfish carrying torpedoes, so that they could strike at the Italian warships silhouetted against the light of the flares. The second wave carried bombs and concentrated on shore installations, including fuel tanks.

Despite the problems, the raid was extremely successful. The battleships

HMS *Attacker* at Taranto in 1945. (*FAAM CARS A/192*)

Littorio, Conte di Cavour and *Caio Duilio* were all sunk, although the *Conte di Cavour* was refloated and repaired at the end of the war. The cruiser *Trento* had a narrow escape, as a bomb crashed through the ship and through the bottom of the hull without exploding. Fuel tanks ashore were damaged. Just two aircraft were shot down and the crew of one of these survived to be taken as prisoners of war.

One of the most spectacular aerial operations of all time, the raid has never been given the recognition it deserved, as senior officers failed to appreciate just how successful it had been. The ship's company tore down the notices announcing the first list of awards, because just six medals were awarded, the highest of these was a DSC for Scarlett-Streatfield. The sailors could be excused for believing that something better was deserved, such as a VC.

BRINGING THE ENEMY TO BATTLE

The Royal Navy's surface fleet was far superior in numbers to those of Germany or Italy, but it was over-stretched, with operations in the Atlantic, the Mediterranean and a presence in the Indian Ocean and Far East. It had convoys to protect. In the face of U-boats and surface raiders, the advantage in the vast expanses of the oceans lay with the predators. German and Italian convoy protection was limited to the Mediterranean, which increasingly resembled a maritime crossroads. German and Italian convoys sought to supply their forces in North Africa, plying north–south in the face of British air and naval attack, often using light forces and submarines based on Malta. British convoys sought to lift the siege that was starving Malta and, at first, supply British forces in North Africa and the Suez

Canal Zone. While the Italian fleet had suffered a major blow after the raid on Taranto, it still presented a threat, and was supported by German and Italian air power that was vastly superior in quantity and quality. Eventually, British supplies and reinforcements for North Africa had to take the lengthy route around the Cape of Good Hope and through the Suez Canal.

Not only did the Fleet Air Arm play its part in convoy protection, it was also involved in many smaller operations against enemy forces. On 17 December 1940, aircraft from *Illustrious* had attacked enemy positions on Rhodes. The following February, Force H raided the Gulf of Genoa, with aircraft from *Ark Royal* bombing Leghorn and dropping mines off the naval base of La Spezia.

Still in the Mediterranean, the Germans managed to convince their Italian allies that the Royal Navy had just one battleship operational, persuading them to send the battleship *Vittorio Veneto* to sea with an escort of cruisers in early 1941. By this time, the Royal Navy had three battleships in the Mediterranean, with the *Warspite* and *Valiant* joined by *Malaya*. *Illustrious* had departed for repairs in the United States, but had been replaced by another new carrier, *Formidable*. She brought a new aircraft, the Fairey Albacore, supposedly an improvement on the Swordfish, but still a biplane, and prone to engine problems. She also had Fairey Fulmar fighters. Altogether, she had just twenty-seven aircraft: thirteen Fulmars, ten Albacores (only half having long-range tanks) and four Swordfish.

As with preparations for the Taranto operation, the encounter with the Italian fleet in the Battle of Cape Matapan raised the problem of confusing enemy agents in Alexandria. On 27 March 1941, many officers were seen to be going ashore with suitcases, awnings were kept spread and

guests were invited to dinner. After dark, those ashore hastily rejoined their ships, awnings were furled and dinner was cancelled. The fleet sailed at 19:00.

At sea the following morning at 06:00, *Formidable* mounted combat air patrols, anti-submarine patrols and sent off her reconnaissance aircraft. At 07:20 four cruisers and four destroyers were sighted by one aircraft, and nineteen minutes later another aircraft reported four cruisers and six destroyers. In fact, at this time, a British destroyer and cruiser force was being pursued by the Italians, led by the cruiser *Trieste*.

Anticipating action, *Formidable* had six Albacores of 826 Squadron ranged on deck from 08:30 and at 09:39 Adm Cunningham ordered these into action, to attack the *Trieste* force of cruisers. By this time, the British cruisers, commanded by Rear Adm Pridham-Wippell, were in trouble, out-gunned by Italian heavy cruisers, who were gaining on them and within range of the heavy guns of the *Vittorio Veneto*. The Albacores arrived at 11:27, escorted by Fulmar fighters, who managed to shoot down one of the two Junkers Ju88 fighter bombers that had appeared and drive off the other one. Pressing home their attack in the face of heavy Italian AA fire, they forced the battleship to break off the attack. A second strike of three Albacores and two Swordfish from 829 Squadron was sent before the first strike returned, keeping the decks clear for the returning aircraft. *Formidable* was attacked shortly after 12:45 by two Italian SM79s, but was not hit by their torpedoes.

In between the attacks by the two waves of carrier-borne aircraft, RAF Blenheim bombers from Greece made four attacks on the Italian fleet, scoring a number of near misses, as they bombed from high altitude, but no hits. Then, at 15:30, Lt Cdr Dalyell-Stead led 829 Squadron into the attack, while the Fulmars distracted the AA gunners and look-outs by machine-gunning the ships. The lead aircraft dropped its torpedo 1,000 yards ahead of the *Vittorio Veneto* as she turned to starboard, only to be hit by the concentrated fire of her AA defences, crashing into the sea just before the torpedo hit the ship. The battleship was holed close to the port outer screw, 15 ft below the waterline, and within minutes her engines stopped. Rapid work by her damage control parties saw her underway again at 17:00, at the reduced speed of 15 knots. Five minutes later, Lt Cdr Gerald Saunt left *Formidable* with six Albacores of 826 and two Swordfish of 829 Squadron, while a Swordfish seaplane from *Warspite* re-established contact with the *Vittorio Veneto* at 18:20. In the gathering darkness, the carrier-borne aircraft, joined by two Swordfish from the naval air station at Maleme in Crete, struck at the Italian fleet, seriously damaging the heavy cruiser *Pola*.

It took the Italian Admiral Iachino, an hour to appreciate just how desperate was the plight of the *Pola*. Not expecting a night battle, he sent the heavy cruisers *Fiume* and *Zara*, with four destroyers, to her aid. Cunningham, meanwhile, had mistaken the radar trace of *Pola* for *Vittorio Veneto*. Before his ships could open fire, the two heavy cruisers and destroyers of the Italian rescue party blundered across the path of the British ships and were hit by the combined 15-in broadsides of the three battleships. Both cruisers were sunk, along with two of the four destroyers, and *Pola* was despatched by torpedoes from two British destroyers.

In the heat of battle, *Formidable* was caught by *Warspite*'s searchlights and the battleship's secondary armament was trained on her, before she was recognised, just in time.

More than 900 Italian survivors were picked up by the British ships the next morning, before German aircraft forced them to retire. In an act of gallantry, Cunningham signalled their position to Rome, allowing Italian ships to take over the rescue, despite the risk of exposing his own position.

Next was the turn of the German Navy, with the Fleet Air Arm again playing an important role in the hunt for and destruction of the German battleship *Bismarck*.

The Kriegsmarine's force of battleships, pocket battleships and battlecruisers presented a serious threat to Britain for the first three years of the Second World War. There was to be no replay of the First World War Battle of Jutland; the Germans knew that they could not win such a confrontation. Instead, the threat came from the danger these ships presented to the convoys. Despite the loss of the *Konigsberg*, the Germans were not too concerned about aerial attack once the ships were at sea, appreciating that a fast moving ship on the open sea presented a difficult target for bombers, while torpedo-bombers were vulnerable to heavy AA fire.

The *Bismarck* and her sister ship, *Tirpitz*, were to be a major preoccupation for the British for as long as the two ships presented a danger. After the war a United States Navy assessment put the *Bismarck* as having a full-load displacement of almost 53,000 metric tonnes, while she had a maximum speed of 30 knots, with two twin 38-cm, approximately 15 in, turrets forward and another two aft. For aerial reconnaissance, she had four Arado Ar196 floatplanes, low-wing monoplanes. Her complement was 2,200, and included German war correspondents.

The first raiding cruise of the *Bismarck* and her escorting heavy cruiser, *Prinz Eugen*, was known to the Germans as Operation Rhine Exercise. The two ships left Gotenhafen in Germany on 18 May 1941, under the command of Adm Gunther Lütjens. Anxious to avoid any encounters with the Home

Fleet, with its northern base now at Scapa Flow, in Orkney, Lütjens sought a route north of Iceland, but called first at Korsfjord, south of Bergen in occupied Norway. This would have been an opportunity for the ship to fill her fuel tanks, which had not been completely filled before leaving Germany, as a hose had given way, interrupting fuelling, but it was not taken. This was to prove to be an incredible blunder.

Once at sea, the German ships were shadowed by the heavy cruisers, *Suffolk* and *Norfolk*, making good use of their radar in heavy weather. Vice Adm Holland took the battlecruiser *Hood* and the new and not fully operational, battleship, *Prince of Wales*, to confront the Germans. On 24 May, the British intercepted the Germans and a classic naval gun battle broke out, during the course of which the *Hood*, with Holland aboard, exploded, with the loss of some 1,500 men, leaving just three survivors. The *Prince of Wales* was forced to break off the fight after receiving several heavy hits from the two German ships. Despite these setbacks, the British had managed to damage the *Bismarck*, hitting her three times and causing a fuel leak that forced Lutjens to break company with the *Prinz Eugen* and attempt to head for St Nazaire, with Brest as an alternative, in occupied France. These problems were bad enough, but they were compounded by battle damage having severed the connections with the ship's forward fuel tanks.

Despite her damage, the *Prince of Wales* joined *Suffolk* and *Norfolk* in shadowing the *Bismarck* throughout 24 May. That evening at 22:30, nine Fairey Swordfish of 825 Squadron, from the new carrier, *Victorious*, found the *Bismarck* and launched a torpedo attack. As the ship increased her speed to 27 knots and zigzagged, the Swordfish launched their torpedoes so that these were heading for the ship from different directions, with at least one hitting the ship,

killing a warrant officer and injuring six ratings. This was followed by a brief gunnery exchange with the *Prince of Wales*, before this was broken off in the fading light.

On 25 May, Vice Adm Somerville left Gibraltar with Force H, which included the aircraft carrier *Ark Royal*, with 800, 808, 818 and 820 Squadrons embarked: the first two operated Fulmar fighters, 818 and 820 operated Swordfish.

Contact with the *Bismarck* was lost early on 26 May, but an RAF Catalina flying-boat rediscovered her later that morning. In rough weather, fifteen Swordfish took off from *Ark Royal* in the early afternoon, while the cruiser *Sheffield* shadowed the German ship. Unfortunately, the Swordfish crews had been briefed that the only ship that they would see would be the *Bismarck*, and dropping out of the clouds, initially attacked *Sheffield* before realising their mistake. Prompt evasive action by the cruiser and problems with the magnetic detonators on the torpedoes, meant that no damage was done.

Again, in low cloud and with poor visibility, a further strike by fifteen Swordfish from *Ark Royal* was launched at 19:15, with the aircraft carrying torpedoes with contact detonators. Directed to the target by *Sheffield*, the aircraft had to return for further directions in the poor visibility, but on the second occasion the sound of *Bismarck*'s heavy AA fire told those aboard the British cruiser that the Swordfish had found their target. Aboard the battleship, Capt Lindemann attempted to zigzag once more, but first two torpedoes struck the ship forward, and then one struck aft, jamming the twin rudders and forcing the ship into a continuous turn to port. All of the Swordfish returned to the carrier.

During the night, British destroyers carrier out a torpedo attack, but failed to inflict any further serious damage on the stricken battleship. During the morning of

Swordfish, armed and ranged on the flight deck of *Ark Royal.* (*via S.H. Wragg*)

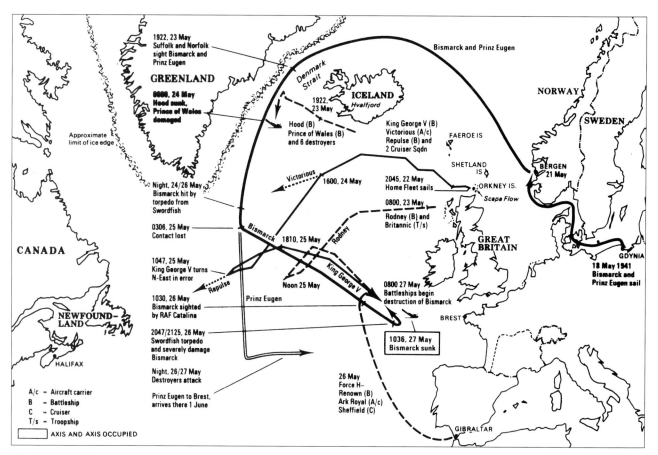

The hunt for the German battleship *Bismarck.* (*FAAM Cars B/81*)

A Fairey Swordfish takes off from *Victorious* for a torpedo attack on *Bismarck*. (*FAAM CARS V/53*)

27 May, the battleships *Rodney* and *King George V* engaged the *Bismarck*, and within ninety minutes she was burning fiercely. Two cruisers attacked with torpedoes, but a further Swordfish attack had to be abandoned, because of the danger of attacking while heavy shellfire was falling on the target from the British battleships.

Eventually, the Germans were forced to abandon ship. Many of her crew reached the water, but the cruiser *Dorsetshire* was forced to cut short a rescue attempt after one of the survivors told his rescuers that U-boats were coming, so that just 115 of the 2,200 men aboard survived.

HELPING THE RUSSIANS

Shortly after the loss of the *Bismarck*, Germany invaded the Soviet Union in Operation Barbarossa. Overnight, the USSR moved from the status of a pariah state, an ally of Germany and partner in the occupation of Poland, to an ally of Britain. Despite the poor performance of the Soviet armed forces, and especially the Soviet Navy, during the invasion, there was political pressure on the British 'to do something'. This fell entirely on the Royal Navy, since there was no opportunity for the Army to relieve the pressure on the Russians, and suitable targets were beyond the reach of RAF Bomber Command. The reluctant Commander-in-Chief, Home Fleet, Adm Sir John Tovey, was urged by Winston Churchill to carry out an attack 'as a gesture in support of our Russian allies to create a diversion on the enemy's northern flank.' The Russians wanted an attack on German shipping.

The most obvious targets were north of the Arctic Circle, at the ports of Petsamo and Kirkenes, since an attack on the Baltic

Victorious in Seydisfjord, Iceland, June 1941, ready for the raid on Petsamo. (*FAAM CARS V/157*)

ports was out of the question. Just two ships were available, *Victorious*, that would attack Kirkenes with the Albacores of 827 and 828 Squadrons and Fulmars of 809 Squadron, and *Furious*, that would attack Petsamo with Swordfish in 812 Squadron, Albacores in 817 Squadron and Fulmars in 800.

However, this was not a re-run of the raid on Taranto. It took place in broad daylight on 22 and 25 July 1941. The terrain around Kirkenes forced aircraft to fly high enough to encounter anti-aircraft fire on the run into the targets, and indeed, good targets were scarce. Worse still, the aircraft from *Victorious* had to fly over a German hospital ship on the way to the target and while they could not attack the hospital ship, it was able to warn the shore defences of their approach. In each case, the Germans were expecting the attackers, and contrary to

briefings that they would only find training aircraft – despite the proximity of the Russian-German front – fighters were waiting. In return for sinking one cargo vessel of just 2,000 tons and setting fire to another at Kirkenes, *Victorious* lost thirteen aircraft. At Petsamo, there were no ships, just empty wharves for the torpedo-bombers to attack, and three aircraft were lost. Worse still, forty-four aircrew were lost, seven of them killed and the rest taken prisoner.

LOSS OF *ARK ROYAL*

At this difficult, early stage of the war, the loss of any major fleet unit was a disaster. In postwar years, the Royal Navy devoted much time and attention to damage control, and even before this, during the war in the Pacific, good damage control did

Ark Royal, crippled after being torpedoed, remained afloat until the following day. (*IWM A6334*)

much to minimise the effects of Japanese Kamikaze attack. It can be argued that poor tactics resulted in the loss of several aircraft carriers during the first two or three years of war, but that others were lost simply due to the fortunes of war.

The sinking of HMS *Ark Royal* off Gibraltar, on 13 November 1941, after being torpedoed by *U-81*, could be seen as sheer bad luck. On the other hand, the ship remained afloat until the next day and many naval officers believe that poor damage control was to blame for her loss when just one life was lost.

THE CHANNEL DASH

As the war progressed, the Fleet Air Arm gained a reputation for effectiveness. Naval air power was something that could never again be dismissed out of hand.

However, surface vessels still posed a threat, including the fast battlecruisers *Scharnhorst* and *Gneisenau.* In 1940, these

ships sunk twenty-two ships, totalling 116,000 tons, as they preyed on the North Atlantic convoys. The Royal Navy had forced them to take refuge at Brest, in occupied France, with the heavy cruiser *Prinz Eugen,* where they were bombed by the RAF. Although the size of bombs and bombing techniques used at this stage meant that they were unlikely to be sunk, damage was inflicted. The German Navy's natural instinct was to bring the ships home in an exercise named Operation Cerberus. However, at this stage, Hitler intervened. He ruled against taking the most obvious route into the Atlantic and around the west of Ireland, instead ordering the ships to take the shortest route, through the English Channel.

The British expected the three ships to be moved and had prepared contingency plans under the heading Operation Fuller. A close watch was maintained on the three ships. In the event, the planning failed, mainly due to intense secrecy, so that too few people who were to have an important role in its

Officers and ratings of the Fleet Air Arm decorated for the part they played in sinking the *Bismarck*. Second from left is Lt Cdr Eugene Esmonde, who was to win a posthumous VC for his action against *Scharnhorst* and *Gneisenau*. Of interest, of the two ratings on the right, the AB has retained his pre-war cap ribbon, and the TAG is wearing white socks and shoes. (*FAAM Personnel/1878*)

implementation even knew of its existence. There were other factors, including a number of those involved playing everything strictly according to orders. There was a lack of initiative, poor communication between the Admiralty and the Air Ministry, poor weather and technical failures, many of which could be ascribed to bad luck.

The RAF failed to detect the break out as the ships sailed from Brest, when technical failures hampered operations on 11 February 1942. When RAF fighter pilots discovered the ship, one pair maintained strict radio silence, wasting valuable time, although when the other pair radioed a warning, they were not believed. Bad weather grounded Coastal Command's torpedo-bombers in Scotland until it was almost too late, while secrecy meant that when they did arrive, it was with bombs rather than torpedoes. Thick fog meant that the heavy coastal artillery at Dover was unable to engage the German force.

It fell to a detachment of 6 Swordfish of 825 Squadron, based at Lee-on-Solent, to face the 3 ships, escorted as they were by a strong CAP of 30 Luftwaffe fighters, continuously refreshed out of a force of 280 aircraft assigned to the operation. Having been moved forward to Manston in Kent, they were put on standby on the afternoon of 12 February, and promised an escort of sixty Spitfires from Fighter Command.

In the gloom of a late winter afternoon, Lt Cdr Eugene Esmonde took his six aircraft into the air. A communications breakdown meant just ten Spitfires turned up. In poor light, they found the three warships and their escort of ten destroyers, several of which were larger than any of their British counterparts. The lumbering Swordfish were caught in a hail of fire from the fighters above and the warships below, but they pressed home a torpedo attack. His aircraft badly damaged as pieces were knocked off it in the heavy fire, Esmonde managed to keep the aircraft airborne long enough to launch its torpedo and then it crashed into the sea. His target, the *Prinz Eugen*, managed to avoid the torpedo. All six Swordfish were shot down, with the loss of Esmonde and twelve others out of the eighteen naval airmen involved in the attack. Esmonde was awarded a posthumous VC.

Having originally planned to have 300 aircraft available for Operation Fuller, the British now panicked and 700 aircraft were put on standby. However, the only aircraft to find the ships after the attack by 825 Squadron were 2 RAF Beauforts, who also missed the ships. In fact the only damage suffered by the ships as they raced for home was when *Gneisenau* hit a mine as the trio approached Kiel.

SINK THE TIRPITZ

If the definition of a truly successful deterrent is one that never has to be used, the German battleship *Tirpitz* can probably count among the most successful of all time, second only to the postwar nuclear deterrent. This ship was never involved in a surface action and spent most of her short life hiding in Norwegian fjords, but she was a constant thorn in the flesh of the British. She suffered the attentions of the best that the Fleet Air Arm and the RAF could put into the air. A sister ship of the *Bismarck*, *Tirpitz* differed in a number of respects, mainly by having an even heavier AA armament and eight torpedo tubes.

Tirpitz sailed from Wilhelmshaven for Norway on 16 January 1942. From this port she was an ever-present threat to the Allied convoys making the long and hazardous passage round the North Cape to the Soviet Union. Her first operational sortie was on 9 March 1942, when Vice Adm Ciliax took her to sea to destroy convoy PQ12 bound for Russia. Having missed the convoy in bad weather, *Tirpitz* and her three escorting destroyers were discovered by the Royal Navy and attacked by Albacore torpedo-bombers of 817 and 832 Squadrons flying from the *Victorious*. The ship escaped unscathed, but Hitler was so alarmed that he ruled that she must stay in port if there was any risk of her encountering a British carrier.

On 4 July 1942, she moved her berth, causing the Norwegian resistance to believe that she was being readied for sea. When this was communicated to the Allies, it persuaded Adm of the Fleet Dudley Pound to order the Russia-bound convoy PQ17 to scatter, with disastrous results, as merchantmen were left at the mercy of U-boats and the Luftwaffe. A more effective sortie by the ship was in late 1943, when she accompanied the battlecruiser *Scharnhorst* and ten destroyers north to bombard shore installations at Spitzbergen on 6 September. After this, she was moored in the Altenfjord, where she was attacked by British X-craft on 22 September.

Ugly in appearance and a maintenance nightmare, the Fairey Barracuda did much useful work, especially in operations over Norway, but lacked the performance for tropical operations. (*FAAM CAMP/266*).

Their two-ton charges put her machinery and main armament out of action for six months.

In the far north of Norway, the Altenfjord was undoubtedly the safest berth any ship has ever enjoyed. The steep sides of the high mountains on either side meant that attacking aircraft could not see the ship until it was too late, by which time they were in clear view of her AA armament. During an attack, aircraft had to dive steeply and at all times were in real danger of flying into the sides of the fjord. Even so, the Fleet Air Arm mounted nine attacks against the ship

and RAF Bomber Command mounted another seven, mainly flying from airfields in the Soviet Union.

The attacks were often of considerable strength, with the heaviest being on 3 April 1944, in Operation Tungsten, when aircraft were flown from the carriers *Victorious, Furious, Emperor, Fencer, Pursuer* and *Searcher*. The raid was carried out by the Barracudas of 827, 829, 830 and 831 Squadrons. A strong fighter force was sent to provide the essential cover against German fighter defences, with a mixed force of Seafires, Hellcats, Corsairs, Wildcats and Martlets

Fairey Fulmars ranged on the deck of *Victorious*. Despite being outclassed by the German and Italian opposition, this aircraft did much useful work in the hands of skilled and determined pilots. (*FAAM Fulmar/63*)

provided by 800, 801, 804, 880, 881, 882, 896, 898, 1834, 1836 and 1840 Squadrons. Other squadrons remained close to the carriers, providing anti-submarine cover. Fourteen bombs from this force hit the ship, causing more than 400 casualties, but did not sink her, possibly due to the maximum weight of bomb employed being no more than 1,600 lbs. Nevertheless, the attack caused enough damage to put the *Tirpitz* out of action for three months.

With such a large ship so well protected, different tactics were needed. On 15 September 1944, Lancaster bombers of the RAF's 617 Squadron damaged the *Tirpitz* using 12,000-lb 'Tallboy' bombs, damaging her so severely that she could not be repaired *in situ*. She was moved south to Tromso, where bombers operating from Britain were able to reach her. On 12 November 1944, 617's Lancasters attacked again, using Tallboys once more. This time three of the large bombs hit the ship, causing her to capsize, trapping 1,000 of her crew below decks. It was not until after the war that it was discovered that the ship had not been taken to Tromso for repairs, but to act as a large unsinkable fortress.

CHAPTER 3

THE CONVOY WAR

and a security for such as pass on the seas upon their lawful occasions . . .

The Naval Prayer

One of the most important tasks of the Royal Navy has always been the protection of trade, and in wartime that means convoys. There is nothing new about convoys. They were used to protect Roman shipping against Mediterranean pirates; by the Spaniards to protect shipping to and from their American colonies and by the British during the Napoleonic wars. The difference during the Second World War was that the Royal Navy was also actively involved in attacking enemy convoys: German ore convoys along the Norwegian coast; German and Italian convoys across the Mediterranean to support Rommel's *Afrika Korps*; and Japanese convoys carrying oil and rubber from their Asian empire.

At first, the convoy war went badly against Britain until first the merchant aircraft carrier, or MAC-ship, and then the escort carrier, combined with ever longer-range maritime reconnaissance aircraft to close the Atlantic Gap, that part of the ocean without air cover, to end the U-boat menace. During the war years there were 2,889 escorted trade convoys to and from the UK, with a total of 85,775 ships. Out of these, 654 were sunk, a loss rate of 0.7 per cent. There were in addition another 7,944 coastal convoys, comprising 175,608 ships, of which 248 were

sunk, a loss rate of 0.14 per cent.[1] This latter figure has to be put into perspective, for after the fall of France coastal convoys did not operate through the English Channel because of the danger of enemy attack and instead their cargo went by rail.

The convoy system was not compulsory and not universally accepted. Fast troopships, such as the former liners *Queen Mary* and *Queen Elizabeth* sailed alone, relying on speed to keep them safe. The independent sailing of ships not in convoy has to be added to the convoy losses. In 1942 alone, this accounted for 840 merchant vessels lost to U-boats, against 299 from convoys, and at least 60 of the convoy losses were stragglers; ships that for one reason or another could not keep up with the rest of the convoy.[2]

The most dangerous convoys were those through the Mediterranean in the struggle to sustain the defence of Malta. This situation was so bad that fast minelayers and large mine-laying submarines were pressed into service to keep the Maltese islands going.

[1] Roskill Capt, S.W., RN, *The War at Sea* (HMSO, 1960)

[2] Lord Kilbracken, *Bring Back My Stringbag* (Pan, 1980)

Grimmest of the convoy routes were those to Russia, sailing past occupied Norway and north of the Arctic Circle; the weather was as much an enemy as the Kriegsmarine and the Luftwaffe. A total of 811 ships sailed in the Arctic convoys to Russia, of which 720 completed their voyages, another 33 turned back for one reason or another, and 58 were sunk, giving a loss rate of 7.2 per cent. Of the ships that reached Russia, 717 sailed back (some were being delivered to the Soviet Union) and of these, 29 were sunk, a loss rate of 4 per cent. This was the price of delivering to Russia some 4 million tons of war stores, including 5,000 tanks and more than 7,000 aircraft.[3]

In the battle to protect the convoys, the Royal Navy was joined by other allies and by the free forces of countries occupied by the Germans. It was the convoy war that saw the birth of Canadian and Dutch naval aviation brought into being as part of the Fleet Air Arm and at first fully integrated with it. Later, Australian squadrons were to emerge in the same way.

The small number of aircraft carriers available to the Royal Navy at the outset of war was not enough to provide convoy protection, and in any case, these major fighting units of the fleet were often needed elsewhere. Major units were sometimes provided to cover convoys, and especially those to Malta, but these were in exceptional, even desperate, circumstances. Yet, some of the ships lost in the early years might have been better used as escort carriers, especially the small *Hermes*.

During the late 1930s, the Admiralty's Trade Division had advanced a scheme to provide small 'trade protection carriers' and conversion of the new fast liners RMS *Queen Mary* and *Queen Elizabeth* to aircraft carriers was mooted, but rejected because of the lack of suitable aircraft. In 1940, Capt, later Rear Adm, M.S. Slattery, Director of Air Material, proposed two solutions to the problem, both involving the use of merchantmen. One idea was to use merchant vessels with simple flight decks placed over their holds; the other was to equip other merchant vessels with catapults for fighters. The problem with the first idea was that the ships would be too small and too slow to operate fighters, so anti-submarine Swordfish would be all that could be carried. On the other hand, the catapult-launched fighters would be expendable, since there would be nowhere for these aircraft to land after their one and only sortie against German bombers and maritime reconnaissance aircraft. Nevertheless, a combination of these two ideas would provide a cost-effective solution to convoy protection.

The conversion of merchant ships to provide escort carriers is dealt with later. Suffice it to say, these took some time to arrive, being conversions into warships. Truer to Slattery's vision were the MAC-ships, of which there were two kinds: tankers, capable of carrying three Swordfish, and grain ships, capable of carrying four Swordfish. The grain ships had the advantage of having a hold aft-converted as a hangar, with an aircraft hoist so that all four aircraft could, with wings folded, be struck down into the hangars. The grain ships had a shorter flight deck, at between 413 and 424 ft, than the 460 ft of the tankers, but the extra length of the tanker deck was offset by having aircraft parked on the deck, reducing the take-off run. The lack of a hangar also made maintenance work difficult and unpleasant in bad weather and often dangerous, if not altogether impossible. The width of the flight deck was a standard 62 ft.

[3] Capt S.W. Roskill, RN, *The War at Sea* (HMSO, 1960)

On the North Atlantic, MAC-ships provided vital anti-submarine protection and continued even after the escort carriers arrived. This is the converted tanker *Adula*, turning to receive Lt John Godley's aircraft, from which this photograph was taken by Jake Bennett. (*via Lord Kilbracken*)

Thirty-five merchant vessels were rapidly converted with catapults, becoming Catapult Aircraft Merchant Ships, CAM-ships, sailing under the Red Ensign, and still carrying their normal cargo. With one exception, RAF aircraft were flown from CAM-ships.

Work on converting the first two MAC-ships, *Empire MacAlpine* and *Empire MacAndrew*, started in June 1942, and by October, work had started on ten more, although the original plan to have thirty-two such ships was cut back to nineteen as escort carriers started to arrive. The first two ships were both grain ships, but the October batch included the first tanker, *Rapana*. The simpler tanker conversion took much less time and ships were converted in as little as five months.

The ships' flights belonged to 836 and 860 Squadrons, based at Maydown in County Londonderry. These two squadrons came to comprise the MAC-ship Wing, with 836 being the larger squadron manned by Royal Navy personnel, while 860 was manned by members of the Royal Netherlands Navy, who operated from the Dutch MAC-ships, MV *Acavus*, *Macoma* and *Gadila*.

A 860 Squadron Swordfish in flight. (*Royal Netherlands Navy Maritime Institute*)

Macoma from the air, showing the limited deck space, and just how much of it two Swordfish could use. (*Royal Netherlands Navy Maritime Institute*)

Maydown was a convenient base, with ships' flights disembarked to Maydown as the convoy approached the Clyde. On the other side of the Atlantic, the MAC-ships used Halifax, Nova Scotia and their aircraft disembarked to RCAF Dartmouth.

From May 1943 until VE-Day, MAC-ships made 323 crossings of the Atlantic and escorted 217 convoys, of which just one was successfully attacked. The Swordfish they carried flew 4,177 patrols and searches, an average of 13 per crossing, or 1 per day at average convoy speed. Usually, the mere sighting of an aircraft was enough to force any U-boat to submerge, although there were occasions when U-boats caught on the surface, possibly while charging their batteries, did make a fight for it.

CONVOYS TO RUSSIA

The main convoy routes were across the North Atlantic, usually terminating on the Clyde or at Liverpool; from Scotland and Iceland to the Soviet Union; from Southampton and Plymouth to Gibraltar; to Malta from Gibraltar; and from Gibraltar to Cape Town. Coastal convoys were usually looked after by RAF Coastal Command, often aided by Fleet Air Arm shore-based squadrons, sometimes under RAF control. For mine-laying and other operations with Coastal Command, it was not unknown for Swordfish to be painted black for night operations. MAC-ships were kept on the North Atlantic because the 'Arctic convoys', needed the larger aircraft capacity of the escort carriers as both anti-submarine and fighter protection was needed. CAM-ships appeared on both routes.

Most famous of the Arctic convoys was the ill-fated PQ17, which had sailed from Hvalfiordur, in Iceland on 27 June 1942, without a carrier among its escorts and had such a presence been available, the tragic events might not have occurred. In his book, *Arctic Convoys*, Richard Woodman explains that 'the sinking of a 10,000 ton freighter, was the equivalent, in terms of material destroyed, of a land battle.' The only route for the convoys was around the northern tip of occupied Norway to Murmansk and Archangel. In summer, the almost constant daylight left the ships open to attack from the air, U-boats and surface raiders. In winter, the weather was another hazard in the almost constant darkness with just three hours of weak twilight in the middle of the day. One officer having difficulty eating a meal as his cruiser rolled to angles of thirty degrees consoled himself with the thought that life must have been even more difficult in the destroyers and corvettes, which rolled as much as fifty degrees and sometimes even more. For the airmen, life was hard. The cold meant that they tried to wear as much as possible, limited only by the need to get into and out of the cockpit. Metal became so brittle that tail wheels could break off on landing.

Convoy PQ18 was the first Arctic convoy to have an escort carrier, the US-built HMS *Avenger*. She carried three radar-equipped Swordfish from 825 Squadron for anti-submarine duties, as well as six Sea Hurricanes, with another six dismantled and stowed beneath the hangar deck in a hold, for fighter defence. The fighter aircraft were drawn from 802 and 883 Squadrons. Another Sea Hurricane was aboard the CAM-ship, *Empire Morn*. These were not the only ships with the convoy, which also had the cruiser *Scylla*, two destroyers, two anti-aircraft ships converted from merchant vessels, four corvettes, four anti-submarine trawlers, three mine-sweepers and two submarines. There was a rescue ship, so that the escorts would not be distracted from their work to rescue survivors, a matter of

The Arctic convoys suffered heavy losses until escort carriers could be provided, and even then some ships were unlucky, such as this ammunition ship that blew up taking her German attacker with her. (*IWM A12275*)

urgency in the cold seas. Three American minesweepers being delivered to the Soviet Union also acted as rescue ships.

Getting to the rendezvous off Iceland was difficult. Seas were so rough that a Sea Hurricane was swept off *Avenger*'s deck, and the steel ropes securing the aircraft in the hangar failed to stop the aircraft breaking loose, crashing into one another and into the sides of the hangar. Fused 500-lb bombs stored in the lift well broke loose, and had to be captured by laying down duffle coats with rope ties, to be quickly tied up as soon as a bomb rolled on to the coats. The ship suffered engine problems due to fuel contamination. Iceland, some distance from the nearest German air base, was still not completely safe, for here the carrier was discovered and bombed by a Focke-Wulf Fw200 Condor long-range maritime

reconnaissance aircraft, which dropped a stick of bombs close to the ship, but without inflicting any damage.

The engine problems meant that the convoy, already spotted by a U-boat while on passage to Iceland, had to sail without the carrier; on 8 September, the convoy was discovered by another Condor. Low, overcast weather protected the convoy from German aircraft until 12 September, when a Blohm und Voss Bv138 flying-boat dropped through the clouds. By this time *Avenger* had caught up with the convoy and was able to launch a flight of four Sea Hurricanes, but not in time to catch the German aircraft before it disappeared. The fighters were not simply concerned with protecting the ships, they also had to cover the Swordfish. At 04:00 on 9 September, the Sea Hurricanes were scrambled after

Landing on any carrier could be difficult in bad weather, and especially with heavier aircraft and smaller escort carriers. This is a fire aboard *Tracker*, after one of her Avengers crashed on landing in April 1944. The work of the fire teams has added urgency as they struggle to stop the fire reaching the ready-use ammunition locker for the aft AA armament just below the flight deck. (*IWM A22863*)

Swordfish on anti-submarine patrol were discovered by another two Luftwaffe aircraft, a Bv138 and a Junkers Ju88 reconnaissance aircraft, but again, these disappeared into the low cloud before the fighters could reach them.

The Swordfish also kept a general reconnaissance for the convoy, noting that Bv138s were dropping mines ahead of the ships. Sometimes, U-boats were discovered on the surface, but attempts to attack them were foiled by heavy AA fire from the U-boats.

Later on 13 September, a formation of Ju88 medium-bombers made a high-level bombing attack on the convoy. Again, the convoy's fighters were unable to shoot down a German aircraft, largely because the early Sea Hurricane's machine guns could not concentrate enough fire on the bombers to have any effect. While the fighters were refuelling and rearming aboard the carrier, the next Luftwaffe attack came at 15:40. As twenty Ju88s flew over the convoy in a high-level attack, distracting the defences and causing the ships to take evasive action, twenty-

Biter and *Avenger*, two escort or auxiliary carriers, astern of *Victorious*. (*FAAM CARS B6*)

eight Heinkel He111 and eighteen Ju88s made a low-level torpedo attack, following by a second wave of seventeen Ju88s. Sweeping in at around 20 ft above the waves, the attackers ignored the escorts and concentrated on the merchant vessels. The Sea Hurricanes, however, were still on the carrier's deck and could not take part in the operation.

A mass forty-five degree turn was attempted by the convoy, but the inexperience of many of those aboard and the large size of the convoy meant that not all of the ships managed this manoeuvre. The American ships had had little experience at this time of being under determined enemy attack, and the wild anti-aircraft fire against the low-flying aircraft meant that the anti-aircraft crews on other ships were exposed to fire from shells and

bullets. Pressing home their attack with considerable courage, the Germans sank eight ships, the more fortunate crews being able to jump direct from their ships onto the ice-encrusted decks of the escort and rescue vessels. The less fortunate had minutes in which to be rescued or die in the freezing water. Those aboard the *Empire Stevenson*, which was loaded with explosives, disappeared with the ship in one huge explosion. Five aircraft were shot down by AA fire.

The Sea Hurricanes drove off a later attack by Heinkel He115 floatplanes, but one of the four fighters was shot down. In a change of tactics, the Sea Hurricanes rotated, each spending twenty-five minutes in the air before landing to refuel, keeping a constant CAP over the convoy.

On 14 September, the first Swordfish of the day found *U-589* on the surface, but she dived leaving the Swordfish to mark the spot with a smoke flare. Once the aircraft had gone, the submarine surfaced and continued charging her batteries. Alerted by the Swordfish, the destroyer *Onslow* raced to the scene. Once again, *U-589* dived, but the destroyer attacked with depth charges and destroyed her. Now, the Germans changed their tactics. Reconnaissance Bv138s and Ju88s were sent to intimidate the Swordfish, forcing them back onto the convoy, until the Germans were driven away by heavy AA fire. The Swordfish would then venture out, only to be found and driven back again.

A further attack by Ju88s later that day was detected by the duty Swordfish. This time *Avenger* herself was the target, moving at her maximum 17 knots. The Sea Hurricanes broke up the attack and no ships were lost, but eleven Ju88s were shot down, again mainly by AA fire. Further attacks that day, including dive-bombing, saw another German aircraft shot down, without any losses to the convoy. In a final attack, three of the four patrolling Hurricanes were shot down by friendly fire, although all three pilots were saved after five Luftwaffe aircraft were shot down and another nine damaged beyond repair, five by the Sea Hurricanes. In this attack, *Avenger*'s commanding officer, Cdr Colthurst, successfully managed to comb the torpedoes dropped by the Germans, but the ammunition ship, *Mary Luckenbach*, blew up, taking her attacking aircraft with her.

The following day, the remaining Sea Hurricanes and the Swordfish were again in the air, with the former breaking up further attacks. It was not until 16 September that the Swordfish were relieved of their patrolling by shore-based RAF Consolidated Catalina flying-boats operating from Russia. However, the break was short-lived. Later

that day, the convoy crossed the homeward convoy, QP14, with the survivors of the ill-fated PQ17 and *Avenger*, with her aircraft and some of the other escorts transferred to this convoy. The interval had been used by the ship's air engineering team to assemble five Sea Hurricanes, more than replacing the four lost on the outward convoy. All in all, the Sea Hurricanes had accounted for a total of five enemy aircraft and damaged seventeen others.

THE MALTA CONVOYS

Italy's entry into the Second World War on 10 June 1940 found Malta isolated. The situation was not unexpected and the British Government and armed forces had already considered what to do once Italy entered the war. It was clear that Malta would be a target, in effect sitting on the crossroads of the Mediterranean, roughly halfway between Gibraltar and Alexandria, and between southern Italy and Italian forces in North Africa. This was a vital strategic situation, but Malta was a fortress of the past, not the present. Her extensive fortifications had been built with earlier conflicts and armaments in mind, while the island could not provide enough food to feed its own people, even without taking the needs of a garrison into account. Even more so than the British Isles, Malta was dependent on external sources to survive.

The British Army and the Royal Air Force were in no doubt that the Maltese islands could not be defended. The sole dissenting voice in this debate was that of the Royal Navy, seeing Malta as of vital strategic importance in controlling the Mediterranean and as a base for light forces and submarines. Most British civilians were evacuated well in advance of the Italian declaration of war, but the Royal Navy had won the argument, and the armed forces stayed.

Malta's survival was a mixture of luck and pluck. Luckily, the Germans and the Italians held back from their plan to invade the islands until after the invasion of Crete. That operation proved so costly, and was such a close run thing, that Hitler forbade any further massive airborne invasions. Malta would have been a difficult landing ground for assault forces, with few large beaches, while road access to the rest of the island could be easily blocked. Apart from the airfields and a racecourse, there were few areas of open ground on which gliders could land, since Malta, Gozo and Comino have their agricultural land divided into small fields by 'stone hedges'.

The pluck was the sheer resilience and fortitude of the defenders, British and Maltese alike, and of those running convoys to Malta. The convoys were far smaller than on the Arctic routes, but at times convoys could not get through, despite attack carriers and battleships operating with them. Malta had to rely on fast runs by fast minelayers, the occasional fast merchant-man with a cunning master and large mine-laying submarines. Submarines using Malta as a base for a series of successful operations against Axis convoys, and those bringing supplies, had to submerge in port during the day to avoid destruction in the heavy air raids.

Aircraft were flown from carriers, including the USS *Wasp*, to provide Malta with a fighter defence, but at first these fighters were often destroyed as they landed to refuel and re-arm in the middle of almost continuous Axis air attack. Earlier, Malta depended on four Gloster Sea Gladiators left behind by the carrier *Eagle*, three of which were flown by RAF pilots and became famous as *Faith, Hope* and *Charity*. However, someone at the Admiralty sent a signal demanding to know why Fleet Air Arm property had been handed over to the RAF.

The Royal Navy's great achievement at Taranto still left Malta convoys vulnerable to air attack. This point was brought home with a vengeance when Operation Excess ran into trouble early in 1941. The convoy had been delayed from December, but the eastbound convoy, with ships for Malta and Greece, had been held back because of the presence of the cruiser *Hipper* in the Atlantic. The eastbound convoy, escorted towards Malta by Adm Somerville's Force H, consisted of just four large merchantmen, three for Piraeus and one, carrying 4,000 tons of ammunition and 3,000 tons of seed potatoes, for Malta. The westbound convoy consisted of two merchantmen, one with general supplies and another with fuel for Malta, while at the same time Cunningham was also sending an oiler to the anchorage at Suvla Bay in Crete. It was always important in convoy planning to look after 'the empties', and part of the plan was to escort merchantmen from Malta to safety in Alexandria. Wellington bombers from Malta had raided Naples on the night of 8/9 January, damaging the battleship *Guilio Cesare*, and forcing her and the *Vittorio Veneto* to withdraw north to Genoa.

On Malta convoys, escorting warships often outnumbered the escorted merchantmen. Force H included *Ark Royal*, the battleship *Malaya*, the cruisers *Southampton, Gloucester* and *Bonaventure*, and five destroyers. The Mediterranean Fleet included *Illustrious* and the battleships *Warspite* and *Valiant*. After initial skirmishes on 9 January, when Force H was bombed, but *Ark Royal*'s Fulmars accounted for two bombers, the real action came at the hand-over the following day. The Axis reconnaissance aircraft knew of the Mediterranean Fleet's presence in the area, but the bombers had failed to find them until 10 January. Both carriers kept their Fulmar fighters on constant CAP.

The first attack came at 12:20, with a torpedo-bomber attack on *Illustrious*, but the

Even the fast armoured carriers could meet their match, but at least they survived. Damage to the flight deck of *Illustrious*, caught off Malta in early 1941. (*FAAM Carrier I/43*)

ship wheeled to avoid the attacks and combed the torpedoes, which passed close astern of *Valiant*. Fulmars of *Illustrious*'s 806 Squadron chased the two Savoia torpedo-bombers away, but left the sky empty until the next flight took off at 12:35. At 12:30, the carrier's radar picked up a massive formation of aircraft. Her CO, Capt Boyd, had just asked Cunningham

permission to turn into the wind to launch his fighters, when forty-three Junkers Ju87 Stukas were spotted, followed by a wave of Ju88s, of *Fliegerkorps X*. Thirty aircraft in the first wave aimed for the carrier, leaving just ten to mount an attack on the two battleships.

Diving from 12,000 ft, releasing 1,000-lb and 500-lb bombs as they passed down between 1,200 ft and 800 ft, the Stukas quickly scored six direct hits and three near misses on *Illustrious*, whose deck was designed to take a direct hit of 500-lbs. The first two 1,000-lb bombs hit a gun position and a paint store, after plunging through several decks. Then a 500-lb bomb hit the after lift, which was not armoured and blew the lift platform into the hangar, while a second followed it and exploded inside the hangar, setting fire to several aircraft. Another bomb struck the forward lift, before a 1,000-lb bomb penetrated the flight deck and exploded inside the hangar.

Within minutes, the hangar was an inferno, while the near-misses put the steering out of action. Yet, despite the severity and accuracy of the attack, the ship's machinery remained intact, so that her speed never fell below 18 knots and her pumps and fire-fighting mains remained operational. The tanks of highly explosive aviation fuel were undamaged. Between them, her anti-aircraft guns and Fulmar fighters shot down four of the attackers.

The ship was forced to put into Malta for emergency repairs, where she remained vunerable to attacks from the Luftwaffe and Regia Aeronautica until she was able to sail to the United States for repairs. Those of her aircraft that were airborne at the time of the attack, managed to reach Malta, where for a while the Fulmars augmented the RAF Hurricanes in defending the island. Five of the carrier's Swordfish also survived to be based on Malta.

On this occasion, the merchantmen all reached Malta safely. It was not always to be the case. It also became apparent that Malta lacked the port facilities to receive and discharge the cargoes of a number of ships at once. When four ships reached Grand Harbour on 23 March 1941, two were sunk at their moorings before they could even be unloaded.

Most famous of the Malta convoys was that from 10 to 15 August 1942, known to the Allies as Operation Pedestal, but to the Maltese as the 'Santa Maria Convoy', arriving in Malta on 15 August, the feast day of the Assumption of the Virgin Mary. Operation Pedestal was the largest of the Malta convoys; it had fourteen merchant vessels, reflecting both the desperate plight of those on Malta and the reality that not all of the ships could make it. Under the command of Vice Adm Syfret, the escorts included the battleships *Nelson* and *Rodney*, with their 16-in guns in three triple turrets forward, the aircraft carriers *Eagle, Furious, Indomitable* and *Victorious*, seven cruisers and twenty-seven destroyers. *Furious* was carrying forty-two Supermarine Spitfire fighters to be flown off to augment Malta's defences.

The fleet itself was largely dependent on forty-three Sea Hurricanes for its air defence, although it also had a number of Fulmars and Grumman Martlets. *Victorious* had sixteen Fulmars of 809 and 884 Squadrons, five Sea Hurricanes of 885 and twelve Albacores of 832 Squadron. *Indomitable* had nine Martlets in 806 Squadron, twenty-two Sea Hurricanes in 800 and 880 Squadrons and sixteen Albacores in 827 Squadron. *Eagle* had sixteen Sea Hurricanes in 801 Squadron and another four in 813. In addition to her Spitfires, *Furious* had four Albacores of 823 Squadron as spares.

The operation got off to a bad start when, after passing Gibraltar on the night of 10/11 August, the *Eagle* was torpedoed at 13:15 on 11 August by *U-73*. All four torpedoes hit the carrier, sinking her quickly, and her four Sea Hurricanes flying CAP at the time had to land on the other carriers. The elderly carrier, regarded as too slow for frontline duty, was no stranger to the Malta run, and had flown 183 fighters safely to the island from her deck.

Later that day, the Luftwaffe started the series of heavy aerial attacks that the convoy was to suffer on its run across the Mediterranean. At 20:45, thirty-six aircraft attacked from bases in Sardinia. The following morning, at 09:15, twenty German aircraft attacked, before a combined Luftwaffe and Regia Aeronautica force of seventy aircraft attacked at noon. The fighters on patrol succeeded in bringing down some of the attackers. The escort vessels sank an Italian submarine at 16:00, before another combined strike of a hundred aircraft attacked at 19:00, sinking a merchantman and so seriously damaging *Indomitable* that she was put out of action, leaving her aircraft to be recovered by *Victorious*. An hour later, twenty Luftwaffe aircraft attacked, sinking the cruiser *Cairo* and two more merchant vessels, as well as damaging the cruiser *Nigeria* and three other ships, including the tanker *Ohio*. Those ships sunk had been badly damaged in earlier attacks.

Darkness brought no respite: An attack by E-boats sank another five ships, and so badly damaged the cruiser *Manchester* that she had to be sunk later.

On 13 August, at 08:00, twelve Luftwaffe aircraft flying from Sicily sank another ship and caused still more damage to the *Ohio*. After an Italian air raid at 11:25 damaged the tanker further and fires burned out of control, her master ordered her to be abandoned. Before they could be picked up, the crew re-boarded the ship as she was still afloat. By this time the convoy was badly scattered. The leading ships reached Malta on 13 August, but *Ohio*, aided by an escorting destroyer, did not arrive until 15 August, one of just five out of the fourteen merchant vessels to survive the ordeal. Her master and crew were valiant, but they were also lucky, as another straggler behind the main convoy was promptly despatched by a U-boat. *Ohio*'s cargo of fuel was to prove invaluable in the defence of Malta. Strangely, this time there were no attacks on the ships as they unloaded.

One aircraft carrier, a cruiser and a destroyer were sunk in the operation, with serious damage to two carriers, *Indomitable* and *Victorious*, and two cruisers. Part of the problem was the quality of the fighters. While the Sea Hurricanes could tackle a Stuka, the Ju88s were far more difficult, making 'the fleet fighters' task a hopeless one', according to Syfret. Yet, this marked the beginning of the lifting of the siege. The tide was turning against the Axis Powers, and nowhere sooner and more sharply than in the Mediterranean theatre and North Africa.

ON THE ATTACK

The convoy war was not simply one-sided. Germany had few true overseas trade routes, so the invasion of Norway and Denmark had been largely to secure supplies of Swedish iron ore. The ore was shipped through Norwegian ports after a railway journey, because the Gulf of Bothnia in Sweden froze during the winter. On several occasions, the Home Fleet sent carrier-borne aircraft to attack coastal shipping off occupied Norway, accounting for 100,000 tons of shipping. Further losses came from mines laid by the aircraft. These attacks also helped to foster a belief among many in the German leadership, including Hitler, that the planned invasion of Europe would start in Norway.

In the Pacific, Japanese ships, especially tankers, often fell prey to the Fleet Air Arm's attacks, especially in Sumatra and then, towards the end of the year, in Japanese ports, where the Fleet Air Arm earned its second VC of the war. Nevertheless, the bulk of Japanese shipping losses during the war were to American submarines.

CHAPTER 4

SUPPORTING THE ARMY

Their honour and courage remained throughout as dazzling as the snow-covered mountains over which they so triumphantly flew.

Capt Troubridge, on *Furious*'s airmen during the Norwegian campaign.

It is an old maxim for the Royal Navy that it must never let the Army down. In times past, this meant providing shore bombardment and ensuring that soldiers were not left ashore in the face of an advancing enemy. In the Second World War, it came to mean the close air support of ground forces, both from carriers at sea and from bases ashore.

Support of the Army had begun early in the war with the Norwegian Campaign. The early involvement of the carrier *Furious* has already been mentioned, and during a period of eighteen days, her aircraft flew 23,870 miles and dropped eighteen torpedoes and eighteen tons of bombs. All this in fog and snow, with aircraft operating from a flight deck that quickly became covered in an icy slush.

For the evacuation of Dunkirk, several squadrons, including 815 and 826, provided anti-submarine patrols, while the latter also attacked E-boats at Zeebrugge. The narrow confines of the English Channel at this point meant that carrier-borne aircraft could not be used, because of the lack of room for manoeuvre.

Army co-operation grew in importance as the war progressed, with squadrons undergoing training at Sawbridgeworth in Army co-operation work. Dekheila in Egypt became an important shore station, from which naval aircraft flew to support the Eighth Army fighting in the desert. Often, these squadrons would operate under the control of the RAF's Desert Air Force. In early 1941, 815 was flying Albacores and two radar-equipped Swordfish over the Western Desert, attacking enemy airfields and formations. Operations by the Fleet Air Arm in Egypt included flare-dropping and target marking, and laying mines in the approaches to ports used by Axis forces. At one stage, units, including 805 Squadron, operated as part of the Naval Fighter Squadron in the desert, attached to a succession of RAF wings. Dekheila grew in importance as the war progressed, Malta became inhospitable and dangerous for surface ships, and the Mediterranean Fleet found itself confined to the Eastern Mediterranean, so that the ships were based on Alexandria with Dekheila as the main shore station for disembarked aircraft.

Operating from HMS *Formidable*, 806 Squadron provided fighter cover and 826 operated from Dekheila in support of the withdrawal of British and Greek troops from Crete, following the German invasion that started on 20 May 1941. Cunningham, in command of the Mediterranean Fleet,

JUST received from Norway, this picture, taken from the snow-covered flight deck of H.M. Air raft-carrier Furious while on patrol in a fiord near Tromsc, shows something of the conditions with which the Fleet Air Arm had to contend during the Norwegian operations.

The first time the Fleet Air Arm operated in support of the Army was during the Norwegian campaign of 1940. This is a newspaper photograph of *Furious*, with her flight deck covered in snow. (*via S.H. Wragg*)

continued with the evacuation well beyond the deadline set by London. Even so, about half the British troops defending Crete, many of them having been moved there on the fall of Greece, had to be left behind to become prisoners.

As the tide turned, naval aviation was often the only way to ensure air cover for the series of invasions, simply because friendly airfields were rarely available, other than for the invasion of Sicily. This saw the Allies invade first Madagascar in the Indian Ocean and then North Africa, Sicily, the mainland of Italy and finally the South of France.

Although German defeat was not inevitable until the end of 1943, the tide started to turn in 1942. Escort carriers were closing the Atlantic Gap, while in the Pacific the United States Navy inflicted a serious defeat on the Imperial Japanese Navy, which lost four of its aircraft carriers in the Battle of Midway. Stalin demanded a second front, but a direct invasion of mainland Europe was impossible at this stage, so the British and Americans had to depend on an air offensive to take the war to Germany.

The large island of Madagascar, off the coast of East Africa, was of vital strategic importance to the Axis Powers. Under Vichy French administration, it provided a base for commerce raiders in the Indian Ocean, and with the Mediterranean all but impassable, it was close to the long convoy route around the Cape of Good Hope and through the Suez Canal to Egypt. Nevertheless, its position meant that the Axis Powers could never establish a strong defence. On 5 May 1942, in Operation Ironclad, British forces were landed at Diego Suarez, in the far north of the island. Aircraft from 800, 806, 810, 827, 829, 831, 880, 881 and 882 Squadrons provided air cover and ground attack, operating from the carriers *Indomitable* and *Illustrious*, now back from her repairs in the United States. The carriers were part of a strong naval force that included the battleship *Ramillies*, as well as two cruisers and eleven destroyers. While the landings took until 8 May to become fully established, little resistance was met.

Despite its strategic position, Madagascar was far removed from the harsh realities of the war and the vital objective of securing Axis defeat. This had to come through North Africa and southern Europe before a head-on clash in northern Europe could be contemplated.

In North Africa, the British Eighth Army had inflicted a major defeat on the German *Afrika Korps* at the Battle of El Alamein, which lasted from 23 October to 5 November 1942. Even before this victory, landings had been planned in North Africa, to squeeze the Germans between British and American forces. The landings were known as Operation Torch and involved landing almost 100,000 men in Vichy French territory on the Atlantic coast of French Morocco and in Algeria. While Force H, with the aircraft carriers *Victorious* and *Formidable*, and three battleships defended the eastern flanks of the invasion force from the Italian fleet and German U-boats, the elderly *Argus* and *Furious*, with two escort carriers, covered the landings in Algeria. The landings in Morocco had air support provided by the USS *Ranger* and four American escort carriers.

The landings started at around 01:00 on 8 November at Oran, and then a little later at Algiers, while those in Morocco started at 04:30. Aircraft from a large number of Fleet Air Arm squadrons were involved, including 700, aboard the battleships and cruisers, and

800, 801, 802, 804, 807, 809, 817, 820, 822, 832, 833, 880, 882, 883, 884, 885, 888, 891 and 893. Aircraft used included high performance fighters for the first time, with Supermarine Seafires and Grumman Martlets, as well as the Fulmar and Albacore.

The North African landings marked the end of German and Italian ambitions in Africa, tipping the balance of power in the Mediterranean and considerably easing the plight of Malta. They laid the foundations for the next step in the war, taking ground forces into Axis territory for the first time in Operation Husky, the Allied landings in Sicily. Again naval aviation was to be at the forefront, but augmented by ground based Fleet Air Arm and RAF aircraft operating from bases in Malta and in North Africa. As a preparation for the operation, the small Italian islands of Pantelleria and Lampedusa, to the west of Malta, were taken on 11 and 12 June 1943. The scene was set for Husky, scheduled for 10 July.

On this occasion, just two aircraft carriers, *Indomitable* and *Formidable*, were used, both from Force H, now under the command of Vice Adm Willis, with aircraft from 807, 817, 820, 880, 885, 888, 893 and 899 Squadrons. While the close air support of carriers was welcome, the vast majority of the 3,700 aircraft available to the Allies could be based ashore. They also heavily outnumbered the Axis forces, which had just 1,400 aircraft. The landings on 10 July took place in bad weather and at one stage postponement was considered. The adverse weather may have lulled the defenders into a false sense of security, but it also played a part in heavy losses among the paratroops and glider-borne forces. Apart from a single Ju88, shot down by a Spitfire, many pilots did not recall seeing an enemy aircraft for the first four days after the invasion.

Unfortunately, it seems that the Allies became too relaxed, with an Italian aircraft successfully attacking and seriously damaging *Indomitable* with an air-launched torpedo, after those aboard mistook the aircraft for a Swordfish.

Despite the strength of the Allied onslaught and growing mastery of the air and of the seas, the bulk of the Axis forces escaped from Sicily across the Straits of Messina. Meanwhile, a major political advance had taken place between Montgomery's Eighth Army crossing the Straits of Messina into Calabria on 3 September and Operation Avalanche, the Allied landings at Salerno, on 9 September. Mussolini had been deposed in late July and his successor, Marshal Badoglio, had signed a secret armistice with the Allies on 3 September, that was publicly announced on the eve of the Salerno landings. The landing was coordinated with a British airborne assault on Taranto to seize the port.

Salerno was chosen because it was within range of Allied aircraft using airfields in Sicily, but it was only just within range for fighter aircraft, so that a Spitfire was limited to no more than twenty minutes on patrol over the beachheads. In practical terms, this meant that the number of aircraft available and flying time to and from the operational zone ensured that no more than nine aircraft could be present at any one time. Once again, this was an operation designed for the aircraft carrier and Willis brought Force H, with the carriers *Illustrious* and *Formidable*. Additional support for the landing forces came from Force V, with the maintenance carrier, *Unicorn*, operating as a light fleet carrier, and also the escort carriers *Attacker, Battler, Hunter* and *Stalker*. Fleet Air Arm squadrons present included 807, 808, 809, 810, 820, 834, 878, 879, 880, 886, 887, 888, 890, 893, 894, 897 and 899. The landing fleet was also accompanied by one of the United States Navy's Independence-class light fleet carriers and four escort carriers, giving a total of twelve flight decks in all.

Aircraft aboard the escort carriers and *Unicorn* were Seafires, for the air defence of the landings, after which they would provide fighter-bomber support to help suppress the defences. Each escort carrier had a single large Seafire squadron with thirty aircraft, while *Unicorn* had sixty of these aircraft in 809 and 887 Squadrons. The Seafire L2C's Merlin engines were tuned to provide maximum power below 5,000 ft rather than the 15,000 ft of the original, making them better suited for naval operations and for ground attack work. There were local alterations, with many of the aircraft having catapult knobs removed to reduce drag, since the Seafire seldom needed catapult assistance and exhaust manifolds were replaced by stubs to reduce drag further.

Aircrew were awakened at 4:30 on the morning of 9 September and before dawn *Unicorn* had flown off eight Seafires, four to provide high cover and four to provide low cover. All of the aircraft had extra fuel tanks, that they had to use first and that were to be dropped as soon as the Luftwaffe appeared to avoid the drag affecting the aircraft's performance. While there was little sight of the Luftwaffe initially, the troops ashore encountered fierce resistance, later supported by heavy Luftwaffe aerial attack.

Force V faced a major problem. The carriers had been given a 'box' in which to operate while flying off and recovering their aircraft, but the box was too small, causing difficulties for the commanders of the carriers. The situation was even worse for the pilots. Large numbers of aircraft were circling, waiting to land, while others having taken off were getting into formation, giving rise to a very real risk of collision with ships steaming in close proximity to one another. These problems were intensified by the dead calm weather conditions, by the short flight decks of the escort carriers and their slow speed, just 17 knots when a Seafire needed

25 knots wind over the flight deck for a safe take-off or landing. Arrester wires had to be kept tight, as did the crash barrier two-thirds of the way along the deck, aggravating the Seafire's tendency to bounce and pitch forward on landing. Haze added to the problems.

High casualty rates among Seafire pilots were soon discovered to be due to their using the RAF-recommended means of leaving the aircraft. This entailed inverting the aircraft, opening the canopy and undoing their seat belt to eject, but this did not work with the Seafire, possibly because of its greater weight compared to the Spitfire. Matters improved once pilots were told to jump from the wing of the aircraft.

The Luftwaffe turned its attentions to the carriers on 11 September, forcing them to race up and down the box at maximum speed. Fuel became critical, but the carriers were asked to remain on station because of the desperate need for air cover. The original plan had expected the carriers to be on station for two days, three at the most, while bases ashore were secured and RAF units could be brought forward from Sicily. In the end, they remained for five days, helping the guns of the fleet break determined German counter-attacks on 12 and 14 September. By this time, the original 180 Seafires had been reduced to just thirty, having made more than the planned number of sorties. The attrition rate was due more to deck landing accidents than the Luftwaffe's fighters, and this led many senior naval officers to hesitate to commit the Seafire to future operations, even though it had its adherents.

The final operation in this series of invasions around and near the Mediterranean did not come until almost a year later, in August 1944, after the Normandy Landings. This was Operation Dragoon, the Allied landings in the South of France between 15 and 24 August 1944. This came after the bottlenecks in the Allied advance northwards through Italy had been overcome and Rome liberated. It was an attack on the soft underbelly of German resistance. The Germans had not invaded the South of France until late 1942 and had lacked the resources to build massive coastal fortifications along the lines of the 'Atlantic Wall' in the north of France. An invasion of the South of France had been considered by the Allies the previous year, but the British had objected, due to the necessary diversion of resources from the advance through Italy, which some saw as leading to the invasion of Germany through Austria. When these hopes were foiled, it was decided to give priority to the Normandy Landings. Meanwhile, some of the ships and air squadrons involved in the earlier campaigns had spent time harassing Axis forces in the Adriatic, before moving to the Far East.

Carrier air power was to be the key to the success of the operation. The build up in the numbers of escort carriers and the growing control of the major sea routes meant that there were nine of these ships, drawn from the British and US Navies, with aircraft for fighter and ground attack duties during the invasion. British escort carriers included *Attacker, Emperor, Hunter, Khedive, Pursuer, Searcher* and *Stalker,* while Fleet Air Arm squadrons included 800, 807, 809, 879, 881, 882 and 899, some of whose pilots were becoming very experienced in this kind of warfare.

Relatively little resistance was met, and within a few days, the naval port of Toulon and the major port of Marseilles were in Allied hands. Instead of concentrating on fighter cover, the Fleet Air Arm pilots found themselves harrying the retreating German Army as it moved north and providing reconnaissance for the ground forces. Both RN and USN pilots continued this work until 24 August, by which time the German forces were beyond the effective fighter range of carrier aircraft, and shore-based USAAF units took over.

CHAPTER 5

THE WAR IN THE EAST

On the road to China Bay,
Where the flying Corsairs play ...

The Fleet Air Arm Songbook

Conflict in the Far East had not been unexpected, but the Royal Navy, in common with the other British services, had been unable to do much about it. There were mistakes, but the main problem was simply that successive British governments had always assured Australia and New Zealand that any threat would be met by sending a British fleet. No one seemed to have considered the possibility that the fleet might be heavily engaged elsewhere. Many historians have made much of the poor contribution made to Imperial defence before the war by both Australia and New Zealand. There is some evidence for this in the case of Australia, however, the then small populations of both countries before mass immigration, especially in the case of New Zealand, would have made a major contribution difficult.

The war in the East started badly for the British, with the Japanese rapidly gaining a strong foothold in Malaya, before advancing towards Singapore. On 10 December 1941, Japanese aircraft found and sank the new battleship, HMS *Prince of Wales* and the elderly battlecruiser *Repulse*, gaining complete control of the seas. It had been intended that the two ships should operate with the new aircraft carrier *Indomitable*, but she had run aground and was not available. It is unlikely that she could have made a big difference since Rear Adm Tom Phillips was anxious to attack the invasion fleet and had discounted the threat of aerial assault, even maintaining radio silence and making it difficult for the RAF to provide air cover.

By early 1942, the British Eastern Fleet, under the command of Vice Adm Somerville, included the aircraft carriers *Hermes*, *Indomitable* and *Formidable*. The last two were at Addu Atoll, now known as Gan, a hastily constructed refuelling anchorage, when the Japanese First Air Fleet, aboard five carriers, sailed towards Ceylon. On 5 April, Easter Day, aircraft from the *Soryu* found and sank the heavy cruisers *Dorsetshire* and *Cornwall* in just twenty minutes. Meanwhile, the one carrier in the area, *Hermes*, escaped Japanese notice until 9 April. By this time, her normal complement of aircraft was simply a squadron of Swordfish and even had she had aircraft aboard, she would have been without fighter protection. Once spotted, the ship was recognised as being vulnerable and was ordered to head for

En route to the Far East, British carriers called at Alexandria. Here, officers from *Khedive* entertain King Farouk of Egypt, with a Seafire providing a backdrop. Note the battledress worn by Lt Cdr George Baldwin, second row, second from right, and the captain, front row, right, with wings, an unusual distinction for such a senior officer at this stage. (*IWM A28114*)

Trincomalee and the protection of the shore defences. She was within sight of the coast with her escorting Australian destroyer, *Vampire*, when she was attacked by eighty Japanese aircraft, many at such low height that some of the carrier's AA gunners claimed to have been firing downwards. Within minutes, she was ablaze, with her forward lift blown out of position and sinking.

Despite the setbacks, the Japanese advance was not unstoppable, and was brought to a halt in the jungles of Burma and New Guinea. In bringing the United States into the war, the Japanese had made

a fatal mistake, for less than six months passed between the surprise attack on the US Pacific Fleet's forward base at Pearl Harbor and Japanese defeat at the Battle of Midway. As the tide started to turn in Europe and on the North Atlantic, resources could be spared to ensure that the Royal Navy played an active role in the Far East and then in the Pacific. This was to prove controversial at first. Many senior USN officers felt that they could finish the job without British help. On the other hand, the British had strong political reasons for wishing to play an active part. They did not want to be seen to be leaving an ally on its own or abandoning Australia and New Zealand. They also needed to put pressure on the Japanese to relieve British forces, who were fighting to protect India from Japanese attack in Burma. Finally, it must not be forgotten that much of the territory overrun by Japan was British, including Hong Kong, Singapore, Malaya and Burma.

There were practical difficulties to be resolved, such as coordination and liaison, and this could be difficult with any large force, even within a single Navy. In the Battle of Leyte Gulf, parts of the US Navy had not been where they were expected to be. A condition laid down by the US Navy was that the Royal Navy could not expect to use American facilities in the Pacific. Two of

the senior American commanders, Chester Nimitz and Ernest King, felt that the British lacked the experience of mounting mass air attacks from carriers and the means of supporting a fleet so far from its bases. The British had little experience of putting together a modern fleet that was both balanced and adequate in strength, which was why they lost so many important ships early in the war. British ships also tended to be short on range and some eye-witnesses could attest to the Royal Navy's slow progress when refuelling at sea compared to the Americans. The distances over which the war in the East was fought have to be taken into account; from Japan to Singapore was about the same distance as Southampton to New York.

In preparation for the big British naval build-up in the Far East, *Illustrious* operated with the USS *Saratoga* against targets in Sumatra. Here are the two ships at Trincomalee, or 'Trinco', in Ceylon, April 1944. (*IWM A23475*)

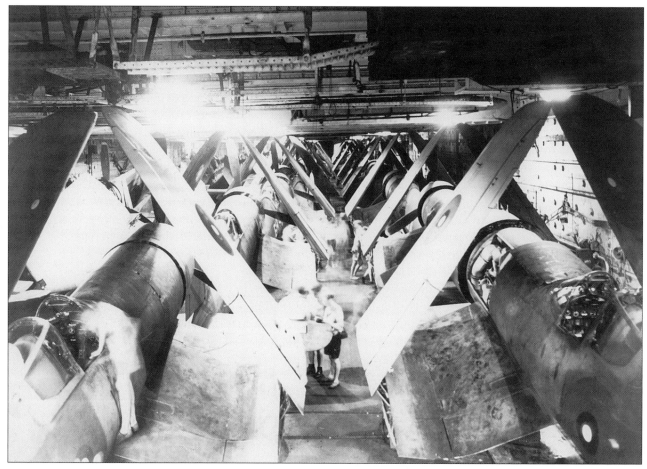

The war in the Far East saw the Corsair fighter-bomber, rejected at first by the USN as too big and heavy for carrier operations, well to the fore. It was a tight fit, as can be seen by 1833 Squadron's aircraft tucked into the hangar of *Illustrious*. (*FAAM Corsair/109*)

However, the British started to resolve these problems. They were able to use Simonstown in South Africa as a base, with South African Air Force airfields available for carrier aircraft disembarking as the carriers went into port. Ceylon provided a forward base with many naval air stations ashore, and others in southern India played a part. Australia became another base, especially important for the British Pacific Fleet, using Sydney and Brisbane with air stations ashore. Nevertheless, the prospect of having additional ships and aircraft appealed to many senior American officers. The problems of cooperation were resolved, partly by ensuring that at first the British Eastern Fleet operated in one area, while the US Fifth Fleet operated elsewhere. This did not mean that there was no cooperation; British, Australian and New Zealand ships sometimes operated with the Americans and under their command, and liaison officers were exchanged.

Cooperation on a small scale was attempted at first, so that the two navies could get used to each other. During the spring of 1944, the USS *Saratoga* was attached to the British Eastern Fleet, joining *Illustrious* for the early raids on Sabang in Task Force 70. This was to prove to be the ideal target for the Fleet Air Arm to hone its techniques on massed aerial attack. It was far enough away from the Americans and posed no threat to them, but it was also a useful target, a small island off the northern end of Sumatra, with a harbour and airfields vital to the Japanese war effort in Burma. This was also to prove to be the baptism of fire for a new high performance fighter for the Fleet Air Arm, the American Vought Corsair, sometimes described as the 'best American fighter of World War II.'

The first attack was made on 19 April 1944, with Corsairs escorting Barracudas, aircraft that had seen action in Europe, notably against the *Tirpitz*, but it proved ill-suited to tropical conditions. Operating under the command of Adm Sir James Somerville, the British Eastern Fleet was to be a thorn in the Japanese flesh. The initial raid was unexpected by the Japanese, and was devastating, despite the poor performance of the Barracudas, which were quickly exchanged for the more capable and reliable Grumman Avenger. Both *Saratoga* and *Illustrious* were able to launch a second successful attack in May against an oil refinery outside Surabaya, on the island of Java, with the loss of just one aircraft.

Operating together quickly exposed weaknesses in British organisation. The British carrier air group was smaller than the American, but even more important, the Fleet Air Arm had to learn the importance of a fast turn-round of aircraft on the flight deck and in the hangar. Fortunately, these lessons were learnt very quickly. Completely integrated carrier operations by the two

navies took time, but coordination became increasingly important and as the war progressed was much in evidence. The Americans also came to appreciate the strength of the Illustrious-class carriers, especially under Kamikaze attacks. As one American officer aboard a British carrier put it: 'When a Kamikaze hits an American carrier, it's six months repair at Pearl. In a Limey carrier, it's a case of "sweepers, man your brooms!"'

Several targets fell to the Fleet Air Arm. One of these was Palembang, with oil refineries and port facilities on Sumatra. The most important of these was on 24 January, 1945, in Operation Meridian I, which involved aircraft from 820, 849, 854, 857, 887, 894, 1770, 1830, 1833, 1834, 1836, 1839, and 1844 Squadrons, operating from *Illustrious, Indefatigable, Indomitable* and *Victorious*. The Japanese were subjected to heavy attacks throughout December 1944 and January 1945.

As the war moved eastwards and ever closer to Japan, a British Pacific Fleet was formed, commanded by Vice Adm Rawlings. The entire operation was under overall American direction, with the BPF becoming Task Force 57, part of the US Fifth Fleet. Rear Adm Sir Philip Vian commanded the British carriers *Illustrious, Indefatigable, Indomitable* and *Victorious*, although *Illustrious* had to be replaced by *Formidable* after suffering heavy damage from aerial attack. The squadrons included those already mentioned, with additional aircraft from 848, 885, 1840, 1841, 1842 and 1845 Squadrons.

Changes continued to take place, so that organisationally the British could match the Americans. The concept of the naval air wing had evolved in 1943, but in 1945 the Royal Navy formed the squadrons embarked in both the fast fleet carriers and the new light fleet carriers into carrier air groups.

A Corsair approaches *Illustrious* at a tight angle – notice the batsman and the AA armament almost, but not quite, flush with the flight deck! (*IWM A20995*)

Missing the arrester wires meant collision with the crash barriers – a not infrequent occurrence given the Corsair's tendency to bounce on landing and the long nose. This one came to grief aboard HMS *Victorious*. (*via Mrs M.J. Schupke*)

The BPF was able to take the war home to Japan, as in this attack by Avengers from *Formidable*, in August 1945. To avoid AA gunners being confused, instead of the usual red and blue roundels which might have been mistaken for the red on Japanese aircraft, the BPF adopted a blue roundel with a pale blue centre. (*FAAM CAMP/463*)

On a more practical level, changes to make inter-operability between the two navies easier included changes to the batsman's signals so that the two navies were in accord. Before this, some directions had had precisely the opposite meaning.

The BPF, or Task Force (TF) 57, when part of the integrated Allied force, operated against the Sakashima Gunto group of islands, through which the Japanese ferried aircraft to Okinawa and did much to cut Japanese reinforcements. On and off, the carriers sent their aircraft to targets in the Sakashima Gunto from 26 March to 25 May 1945, as the BPF took part in Operation Iceberg, the attack on Okinawa.

Operations in the Pacific, as the Allies closed in on the Japanese, had more than the usual hazards for the naval aviator, or even those additional hazards of flying over inhospitable terrain. The Japanese never felt bound to observe the rules of the Geneva Convention, and the fate of pilots shot down could be grim. Many squadron commanders wore uniforms of a lower rank as some means of protection against

Wildcats fly over the escort carrier *Ruler* in the Pacific – again note the two tone blue roundels. (*FAAM Carrier R/6*)

interrogation and torture and to avoid providing a propaganda coup for the Japanese.

The role of the aircraft carriers in the US Navy's Task Force TF58 was to provide air support for the assault on Okinawa. The Royal Navy's TF57 protected the left flank of the US Fifth Fleet and especially TF51, the escort carriers providing close air support for ground forces. The initial landings on Okinawa were on Sunday 1 April 1945, when the US Tenth Army landed with four divisions on the west coast of the island. A breakdown in the Japanese chain of command proved helpful, with initial resistance being light, but on 6 April, British and American forces started to suffer from the attentions of the Japanese Kamikaze

suicide aircraft. In all, between 6 April and 29 May, 1,465 aircraft from one of the Japanese home islands, Kyushu, were used in ten massed Kamikaze attacks, with another 250 aircraft from Formosa. On top of this, there were almost 5,000 conventional sorties. The main target for the Japanese aerial attacks were the ships of the combined British and American fleet and in six weeks, twenty-six ships of destroyer size and below were sunk, and another 164 damaged, including *Illustrious, Formidable, Indefatigable* and *Victorious*.

Within days of the attacks starting, on 9 April, TF57 was ordered to attack airfields in northern Okinawa, while TF51 attacked the airfields of the Sakashima Gunto. A pattern then developed, with the carriers

Menacing the BPF were the Japanese Kamikaze suicide pilots. This is the scene on *Formidable*'s flight deck after the attack of 4 May 1945. At one stage, the ship disappeared behind the smoke generated by the blaze. (*FAAM CARS F/36*)

striking hard at their targets and then being rotated out of battle every few days to replenish their rapidly exhausted fuel and munitions. The demands on the ships of TF57 varied, according to the overall strategic situation, so that by 4 May, TF57 found itself off Miyako in the Sakishima Gunto again. This was when *Formidable* was struck by her first Kamikaze, finding the ship relatively lightly protected, since the battleships, which could do so much to provide a dense curtain of AA fire around the fleet, were away shelling coastal targets. Unfortunately, the attack, at 11:31, came while the flight deck was crowded, as aircraft were ranged for launching and so while the ship merely suffered a 2 ft dent in the flight deck near the base of the island, eight men were killed and forty-seven wounded. It might have been worse. The Medical Officer had moved the flight deck sick bay from the Air Intelligence office at the base of the island, which was the scene of many casualties.

Just five days later, they were back, but again *Formidable* survived. (*FAAM CARS F/39*)

Worse was to come. On 9 May, *Formidable* was struck yet again. On this occasion, the Kamikaze hit the after end of the flight deck and ploughed into aircraft ranged there. A rivet was blown out of the deck and burning petrol poured into the hangar, where the fire could only be extinguished by spraying, with adverse effects even on those aircraft not on fire. Seven aircraft were lost on deck, with another twelve lost in the hangar: The ship had to refuel and obtain replacement aircraft. Nine days later, on 18 May, an armourer working on a Corsair in the hangar, failed to notice that the aircraft's guns were still armed. He accidentally fired the guns into a parked Avenger, which blew up and started another fierce fire. This time, thirty aircraft were destroyed. Even so, the ship was fully operational by the end of the day.

The BPF continued to operate alongside the US Fifth Fleet as the war was taken to the Japanese home islands. In the closing days of the war in the Pacific, the Fleet Air Arm was striking at targets in the Tokyo area

The FAA gained its second VC in the final days of the war against Japan, when Lt Robert Hampton 'Hammy' Gray, RCNVR, lost his life pressing home an attack against Japanese shipping in the face of heavy AA fire. (*FAAM PERS/38*)

The 1st Aircraft Carrier Squadron of the BPF, at peace in Leyte Gulf, 1945. (*FAAM*)

and it was then that it earned its second Victoria Cross of the war, but again, posthumously. On 9 August, Lt Robert Hampton Gray, RCNVR, was leading a strike of Corsairs from *Formidable*'s 1841 and 1842 Squadrons to attack a destroyer in the Onagawa Wan, when he came under heavy AA fire from five warships. He pressed ahead with his attack, even though his aircraft was damaged, and succeeded in sinking the destroyer before his aircraft crashed into the harbour.

CHAPTER 6

RECRUITMENT AND TRAINING

They say in the Air Force the landing's OK,
If the pilot gets out and can still walk away,
But in the Fleet Air Arm the prospects are grim,
If the landing's piss poor and the pilot can't swim.

The Fleet Air Arm Songbook

The outbreak of war did not take the Royal Navy or the Fleet Air Arm by surprise. Nevertheless, the service was still constrained by its almost complete dependence on the Royal Air Force for training both naval aviators and ground crew. Indeed, many naval air squadrons were still heavily dependent on RAF personnel at the time, although around 1,500 transferred to the Royal Navy. During the first year or so of war, civilians who volunteered for the RAF and were accepted had to return home and wait, often several months, before being called forward for training. While the RAF has been criticised for its treatment of the needs of the Royal Navy, under the pressures of building up its own strength to meet wartime needs, its systems came under considerable stress.

One advantage that the RAF did not share with the senior service was the Royal Auxiliary Air Force, that body of weekend enthusiasts who were to prove so valuable to the RAF during the early years of the war, especially in the fighter squadrons. RAuxAF squadrons were organised with distinct local affiliations, mirroring the way in which the

Territorial Army was raised, so that, for example, 603 Squadron was known as 603 (City of Edinburgh) Squadron.

The Royal Navy and Royal Marines in June 1939, totalled 129,000 men, of whom just under 10,000 were officers. To bring it up to maximum strength in wartime, it could depend on recalling recently retired officers and ratings, as well as two categories of reserves, the Royal Naval Reserve (RNR), and the Royal Naval Volunteer Reserve (RNVR), which between them provided another 73,000 officers and men in 1939. The RNR consisted mainly of people drawn from the merchant navy, often bringing with them outstanding navigation and ship handling capabilities, although, of course, there were other branches, notably marine engineering. The RNVR, consisting of people from all walks of life, was to undergo massive wartime expansion as most wartime recruits went into the RNVR. The old saying was that Royal Navy officers were 'gentlemen trying to become sailors, RNR officers were sailors trying to become gentlemen, and the RNVR were neither trying to become both!' Doubtless, RNR

Those selected for officer training wore white cap ribbons. Initially, this started at *St Vincent* at Gosport, but as the war progressed, a new camp was set up at HMS *Medina*, on the site of a holiday camp at Puckpool Park, between Ryde and Seaview on the Isle of Wight. Far right of this cheerful group is Gordon Maynard. (*via Mrs M.J. Schupke*)

officers from the smarter shipping lines, such as P&O, would probably have refuted any question that they were not gentlemen.

Included in the 1939 total were 12,400 officers and men from the Royal Marines. The Royal Marines had a number of roles aboard ship, including security and the RM Band Service, but on cruisers and battleships they also manned 'X' turret, one of the aft turrets. The Fleet Air Arm included a significant number of RM pilots and some observers, the naval term for an aircraft navigator.

Under wartime pressures, the traditional means of recruiting naval officers had to change. In peacetime, regular officers had joined as early as thirteen years old, spending four years at the Royal Naval College at Dartmouth, which operated as a fee-paying public school. Those who had attended other schools joined at seventeen or eighteen years, spending a term at Dartmouth. In both cases, after graduating from Dartmouth, they would spend eighteen months as a midshipman. Despite the cap badge, midshipmen were not regarded as being officers in the full sense, being addressed as 'mister' and not joining their seniors in the wardroom, the naval term for the officers' mess, but instead being confined to the gunroom mess. In peacetime, a midshipman who wanted to fly would undergo most of his training with the RAF, with the Royal Navy providing catapult training so that he could fly seaplanes and amphibians from battleships, battlecruisers and cruisers. Training for pilots and observers that had taken two years in peacetime was compressed into ten months in wartime.

While commissioning from the ranks was significant during and after the Second World War, it had been rare in the pre-war Navy. To obtain a sufficient number of experienced officers for the rapid wartime expansion, many senior ratings, normally chief petty officers, the naval equivalent of a staff sergeant or flight sergeant, were commissioned under the 'Upper Yardman Scheme'. The importance of this can be seen from the fact that, by June 1944, the Royal Navy in all of its categories had 863,500 men and women, a number that fell slightly to 861,000 the following June as the end of the war in Europe started to have an effect.[1]

PILOTS

Under wartime conditions, everyone had to register for National Service, but those who were interested in naval aviation did not leave matters to luck, but instead presented themselves at a recruiting office. There was chaos at first. One man ended up in the Fleet Air Arm because he had been told that he would have to wait until he was called, unless he wanted to short circuit the system by volunteering for the Royal Marine Commandos or the Fleet Air Arm. Even then, they had run out of forms. He thought that he might become an aircraft mechanic, but when the forms arrived, they were stamped PILOT OR OBSERVER. Another volunteered for the RAF, but was told that there was a waiting list of almost a year, but if he tried the Fleet Air Arm, he would be flying within a couple of months.

There was a substantial proportion of RNZNVR personnel in the FAA during the war. This was because the Royal Navy had a recruitment office in New Zealand, while

Completing the first solo flight is the highlight of any pilot's life. Here a delighted Gordon Maynard stands by his Tiger Moth at RAF Elmdon, now Birmingham Airport. (*via Mrs M.J. Schupke*)

those wishing to join the RAF had to make their own way to the UK to volunteer.

This first hurdle surmounted and the forms submitted, the applicant would be summoned to HMS *St Vincent*, the barracks at Gosport, a small town across the harbour from Portsmouth. Here, groups of forty or so were given a medical, the whole process taking a couple of hours. An interview board followed, a triumvirate chaired by a senior officer, up to and including a rear admiral,

[1] Wartime statistics from *The War at Sea* (HMSO)

supported by an instructor lieutenant commander and an engineer, usually a lieutenant commander or commander. At this stage, the candidate would be offered the choice of becoming either a pilot or an observer. If successful, he would be sent home until he could be accommodated on a course.

For the aspiring naval airman in wartime, training started with a return to HMS *St Vincent*, although sometimes nearby HMS *Daedalus*, RNAS Lee-on-Solent, had to be used as well for a week or so until accommodation was available. Here, the recruits joined in batches of fifty or sixty every four weeks, forming into courses with those for observers given even numbers and those for pilots odd numbers. They were kitted out with standard naval ratings' uniform, as Naval Airmen 2nd Class, including bell bottoms. In wartime, ratings' cap ribbons no longer showed the name of their ship, but just the simple 'HMS'. Some found a supplier able to produce ribbons showing 'FLEET AIR ARM', but this was unofficial and could only be swapped for the correct ribbon once away from base.

Pay for the new recruits was just 14s per week, but a cup of tea in the NAAFI cost just 1d, and bed and board was free. Cigarettes were 1s per 100, and traditionally duty free for naval personnel.

Recruits spent seven weeks at *St Vincent*, learning to march, salute and look after their kit, machine gun handling and navigation, Morse, semaphore and meteorology. They would also have become familiar with naval terminology and know that whenever they left a shore station, they were still officially 'going ashore'. At the end of their basic training, an examination would have to be passed, before starting elementary flying training, which, initially, was handled by the RAF, at either Elmdon, now Birmingham International Airport, or Luton, now London Luton Airport. These were additional training facilities set up by the RAF in an attempt to increase the flow of pilots, but a further stimulus came with additional training bases overseas, initially in Canada and then at Pensacola, where training was provided by the United States Navy. This was known as the Towers Scheme, set up by Admiral Towers of the USN, initially planned to train 30 pilots a month for the Fleet Air Arm and another 100, mainly flying-boat crews, for the RAF. Training overseas not only increased the output of pilots and observers, it often enabled training to become more concentrated with better flying weather. Most important of all, the vulnerable training aircraft were away from the threat of being bounced by a Luftwaffe fighter. The RAF also had many of its pilots trained abroad, often in southern Africa under the Empire Flying Training Scheme.

Graduating from *St Vincent* as Leading Naval Airmen with anchors on their sleeves, it was either the train to London for those going on to Elmdon or Luton, or a troopship to the United States for those on their way to Pensacola. At Luton, basic training was given on Miles Magisters, streamlined monoplanes, while at Elmdon, the training was on de Havilland Tiger Moths. Here, the RAF instructors believed that they could tell whether or not someone was pilot material within a week. On the Tiger Moth, some went solo after as little as five hours and few took more than ten hours; on the Magister, 'Maggies', it took longer, but anyone taking twelve hours started to worry about his chances. This stage of training usually took eight weeks and the student pilots would spend between fifty and sixty hours in the air. Pay at this stage was 6s 6d a day, of which 3s 6d was flying pay, but being based on an RAF station, cigarettes now cost 6d for ten, and half a pint of bitter was 6d.

Elmdon was already an airport before the war, with a new terminal building opened just before the war, seen here in 1939. (*Birmingham International Airport*)

Graduating from Luton or Elmdon, still as Leading Naval Airmen, the next stage was the RAF's No. 1 Service Flying Training School at Netheravon. Here, the student pilots were streamed to become fighter or bomber pilots. The former continued their training on Fairey Battles as a prelude to Skuas and Fulmars in the early days, although later they would have graduated to Sea Hurricanes, Seafires, an American fighter or, towards the end of the war, Fireflies. The latter were trained on Hawker Harts, and would expect to fly Swordfish or Albacores, and later, Barracudas or Avengers. Despite their lowly rank, at this stage, the student pilots were accommodated in the officers' mess and had WAAFs to make their beds and white cap ribbons to show that they were future officers.

This was another difference between the RAF and the Fleet Air Arm. Most naval pilots and observers were commissioned, while the RAF had a substantial number of sergeant pilots and navigators. One way of becoming a rating pilot in the Fleet Air Arm was to blot one's copybook. Two student pilots were stealing petrol from the aircraft and selling it. Fuel was eventually died red to stop such activities, and the two who were caught were imprisoned for six months and emerged to complete their training and fly as petty officer pilots.

The time spent at Netheravon was meant to increase a student's flying hours to well over a hundred, but during the early years at

A student pilot's view of the North American Harvard trainer. (*via Mrs M.J. Schupke*)

least it suffered from a shortage of aircraft. It was not unknown for half a dozen keen would-be fliers to arrive at dispersal to find just one aircraft and sometimes none at all. The weather could also play a part in reducing the number of hours flown, so that sometimes the new pilot would have as little as eighty-eight hours of solo flying. This was where they were supposed to learn formation flying and aerobatics, night flying, navigation and instrument flying, with dive-bombing for the bomber pilots and fighter tactics for the rest. They also shot at towed targets. On leaving Netheravon, the new pilots received their wings. The pass rate must have varied, but it seems that on average about half failed, or 'dipped' in naval slang. There were also casualties from accidents and, occasionally, from enemy action.

New pilots went on leave for a week, their first since joining, and their commissions were dated from the end of the leave. Then they were all commissioned into the RNVR. Those over twenty-one became temporary sub-lieutenants, those under twenty-one, temporary acting sub-lieutenants, and those under twenty became temporary mid-shipmen.

It was at this stage that they were returned to the Royal Navy for their operational training. They would learn how to fly naval aircraft and how to fly from aircraft carriers or from the catapult of a cruiser or other major fleet unit. Here they would come across another FAA/RAF difference. The RAF had operational training units, the Fleet Air Arm treated theirs as naval air squadrons, with numbers in the 700 series, along with squadrons handling a miscellany of other supposedly non-operational tasks.

Their counterparts destined to train in the United States started with passage in a troopship, often boarded not in one of the pre-war liner ports, but in some point convenient for convoy assembly, such as Gourock on the Clyde. Accommodation aboard was Spartan, but they did at least known how to sling the hammocks with which they were issued, unlike their RAF counterparts. Food, on the other hand, seems to have been good.

On arrival, usually via Canada, the early students found that the US Naval Air Station at Pensacola, was under the command of the famous pioneer, Capt A.C. Read, who as a lieutenant-commander, in 1919, had led the famous flight of flying-boats across the Atlantic, via the Azores. They also found what amounted to a self-contained town of 16,000 people, with recreational facilities that few major cities in the UK could match.

This superior setting extended to their accommodation, in comfortable dormitories with eight beds each and a spacious dining room with black stewards. Then there was the climate, for Pensacola was in Florida and on the Gulf of Mexico. Liaison officers were appointed to look after the British cadets. They took no part in training recruits, but were there to represent their interests and look after their welfare. Not surprisingly, given its facilities, which included four airfields and many emergency strips, Pensacola was known to the USN as the 'Annapolis of the Air'.

Naval cadets at Pensacola found themselves integrated into classes with USN and USMC cadets. Destined to be fighter pilots, for the first six weeks, they attended

And so is this, as they fly over the United States in formation. (*via Mrs M.J. Schupke*)

Another view of student pilots in formation, twenty-seven aircraft in all. In photographs home it was important to show just who was where! (*via Mrs M.J. Schupke*)

ground school, studying navigation, including celestial navigation, meteorology, theory of flight, and fuel, oil and hydraulic systems. There were instructional films, a compulsory period of physical training, lasting two hours every day, and a written test every Friday afternoon. Everyone had to undergo a spell in a decompression chamber, so that they could appreciate the effects of a lack of oxygen at altitude. This extended to them sitting at desks inside the chamber and taking written tests while pressure was reduced to the equivalent of an altitude of 18,000 ft. Only once this altitude was reached were they fitted with

oxygen masks, while pressure was reduced to the equivalent of 30,000 ft, when they took more tests.

Just as those trained by the RAF soon discovered differences in practice between the two services, so too did those trained by the USN. Being on parade in the Royal Navy was far more demanding than in the USN, but the drill for taking over the two-hour watch as 'Mate of the Deck' in their living quarters had evolved into a ceremony taken very seriously by the USN, but not by their RN guests.

After ground school, flying training started. Basic training was in a Naval

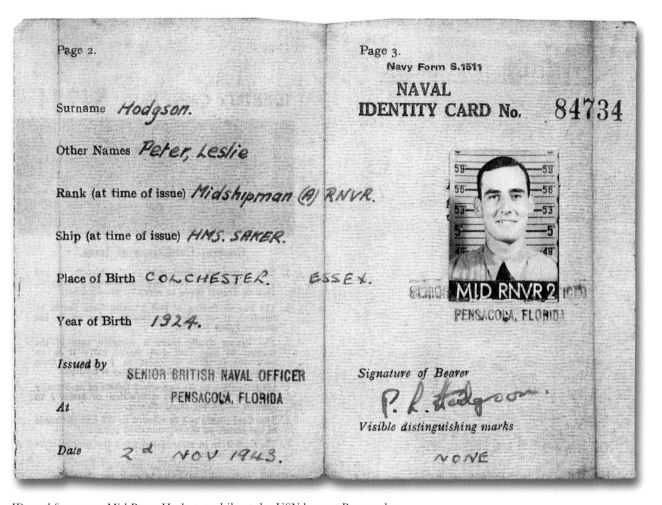

Page 2.

Surname *Hodgson.*

Other Names *Peter, Leslie*

Rank (at time of issue) *Midshipman (A) RNVR.*

Ship (at time of issue) *HMS. SAKER.*

Place of Birth *COLCHESTER. ESSEX.*

Year of Birth *1924.*

Issued by

SENIOR BRITISH NAVAL OFFICER

At PENSACOLA, FLORIDA

Date *2d NOV 1943.*

Page 3.

Navy Form S.1511

NAVAL
IDENTITY CARD No. 84734

MID RNVR 2

PENSACOLA, FLORIDA

Signature of Bearer

P. L. Hodgson.

Visible distinguishing marks

NONE

ID card for young Mid Peter Hodgson while at the USN base at Pensacola.

Aircraft Factory N3N-3 biplane with dual controls, and unusually for such aircraft, the instructor sat in the front seat. The student pilot was expected to be able to fly solo at around ten hours. One pilot who went through the process remembers a steady stream of his class mates being dropped from the course and returned to the UK for medical reasons, including air sickness, which USN doctors maintained would never disappear given time. Another was poor depth perception, which could result in the student pilot attempting to land 50 or 60 ft above the runway.

After more than thirty hours of solo flying, the training extended to flying in bad weather. This started with many hours under the hood of a ground-based Link trainer, the crude predecessor of today's flight simulators, where the students practised 'flying' along radar beams, timed approaches to airfields and let-downs in simulated bad weather. The next stage was to fly in a Harvard dual control trainer, with the student sitting in the rear cockpit under a hood, so that he did not have so much as a chink of light. The instructor sat in front, also acting as safety pilot. The instructor would fly the aircraft to within

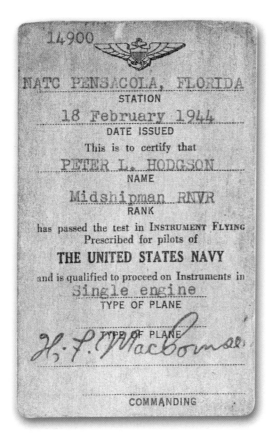

14900

NATC PENSACOLA, FLORIDA
STATION

18 February 1944
DATE ISSUED

This is to certify that

PETER L. HODGSON
NAME

Midshipman RNVR
RANK

has passed the test in INSTRUMENT FLYING
Prescribed for pilots of

THE UNITED STATES NAVY

and is qualified to proceed on Instruments in

Single engine
TYPE OF PLANE

TYPE OF PLANE

H. F. MacComal

COMMANDING

Proof that Peter Hodgson had passed his instrument flying test.

radio distance of a small civil airfield, then turned on the radio and left the student pilot to fly the approach. This entailed the student finding the beam, tracking it down to the right altitude and speed and finally positioning the aircraft to land on the duty runway. Even harder than it sounds, the student achieved all this by listening to the radio signals and interpreting them, and also reading the instruments and using a stopwatch correctly, while at the same time controlling the aircraft. At the end of this exercise, the instructor would snap up the hood so that the student could see whether or not the airfield was ahead.

The next stage was flight in a Vought Sikorsky O3U-1 biplane, similar to a Swordfish, before moving on to a landplane

version of the Vought OS2U-3 Kingfisher, with more sophisticated flying controls, and formation flying and aerobatics. Then it was time to be commissioned and move on to the fighter course at Miami, further south and almost at the other end of the state.

Fighter training took place at the USN's Fighter Training School at Opa Locka, fourteen miles north of Miami. Training here was intensive, working eight days without a break before a night and the following day at liberty. Their new aircraft was the Harvard, known to the USN as the SNJ-3. It marked a considerable advance in sophistication compared to aircraft previously flown, and was equipped with radio. The only real worry for the aspiring aviator was that so much of the training took place over the Everglades, the vast areas of swamp and scrub around Miami. The training included ground strafing, air-to-air firing at drogues and gun-camera attacks on simulated bomber formations or individual aircraft flown by other students.

After the Harvard, the students moved on to the Brewster Buffalo, fighters that had only just been discarded by the USN. At this stage, the Royal Navy resumed responsibility for their training, and not only did they have to become accustomed to a fighter, but they also had to start learning the Fleet Air Arm, as opposed to the USN, way of doing things. This meant not only learning British flying methods and phraseology, but also learning map reading, flight information, patrol formation, simulated forced landings and dummy deck landings, known as ADDLs (aerodrome dummy deck landings), as well as navigation exercises over the sea, anti-submarine bombing and night flying. They would soon be ready to convert to their operational aircraft. Lacking dual control aircraft for conversion training, pilots adapted to new aircraft types by studying the handbook and spending time in the classroom and the cockpit before attempting a first flight.

Apart from the climate and vastly superior accommodation, with higher performance aircraft on which to learn, training in the United States had other advantages compared to war-torn Britain. Petrol cost just 11 cents a gallon at a time when there were four US dollars to the pound, and serviceable old cars were also easily and cheaply available. Many bought cars and enjoyed a spell of independence during their time off that would not have been possible with strict rationing in Britain. At first, many Americans resented the presence of the Britons, jeering and shouting not just off base, but on it as well, as many felt that Churchill was attempting to draw the United States into the war. However, attitudes changed overnight with the Japanese attack on Pearl Harbor.

While these were the standard training programmes, the system was capable of variation. Initial training took into account any previous significant experience. Airline pilots, for example, were sent on a conversion course with 780 Squadron at Eastleigh, now the airport for Southampton, to familiarise themselves with the very different conditions of naval flying, using a variety of aircraft, including Hart Trainer, Nimrod, Shark, Gipsy Moth, Hornet Moth and Tiger Moth, Proctor, Shark, Swordfish and Vega Gull. From this, the younger recruits would go onto to carrier or catapult training. In some cases, conversion training was unnecessary, as with the former Jersey Airways pilots who signed up for naval commissions and flew airliners conscripted into the Royal Navy on communications duties.

Carrier deck landing training was given when needed, with refresher training after any lengthy period spent flying from a naval air station. For those trained in the United States, the USN also helped with deck

landing training. After using a runway marked out as a carrier deck, the new pilots would have a chance to learn on the real thing. For most, this meant using the USS *Challenger*, an escort carrier originally intended for the Royal Navy, but retained by the USN for just this purpose. A small number were able to use the USS *Wolverine* or *Sable*, two lake paddle steamers converted to training carriers to avoid using an operational carrier.

Fighter training for those being taught in the UK was no less intensive. The fighter school was initially at RNAS Yeovilton, where the circuit became so congested and overcrowded with inexperienced pilots that an unacceptably high number of accidents occurred. So a second training airfield was soon established at Zeals.

Other bases provided specialised training for other types of naval aviation. In the UK, the deck landing school was at RNAS Arbroath, HMS *Condor*, known to some as Aberbrothock, where there was also an observers' school. Torpedo training took place at RNAS Crail, in Fife, HMS *Jackdaw*. Advanced instrument training took place at Hinstock, HMS *Godwit*. Those destined to operate from MAC-ships also had their own special training centre at RNAS Maydown, which was initially a satellite of Eglinton before becoming HMS *Shrike*. It also housed the anti-submarine school.

Catapult training for the flights embarked in major warships passed to 700 Squadron in 1942. After initial and advanced training, seaplane and amphibian pilots would have three weeks at Donibristle learning aerodrome circuits, wireless telegraphy, water landings, photography, anti-submarine attacks and dive-bombing. This was followed by three weeks at Dundee, with crew training, navigation and night landings. Then a week of catapult training aboard HMS *Pegasus* in the Irish Sea, before

Most deck landing training in the United States was aboard the escort carrier USS *Challenger*, but a few trained on the *Wolverine*, a converted lake paddle steamer, saving scarce escort carriers for operations. Notice her low freeboard. (*US Naval Institute*)

a week at Donibristle and two weeks at Twatt in Orkney before embarkation. As the war progressed, catapult training ceased.

There were other specialised courses, with one of the more unusual being for maintenance test pilots. Early in the war, this was a course of just four weeks, but later it was extended to ten weeks and was held at RNAS Worthy Down, HMS *Kestrel*. On the extended ten week course, the pilot had a minimum of five weeks flying on the main types of aircraft in service, which by this time included the Avenger, Barracuda, Corsair, Firefly, Hellcat, Seafire and Wildcat. This was another task that fell to 700 Squadron in October 1944, after catapult training had ceased, with eighty-four test pilots trained in the following eleven months.

OBSERVERS

Much of the initial training for observers was similar to that for aspiring pilots, including the spell at *St Vincent*. The role of the observer was especially significant for naval aviation, since it was felt that even fighter aircraft needed an observer, given the greater problems of finding a fast moving carrier at sea. This, of course, also affected the performance of the aircraft, having two seats instead of one. At the same time, the work of an observer was more than just that of a navigator. The observer observed, often took photographs and in the catapult flights could be called on to help relay the fall of shot in a naval gun battle. It was also important that the observer could handle the radio, especially in aircraft without a TAG (telegraphist air gunner), or when the TAG was replaced by a fuel tank, as often happened with the Swordfish.

There were two main observer schools. The first was No. 1 Observer School, initially based at Ford and then Yeovilton, before moving to Piarco in Trinidad, where 749, 750 and 752 Squadrons provided training using a variety of aircraft, including Percival Proctors, Albacores, Barracudas, Walruses and Grumman Gooses. The second, based at RNAS Arbroath, HMS *Condor*, was No. 2 Observer School and consisted of 740, 741, 753 and 754 Squadrons, again with a mixture of aircraft, including Proctors, Walruses, Swordfish and Kingfishers. In the early years some Seafoxes, Sharks and Seals were also operated there. At one point, 754 Squadron operated a substantial number of Lysander target tugs.

DECK LANDING CONTROL OFFICERS

Deck landing control officers, or batsmen, as they were known, trained at East Haven, which also had the Deck Landing Training School. They were all experienced naval pilots. Initial training consisted of aircraft from the training squadron, 731, flying circuits, involving dummy deck landings. This routine gave rise to the nickname 'clockwork mice' for the pilots. Not surprisingly, the pilots sometimes relieved the tedium by occasionally making an irregular approach to make life more difficult for the aspiring batsmen. At least at this stage, they were in no danger of getting wet.

TELEGRAPHIST AIR GUNNERS

TAGS were naval ratings, with the highest rank on a squadron usually being a chief petty officer. Training took six or seven months, during which they would be expected to accumulate sixty hours' flying time. Initial training was at Worthy Down, home of No. 1 Air Gunners School, where 755 Squadron provided the early part of their wireless course and 757 did the same for air gunnery, with 756 providing the more advanced element of the wireless course, including cross country flying and beacon flying. The advanced element of the air gunners' course was provided by 774 Squadron, with live firing at St Merryn in Cornwall.

These arrangements were augmented by training in Canada, when a second school opened in 1943, at Yarmouth, Nova Scotia, an RCAF base handed over to the Fleet Air Arm. Confusingly, while the RN referred to this as No. 2 Air Gunners School, the RCAF referred to it as No. 1 Naval Air Gunners School.

NAVAL ANTI-AIRCRAFT GUNNERS

Naval anti-aircraft gunners were not part of the Fleet Air Arm, but the FAA was involved with their training. The prime task of aircraft in the fleet requirements unit squadrons was to provide practice for anti-aircraft gunners, usually by towing target drogues, as well as helping to calibrate ships' radar. 723 Squadron dived towards fleet units whose gunners fired back using live ammunition, although with gun sights offset 15 degrees to port.

AIR MECHANICS AND ARTIFICERS

The Royal Navy operated a two-tier system for technical personnel, and this was not unique to the Fleet Air Arm. The skilled tradesmen were known as artificers, and their work was supported by the less skilled naval air mechanics. This was a system designed to both increase the manpower available in the shortest possible time and to make the best use of the more highly

Deck landing officers, or 'batsmen', were experienced pilots moved on to an even more hazardous duty. Here is one in training at RNAS Yeovilton. The pilots giving the training nicknamed themselves the 'clockwork mice'. The holes in the bats are to reduce wind resistance, vital when standing on a flight deck in a wind of more than 30 knots. (*FAAM LANDING AIDS/47*)

skilled recruits. The less skilled air mechanics were often at leading rank, but could advance to the senior rates. Artificers were normally petty officers, POs or chief petty officers, CPOs, and had either served an extended service apprenticeship, at this stage provided at RAF Halton, or were reservists bringing their civilian skills with them. To encourage volunteers, skilled men were usually paid their pre-war civilian rates. Heading the artificers and mechanics on any squadron would be an air engineer officer.

Recruitment of the desperately needed technical personnel started well before the outbreak of war. The Admiralty knew that it not only needed to allow for dramatic wartime expansion, it also had to replace the many RAF personnel looking after the aircraft of the fleet. An Admiralty Fleet Order in the late spring of 1938 sought volunteers for the FAA from those already serving. Many volunteered in the belief that promotion would be quick. After some waiting, the applicants were interviewed by senior officers. One applicant, who wanted

Destined to become air mechanics (E), these young ratings are under instruction at Speckington in 1942, and are learning the rudiments of the four stroke engine cycle. (*FAAM*)

to be a naval air mechanic (E), working on aircraft engines, was told: 'You are an AB [able seaman], so you know about knots and splicing, so you'll be better off as an air mechanic (A), a rigger.' This was an apt reflection of the needs of aircraft such as the Swordfish and Sea Gladiator. He heard nothing more that summer. In September, when the Munich crisis broke, he was drafted to a destroyer, but as he prepared to join his ship, the First Lieutenant asked for all volunteers for the FAA to assemble outside the drafting office.

As with the rest of the Fleet Air Arm, the new recruits were dependent on the Royal Air Force for their training. The RAF, accustomed at worst to training relatively raw naval recruits, thought these ex-

perienced seamen to be a motley crew, since it did not understand their ways and their adherence to their own routines. They were divided up by specialisation, airframes, engineers, electrical and ordnance, with training at RAF Henlow, St Athan, in South Wales and Eastchurch, on the Isle of Sheppey. Training took about a year and for the naval air mechanics (A), was divided between six months at Henlow and four months at RAF Locking, near Weston-super-Mare.

For the naval air mechanics (A), training included the theory of flight as well as aircraft repairs and general maintenance, including work on the fabric covering many airframes and studying aircraft hydraulic and pneumatic systems.

However, there was no automatic promotion to a higher rate on completing the courses. The naval air mechanics of all kinds were posted to HMS *Daedalus* at Lee-on-Solent to await drafting to their squadrons. In contrast to modern practice, where special training is regarded as vital for working on different types of aircraft, no special training was given in most cases, although handbooks were usually available. Even when the FAA introduced the relatively sophisticated Sea Hurricane, the Royal Navy's first high performance aircraft,

no special training was given. The first time this was thought necessary came with the all-metal Seafire, where the air mechanics went to Supermarine at Eastleigh for two weeks. The Seafire also introduced hydraulically-operated folding wings to the FAA, a marked advanced on the mechanically-folding wings of the Swordfish. When American aircraft joined the fleet later, their greater sophistication was compensated for by being much easier to work on and by having standardised layouts for the positioning of components.

NAVAL OFFICERS' BADGES OF RANK AND INSIGNIA

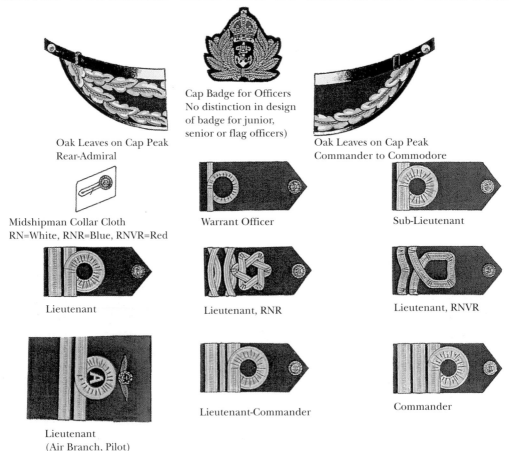

Oak Leaves on Cap Peak
Rear-Admiral

Cap Badge for Officers
No distinction in design
of badge for junior,
senior or flag officers)

Oak Leaves on Cap Peak
Commander to Commodore

Midshipman Collar Cloth
RN=White, RNR=Blue, RNVR=Red

Warrant Officer

Sub-Lieutenant

Lieutenant

Lieutenant, RNR

Lieutenant, RNVR

Lieutenant
(Air Branch, Pilot)

Lieutenant-Commander

Commander

Notice the difference between the wings for pilots and for observers. (*Sources: Various*)

Captain

Commodore (2nd Class)

Commodore, RNVR

Commodore, RNR

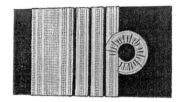

Admiral

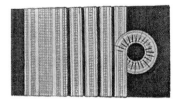

Admiral of the Fleet

Observer Wings

Rings for Rear Admiral are one broad and one narrow with a loop, and for Vice Admiral, one broad and two narrow, the upper having a loop. (*Sources: Various*)

Although flag officers did not have epaulettes on their blue uniform jackets, they did on white tropical kit. Here are the epaulettes for (left to right) Commodore 2nd Class; Rear Admiral; Vice Admiral; Admiral and Admiral of the Fleet. (*Sources: Various*)

Rating Cap Badge
(Stewards, Sick Bay Attendants)

Rating Wartime Cap Ribbon

Petty Officer
(Blue Uniform)

Chief Petty Officers Cap Badge

Petty Officer Cap Badge

3 years   8 years   13 years

Good conduct chevrons for junior rates

Leading Seaman
('Leading Hand')

Chief Petty Officer – worn on both cuffs

Petty Officer
(White Uniform)

Badges of rank for ratings. The rating cap badge was red, as were the good conduct chevrons worn by those of petty officer rank and below. (*Sources: Various*)

NAVAL RATINGS' TRADE BADGES

Telegraphist Air Gunner 2nd Class
(Leading Airman)

Air Mechanic Engines
(E for Engines, A for Airframe)

Air Fitter Electrical

Leading Photographer

A selection of naval ratings' trade badges of most relevance to the Fleet Air Arm. (*Sources: Various*)

ROYAL MARINES' AIRCREW INSIGNIA

Pilots' Wings
(Observers' Wings an 'O' with one wing attached similar to RAF
'N' Navigator)

Officers' Cap Badge

Insignia of rank similar to British Army practice, using pips and crowns.

Royal Marines' aircrew insignia, which would have been gold. (*Sources: Various*)

CHAPTER 7

THE FAA AND THE ROYAL NAVY

High, high in the sky,
Where the Swordfish and the Albacores fly;
Now we've all got our wings
We'll be doing such things
That Taranto will seem like small fry.

The Fleet Air Arm Songbook

Except while under RAF control, the Fleet Air Arm has never been a service within a service. The Admiralty would not allow such a thing. Indeed, the term 'Fleet Air Arm' was retained unofficially, since officially it was the 'Air Branch of the Royal Navy'. After the Second World War the case for full integration had to be carried to its logical conclusion by ensuring that pilots and observers would be able to obtain their watch-keeping certificates, without which eventual command of a warship would be impossible. Command of a warship is a necessary prerequisite for anyone who wants to become First Sea Lord, the highest service position on the Board of Admiralty. On regaining control of the Fleet Air Arm, the Admiralty integrated its new acquisition into the service by appointing a new member, the Fifth Sea Lord, with responsibility for naval aviation. So it fell to Vice Adm Sir Lumley Lyster to visit his USN opposite number, Vice Adm Jack Towers, shortly before the United States entered the Second World War, to discuss collaboration. The first thing they did was agree to standardise deck landing signals, although this was not implemented until later in the war when the British Pacific Fleet was operating alongside the US Fifth Fleet.

Under wartime conditions, corners had to be cut to ensure that an adequate number of aircrew were available for training. The massive wartime intake did not need watch-keeping certificates, probably did not want them and in any case, under the intensity of operations, would have had little time for such duties. Warships had peacetime and wartime complements, so that additional bodies were around. This again was in contrast to the situation after the war, when officers on an aircraft carrier would be glad to have their squadrons aboard, with the pilots and observers helping to take turn with the tasks of running the ship. Much the same happened at naval air stations ashore, when the gruelling twenty-four hour stint of officer of the day came up less frequently when the squadrons were ashore.

At all stages, the Fleet Air Arm was subordinate to the local commander, in

The formal side of naval life. Sunday Divisions parade aboard *Victorious*, March 1942, with the ship's CO taking the salute. (*FAAM*)

naval terms this meant generally the flag officer, flag rank being the Royal Navy's equivalent to a general officer in the British Army, or air rank in the RAF. In some cases, there would be a commander-in-chief over and above any flag officers, which was often a tri-service appointment, rather than purely naval. The term 'flag officer' meant those holding the rank of rear admiral and above, there were many occasions when the Fleet Air Arm would be under the command of a flag officer subordinate to a more senior flag officer. This happened with the flag officers on aircraft carriers for the Home Fleet and the Mediterranean Fleet and also when there was a naval Commander-in-Chief. In the case of a convoy, command would be vested in a senior officer, often a commodore, while the aircraft carrier or carriers would be under the command of their commanding

officers, usually a captain, but escort carriers sometimes had a commander.

The admiral's flag always indicated the presence of a senior officer aboard any warship. This consisted of the Standard of St George, with red balls in the quarters to show the precise rank. A single red ball in the left upper quarter meant a rear admiral; red balls in each of the left quarters mean a vice admiral; while a plain Standard meant an admiral. Admirals of the fleet were a rarity at sea. The system was not confined to those of flag rank, with commodores having a pennant flown from their ship based on a plain Standard of St George.

A clear pattern emerges. The relevant flag officer would be responsible to the First Sea Lord and below him there would be someone in command of naval aviation, who might be a flag officer or a captain if there was just one aircraft carrier. For convoys, the convoy commodore would be under the command of a flag officer, usually at a major naval base. For support facilities, such as training and material, the most senior Fleet Air Arm officer would be under the control of his general service superior. (Wartime Fleet Air Arm Flag Officers are shown in Appendix Two).

The most senior rank attainable by members of the RNR or RNVR was commodore. Many convoy commodores were senior officers recalled to the active list from retirement; some took a demotion to carry out this important duty. For naval aviators, there was none of the comfort of the RAF's promotion structure to look forward to. RAF squadrons could be led by a squadron leader or, especially in the case of a bomber squadron, a wing commander. Naval air squadrons were led by a lieutenant-commander and occasionally a lieutenant, especially if it was a temporary appointment after the commanding officer had become a casualty. Even when the Royal Navy introduced carrier air wings, command was normally vested in a lieutenant-commander, or the Royal Marine equivalent, a major. Carrier air groups were normally led by a commander. This became the most senior flying rank effectively, again in contrast to the RAF, where group captains were often engaged on operational sorties.

Aboard a ship, many, and sometimes most, of the complement would not be Fleet Air Arm at all, but mainly general service. Those running the ship, navigating, manning the guns, including the anti-aircraft armament and the radar, as well as providing catering and medical services and most of the Royal Marines aboard, were not Fleet Air Arm. Even naval air stations contained a substantial number of general service people. Photographers were Fleet Air Arm, along with all those responsible for maintaining the aircraft, as well as those

flying them, as were fighter direction and air traffic control, once these luxuries appeared.

On a personal level, attitudes to naval aviation varied as much as individuals differ. Many commanding officers did their best to accommodate the needs of their aviators, but others could be difficult. Flag officers could also differ. For every one who appreciated the efforts and bravery of the naval airmen, and especially their struggle to make the best of outclassed equipment during the early years of the war, there were others who resented the Fleet Air Arm. Some did not like the commanding officer of a carrier requesting permission to change course to either fly-off or land his aircraft. As more officers of flag rank assumed responsibility for naval aviation, even if they were not aviators themselves, the position improved.

Aboard an aircraft carrier or at a Royal Naval Air Station, the command structure started with the commanding officer, usually holding the rank of captain. There would be a chain of command below the commanding officer running the ship, with the second in command being a commander, then a first lieutenant, carrying out the same role as an adjutant in the other two services. The senior aviator on board was commander flying (becoming commander air after the war), and his deputy would be lieutenant-commander air. Neither of these officers flew operationally. Apart from the squadrons, the rest of the ship's company were organised into 'divisions', the naval equivalent of a department within a large organisation. Sunday inspections by the commanding officer were known as 'Divisions'.

In each squadron, there would be a squadron commander. The second in command of a squadron was known as the senior pilot, and there was usually a senior

The less formal side, as this relaxed group discusses a letter from home beside a Seafire fighter. (*IWM A24774*)

A Walrus amphibian, or 'Shagbat', after landing aboard *Ark Royal*. Aboard carriers, aircraft handling was still done by hand, or very many hands! Judging by the flag painted on the nose, this is an 'admiral's barge'. A single red dot on the Standard of the St George denotes a rear admiral. (*via S.H. Wragg*)

observer as well, both of whom would usually be lieutenants. Squadrons were divided into flights, and for those squadrons providing aircraft for the MAC-ships or catapult flights, there could be an extremely large number of flights, all given a suffix letter. Squadrons would have an air engineering officer looking after their aircraft.

Aboard the MAC-ships, which were still Merchant Navy vessels, the small Royal Navy contingent would have their own accommodation, built beneath the flight deck when the ship was converted, but the officers came together in the saloon for meals. Mixed crews like this usually worked fairly well, but there could be problems.

The trade union structure of the Merchant Navy did not always work well with the ethos of the Royal Navy. The naval ratings resented the higher pay of the merchant seamen, but they in turn resented the fact that when a merchant ship was sunk, the merchant seamen had their pay stopped, while the naval man continued to receive his, including the all-important allotment, or allowance, to his dependants.

The decision over whether or not a MAC-ship, commanded by a Merchant Navy captain, or master, flew off its aircraft rested with the commodore of the convoy. The commodore was usually in a cruiser, although often this would be an armed merchant cruiser, a converted liner.

CHAPTER 8

PERSONAL AND PERSONNEL

Let's get back to sea again and catch up on our sleep,
Let's get back on the bosom of the rolling deep,
Let's get back to sea again and get our piss-ups cheap . . .
Credited to Bob LePage, from *Bring Back My Stringbag*, by Lord Kilbracken

Life for the Royal Navy during the Second World War had its compensations, of which duty free alcohol while at sea and tobacco products even while in the UK, were just a part. However, naval discipline also imposed restrictions. Only officers were allowed spirits other than the traditional daily issue of 'grog', watered-down rum, and ratings were restricted to three pints of beer while aboard, which, of course, included air stations and barracks ashore. Midshipmen were not allowed spirits. It must have been hard for a midshipman pilot to have been paid just 9s a day, of which 4s was flying pay. Someone with the same training and experience but just a year older was ranked as temporary sub-lieutenant and received 13s 6d a day.

UNIFORMS

Uniforms were issued to ratings, while officers had to buy their own. The uniforms for ratings were made from navy blue serge, while those for officers were double-breasted navy blue barathea jackets, a style and cut copied by many navies and by the British Merchant Navy. At first, there was no naval equivalent of the battledress issued to the Army and the RAF. For aircrew this was a nuisance, because the standard naval uniform, worn under a flying jacket, snagged as they climbed into their cramped cockpits. It was not until the war was well advanced that the pilots of 832 Squadron ordered and paid for their own Royal Navy battledress uniforms in serge. As with the Army officers' battledress, it was still worn with a collar and tie – a privilege enjoyed by all ranks in the RAF. Naval officers could ask their tailor for a uniform in fine serge, which was lighter in weight than barathea, but this was frowned upon by many senior officers if worn on parade.

The standard naval ratings' uniform gave a clear indication of the trade of the rating wearing it, as well as his rank and his length of good conduct. For wartime, the rank, good conduct and trade badges were always red on the standard blue uniform and blue on white tropical uniforms. The pre-war practice of having these badges in gold on the No. 1 blue uniform was not reinstated for many years after the war. Trade badges were worn on the right arm of all ratings, with the exception of CPOs, who wore two

RNVR pilots beside a Sea Hurricane, the fleet's first high performance fighter. Gordon Maynard, far right, is in the uniform of a midshipman, his red collar cloth not showing in this black and white print. (*via Mrs M.J. Schupke*)

identical badges on the collars of their blue uniform, or on the right cuff of the tropical white uniform or on the right sleeve if a short-sleeved shirt was worn. The rank of a rating, ordinary seaman, AB (able-bodied) seaman or airman, leading airman or leading hand and petty officer was worn on the left arm, above any good conduct stripes for regular personnel and good service stripes for reservists. Good conduct stripes were awarded with one for the first three years of good conduct or good service in the reserves, two for eight years and three for

thirteen years. Good conduct was often referred to as 'undetected crime' by the more experienced and cynical naval people. This meant that an experienced man with good conduct would eventually be a 'three badger', that is, he would have three stripes and confuse the uninitiated who might think that he was a sergeant. Young junior ratings were always wary of a 'three badge PO', who would be, by definition, an old salt, wise in the ways of the world and, more importantly, those of the Royal Navy. After the war this changed, with each stripe

The need for battledress was driven by the damage done to traditional uniform, such as this, when getting into and out of cramped cockpits. This is an RNVR lieutenant.

walking out, a rope lanyard would be added. On his head, the rating wore the standard naval cap without a peak, known as a 'lid'. The peacetime tradition of having the name of his ship in gold on the ribbon was replaced with the simple letters 'HMS' in gold, partly for security and partly for economy, as personnel could change ships very frequently, while naval airmen were constantly switching between ships and shore stations. Petty officers wore a single-breasted pea jacket in fine serge, with collar and tie, while CPOs had double-breasted jackets; both wore peaked caps with gold badges, although the one for CPOs was more elaborate. The only junior ratings who

denoting a straight four years good conduct. CPOs did not wear good conduct badges; their badge of rank was the three brass buttons around the cuffs of their jackets.

The cut of the uniform varied with rank. Below the rank of petty officer, ratings wore the traditional 'square rig', a serge jumper with collar and vest and serge bell bottom trousers. The vest was usually white, but in northern conditions would be navy blue. The blue collar which hung over the shoulders of the jumper was bordered by three white stripes, for each of Nelson's great victories, while there was also a black ribbon, in mourning for Nelson, although this was swapped for white when the rating was being married. On parade and for

Eugene Esmonde's uniform, that of a regular lieutenant commander.

Khaki was sometimes worn, especially when operating ashore in support of the Army.

were only issued with tropical kit in wartime and for some years afterwards. Occasionally, usually for those deployed ashore in the desert or the jungle, often in support of the Army, khaki uniforms were issued and except for badges of rank, this was similar to the uniform issued to personnel in the other services. Cotton overalls were worn by those engaged in messy jobs, blue for ratings and white for officers. This would be worn, for example, by naval air mechanics and while outside the standard issue hat would be worn.

Warrant officers wore a thin version of the traditional sub-lieutenant's ring and loop, with an officer's cap badge. Midshipmen wore a piece of cloth and a brass button on each lapel, with the cloth white for regulars, blue for the RNR and red for the RNVR. The straight rings and loops were for the regulars, with a complex double ring for RNR officers, and a simple single wavy ring for the 'Wavy Navy' RNVR officers. Certain specialists had coloured cloth between the rings, including red for doctors, always known in the Royal Navy as surgeons, orange for dentists, purple for engineers, green for electrical and electronics, and white for paymasters. Paymasters were general administrators, since secretaries were members of the paymaster branch. Instructors had light blue cloth between their rings.

Pilots and observers had their wings, which differed, above the loop on the rings of their cuff. Not all aircrew were recognised as belonging to the Air Branch, since many were regarded as general service officers, in effect sailors who flew rather than fliers who went to sea. Those in the Air Branch had a capital letter 'A' within the loop of their rings. All RNVR officer pilots and observers were treated in this way, but there were a number of regular officers as well, usually those who had transferred from the RAF.

did not wear the square rig were stewards and sick bay attendants, who wore a single-breasted serge jacket and tie and ordinary trousers, but with a red cap badge. When marching or on guard duty, khaki webbing and gaiters were worn.

In tropical kit, which was usually white, the standard issue for junior ratings consisted of white shorts, while the white vest would be worn without the jacket. Stewards, petty officers and chief petty officers wore open-necked tropical white shirts. Ratings up to and including petty officers wore navy blue knee socks and black shoes, chief petty officers had white knee socks and white shoes. White cap covers

Many senior officers dressed formally, here is Rear Adm Sir Philip Vian, commanding the carrier force, with a cynical bunch of war correspondents, somewhere in the Far East. (*IWM A28072*)

When wearing tropical kit or battledress, the wings were worn on the left breast above any medals.

The cap badge for warrant officers, midshipmen (nick-named 'snotties' in the Royal Navy) and officers was more elaborate than that for senior ratings. The use of gold oak leaves on the peaks of officers' caps differed slightly in the Royal Navy from the practice in the RAF, with commanders, captains and commodores having one row of oak leaves, with two rows for rear admirals and above. As with all other ranks, white cloth covers were not usually issued

for wear with blue uniforms during the war years, or for some years afterwards, with an exception being made in the sub-tropical areas, where the armed forces changed into blue uniform for the winter months. Another wartime utility measure was the suspension of the traditional mess kit for formal dining evenings.

For tropical kit, officers usually wore a white shirt and shorts, but in some cases khaki was worn, with white or khaki cap covers, white or khaki knee socks and white shoes, unless wearing khaki, when black shoes were worn. Markings of rank were

Contrast the formality of Vice Adm Sir Henry Rawlings, in command of the British Pacific Fleet, with that of Adm Chester Nimitz. Strangely, many US servicemen were unfamiliar with shorts! (*IWM A29263*)

worn on shoulder epaulettes when wearing tropical kit. Some senior officers, including Adm Sir Andrew Cunningham, persisted in wearing peacetime 'Number Ones', white with buttoned up jacket and trousers, as a further mark of their authority.

Normally, Royal Marines wore blue uniform, with a jacket that buttoned up to the neck for non-commissioned men, but with a shirt, collar and tie for officers. Wings were worn on the left breast. Officers wore their badges of rank, similar to those of the Army, on their shoulder epaulettes. Tropical uniform was khaki, except for ceremonial duties, when it was white.

FOOD AND ACCOMMODATION

Wartime conditions in the Royal Navy varied. There was the obvious discomfort of being in cramped conditions aboard a ship, where even officer accommodation was cramped by the standards of those living ashore, and this situation was worsened by the increase of ships' companies in wartime. There was strict segregation between the lower deck, the ratings, and the upper deck, the officers. Aboard a carrier, priority was given to the aircraft, to their munitions, fuel and spares, then to the ship's own armament, leaving the ship's company and

Ratings take a meal aboard *Avenger*. The ship clearly has cafeteria messing, marking the change from the old practice of eating and sleeping in the same quarters. (*IWM A10960*)

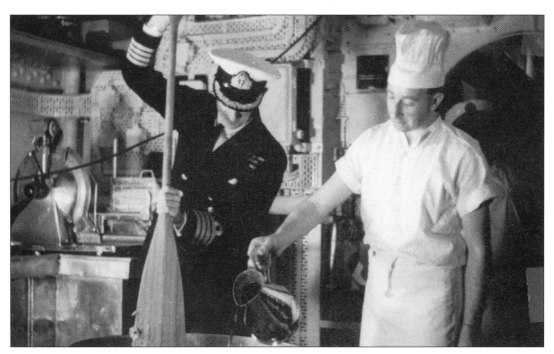

One Royal Navy tradition is the ship's captain giving the Christmas pudding a stir. This is Capt Holland giving a hand with an oar aboard *Ark Royal*. (*via S.H. Wragg*)

the personnel of the embarked squadrons to fit in around it. For the ratings, there were hammocks, often in large mess decks; for the officers, there were cabins, but it was not unusual for these to be shared by two or three officers, sometimes more. Even officers' cabins could be noisy, and usually being higher up in the hull of the carrier, they would be more likely to be disturbed by flying, and especially the thump of an aircraft landing.

There were few concessions to the Fleet Air Arm at first, and naval aviators, especially the non-commissioned, landing back aboard after a night patrol, could find sleep difficult in the cramped and often noisy conditions of a warship mess deck in daytime. Unlike the RAF, where the whole base revolved around the needs of the aircrew, and where in most cases entire squadrons were scrambled or sent on a mission, in the Royal

Navy for much of the time, the airmen were seen as a nuisance. It was not just sleep that the returning aviator might find difficult, meal times were at first very rigid, especially for rating airmen, usually TAGS. Ratings were fed for free, but officers had to pay a small amount for their food.

Meal times for ratings were breakfast at 7:00, lunch at noon, afternoon tea at 16:00 and supper at 18:00. During the early years, if a TAG happened to be flying at these times, that was his bad luck. If he was lucky and someone remembered, a meal would be set aside for his return, by which time it would be a congealed, greasy mess. On one occasion, after a long cross-country flight and several missed meals, one TAG recalled how he had to go to the officers' wardroom to get a chit signed so that the duty cook could prepare some food.

There were three different types of messing arrangements for ratings. There

It looks as if the Christmas pudding will be fine! (*via S.H. Wragg*) (*Opposite*): The end result, *Ark Royal's* Christmas Day menu, 1940. Many recall food being better than that of the civilian population. (*via S.H. Wragg*)

was general messing, in which the paymaster or his deputy would draw up a menu for all the lower deck and each mess sent a duty cook, chosen by roster, to collect the meals for the agreed number of men in the mess. The meals would be served and eaten on the mess deck at a wooden table, with the men sitting on wooden stools or benches and at night the mess became the sleeping accommodation for the men. A variation on this would be canteen messing, in which supplies were drawn, including a ration of meat, potatoes and any other vegetables, from the ship's provision store and prepared in the mess, again by a duty cook and then taken to the galley to be cooked. Once the meals were cooked, they would be collected and served as in general messing.

This system was applied in HMS *Argus*, for example. Then, on the later ships, including the escort carriers, there was cafeteria messing, in which eating and sleeping took place in different areas of the ship and the ratings had their meals in a self-service cafeteria, as they would ashore.

Most accounts of the war years suggest that the standard of catering was good, and that even for the lower deck, the ratings, rationing had little impact and that those at sea fared better for food than the civilian population. Nevertheless, there were some hardships. The carriers may have been large ships, for the most part, but they also had large complements and soon ran out of potatoes. At a time when the civilian population had very conventional meals with little sign of today's international cuisine, rice was a staple part of the naval diet.

People had their favourites, made even more glamorous by naval slang. A 'cackleberry' was an egg, 'Spithead pheasant' a kipper and 'train smash' tinned pilchards in tomato sauce. The rations could be augmented by treats from the NAAFI (the Naval, Army, Air Force Institute) aboard every ship and in every air station and barracks.

Fresh water was another problem, especially on the older ships, such as the converted battlecruiser *Furious*. Never designed for the number of men aboard, and in any case designed to operate with the Home Fleet, she soon ran out of fresh water for washing, shaving or bathing. Salt water had to be used for these functions and special salt water soap was issued, which took a long time to lather. Experienced sailors soon adjusted and habitually became very careful in their use of water, even though the newer carriers were much better in this respect, including *Ark Royal*, where fresh water seemed to be plentiful. The escort carriers, with their merchant hulls, also tended to be

better able to meet the freshwater needs of their crews. This may well have been because the vast majority of these ships were US conversions, and as befitted a Navy with relatively few overseas bases and the vast expanses of the Pacific, American warships had very good fresh water provision.

Accommodation in the escort carriers could be Spartan, nevertheless. Even officers sometimes found themselves accommodated next to the side of the hull. One recalled how they were blown out of their bunks when an escorting destroyer swept past making a depth charge attack. One especially Spartan feature on the escort carriers were the ratings' lavatories, which consisted of wooden benches with holes cut in them and water running underneath. The younger members of the crew could be relied upon to put oily rags or screwed up newspapers into this stream, light them and then wait for the panic that ensued. Normally, the only real victim was the first to be reached by these improvised fire ships.

None of this should disguise the fact that many naval airmen of all ranks were often anxious to return to sea, despite the discomforts and the dangers. The Fleet Air Arm had few bases of its own at the start of the war and these quickly became overcrowded. Yeovilton was still not complete at the time of the Battle of Britain. As its needs changed, the RAF released some bases to the Admiralty, but much depended on the location. This was part of the problem. The Fleet Air Arm needed air stations close to the ports and anchorages used by the fleet. Aircraft could not be kept on board while in harbour because they were vulnerable and could not be flown from a ship not under way. The Home Fleet was moved north to Scapa Flow and this meant that an air station had to be quickly improvised at Hatston, just outside Kirkwall, on the mainland of Orkney. A bleak position

The officers' wardroom aboard *Atheling*. The presence of ladies shows that the ship is in port. (*via Mrs M.J. Schupke*)

in winter, it was muddy, wet, windy and it snowed often, but the men were quartered in bell tents. A warm climate did not always guarantee ideal conditions either. Hal Far, then an RAF base on the southern end of Malta, also provided tented accommodation through the heat of the Maltese summer.

For officers, it was different. Meals were served in the wardroom, which usually had an ante-room with a bar and would be provided to match the flying programme, including serving bacon and eggs in the small hours if a major bombing raid required an early start. Most accounts suggest that the effort probably was not worth it, since, understandably, many aircrew had little appetite before a major operation. Wardroom meals were served by stewards and officers would also have a steward to look after their other needs, such as laundry, although usually it would be one steward to two or three officers in the same cabin. The gunroom mess was also comfortable, a bit like a prefect's common room. On most ships, the wardroom had a hierarchy. Many senior officers would have a distinct corner of their own and so too would the Royal Marines if there were a substantial number aboard. The commanding officer was not a member of the

A game of deck hockey, one of the limited sporting events aboard a warship. (*via Mrs M.J. Schupke*)

wardroom and would only appear when invited by the wardroom president, usually his second in command.

Accounts differ over whether wardroom life was boozy or not. Only a fool would get seriously drunk before flying early the next day and doubtless some did not drink when flying was possible. Nevertheless, wardroom life was sociable and when operating with the United States Navy, with its 'dry' ships, visits by American officers to the more relaxed Royal Navy must have helped oil the wheels of collaboration. Little money changed hands in the wardroom. Officers had an account, which had to be settled monthly. Senior officers kept an eye on this, and if anyone appeared to be drinking heavily, there would be a quiet word, and if notice was not taken, the account could be restricted or even closed. A popular feature of wardroom life was the sing-songs around the piano. This was a time when most well-educated young men could play the piano and in the Fleet Air Arm, there seemed to

One popular pastime was 'goofing', watching aircraft come in to land. It could be an exciting, and sometimes dangerous, experience. (*via S.H. Wragg*)

While in port, ships were sometimes visited by professional entertainers from ENSA, although it looks as if a little amateur help is being offered here by a member of *Ark Royal*'s ship's company! (*via S.H. Wragg*)

Such entertainments were obviously popular. (*via S.H. Wragg*)

be many lyricists able to pen a few words to a popular tune, many of these eventually appeared in the *Fleet Air Arm Songbook*.

There was another aspect to life aboard ship. In common with every ship, naval or merchant, aircraft carriers kept a ship's log. There were also squadron logs, and individual pilots and observers also maintained a logbook. In the Fleet Air Arm, colour was added to the dry official accounts of life afloat by the existence in many ships of the 'line book', an informal and sometimes irreverent account of life aboard ship and the deeds and misdeeds of the ship's officers.

PERKS OF THE JOB

Officially, there were few perks for the Royal Navy. There was duty free drink while at sea, and duty free cigarettes and tobacco, even when in the UK. Cheap drink and tobacco products while stationed abroad were something shared by all three services. Stationed at home or abroad, or serving in a ship at sea, the usual UK income tax was still payable.

Nevertheless, given the visits by many ships, including those on convoy escort duty, to North America and the austere wartime rationing at home, some smuggling was to be expected. The Fleet Air Arm played its part in this. Ships were met by customs officers on reaching port and sometimes just before entering harbour, but by this time the aircraft had flown off. Some accounts suggest that these were sometimes fairly heavily laden and customs inspection at the naval air stations receiving these aircraft varied in its intensity, and, most importantly, in how promptly customs would arrive. In any event, many officers would buy a bottle of spirits before leaving the ship.

But there was another way in which the acquisitive seafarer could improve his lot. When an aircraft was lost, all of its equipment was written off. Some stores officers would work hard to ensure that any shortfall in their stores just happened to be on the most recently lost aircraft. The aircrew could benefit as well. On seeking a fellow member of his squadron who had just been rescued after ditching, one naval officer found him celebrating the acquisition of a fine pair of binoculars which he had managed to save as his aircraft sank beneath the waves.

CHAPTER 9

OPERATIONS

There's a ballsup on the Flight Deck and the Wavy Navy done it,
There's a ballsup on the Flight Deck and they don't know who to blame,
Reds galore from an Albacore, Helldiving for the drink,
Di-da Di-da comes from afar as a Fulmar starts to sink.
There's a ballsup on the Flight Deck and the Wavy Navy done it,
There's a ballsup on the Flight Deck and they don't know who to blame.
    Wings at Sea, A Fleet Air Arm Observer's War 1940–45, Gerard A. Woods

Naval aviators had to be flexible. The limited size of an aircraft carrier's complement of aircraft meant that what would today be described as 'multi-tasking' was the order of the day. Even the descriptions given to aircraft and to squadrons emphasised this. Initially there were TSR squadrons, meaning torpedo, spotter, reconnaissance, although these eventually became TBR squadrons, torpedo, bomber, reconnaissance. Such a squadron would undertake all three roles, although it has to be admitted that the reconnaissance aspect of the operation was not to be compared with the work of a high-flying photo-reconnaissance Spitfire or Mosquito. Instead, it was a case of keeping an eye open for the enemy, especially submarines and surface raiders. The aircraft in such a squadron could be used to drop bombs, depth charges and torpedoes, which could be contact or magnetic, exploding close to the target and not needing to hit it to inflict damage, and to drop mines in enemy waters. Later in the war, they would

also fire unguided air-to-surface rockets at submarines.

Of course, some of the descriptions afforded the aircraft were highly optimistic. The Skua was a fighter/dive-bomber. In reality, it was more dive-bomber than fighter and a sitting duck if pounced upon by a Messerschmitt Bf109.

Pilots and observers were often 'rested' at second line squadrons. The role of the second line squadron went far beyond training and communications duties. One of the most important tasks for any naval air arm is the fleet requirements unit, or FRU, whose duties include target towing and simulated attacks, as well as radar calibration, which grew in importance during the war years with the use of radar for gunnery control.

ABOARD SHIP

As with most service aviators, for the naval pilot and observer, a sortie would usually be

SAINT
VALENTINE'S
DAY
1945.

The single-engined Stringbag
Has flown for quite a time,
Its prehistoric silhouette
Is known in every clime.
How different the 88,
With fuselage so slim—
A monoplane with motors two;
Don't make mistakes with him!

Yet what a metamorphosis
A bit of action brings,
When Junkers fly at 80 knots
And grow some second wings;
And Stringbags (clearly Nazified)
And Wildcat sixes too
Become the targets of all guns
Whilst 88's fly through....

The leopard cannot change his spots,
Nor I (alas!) change mine:
Remember this, and I'll be pleased
To be your Valentine.

Another festive occasion, a Valentine with a timely warning for any Swordfish pilot unlucky enough to meet a Junkers Ju88! (*via Lord Kilbracken*)

preceded by a briefing, for which aircraft carriers had a briefing room, often of some size for the fast armoured carriers that could be sending a considerable force on a major operation. There was also in such ships an air intelligence office, or AIO, where the available information on enemy movements was up-dated continuously.

By the outbreak of war, most of the Royal Navy's aircraft carriers had been fitted with accelerators, a hydraulic catapult, to help aircraft into the air. Not all aircraft needed this help and much depended on the speed of the ship and wind conditions, but it was still necessary, even with the accelerators, for the ship to have to turn into the wind and increase her speed before aircraft could be flown off. The waiting pilots could see whether the ship was in fact turning into the wind by watching a jet of steam at the forward end of the flight deck, with markings to show the angle of the wind across the deck. During take-off and landing it was advisable to keep the cockpit hood, if there was one, well back in case a quick escape was called for. The aircraft all had tail wheels, so the pilot could not see ahead, and he was completely dependent on signals from the team on the flight deck. Taxiing in a zigzagging movement, the normal practice with tail wheel aircraft on the ground, was not an option in the cramped confines of a carrier's flight deck. Once waved into position for take-off, by the flight deck officer, the pilot could not see directly ahead until the aircraft had gathered enough speed for the tail to rise and the nose to come down. The flight deck officer used bats by day and wands by night to direct aircraft.

The accelerators were far less powerful than the postwar steam catapults, but they were a help, especially if aircraft were heavily loaded. It was not unknown for aircraft to ditch after taking off, usually because of engine failure, but on at least one occasion, a Swordfish suffered severe structural fatigue and collapsed into the sea. Once in the water, there was a serious risk of being run down by the ship, but in this case, the three-man crew was thrown clear, only to be killed as their aircraft with its load of depth charges reached the depth set for detonation.

The MAC-ships and many of the escort carriers lacked accelerators, and compounded this omission by having both shorter flight decks than the purpose-built carriers and a lower speed. This was a particular problem with the MAC-ships, which could not carry fighters as a result. One solution was to fit rocket-assisted take-off gear (RATOG) to the Swordfish, which helped if all the rockets fired correctly, otherwise the aircraft could become unstable at a critical time. Another system,

An unhappy episode. The funeral at sea of a rating struck by an aircraft propeller while working on the flight deck of *Attacker*. (*FAAM CARS A/238*).

also used aboard escort carriers, was to tether the aircraft while full power was applied, then release it, although it was generally believed that this only contributed an extra mile or two per hour to take-off speed. Aircraft that were making a free take-off, that is, without assistance, had to be carefully chocked, and chockmen would pull these away at the last minute when signalled to do so. The chockmen had to be careful not to walk into a rotating propeller or the wings of an aircraft, a hazard on a congested and busy flight deck, especially at night. Take-off would be under the strict control of 'Wings', either the Commander Flying or Lieutenant-Commander Air.

As the war progressed the aircraft became heavier. The more powerful American fighters were an obvious example of this, but even the Swordfish managed to put on weight by adding radar. There were two main types of radar fitted, both air-to-surface vessel radars, but the British system was known as ASV and the American as ASH. Once away from the ship, good navigation was necessary if she was to be found again. Carriers were quickly fitted with homing beacons by the beginning of

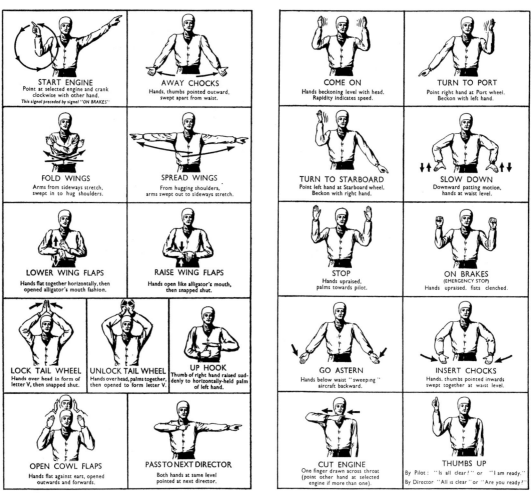

Left: Manoeuvring on a carrier deck was difficult, given the congestion and lack of space, and the movement of the ship, all compounded by the fact that all aircraft had tailwheels, so a pilot could not see directly ahead, and could not zig zag as he would on an air station. These are the Deck Director's signals. (*FAAM*) *Right*: More signals. At night, lighted wands were used. (*FAAM*)

the war, which made finding the ship easier. This was a dustbin-shaped device at the top of the mainmast, transmitting a narrow beam of radio signal through 360 degrees once every minute. The maximum range of the beacon was seventy miles, although fifty miles was more effective. Often, strict radio silence was enforced, both to protect the aircraft on their sorties and the mother ship. The carriers were at the back of the

queue when ships were fitted with radar and could not direct their own aircraft down. Indeed, during the Salerno landings, fighter direction came not from the carriers but from another ship.

Approaching the carrier required caution, over and above that needed as the stern dipped and rose by up to 50 ft in a heavy ocean swell. If the ship had been under heavy aerial attack, if visibility was not too good, or if aircraft recognition was poor, the AA gunners might be jumpy, this was a common hazard. Getting the aircraft safely down was the responsibility of the carrier deck landing officer, the batsman, himself a former pilot. The batsman would stand at the after end of the flight deck, a lonely figure doing a hazardous and tiring job, especially when standing in a stiff breeze. The wind pressure on the bats was such that holes had to be cut in them to allow them to be used. It was not unknown for two aircraft to approach a ship from different directions, not to see each other and both believe that the batsman's signals were meant for them. If an aircraft made an uncertain landing, the batsman often had to jump for it, over the side. All this, and yet these men lost their flying pay when they stopped flying and started training to be a batsman.

All of the carriers had arrester wires to help aircraft to land; it was usual to have four wires laid out across the flight deck so that when raised, the landing pilot would hope to engage one of these. If he failed, the risk was that he would hit aircraft parked forward in the deck park, but this problem was considerably reduced by the introduction of the wire mesh barrier.

Left: The original batsmans' signals for an approaching aircraft. (*via FAAM*) *Right*: For operations with the USN, the signals had to be modified in 1945. (*via FAAM*)

The barrier could be raised and lowered, so that as an aircraft landed, the barrier was dropped, the aircraft taxied over it, and the barrier was raised again, protecting the aircraft from the next one to land. Missing the arrester wires and hitting the barriers was not a soft option for the careless or unlucky pilot. The force of hitting the barrier could break a pilot's neck and on more than one occasion, aircraft blew up after hitting the barrier as fuel pipes were ruptured by the force. Then there were those occasions when aircraft leapt over the barrier and hit aircraft on the other side of it.

For those off-duty, watching aircraft landing was a spectator sport, with many of the ship's company lining the superstructure in what was known as 'goofers' gallery' in the Royal Navy, and perhaps even more aptly, 'vultures' row' in the US Navy. Despite these problems, at the height of the war in the Pacific, some ships of the British Pacific Fleet managed to land an aircraft every forty-three seconds. This required highly skilled work by the batsman, the pilot and those operating the crash barrier, as well as a strong and well-drilled flight deck crew.

Part of the problem was that few aircraft were designed with naval aviation in mind. The Seafire had speed, but its long nose meant that it could easily topple forward during landing. The sturdy Vought Corsair, which also suffered in this way, had been rejected by the US Navy as too big to operate from aircraft carriers and was passed to the US Marines Corps and the Royal Navy. The Seafire also had a bouncy undercarriage, which added to its problems. The Martlet (or Wildcat) had a narrow undercarriage, and in bad weather these aircraft could be seen bouncing from one leg to another. Writing off an aircraft was not uncommon, and if he survived, the pilot had to complete an accident report on form A25, which needless to say, soon became immortalised in song.

Aircraft had to be secured whenever the weather was bad, using big screw pickets if ashore, or ring bolts on the flight deck and hangar deck if aboard a carrier, using wires with quick release attachments. Even this did not always prove to be sufficient, and it was the job of the hangar sentries to keep a close watch and raise the alarm if an aircraft broke loose. It was also important that all equipment, including tool boxes, trestles and trolleys, was secured to the hangar walls.

Keeping the decks clean was an important chore, as fuel and oil, including unburnt particles of fuel from aircraft exhausts and rubber from aircraft being sharply decelerated on landing, could produce a treacherous surface. This was most apparent on the hangar decks, where most maintenance was done, but also to keep the flight decks clear for operations, and because of the difficulty of working on the flight deck, even in good weather if the ship was moving at speed. The tanker-based MAC-ships provided the fitters and mechanics with trying working conditions, as they did not have a hangar.

If a slippery hangar deck was a hazard, fire was an even greater fear. The hangar deck was the most vulnerable area, often with fuelled and armed aircraft present. During the early 1930s, salt water sprays were introduced, recognising that while this would have a corrosive effect on airframes, fire was still the greater hazard. Heavy fire curtains to isolate a blaze were another innovation from the same time. After a refit *Eagle* could cover the flight deck with foam within minutes. Even so, the fire safety officers aboard some British Pacific Fleet carriers learnt from American experience, and one way or another, acquired additional fire fighting equipment for their ships – in one case even purchasing some items from a department store.

While the fast armoured carriers had heavy armour plating to protect the hangar, the smaller ships did not, such as the escort carriers and even *Ark Royal*. On one occasion, a fused 40-lb bomb fell off a Swordfish landing on *Ark Royal* and blew a hole in the flight deck, killing the crew of the aircraft and four members of the deck handling party.

Initially, every aircraft had its own maintenance team, usually a naval airman (A) and a naval airman (E), a system that lasted for some time. It made for good rapport with the aircrew. Nevertheless, pressures on accommodation and a dire shortage of trained personnel of all kinds until the last year or so of the war, led to what some described as a 'garage' system, whereby personnel maintained any aircraft allocated to them.

The Fleet Air Arm has always been more flexible in the use of its maintainers than the RAF, with a less rigid trade system; this continues today, with electricians handling electronics and ordnance. Airframe fitters in wartime were also trained to handle torpedoes, for example. This is probably a by-product of life aboard ship, where everyone has to chip in. In wartime, for example, a paymaster might find that at action stations his place would be on one of the ship's AA guns.

ACTION STATIONS

In wartime, warships were often at defence stations, a lower rate of readiness than action stations. Defence stations meant that all ready use ammunition lockers would be fully stocked and some of the ship's guns would be manned, so that even a surprise attack would not necessarily succeed.

Watertight doors in certain vulnerable positions would be closed, but most would be open so as not to restrict the work going on aboard the ship. Action stations denoted a far higher state of readiness. As soon as action stations sounded over the tannoy, the remaining watertight doors and hatches would be closed, so that the ship was divided into watertight compartments. These could not be re-opened again without permission from the officer of the watch. Combat air patrols would be mounted and all non-operational aircraft would be struck down into the hangar.

Apart from the ship's aircraft and the defending fire of escorting warships, which in the case of a battleship could be extremely heavy, aircraft carriers had their own anti-aircraft defences. This varied considerably, especially between classes of ship, but also between ships of the same class, partly due to availability and sometimes due to the policy in force at the time of a major refit. The *Ark Royal* and the ships of the Illustrious-class had standardised on a main AA armament of sixteen 4.5-in guns in twin turrets, with two turrets aft and two turrets forward on each side of the ship. Many ships had Oerlikon or Bofors guns, and small 0.5 in machine guns. However, many believed that the most effective defence against low-flying aircraft, such as a torpedo-bomber, was the multiple pom-pom, each with eight barrels firing 2-lb shells.

Under attack, ships would increase their speed and take evasive action, although this could be difficult in a convoy and it was one reason why large convoys extended over several miles of sea. Within the convoy, ships travelled in lanes. It was usual for any aircraft carrier to be in the middle of a convoy, so as to protect its most important asset, but with gaps in the adjoining lanes to allow room for the carrier to manoeuvre, especially when operating her aircraft.

As with any operational sortie, the briefing was important. These are almost certainly members of 1833 Squadron aboard *Illustrious*. (*IWM A28006*)

One trick that commanding officers had to learn was that of combing torpedoes. This meant turning the ship to face the approaching torpedoes, presenting a smaller target than when broadside on to the torpedoes and so hoping to avoid them.

An essential part of wartime operation was to 'darken ship' as nightfall approached. This order was piped at dusk and on deck even lighting a cigarette or pipe was strictly forbidden. 'Slow matches' were used behind screens for those wanting to light up, and these consisted of slow burning hemp that gave a dull glow for anyone wanting to smoke. When aircraft had to be moved into or out of the hangars, the lights in the vicinity of the lift would be dimmed.

IN THE AIR

The British armed forces had to revise many of their tactics during the early years of the war. Many of the lessons learnt, often the hard way from experience of fighting against German veterans of the Spanish Civil War and the Polish Campaign, applied equally to the Fleet Air Arm and the RAF. One of the best examples lay in fighter tactics, where it soon became clear that the German concept of a 'finger four' formation for patrolling fighters was the one that enabled each aircraft in the formation to cover the others while keeping an eye open for enemy aircraft. It was also the one that enabled them to respond most effectively once a threat emerged.

The number of fighter aircraft that could be put into the air to protect the fleet was always limited. A single aircraft carrier could only carry so many aircraft, and would feel just as defenceless without her anti-submarine patrols as she would without her fighters. There was another problem as well. The number of aircraft that could be put into the air quickly was limited by the size of the flight deck, itself often reduced by parked aircraft. It was also considered good practice to have the standing air patrol augmented by aircraft on the flight deck, ready to be launched as soon as a threat appeared and not to wait until those fighters in the air on their CAP were short of fuel before recalling them, otherwise they could be at a serious disadvantage when enemy aircraft approached. Even when several carriers were operating together, rather than put additional aircraft into the air, it was seen as a better idea to conserve fuel and aircraft. There was also the need to keep a flight deck free to launch aircraft and another carrier's flight deck free to receive them. Launching and receiving aircraft at the same time was hardly a practical proposition before the introduction of the angled flight deck.

When possible, fighters would provide cover for the bombers or torpedo-bombers. This was not always possible at first, but it became increasingly commonplace later in the war, once high performance fighters became available to the fleet. A good example was Operation Lentil, the raid on

Pankalan Brandan on 4 January 1945, when Hellcats from *Indomitable* flew top cover and low cover, while middle cover was provided by Corsairs from *Victorious*, for Avengers from both ships. This was not the only task falling to fighter aircraft as the fleet went onto the offensive. This particular formation included 'fighter ramrods', the Royal Navy's code name for offensive fighter sweeps, which usually included airfields, harbours and shipping. The effect of the fighter ramrods could be significant, on Operation Lentil they discovered twenty-five Japanese aircraft on an airfield and destroyed seven of them, while also shooting down two aircraft in the air.

Using fighters to strafe ground targets was often the ideal way to attack soft targets, such as aircraft, hangars, accommodation, especially lightly-built tropical structures and vehicles, while it also helped to keep the heads of the anti-aircraft gunners down. This technique had already been used on attacks against the *Tirpitz*, where, after escorting the bombers, in this case Barracudas, to the target, the fighters would attack the ship to discourage the AA gunners, and at least it caused them to divide their fire. There could be drawbacks to such activities, especially against open targets such as airfields. The instruction was given that when attacking airfields, fighter ramrods should make just one pass over the target. This was because on the second pass the defenders knew what to expect and had the fighter's height and direction, so had a much better chance of shooting him down.

Getting the balance between being a ramrod and providing cover for the bombers was always difficult, even when different units were allocated to these duties. Coordination between fighters and bombers was essential, but so too was good discipline on the part of the fighter pilots who could easily be tempted into a dog fight.

A batsman literally runs for his life as a Fulmar misses the wires while attempting to land on *Ark Royal*. (*via S.H. Wragg*)

This was a problem not unique to the Fleet Air Arm. In aerial combat, the aim was to ward off fighters attempting to attack your bomber formation, and not to leave them alone and vulnerable while testing your skills against an opponent. When defending a target, be it a convoy, a task force or a shore target, the aim was to ignore the escorting fighters as far as possible, and attempt to destroy, or at least scatter, the bombers.

In these cases, the numbers of fighters deployed tended to be substantial. On Operation Lentil, thirty-two fighters provided cover at all levels for the same number of Avengers on bombing duties, and twelve rocket-firing Fireflies, as well as another sixteen Corsairs as fighter ramrods. On Atlantic and Arctic convoys, the number of fighters could be very small indeed, with round the clock protection provided by just six aircraft. Fighters were there to protect the convoy from long-range maritime reconnaissance aircraft, such as the Focke-Wulf Fw200 Condor and the Junkers Ju290, which could be found well out to sea. On the Malta convoys, which were often very heavily protected, and the Arctic convoys, fighters had to contend with Luftwaffe dive-bombers, meaning the Ju87 Stuka, and bombers, such as the Dornier Do17, the Heinkel He111 and the Junkers Ju88, the latter being particularly fast. As well as protecting the ships of the convoy and the carrier, they also had to look after the Swordfish on their anti-submarine and anti-shipping patrols, which were vulnerable.

For their part, aircraft on anti-submarine and anti-shipping patrols had their own pattern of operations, all of which were given reptile code-names.

This helped to keep instructions brief, and also helped maintain some degree of security if the instruction had to be amended while the aircraft was in the air. It was not unknown if the aircraft was within sight for this to be conveyed by Aldis lamp. The table below shows the standard convoy air patrol patterns. All of these patrol patterns were suitable for one aircraft at a time, reflecting the reality that few aircraft were available on an escort carrier. Only *Cobra* and *Viper* were suitable for more than one. This was inevitable, with a convoy often entrusted to a single MAC-ship with just three or four Swordfish, not all of which might be fully operational.

STANDARD CONVOY AIR PATROL CODENAMES

ALL SUITABLE FOR A SINGLE AIRCRAFT

COBRA 'Y' Patrol around convoy at a distance of Y miles, with Y being the distance from the convoy so that the instruction Cobra 12, would mean patrol at a distance of twelve miles.

VIPER Patrol around convoy at distance of visibility.

ADDER Patrol ahead of convoy at distance of eight to twelve miles, with the length of patrol thirty miles, that is, fifteen miles on either side of the centre line.

'X ' PYTHON 'Y' Given when a submarine had been spotted, so that the aircraft would patrol on bearing 'X' at a distance of 'Y' miles, and would carry out a square search around the indicated position for twenty minutes.

'X' MAMBA Search along bearing 'X' to a depth of thirty miles and return.

'X' LIZARD 'Y' Search sector bearing 'X' to a depth of 'Y' miles.

FROG 'Y' Patrol astern of convoy at distance of 'Y' miles. Length of patrol would be 2 'Y' miles, that is 'Y' miles on either side of the centre line. This was to stop U-boats trailing the convoy, often shortly before dusk. It was also essential prior to any change of course so that the U-boat commander would keep his craft submerged and not realise that the change had taken place until it was too late.

ALLIGATOR, port or starboard Patrol on side indicated at distance of ten miles from the convoy along a line parallel to the convoy's course. The length of patrol would be twenty miles, that is ten miles ahead and astern of the aircraft's position on the convoy's beam.

CROCODILE 'Y' Patrol ahead of convoy from beam to beam at radius 'Y' miles, in effect a half COBRA. This was popular with fast convoys since they had little to fear from a U-boat sneaking up from astern.

CHAPTER 10

SQUADRONS, WINGS AND CARRIER AIR GROUPS

Fly off, fly off for Christ's sake,
For the Captain wants a gong,
Fly off, fly off for Christ's sake,
For the Captain can't be wrong.

from *Bring Back My Stringbag*, by Lord Kilbracken

After the formation of the Fleet Air Arm in 1924 as a part of the Royal Air Force, separate blocks of squadron numbers were allocated. Numbers 401–439 were fleet spotter flights, assigned to battleships and cruisers; 440 to 459 being fleet reconnaissance flights, and 460 onwards as fleet torpedo flights.

Many of these squadrons and flights were renumbered in the 700 series in 1936 and retained when the Admiralty regained full control of the Fleet Air Arm. Under this scheme, 700–749 were catapult flights and squadrons, but eventually these merged into 700 Squadron, with a suffix for each flight. This left the numbers 701–710 for amphibian and floatplane squadrons from 1943 onwards. Numbers, 750–799, were assigned for training and ancillary squadrons, in contrast to the RAF practice of not assigning squadron numbers to training units. Combat squadrons were 800–809 for fighter squadrons; 810–819 for torpedo bomber squadrons, later torpedo

spotter reconnaissance (TSR), and torpedo bomber reconnaissance (TBR), squadrons; 820–859 were initially spotter reconnaissance squadrons, later becoming TSR and, finally, TBR squadrons. Originally, the latter included 860–869, but these were assigned to Dutch-manned and then Royal Netherlands Navy squadrons. Numbers 870–899 were initially for single-seat fighter squadrons, but 870–879 were assigned to Royal Canadian Navy squadrons. As numbers ran out, new series prefixed by '1' were assigned for the many squadrons manned by members of the RNVR. Leaving aside unused blocks, 1700–1749 became torpedo bomber reconnaissance squadrons; two-seat fighter squadrons 1770–1799; dive-bomber squadrons 1810–1829 and 1830–1899 were initially assigned to single-seat fighter squadrons.

In June 1943, embarked squadrons were grouped into numbered wings, given the title 'naval' to avoid confusion with RAF wings, followed by a suffix for its purpose,

Having failed to make the day for those in the 'goofers' gallery', this Hellcat waits for the barrier to be lowered so that it can reach the forward deck park. (*FAAM HELLCAT/114*)

either fighter or torpedo bomber reconnaissance, usually abbreviated to TBR. This took effect on 25 October 1943. In contrast to RAF practice, in which a wing usually meant three squadrons, the number of squadrons in a naval wing varied, in one case a wing amounted to a solitary squadron. In most cases, wing leaders were lieutenant-commanders, or Royal Marine majors, equivalent to the RAF rank of squadron leader, rather than the more senior ranks of commander or lieutenant-colonel, the equivalent of the RAF rank of wing commander. From 30 June 1945, the naval wings of the British Pacific Fleet were merged into carrier air groups, often headed by a commander.

The advent of carrier air groups reflected the close coordination with the United States Navy as the war in the Pacific reached its climax. With the war in Europe over and resources concentrated in the Far East, it

made sense to align with American practice. Anticipating heavy losses, it was planned to have spare groups, so that the fleet carriers would have a 100 per cent reserve, and the light fleets 50 per cent.

THE SQUADRONS

Unless otherwise indicated, all officers are RN. RAF officers still in the FAA in the early years of the war also had a dual RN rank. Only wartime commanding officers are mentioned.

Where identification letters are shown as 5A+, for example, it means that subsequent aircraft in a unit carry the letters 5B, 5C, etc. Not all wartime identification letters are known.

700 Squadron Reformed Hatston, 21/01/40, as the HQ unit for all battleship and cruiser flights, with initial strength of

Aboard battleships and cruisers, the Vought Kingfisher brought higher levels of performance, but not long afterwards the value of catapult flights was called into question as the number of carriers proliferated. (*Vought Aircraft*)

42 Walruses, 11 Seafoxes and 12 Swordfish floatplanes. It absorbed the Shetland Flight of Walruses based on Sullom Voe in 07/40. Later detachments included Dekheila in Egypt, which later moved to Beirut, Gibraltar and Algiers. Reached strength of 63 Walruses in 06/42 and moved to Twatt. 700 ran down with the growth in carrier air power and disbanded 24/03/44. Reformed 11/11/44 as Maintenance Test Pilot Training Squadron at Donibristle, before moving to Worthy Down, near Winchester. Battle honours: River Plate, 1939; Norway, 1940; Spartivento, 1940; Atlantic, 1940–41; Matapan, 1941; Mediterranean, 1942; North Africa, 1942–43; Normandy, 1944.

Identification markings: A few aircraft had single letters, also 9A+ for British East Indies Fleet.

Commanding officers:
Lt Cdr A.H.T. Fleming, 29/01/40
Lt Cdr N.S. Luard, DSC, 17/05/41
Lt Cdr G.W.R. Nicholl, 04/02/42
Lt Cdr (A) C.G. Hide, RNVR, 16/10/43
Lt Cdr L.R.E. Castlemaine, RNVR, 11/10/44

701 Squadron Reformed 07/05/40, at Donibristle to provide for temporary units formed ashore, the first of which was set up at Harstad during the Norwegian Campaign, with 6 Walruses. Disbanded 08/06/41. Reformed again on 01/10/42, to take over the 700 Squadron flight at Beirut and operated with 6 Walruses under the control of the RAF's 201 Squadron. A detachment was later assigned to 235 Wing to carry out anti-submarine patrols from Latakia. Disbanded on 15/08/43. Reformed at Heston on 18/04/45, taking over 'B' Flight of 781 Squadron, for communication duties, flying a number of types including Dominies (the military variant of the Rapide), Oxfords and Travellers.

Battle honours: Norway, 1940.
Identification markings: from 1945, LOA+.
Commanding officers:
Lt H.H. Bracken, 08/05/40
Cdr R.S.D. Armour, 18/05/40
Lt Cdr M.A. Everett, 14/03/41
Lt P.C. Chorley, 05 /10/42
Lt Cdr (A) A.B. Cunningham, RNVR, 18/04/45

702 Squadron Merged into 700, 21/01/40. Reformed 27/12/40, as a Long Range catapult squadron operating Seafoxes from armed merchant cruisers, each of which carried 2 aircraft. Shore-base was Lee-on-Solent. First ship was *Alcantara*, followed by *Pretoria Castle, Canton, Queen of Bermuda* and *Asturias*. Sea Hurricane flight formed 10/05/42, to operate 2 catapult aircraft from CAM-ship *Maplin*, previously operated by 804 Squadron and the only example of FAA-catapult fighters. Disbanded 07/43. Reformed out of 758 Squadron on 01/06/45 at Hinstock as Instrument Flying and Checking Unit.

Identification markings: E8A+ on seaplanes.
Commanding officers:
Lt Cdr R.A.B. Phillimore, 24/05/39
None, 40–43
Lt Cdr (A) G.T. Bertholdt, RNVR, 01/06/45

703 Squadron Took over armed merchant cruiser flights from 702 Squadron when formed as a long-range catapult squadron on 03/06/42, equipping with Vought

A happier landing for a Walrus. (*via S.H. Wragg*)

Kingfishers, of which 11 were in use by 04/43, including aircraft on 2 light cruisers. Shore base was Lee-on-Solent, but 3 Walruses were based at Walvis Bay in South Africa. Disbanded 01/05/44, to be reformed 19/04/45, at RAF Thorney Island, as the naval flight of the RAF's Air-Sea Warfare Development Unit, NASWDU, to operate a variety of new aircraft types. Squadron operated without a CO until 1945, when Lt Cdr J.H. Dundas, DSC, appointed 19/04.

704 Squadron Formed at Zeals 11/04/45, as an OTU for the de Havilland Mosquito, with 4 aircraft detached to join 703 in June on NASWDU work.
Identification markings: FD3A+.
Commanding officer:
Lt Cdr (A) S.M.P. Walsh, DSC & Bar, RNVR.

705 Squadron Formed in 1936 from part of 444 (Catapult) Flight and assigned to battlecruisers in the Mediterranean Fleet, with a shore base at Kalafrana, Malta, for its Swordfish and Shark floatplanes. By the outbreak of war, squadron status had been attained, operating from *Repulse* and *Renown*. Absorbed into 700 Squadron, 21/01/40. Reformed at Ronaldsway, IoM, on 07/03/45, as a Replacement Crew Training Unit with Swordfish IIIs providing an anti-submarine course. Disbanded 24/06/45.
Identification markings: B8A+.
Commanding officers:
Flt Lt P.E. O'Brien, RAF, 14/11/38
Lt Cdr (A) G. Bennett, DSC, RNVR, 07/03/45.

706 Squadron Formed 10/04/45, as a pool squadron at Schofields, Australia, providing refresher courses on the main aircraft types operated by the British Pacific Fleet.
Commanding officer:
Lt Cdr R.E. Bradshaw, DSC and 2 bars.

707 Squadron Formed out of 'B' Flight, 735, on 20/02/45, as a Radar Trials Unit at Burscough, the Naval School of Airborne Radar. It was responsible for evaluation of radar and techniques, as well as training. At first, Swordfish, Ansons, Avengers and Barracudas were used. The squadron moved to Gosport on 14/08/45, and merged into 778 Squadron in October.
Commanding officer:
Lt Cdr (A) S.S. Laurie, RNVR.

708 Squadron Formed at Lee-on-Solent on 01/10/44, from 764's 'B' Flight as the Firebrand Tactical Trials Unit, before moving to nearby Gosport the following January. Firebrand used on rocket-firing trials, but problems with the type delayed progress, although deck landing trials were conducted aboard *Glory* in May, 1945. The squadron later moved to Ford, and disbanded postwar.
Identification markings: OA+.
Commanding Officer:
Cdr (A) W.C. Simpson, DSC, RNVR.

709 Squadron Formed at St Merryn on 15/09/44, as part of the School of Naval Air Warfare's Ground Attack School. Initially, Seafire L.IIIs were operated, which were later joined by Hellcats. Disbanded postwar.
Identification markings: S5A+.
Commanding Officer:
Lt K. White, MBE.

710 Squadron Formed as a seaplane squadron for *Albatross* at Lee-on-Solent on 23/08/39. Initially, 6 Walruses were operated, with another 3 in reserve. The squadron was embarked aboard the ship, stationed at Freetown, Sierra Leone, searching for U-boats and commerce raiders. A shore base was established in mid-1940 and aircraft were often operated from this. The ship and her aircraft took part in the Madagascar Campaign in 1942. The squadron disbanded at Lee-on-Solent on 14/10/43. Reformed at Ronaldsway, 07/10/44, as a Torpedo Training Squadron operating Barracudas and some Swordfish. Disbanded postwar.

Identification markings: Walrus, A9A+, then 9A+; Barracudas, AR2A+ to AR7A+.

Commanding Officers:

Lt Cdr H.L. Hayes, 23/08/39
Capt W.H.C. Manson, RM, 08/08/40
Lt Cdr C.E. Fenwick, 14/07/41
Lt Cdr J.E. Smallwood, 10/03/42
Lt E.F. Pritchard, 01/09/42
Lt (A) M.J.J. Harris, RNVR, 13/05/43
Lt Cdr (A) D.R. Conner, RNVR, 07/10/44
Lt Cdr J.F. Arnold, 01/08/45

711 Squadron Originally formed in 1936 as 711 (Catapult) Flight from 447 (Catapult) Flight to support ships of the Mediterranean Fleet and based at Kalafrana, Malta. By the outbreak of war, the unit had achieved squadron status and was operating Walruses from Aboukir. Absorbed into 700 Squadron in 1940. Reformed on 09/09/44, as a torpedo training squadron, based at Crail, Fife, operating Barracudas. Disbanded postwar, having operated Avengers briefly.

Identification markings: F9A+ for Walrus; C5A+ and C6A+, Barracuda.

Commanding officers:

Lt Cdr O.S. Stevinson, 17/01/38
Lt Cdr A.H.T. Fleming, 24/05/40
Lt Cdr (A) J.B. Curgenven-Robinson, RNVR, 09/09/44
Lt Cdr (A) D.M. Judd, DSC, RNVR, 30/07/45

712 Squadron Assigned to the Humber Force and the 18th Cruiser Squadron on the outbreak of war, including *Belfast, Edinburgh, Norfolk* and *Suffolk*, among a total of 9 ships with 18 Walrus aircraft, 712 was merged into 700 Squadron, 01/40.

Reformed at Hatston, 02/08/44, as a communications squadron, taking 'B' flight of 771 Squadron. Aircraft included Dominies, Expeditors, Sea Otters and Travellers. Disbanded 23/08/45. Walrus markings were G9A+. Communications types were H9A+.

Commanding officers:

Lt Cdr G.A. Tilney, 24/05/39
Lt (A) J.U. Reid, RNVR
Lt (A) R.W.M. Williams, RNZNVR, 27/03/45

713 Squadron Operating Seafoxes from Kalafrana on the outbreak of war, merged into 700 Squadron, 01/40. Reformed at Ronaldsway, IoM, 12/08/44, as a TBR Training Squadron, operating Barracudas. Disbanded late 1945.

Identification markings: H9A+ for Seafoxes; Barracudas, R2A+, R3A+, R5A+, R6A+ and R7A+.

Commanding officers:

Lt J. Hamilton, 26/06/39
Lt Cdr (A) A.G. McWilliam, RNVR, 12/08/44

714 Squadron Having developed from a flight to a squadron by 1939, 714 was operating from the cruisers *Gloucester, Liverpool* and *Manchester* by the outbreak of war, with 6 Walruses, and Seletar and Trincomalee as shore bases. Merged into 700 Squadron, 1940. Reformed at Fearn as a TBR Training Squadron, 01/08/44, equipped with Barracudas. Moved to Ratray on 30/10/44, and disbanded a year later almost to the day. Walruses were marked J9A+; Barracudas, F1A+ and F2A+.

Commanding officers:

Lt Cdr A.S. Webb, 24/05/39
Lt Cdr (A) V.R. Crane, RNVR, 01/08/44
Lt (A) P.D. Buckland, RNVR (temp), 15/05/45
Lt Cdr (A) R.J. Godley, DSC, RNVR, 19/05/45

Earlier, the search for a more powerful torpedo-bomber had led to operations with the Vought Chesapeake, but it did not see combat with the Royal Navy. (*Vought Aircraft*)

715 Squadron On the outbreak of war, 715 was operating 7 Walruses from 5 cruisers, with shore bases at Kai Tak and Seletar. Merged into 700 Squadron, 1940. Reformed 17/08/44, at St Merryn, from part of 736 Squadron for School of Air Combat, providing a fighter air combat course and fighter leaders course on Seafires and Corsairs. Reabsorbed by 736 after the war. Identification markings: K9A+ for Walruses; S4A+ for Seafires and Corsairs.
Commanding officers:
Lt P.J. Milner-Barry, 24/05/39
Lt Cdr (A) R.E. Gardner, DSC, RNVR, 17/08/44

Lt Cdr D.G. Carlisle, DSC, SANF(V), 12/12/44
Lt Cdr F.R.A. Turnbull, DSC & Bar, RN, 28/06/45

716 Squadron Operating Seafoxes, with Simonstown, South Africa, as a shore base on the outbreak of war, 716 was absorbed into 700 Squadron, 1940. Reformed at Eastleigh, near Southampton, on 28/06/44, as the School of Safety Equipment, with Sea Otters and, reputedly, a Wellington, to provide instruction on search and rescue operations. Deployed a detachment briefly aboard the escort carrier *Ruler* in 01/45.

Disbanded after the war.

Identification markings: Seafoxes, L9+; Sea Otter, I0A+.

Commanding officers:

Lt A J.T. Roe, 25/04/38

Lt Cdr J.F. Nicholas, 28/06/44

Lt Cdr (A) D.V. Robinson, RNVR, 11/05/45

717 Squadron Formed at Fearn as a TBR training squadron on 01/07/44, 717 operated Barracuda IIs. Moved to Rattray on 30/10/44. After the war, it absorbed 714 and 769 Squadrons, before disbanding.

Identification markings: Sea Otters, I0A+; Barracuda, F1A+ and F2A+, later changing to AT3A+ and AT4A+ after the move to Rattray.

Commanding officers:

Lt Cdr D. Norcock, 01/07/44

Lt Cdr (A) A. Brunt, DSC, RNZNVR, 18/09/44

Lt Cdr (A) J.L. Fisher, RNVR, 26/01/45

718 Squadron Operating 5 Walruses and 5 Sea Foxes from 6 cruisers on the West Indies station at the outbreak of war, then absorbed into 700 Squadron, 01/40. Reformed at Henstridge as an Army cooperation training unit, 05/06/44, later becoming the Army Cooperation Naval Operational Training Unit and also provided an air combat course. Equipment included 9 Seafire IIIs and 6 Spitfire PR XIIIs. The unit became the School of Naval Air Reconnaissance in 04/45. It became No. 4 Naval Air Fighting School immediately after the war. The Seafires and Spitfires were marked G3A+.

Commanding officers:

Lt Cdr J.C. Cockburn, 29/03/39

Lt Cdr (A) W.H. Stevens, RN, 05/06/44

Lt Cdr S.J. Hall, DSC, 26/11/44

719 Squadron Formed on 15/06/44, at St Merryn as a School of Air Combat air firing training squadron, the squadron briefly operated Seafires and Corsairs before disbanding into 794 Squadron on 02/01/45.

Identification markings: S1A+.

Commanding officer:

Lt Cdr J.L. Appleby

720 Squadron Originating as the catapult flight for the New Zealand Division, 720 had squadron status and a shore base at Auckland on the outbreak of war. Absorbed into 700 Squadron, 01/40. Reformed 01/08/45, from an unnumbered photographic flight originally formed in 12/40, at Ford in Sussex, operating four Avro Ansons.

Identification markings: Z1–Z4.

Commanding officers:

Lt B.E.W. Logan, 24/05/39

Lt Cdr (A) G.N. Gladish, RNVR, 01/08/45.

721 Squadron Formed at Belfast, 01/03/45, as a fleet requirements unit for the Pacific Fleet. Initially equipped with 12 Vengeance target tugs, of which 6 were immediately sent to the Far East. Arrived at Ponam on 28/05/45, and commenced operations towing target drogues. The squadron disbanded at the end of the Pacific War.

Commanding officer:

Lt Cdr (A) F.A. Simpson, RNVR

722 Squadron Formed at Tambaram, 01/09/44, as a fleet requirements unit with 12 Miles Martinets, 1 Reliant and 1 Walrus, for target drogue towing for ships and naval air squadrons based in southern India. Two flights operated, X for the west coast, Y for the east coast. Swordfish and Wildcats were added to the squadron before it disbanded in 10/45.

Identification markings: thought to be T9A+.

Commanding officers:

Lt Cdr (A) A.F.E. Payen, RNVR, 01/09/44

Fulmars in flight. (*via S.H. Wragg*)

Lt Cdr (A) K.C. Johnson, SANF (V),
23/10/44
Lt Cdr (A) L.G. Morris, RNVR, 08/03/45

723 Squadron Personnel assembled at
Townhill Camp in Fife, 11/44 and embarked
for Australia, where the squadron formed at
Bankstown, New South Wales, 28/02/45, as
a fleet requirements unit to assist units of
the British Pacific Fleet working up in Jervis
Bay. Initial equipment included 8 Martlets
and 8 Corsairs, to which Hellcats were later
added. After the war ended, the squadron
moved to Schofields and later disbanded.
Identification markings: N8A+.
Commanding officer:
Lt Cdr H.A.P. Bullivant, RNVR

724 Squadron Formed as a naval air
communications squadron at Bankstown,
NSW, with Expeditors and Ansons.
Disbanded after the war.
Identification markings believed to have
been civilian markings.
Commanding officer:
Lt (A) J.H.L. Evans, RNVR

725 Squadron Formed at Eglinton,
27/08/43, as a fleet requirements unit with
3 Blackburn Rocs, although these were
later augmented and Martinets also added.
Small numbers of aircraft were detached to
Ballyhalbert and Ronaldsway (IoM) in
1944, to provide target-towing facilities. A
varied selection of aircraft, including
Hellcats and Ansons, was being operated by
08/45, when it was moved to St Merryn as
an air target towing unit. Disbanded after
the war.
Commanding officer:
Lt Cdr (A) S.J. McDowell, RNVR

726 Squadron Formed at Durban,
07/07/43, 726 had just 2 Kingfishers for
fleet requirements and communications
duties. A variety of aircraft were soon added,
with Swordfish, Fulmars, 1 Walrus, Defiants,
Martinets and 1 Beaufighter being
operated, augmented by 3 Harvards.
Disbanded after the war.
Commanding officers:
Lt Cdr F.G. Hood SANF (V), 07/07/43
Lt (A) W.A. McElroy, RNVR, 04/01/45,

possibly a temporary appointment with another, unnamed officer following before Lt (A) D.C. Langley, SANF (V), 04/06/45

727 Squadron Fleet requirements unit formed at Gibraltar on 26/05/43, with a detachment at Tafaroui and later Blida. Started with 6 Defiant target tugs, although over its first year of existence, this number doubled and some Swordfish were added. Unusually, target towing was provided for all 3 services. The squadron moved to RAF Ta Kali in Malta on 01/11/44, disbanding on 07/12.
Identification markings: Single letters.
Commanding officers:
Lt (A) E.L. Meicklejohn, RNVR, 26/05/43
Lt Cdr (A) M.V. Dyas, RNVR, 01/10/43

728 Squadron Fleet requirements unit formed at Gibraltar, 01/05/43, with 6 Defiant target tugs, but with a detachment at Tafaroui having a Swordfish. Later, Defiants were deployed to Oujda in French Morocco to provide towing for an American AA battery firing range. Moving to Dekheila on 15/06, it was merged into 775 Squadron on 04/07/43. Reformed out of 775 Squadron on 14/08/43, before moving to Ta Kali as a fleet requirements unit, once again with Defiants, and provided target towing both for the Mediterranean Fleet and the British Army, before later providing a detachment to tow targets for the US Navy at Naples. Martinets, Beaufighters and Hurricanes were added as the British Pacific Fleet worked up in the Mediterranean. The Defiants were replaced by Beauforts, Baltimores, Seafires and Mosquitoes in winter 1944–45, with the squadron moving to Luqa postwar.
Identification markings: M8A+.
Commanding officers:
Lt Cdr (A) E.H. Horn, RNVR, 08/05/43
Lt P. Snow, 12/08/43
Lt Cdr (A) P.B. Pratt, RNVR, 08/01/44

728B Squadron Formed as a fleet requirements unit at Ta Kali 01/45, with 5 Martinets and Seafires, and disbanded 07/45.

729 Squadron Formed at Hinstock as an offshoot of 758 Squadron, 01/01/45, for instrument flying training duties in the Far East, but began operations on 15/05 at Coimbatore with Oxfords and Harvards. It moved to Tambaram in 06/45 and Puttalam in 07/45, and then to Ceylon in late 08/45. Disbanded after the war.
Identification markings: K7A+.
Commanding officer:
Lt Cdr (A) H.R. Law, RNVR

730 Squadron Formed at Abbotsinch, 17/04/44, for communications duties, it had previously been the Flag Officer Carrier Training Flight. A variety of aircraft was operated, including Reliants and when it moved to Ayr on 20/11/44, equipment included Sea Otters, Fireflies, Travellers and Walruses. Disbanded, 01/08/45.
Commanding officers:
Lt (A) G. Windsor, RNVR, 17/04/44
Lt (A) C. White, RNVR, 01/12/44
Lt J.C. Kennedy, 24/05/45

731 Squadron Formed at East Haven, 05/12/43, to provide training for deck landing control officers, operated Swordfish as well as smaller numbers of Fulmars, Sea Hurricanes and Seafires. Pilots nicknamed 'Clockwork Mice'. Absorbed into other squadrons after the war.
Identification markings: E3A+.
Commanding officers:
Lt Cdr (A) K. Stilliard, RNVR, 05/12/43
Lt Cdr R. Pridham-Wippell, 01/01/45

732 Squadron An OTU formed at Brunswick on 23/11/43, using Corsairs, to provide aerodrome dummy deck landing, ADDL,

training for pilots who had received basic and advanced training with the USN in Florida. Disbanded, 01/07/44. Reformed at Drem, 15/05/45, as a Night Fighter Training School using 9 Hellcats, 6 Anson flying classrooms, 6 Harvards and some Firefly NHF1s. Disbanded after the war.
Identification markings: D2A+.
Commanding officers:
Lt Cdr (A) M.S. Goodson, RNVR, 23/11/43
Lt Cdr W.N. Waller, 31/01/44
Lt (A) M.B.W. Howell, RNVR, 15/05/45
Lt Cdr (A) A.M. Tritton, DSC, RNVR, 01/08/45

733 Squadron Formed as a fleet requirements unit for the British Eastern Fleet at Minneriya, 01/01/44, before moving to Trincomalee, then known as China Bay. Operated varied range of equipment, including Avengers, Martinets, Wildcats, Beaufighters, Swordfish and Barracudas, later augmented by Defiants, Mosquitoes, Corsairs, Vengeances and Seafires. Tasks included radar calibration, which required pilots to fly at a specific height and speed.
Identification markings: C8A+ and C9A+.
Commanding officers:
Lt Cdr (A) R.A. Beard, RNVR, 01/01/44
Lt Cdr (A) L. Gilbert, RNVR, (temp), 01/04/44
Lt Cdr (A) J. Ansell, RNVR, 06/10/44
Lt Cdr (A) I .O. Robertson, RNVR, 09/08/45

734 Squadron An unusual squadron, formed at Worthy Down, near Winchester, 14/02/44, as an engine handling unit. Operated Merlin-engined Whitley GRVIIs fitted with fuel flow meters and other additional instruments, so that pilots could receive instruction on how to handle the Merlin engine in these 'flying classrooms'. Moved to Hinstock, after the war and disbanded.

Identification markings: W0A+.
Commanding officer:
Lt Cdr (A) R.C. Cockburn, RNVR

735 Squadron Formed at Inskip on 01/08/43, as an ASV training unit, at first operating Swordfish, but later replacing these with Barracudas. Ansons were also used as flying classrooms. While 'A' flight handled training, 'B' flight conducted radar trials. The squadron moved to Burscough in 03/44, and later a third, 'C', flight was added. 'B' flight became 707 Squadron in 02/45. The Squadron disbanded after the war.
Identification markings: Barracudas, AH4A+, then O4A+; Ansons, AH7A+.
Commanding officers:
Lt Cdr E.S. Carver, DSC, 01/08/43
Lt Cdr (A) R.T. Hayes, 15/03/44
Lt Cdr (A) J.H. Mayne, RNVR, 18/08/44
Lt Cdr (A) S.L. Revett, DSC, 31/03/45

736 Squadron Formed at Yeovilton 24/05/43, as the School of Air Combat and equipped with Seafires, it relieved the RAF Fighter Leaders' School of the role of teaching the latest techniques to experienced naval fighter commanders. In 09/43, the squadron moved to St Merryn to become the Fighter Combat School, part of the School of Naval Air Warfare. Masters and Barracudas were added, so that the squadron included a TBR flight and was able to provide an Air Instructors Course and a TBR Air Strike Course. In 03/45, 'B' flight was formed by taking over 'Y' flight of 787 Squadron, a fighter affiliation unit, equipped with Seafires. This embarked aboard *Colossus*, and provided carrier training on gyro gunsight tactics for the British Pacific Fleet working up in the Mediterranean in early 1945; disbanded 09/45.
Identification markings: ACA+.

Commanding officers:
Lt Cdr (A) R.E. Gardner, DSC, 24/05/43
Lt Cdr D.R. Curry, DSC, 17/08/44
Lt Cdr P.D. Gick, 08/02/45
Lt Cdr S.P. Luke, 03/08/45

737 Squadron Originally formed at Dunino on 22/02/43, as an amphibious bomber reconnaissance training squadron using Walruses, the squadron was disbanded on 28/09 as the demand for catapult-launched amphibians had passed. It was reformed at Inskip on 15/03/44 as a ASV radar training unit using Swordfish and Anson flying classrooms. The squadron moved to Arbroath in 08/44, and then to Burscough in 04/45, but did not receive Barracudas until 08/45, 3 months before disbanding.
Identification markings: Walrus D1A+; Swordfish and Anson K4A+.
Commanding officers:
Lt (A) J.R. Dimsdale, RNVR, 22/02/43
Lt Cdr (A) L.P. Dunne, RNVR, 15/03/44
Lt Cdr (A) G.J. Staveley, RNVR; 09 /11/44
Lt Cdr F.V. Jones, 05/03/45

738 Squadron A pilot training squadron formed at Quonset Point, Rhode Island, 01/02/43, with a mixed batch of Corsairs, Martlets and Harvards. The squadron moved to Lewiston on 31/07/43, when Avengers were also added to its strength and advanced carrier training was provided for American-trained RNVR pilots. Later, it provided complete TBR crews for Avenger squadrons. The squadron moved on 14/02/45, to Brunswick, and disbanded on 31/07/45.
Identification markings: Avengers, 1BA+, then 1V17 to 19V17; Harvards, 1BS+; Martlet, 2BA+; Corsair, 3BA+.
Commanding officers:
Lt Cdr J.C. Reed, DSC, 01/02/43
Lt Cdr (A) J.P. Flood, RNVR, 24/10/44
Lt Cdr J.L. Cullen, 16/03/45

739 Squadron Formed as the Blind Approach Development Unit at Lee-on-Solent, 15/12/42, initial equipment was 1 Swordfish and 1 Fulmar for trials. Acquired Oxfords and Ansons before moving to Worthy Down, 01/09/43 and to Donibristle, 10/44. Disbanded 07/03/45.
Commanding officers:
Lt G. Smith, RN, 15/12/42
Lt Cdr G. Bennett, DSC, 17/01/45

740 Squadron Formed 04/05/43, at Arbroath as part of No. 2 Observer School, using Walruses plus a few Swordfish and Kingfishers. Disbanded 05/08/43. Reformed 30/12/43, at Machrihanish as a communications squadron from a flight in 772 Squadron. A wide variety of aircraft was operated, including Reliants, Travellers, Dominies, Oxfords and Ansons. Disbanded 01/09/45.
Identification markings: 1944/–45, M9A+.
Commanding officers:
Lt Cdr D. H Angel, 04/05/43
Lt Cdr (A) L.F. Diggens, RNVR, 30/12/43
Lt Cdr (A) L.T. Summerfield, RNVR, 23/04/45

741 Squadron Observer training squadron formed 01/03/43, at Arbroath as part of 2 Observer Training School. Operating Swordfish, it trained the students to 'wings' standard. Disbanded, 19/03/45. Aircraft markings: A3A+.
Commanding officers:
Lt Cdr (A) O.H. Cantrill, RNVR, 01/03/43
Lt Cdr (A) R. McA Stratton, RNVR, 17/03/44

742 Squadron Communications squadron formed Colombo, 06/12/43, eventually building up to a strength of more than 20 Beech Expeditors, the military version of the Beech 18. Operations included many regular services like those of airlines, with a

4 times daily Colombo-Trincomalee service and daily flights to Madras in India. It moved to Coimbatore on 15/09/44, becoming the Naval Air Transport Squadron, 11/44, with a number of detachments, which increased after a move to Sulur in 02/45. The squadron flew many millions of miles with just one fatal accident. It disbanded in 08/46, after 9 of its aircraft had flown in formation to the UK, a distance of 6,500 miles, in 01/46.
Commanding officers:
Lt (A) T.N. Stack, RNR from 06/12/43
Lt Cdr (A) R. MacDermott, RNVR, 08/01/44
Lt Cdr (A) T.N. Stack, RNR, 29 /09/44

743 Squadron One of a trio of squadrons assembled at Lee-on-Solent and ready for passage to Canada, where all 3 were formed on 01/03/43 as part of No. 2 Telegraphist Air Gunners' School at Yarmouth, Nova Scotia. They were administered by the RCAF (who knew it as No. 1 Telegraphist Air Gunners School) and instructors were a mixture of RCAF and RN personnel. By 06/43, the squadron had 40 Swordfish and 1 Walrus. Training ended on 19/03/45, and the squadron disbanded on 30/03.
Identification markings: letter number combinations.
Commanding officer:
Lt Cdr (A) R. Gillet, RNVR

744 Squadron Second of the trio, operating Seamews intended for the new generation of light fleet carriers, but a difficult aircraft due to a weakness in the tailplane. Redesignated as 754, 06/44, due to the appearance of another 744 Squadron in the UK. The UK-based 744 was also a training squadron, formed at Maydown, 06/03/44, using 12 Swordfish to train crews for 836 Squadron, operating from merchant aircraft carriers. A detachment was established at

Machrihanish for deck landing training, using an escort carrier in the Firth of Clyde. Barracudas were introduced during the winter of 1944/45, and some Fireflies were added in 07/45.
Identification markings: Seamew, letter number combinations; Swordfish, K7A+ and N7A+; Barracuda, N4A+ and N6A+.
Commanding officers:
Lt (A) E.J. Trerise, 10/02/43
Lt Cdr (A) C.M.T. Hallewell, 06/03/44
Lt Cdr (A) D.W. Phillips, DSC, 27/02/45

745 Squadron Third of the trio with a mixture of Swordfish, Seamews and Ansons, it disbanded, 30/03/45.
Identification markings: letter number combinations.
Commanding officers:
Lt Cdr (A) R.H. Ovey, 01/03/43
Lt Cdr (A) F.A.H. Harley, 06/11/44
Lt Cdr (A) E.J. Trerise, 12/44

746 Squadron Formed as the Naval Night Fighter Interception Unit, 23/11/42, at Lee-on-Solent. Moved to Ford 12/42 to join the RAF Fighter Interception Unit. Initially operated 3 Fulmars as night fighters and 3 as targets. These were joined by Fireflies 05/43, when the squadron came under the control of the Naval Fighter Direction Centre at Yeovilton, tasked with the development of tactics and analysis of the experiences of pilots from the carrier squadrons. It moved to Wittering 05/44, with a detachment at Defford for radar development duties. The Firefly night fighters joined operations against the V-1 flying bombs. The squadron returned to Ford in 10/44, and in 01/45, deployed 'A' flight to Hatston to provide ADDL, carrier deck landing training. It became the Naval Night Fighter Development Squadron in 05/45, evaluating aircraft and their equipment, while detachments of pairs of aircraft were deployed aboard escort carriers after 'A' flight became an operational sub-unit.

Identification markings: Fulmars carried L0A+.

Commanding officers:

Maj L.A. (Skeets) Harris, DSC, RM, 23/11/42

Lt Cdr (A) G.L.C. Davies, DSC, 30/07/45

747 Squadron Part of the TBR Pool and formed at Fearn, 22/03/43, initially with 3 each of Swordfish, Barracuda and Anson radar flying classrooms, it evolved into an OTU. On 09/07, it moved to Inskip and became part of No. 1 Naval OTU and added Albacores to its strength. Moved back to Fearn with No. 1 OTU 26/01/44 and then to Ronaldsway 07/44. Disbanded after the war.

Identification markings: Barracudas, K2A+, F2A+ , then R2A to R7A+.

Commanding officers:

Lt Cdr J.A. Ievers, 22/03/43

Lt Cdr (A) F.A. Swanton, DSC, 13/09/43

Lt Cdr T.M. Bassett, RNZNVR, 03/44

Lt Cdr (A) R.D. Kington, DSC, RNZNVR, 06/11/45

748 Squadron Formed as part of the fighter pool, St Merryn, Cornwall, 12/10/42, it provided refresher flying with 4 each of Fulmars, Martlets, Spitfires and Hurricanes. It became No. 1 Naval OTU in 03/43 and received Seafires. It moved to Henstridge 04/02/44, and to Yeovilton 09/03, where it received Corsairs, Fireflies and Hellcats, then to Dale 01/10. Returned to St Merryn in 08/45 and later disbanded.

Identification markings: All types, S7A+ until 10/44, then P7A+.

Commanding officers:

Lt Cdr (A) R.G. French, RNVR, 12/10/42

Lt Cdr B.H.C. Nation, 05/11/43

Lt Cdr J .G. Smith, RNVR, 20/07/44

Lt Cdr (A) P.J.E. Nichols, RNVR, 05/08/45

749 Squadron Formed at Piarco, Trinidad, 01/01/41, as part of No. 1 Observers School, it used Walrus aircraft at first, but in 1942 these were joined by the Grumman Goose. During that year, operational anti-submarine patrols were also undertaken. In 1944, a peak strength of 27 Walrus and 30 Goose aircraft was being operated, plus some of 703 Squadron's Kingfishers. Disbanded after the war.

Identification markings: Walrus,W2QA+ and W2QAA+; Goose, W2A+ and W2AA+; Ansons, A1–A4.

Commanding officers:

Lt (A) J.C. Moore, RNVR, 01/01/41

Lt Cdr (A) G.H. Winn, RNVR, 01/12/41

Lt Cdr (A) A.E. Worby; RNVR, 07/04/43

Lt Cdr (A) P.G. Lee, RNVR, 01/08/45

750 Squadron One of a trio of squadrons formed at Ford, 24/05/39, as part of No. 1 Observers School, it operated a mixture of Sharks and Ospreys. After moving some of its aircraft to Yevilton 05/40, before the station was completed, they were followed by the rest after the major air raid on Ford 08/40. The next move was to Piarco in Trinidad, where the school re-opened on 05/11/40. At Piarco, at the peak, up to 40 Sharks and 70 Albacores were in use. Barracudas were introduced before the squadron disbanded after the war.

Identification markings: Swordfish, W1A+, W1AA+ and W0-A+: Albacore, Nos 1–78; Barracuda B1, B2, B3+.

Commanding officers:

Cdr (A) J.H.F. Burroughs, 24/05/39

Lt Cdr C.A. Kingsley-Rowe, 01/02/40

Lt Cdr (A) T.G. Stubley, 30/09/40

Lt Cdr (A) E.K. Lee, RNVR, 01/12/41

Lt Cdr F.E. Darlow, 01/10/43

Lt Cdr (A) J.H. Crook, RNVR, 06/12/43

Lt Cdr (A) H. Whitaker, RNVR, 15/03/45

Lt Cdr (A) F.B. Gardner, RNVR, 01/08/45

751 Squadron The second of 3 squadrons formed at Ford, 24/05/39, for the new No. 1 Observers School, initially equipped with Walruses and used Yeovilton for dispersal from 05/40. Moved to Arbroath, 19/08/40, after the German air raid on Ford, to became part of No. 2 Observers School, before moving to Dundee, 13/08/41. Disbanded, 02/05/44.

Identification markings: W9A+ to A4A+, and in 1943, AA4A+ to AA5A+.

Commanding officers:
Lt Cdr (A) J.H. Sender, 24/05/39
Lt Cdr (A) F. Leach, RNVR, 01/02/41
Lt Cdr (A) H. Jones, RNVR, 01/12/41
Lt Cdr D.H. Angel, 07/08/43
Lt Cdr T.E. Sargeant, RD, RNVR, 02 /02/44

752 Squadron The third of the trio formed 05/39, at Ford, as part of No. 1 Observers School, it used Proctors, with a few Albacores. As with the other two, Yeovilton was used for dispersal at first, before moving to Lee-on-Solent 30/09/40, after the bombing of Ford. Moved to Piarco, Trinidad and regrouped there on 05/11 using the same equipment, although later Reliants and Tiger Moths were added. Disbanded, 09/10/45.

Identification markings: Proctors, W0-A+, W3A+, W3AA+, W3AB+; other aircraft, W5A+, W5AA, W5BA.

Commanding officers:
Lt Cdr G.R .F.T. Cooper, 24/05/39
Lt Cdr (A) J.H.I. McMalcolm, RNVR, 21/02/40
Lt Cdr (A) B.A.G. Meads, RNVR, 31/03/41
Lt Cdr (A) G.M. Tonge, RNVR, 01/05/43
Lt Cdr (A) P.G. Lee, RNVR, 01/05/45

753 Squadron Formed at Lee-on-Solent, 24/05/39, out of the School of Naval Cooperation, to became part of No. 2 Observers School, operating Sharks and Seals. Moved to Arbroath on 23/08/40,

where the Seals were replaced by Swordfish. Albacores were introduced in 08/41, and ASV radar-equipped Barracudas in 12/44. Disbanded postwar at Rattray.

Commanding officers:
Lt Cdr (A) G.N.P. Stringer, 24/05/39
Capt A.C. Newsom, RM, 22/10/40
Lt Cdr (A) L.A. Cubitt, 06/05/41
Lt Cdr (A) A .C. Mills, RNVR, 30/09/41
Lt Cdr (A) F.R. Steggall, RNVR, 15/07/42
Lt Cdr (A) R.E. Stewart, RNVR, 31/03/44
Lt Cdr (A) A.J. Phillips, 12/08/45

754 Squadron As with the previous squadron, 754 formed at Lee-on-Solent, 24/05/39, out of the School of Naval Cooperation to become part of No. 2 Observers School, initially with Walruses, Seafoxes and Vega Gulls. After Lee was bombed, 754 also moved to Arbroath on 07/09/40 and re-equipped with Proctors to train observers and air gunners in the use of air-to-surface weapons. A change of role came in 06/41, with the arrival of 18 Lysander target tugs, later joined by Albacores in 1943. Disbanded, 27/03/44. Reformed at Yarmouth, Nova Scotia, as No. 1 Naval Air Gunners School by renumbering 744 Squadron. Disbanded, 12/03/45.

Identification markings: W5A, later, A5A+.

Commanding officers:
Lt Cdr (A) E. Esmonde, 24/05/39
Lt Cdr E.J.E. Burt, 31/05/40
Lt Cdr (A) H.E.S. Pritchett, RNVR, 10/01/41
Lt Cdr (A) A.F.E. Payen, RNVR, 22/04/42
Lt Cdr (A) D.A. Horton, RNVR, 02/05/42
Lt Cdr W.E. Dunn, RNVR; 15/10/43
Lt (A) E.J. Trerise, 06/44

755 Squadron One of 3 squadrons formed at Worthy Down, 24/05/39, to train telegraphist air gunners within No. 1 Air Gunners School. It provided the first part of the wireless course using Sharks and Ospreys.

Moved to Jersey, 11/03/40, but was evacuated on the fall of France. Lysanders replaced the Sharks in 07/41. All 3 squadrons were merged into 755 on 01/12/42, giving it 756's Proctors and 757's Lysanders. The few remaining Sharks replaced by Seamews, 10/43, while some Tiger Moths were also operated. Disbanded on 31/10/44. Reformed as a communications squadron, Colombo, 24/03/45, operating Expeditors. Disbanded after the war.

Identification markings: X2A+, and later W6A+.

Commanding officers:
Lt Cdr R.A. Peyton, 24/05/39
Lt Cdr O.S. Stevinson, 17/07/39
Lt Cdr (E) H.P. Sears, 11/03/40
Lt Cdr (A) T. Coates, RNVR, 06/03/41
Lt Cdr (A) R.H. Ovey, RNVR; 01/12/42
Lt Cdr J.J. Dykes, RNVR, 15/01/43
Lt Cdr (A) W.H.C. Blake, RNVR, 10/06/44
Lt Cdr (A) J.G. O'Sullivan, RNZNVR, 24/03/45

756 Squadron Officially formed along with 755 on 24/05/39, but did not become operational until 06/03/41, still at Worthy Down where it provided the advanced element of the TAG course using Proctors. Merged with 755 and disbanded on 01/12/42. Reformed on 01/10/43, at Katukurunda, Ceylon, providing refresher flying and deck landing training, with a mixture of aircraft, including Swordfish, Albacores and Barracudas, as well as Fulmars to provide monoplane training for Albacore and Swordfish pilots. A satellite base established at Colombo, 03/44, when Avengers were also added. Disbanded after the war.

Identification markings: Proctors, X3A+; Albacores, single letters; Barracuda and Swordfish KA+; Avengers, K1A+.

Commanding officers:
Lt Cdr (A) R.H. Ovey, RNVR, 06/03/41

Lt Cdr (A) W.H.C. Blake, RNVR, 18/06/42
Lt Cdr A.D. Bourke, RNZNVR, 01/10/43
Lt (A) W.E. Widdows, RNVR (temp), 01/02/44
Lt Cdr (A) S.M. deL Longsden, 27/02/44
Lt Cdr (A) T.T. Miller, 28/10/44
Lt Cdr (A) R.E.F. Kerrison, RNVR, 07/07/45
Lt Cdr (A) F.W. Baring, RNVR, 12/08/45

757 Squadron Also formed, 24/05/39, with the two squadrons mentioned above, operating Sharks and Ospreys, but disbanded 15/08. Reformed 06/03/41, with Skuas and Nimrods, as part of No. 1 Air Gunners School, providing the initial part of the course, which was completed by 774 at St Merryn. Disbanded into 755 Squadron, 01/12/42. Reformed at Puttalam as a fighter pool squadron, 02/10/43, known as 757 Naval Operational Training Unit. Used Corsairs, Hellcats, Seafires and Wildcats to train pilots in landing these aircraft on escort carriers and moved to Tambaram on 15/07/45, then postwar to Katukurunda, where it disbanded.

Identification markings: initially X6A+; Puttalam, P1-P87+; Tambaram, T93+.

Commanding officers:
Lt Cdr V.J. Somerset-Thomas, 24/05/39
Lt Cdr (A) C.R. Hodgson, RNVR, 06/03/41
Lt Cdr (A) J.J. Dykes, RNVR, 01/07/42
Lt Cdr (A) G.W. Parish, DSC, RNVR, 02/10/43
Lt Cdr (A) R.W. Durrant, DSC, RNZNVR, 05/05/45

758 Squadron Formed at Eastleigh, 01/07/39, from renumbered 759 Squadron as part of No. 2 Air Gunners School, operating Sharks, Ospreys, and then Skuas and Proctors as these were introduced on the outbreak of war. Moved to Arbroath, 14/10/40. Disbanded, 01/02/41. Reformed at Donibristle, 25/05/42, as the Beam

Approach School, using Airspeed Oxfords, then to Hinstock, 15/08/42, to become the Blind Approach School. Became the Naval Advanced Instrument Flying School in 04/43, operating by sending detachments to the specialised flying schools at Crail, East Haven, Fearn, Hinstock and Yeovilton to provide short instrument courses using more than 100 Oxfords and small numbers of other types. Two roving flights, 758X and Y, augmented the work of the detachments, while a third, 758Z, was a calibration flight and also undertook development of homing and landing aids. Disbanded after the war into 780 Squadron.

Identification markings: X5A+ in 1939–41; then U1A+ U3A+, U1AA, U1BB+, U3AA+ and U3BB+.

Commanding officers:
Lt Cdr W.H.G. Saunt, 10/07/39
Lt Cdr J.M. Wintour, 22/05/40
Lt Cdr (A) F. Leach, RNVR, 26/10/40
Lt Cdr (A) J.B.W. Pugh, AFC, RNVR, 25/05/42
Lt Cdr (A) J.C.V.K. Watson, RNVR, 15/08/42; operated as separate flights from 01/44.

759 Squadron Having earlier been renumbered as 758 Squadron, reformed at Eastleigh on 01/11/39, as a fighter school and pool squadron, operating 9 Skuas, 5 Rocs and 4 Sea Gladiators. Absorbed 769 Squadron on 01/12/39, becoming the Fleet Fighter School, moved to Yeovilton on 06/09/40. During 1940, Masters and Fulmars were added, with Martlets before the end of the year, while Sea Hurricanes were added in 1941. In 04/43, it became the Advanced Flying School of No. 1 Naval Air Fighter School, with 66 Sea Hurricanes, 8 Spitfires, 24 Fulmars and 15 Masters, with Seafires arriving in 08/43. On 01/07/43, a detachment was established at Angle to work alongside 794 Squadron as the Naval Air Firing Unit. A sub-unit, 'E' flight, was established in 1944 for instrument flying training. Further change came in 11/44, when the squadron became a mainly Corsair unit, on which 'A' flight provided conversion, 'C' flight camera air-to-air combat instruction, and 'D' flight dummy deck landings; in 04/45, these flights became 760 Squadron. Disbanded in 1946.

Identification markings: initially single letters; later Y1A+ to Y7A+.

Commanding officers:
Lt Cdr B.H.M. Kendall, 01/11/39
Lt Cdr H.P. Bramwell, DSO, DSC, 18/11/40
Capt F.D.G. Bird, RM, 01/08/41
Lt Cdr J.N. Garnett, 13/10/41
Lt Cdr E.W.T. Taylour, DSC, 08/12/41
unknown, 07/04/42
Lt E.D.G. Lewin, DSO, DSC, 12/11/42
Lt Cdr J.M. Bruen, DSO, DSC, 07/12/42
Lt Cdr N.G. Hallett, DSC, 17/05/43
Maj F.D.G. Bird, RM, 20/12/43
Lt Cdr O.N. Bailey, 10/07/44
Lt Cdr J.W. Sleigh, DSO, DSC, 14/12/44

760 Squadron Formed as Fleet Fighter Pool No. 1, Eastleigh, 01/04/40, with 4 Skuas, 2 Rocs and 1 Sea Gladiator, moved to Yeovilton on 16/09/40, as the Fighter Pool, where it received Masters and Fulmars, followed by Sea Hurricanes. In 08/41, it became part of the Fleet Fighter School operating Sea Hurricanes. Disbanded, 31/12/42. Reformed at Inskip as an anti-submarine operational training squadron, 01/05/44, it used Sea Hurricane IICs to train pilots on rocket projectile attacks and anti-flak cannon fire. Disbanded, 01/11/44, into 766 Squadron. Reformed again at Zeals, 10/04/45, out of 759's Corsair Familarisation Unit, part of No. 1 Naval Air Fighter School. Disbanded, 1946.

Identification markings: Sea Hurricanes, W7A+ to W9A+ ; Corsairs, Y1A+ to Y7A+ .

Commanding officers:
Lt J. Casson, 01/04/40

Lt Cdr P.H. Havers, 23/05/40
Lt Cdr G.N. Torry, 18/01/41
Lt K.V.V. Spurway, 01/08/41
Lt E.W.T. Taylour, 22/10/41
Lt O.J.R. Nicolls, 08/12/41
unknown, 03/42
Lt H.P. Allingham, 09/42
Lt (A) J.D. Kelsall, RNVR, 01/05/44
Lt Cdr (A) P.G. Burke, RNZNVR, 21/04/45

761 Squadron Formed out of 760 Squadron's Fulmars at Yeovilton, 01/08/41, as the advanced training squadron of the Fleet Fighter School, Fulmars and Sea Hurricanes used Haldon for air firing practice. Moving to Henstridge as No. 2 Naval Air Fighter School on 10/04/43, the squadron used 18 Spitfires and Seafires, and some Masters, to provide deck landing training on *Argus* and later the escort carrier *Ravager*. By 06/44, no less than 68 Seafires were being operated, as well as small numbers of Oxfords. Disbanded postwar.
Identification markings: Y1A+, G1A+ to G6A+.
Commanding officers:
Lt C.P. Campbell-Horsfall, 01/08/41
Capt R.C. Hay, RM, DSC, 01/01/42
Lt (A) R.B. Pearson, 01/07/42
Lt (A) W.C. Simpson, RNVR, 12/09/42
Lt A.C. Wallace, 10/42
unknown, 11/42
Lt Cdr (A) R.J. Cork, DSO, DSC, 10 /04/43
Lt Cdr (A) R.H.P. Carver, DSC, 15/11/43
Lt Cdr (A) S.G. Orr, DSC, RNVR, 20/09/44
Lt Cdr (A) P.N. Charlton, DFC, 27/04/45

762 Squadron Formed as an advanced flying training school squadron at Yeovilton, 23/03/42, moved 15/04 to St Merryn, where its Fulmars were augmented by Martlets and Masters. It returned to Yeovilton, 08/09 to receive Sea Hurricanes to provide continuation and conversion flying. Disbanded into 761 Squadron, 09/06/43. Reformed, 19/03/44, from part of 798 Squadron at Lee-on-Solent as the Twin Engine Conversion Unit, moving late 03/44 to Dale, using Oxfords and Beauforts. Identification markings: P1A+ and P2A+ in 1944.
Commanding officers:
Lt (A) R. McD Hall, 23/03/42
Lt D.B.M. Fiddes, 09/09/42
Lt Cdr (A) M.J.S. Newman, 29/03/43
Lt Cdr (A) S.J. Hawley, RNVR, 14/03/44
Lt Cdr (A) T.R. Koeller, RNVR, 07/03/45
Lt Cdr (A) J. Mills, RNVR, 20 /07/45

763 Squadron First formed as Torpedo Reconnaissance Pool No. 1 at Worthy Down, 15/12/39. Using just 6 Swordfish, the squadron provided a pool of newly qualified aircrew and provided training for crews required for *Hermes* and *Ark Royal*. Received 6 Albacores when it was deployed to Jersey on 11/03/40, but was repatriated to Lee-on-Solent on 31/05, shortly before the fall of France. After returning to Worthy Down on 04/07, disbanded on 08/07, with its remaining aircraft absorbed into 767 Squadron. Reformed 20/04/42, as a seaplane training squadron equipped with Walruses aboard the seaplane carrier *Pegasus*, preparing crews for the battleship and cruiser flights of 700 Squadron with a week's training in shipboard catapult operations. Disbanded again on 13/02/44, due to the reduced need for crews and aircraft on this form of duty. Reformed again, 14/04/44, out of 766 Squadron at Inskip, as an anti-submarine operational training squadron equipped with Avengers. A photographic flight was added in 03/45, using Swordfish, but the entire squadron was disbanded on 31/07/45 and absorbed into 785 at Crail.
Identification markings: Swordfish, P5A+; Avengers, K5A+.

Commanding officers:
Lt Cdr P.L. Mortimer, 18/12/39
Lt (A) J.R.W. Groves, 09/10/41
Lt S.M. Howard, 20/05/43
unidentified CO from 14/04/45
Lt Cdr (A) R.J.G. Brown, RNVR, 13/07/44
Lt Cdr (A) N.G. Haig, RNVR, 20/12/44

764 Squadron Formed at Lee-on-Solent, 08/04/40, as a seaplane training squadron providing an advanced seaplane conversion course for landplane pilots, equipped mainly with Walruses, with some Seafoxes and Swordfish. The course operated in conjunction with catapult training from *Pegasus.* The Seafoxes were left behind for 765 Squadron when 764 moved to Pembroke Dock on 03/07/40, where the Swordfish were left after an aerial attack forced the squadron to move to Lawrenny Ferry in 10/41. Kingfishers were introduced in 07/42, when its role became known officially as Seaplane Training Part II. Still at Lawrenny Ferry, the squadron disbanded on 07/11/43. Reformed on 19/02/44, at Gosport, as the User Trials Unit, initially with Barracudas and Avengers for torpedo trials, while the Barracudas were also used for trials of other equipment. Detachment was established at Crail 04/44, and a subsidiary unit, 'B' Flight was formed at Lee-on-Solent on 01/09 for tactical trials with the Firebrand, becoming 708 Squadron on 01/10. Torpedo Trials Flight had been established on the Clyde on 27/09, for net defence tests and this merged into 778 Squadron later. Fireflies were introduced in 06/45, before the squadron disbanded, 01/09.
Identification markings: Swordfish, Y9A+; Walrus, Seafox and Kingfisher unmarked.
Commanding officers:
Lt Cdr F.E.C. Judd, 08/04/40
Lt Cdr (A) H.L. McCulloch, 16/07/40
Lt Cdr H. Wright, 17/10/41

Lt M.B.P. Franklin, DSC, 01/08/42
Lt Cdr (A) W.J.R. MacWhirter, 17/01/43
Lt D.H. Angel, 08/02/43
Lt Cdr (A) J.E. Mansfield, RNVR, 10/04/43
Lt Cdr (A) J.O.B. Young, 16/06/43
Lt (A) E.D.J.R. Whatley, 19/02/44
Lt (A) D.L.R. Hutchinson, RNVR, 19/04/44
Lt (A) G.A. Donaghue, RNVR, 15/11/44
Capt D.B.L. Smith, RM, 03/06/45

765 Squadron Formed, 24/05/39, Lee-on-Solent, as a seaplane school and pool squadron, to train pilots and provide a reserve of pilots for catapult flights. Initial equipment included Walruses, Swordfish and Seafoxes, with the latter augmented by aircraft left behind by 764 in mid-1940. In 02/40, a number of Roc seaplanes had been added so that operational squadrons could be created for operations in Norway, but the plan was abandoned. The squadron moved to Sandbanks, becoming the Basic Seaplane Training School, providing Part I of the Seaplane Training Course. The squadron disbanded on 25/10/43, with the fall in demand for seaplane training. Reformed on 10/02/44, with Wellingtons at Charlton Horethorne as a travelling recording unit, to monitor the efficiency of radar units, the squadron moved on 18/03 to Lee-on-Solent, where the runways were too short for the aircraft, which had to be based at Manston. A secondary role was long-range reconnaissance and photography. A detachment was deployed at RAF Hornchurch in 11/44, for naval cooperation duties, this moved to Manston 06/45. Disbanded after the war in Malta.
Identification markings: Swordfish and Seafox, Y8A+; Walrus, L3A+ and LB3A+; Kingfisher BL3A+; Wellington, L8A+.
Commanding officers:
Lt Cdr H.C. Ranald, 24/05/39
Lt Cdr (A) H.L. McCulloch, 08/04/40
Lt Cdr (A) L.B. Wilson, 12/07/40

Lt Cdr G.R. Brown, DSC, 21/04/41
Lt J.W.L.M. Allison, 27/08/42
Lt Cdr (A) L.D. Goldsmith, RNVR,
11/01/43
Lt (A) D.H. Coates, RNVR, 10/02/44

766 Squadron Formed at Machrihanish, 15/04/42, to provide a night torpedo attack course using Swordfish. Moved to Inskip, 07/07/43, becoming part of No. 1 Naval OTU, with more than 31 Swordfish by 05/44. These aircraft were joined by a variety of aircraft including Albacores, Fulmars, Ansons and Defiants, as the role evolved and at one stage a photographic flight of 3 Swordfish was operated. Fireflies joined in 10/44, with 14 being operated initially, augmented by Sea Hurricanes on 01/11. After the war, the squadron moved to Rattray and Lossiemouth.
Identification markings: Swordfish, K1A+ to K3A+; Firefly, K1A+, K2A+ and K5A+; Sea Hurricane, K1A+.
Commanding officers:
Lt Cdr (A) R.E. Bibby, DSO, RNVR,
15/04/42
Lt Cdr (A) W.F.C. Garthwaite, DSC, RNVR,
24/07/43
Lt Cdr E.B. Morgan, RANVR, 03/08/44

767 Squadron A redesignation of 811 Squadron, formed as a deck landing training squadron at Donibristle, 24/05/39, initially operating a mixture of Moths, Sharks and Swordfish, with *Furious* used for advanced training. In 11/39, a detachment was sent to Hyeres de la Palyvestre, near Toulon in the South of France, to use *Argus* for training in the more favourable climate of the Mediterranean. While deck landing training continued even after the German push west, right up to the fall of France, the squadron also embarked on operational service, with 9 of its aircraft bombing Genoa on 13/06, after Italy entered the war.

Afterwards, the squadron had to be evacuated, with 12 aircraft eventually reaching Malta, where they formed the basis of 830 Squadron on 01/07, while the remaining 6 joined *Ark Royal*, and were absorbed into the ship's squadrons. On 08/07, the squadron regrouped, still as a deck landing training squadron, at Arbroath, mainly using aircraft from 763 Squadron, forming the basis of the Deck Landing Training Squadron, with other squadrons added later, and with the Swordfish as its mainstay, supplemented by Albacores. After a move to East Haven on 05/05/43, the squadron was equipped with Barracudas in 06/44 and provided a TBR course for the rest of the war.
Battle honours: Mediterranean, 1940.
Identification markings: Swordfish in 1939–40, T4A+ and T0A+; T4A+ from 07/40; E1A+ and E2A+ for all types, 05/43.
Commanding officers:
Lt Cdr J.A.L. Drummond, 24/08/39;
Lt Cdr D.N. Russell (dates unknown)
Lt A.G. Leatham, 29/11/41
Lt R.L. Williamson, DSC, 17/06/42
Lt R.S. Baker-Falkner, 01/07/42
Lt C.H.C. O'Rourke, 10/10/42
Lt Cdr W.J. Mainprice, 25/03/43
Lt Cdr (A) T.T. Miller, 03/11/43
Lt Cdr (A) J.L. Fisher, RNVR, 07/11/43
Lt Cdr (A) B.W. Vigrass, RNVR, 06/05/44
Lt Cdr (A) D.R. Park, RNZNVR, 04/02/45
Lt Cdr (A) S.G. Cooke, 12/08/45

768 Squadron Also part of the Deck Landing Training School at Arbroath, formed 13/01/41, using Swordfish. Advanced training used *Argus*, for which a detachment was maintained at Machrihanish, where the squadron moved on 01/03/43, by which time it was also operating Fulmars, Martlets, Sea Hurricanes and hooked Spitfires, to which were added Albacores, Barracudas and Seafires. A move to Ayr on 29/09/43, coincided with the arrival of Hellcats, while a further move to Abbotsinch on 19/01/44, coincided with the arrival of Avengers and Corsairs and later, Fireflies. At this time, deck landing used escort carriers on the Firth of Clyde. A detachment was maintained at Ayr throughout this period, and the squadron returned there on 05/07/45. Disbanded after the war at East Haven.

Identification markings: individual letters initially; B2A+ by 1943; M2A+ by 03/43.

Commanding officers:
Lt Cdr V.C. Grenfell, 13/01/41
Lt Cdr (A) F.D.G. Jennings, 26/06/41
Lt N.G. Hallett, 28/09/41
Lt (A) P.B. Jackson, 15/03/42
Lt Cdr (A) D.M. Brown, RNVR, 29/12/42
Lt Cdr (A) D.J.W. Williams, 01/03/43
Lt Cdr (A) J.S. Bailey, 08/07/43
Lt Cdr (A) J.M. Brown, DSC, RNVR, 29/10/44

769 Squadron Formed at Donibristle, 24/05/39, by renumbering 801 Squadron. A fighter deck landing training squadron equipped with Rocs, Sea Gladiators and Skuas, using *Furious* for advanced training. Disbanded, 01/12/39. Reformed, 29/11/41, as a unit within the Deck Landing Training School at Arbroath, using Swordfish and Albacores. Received Barracudas, 07/11/43, on moving to East Haven, where a course for deck landing training officers was also provided, until this responsibility passed to 731 Squadron on 05/12. Changed to TBR training in 1944, before moving to Rattray on 28/07/45. Merged with 717 Squadron after the war.

Identification markings: Sea Gladiators, T6A+; Swordfish, individual letters; Albacores, numbers up to 78; Barracudas, E1A+ and E2A+, then I4A+ to I6A+.

Commanding officers:
Lt Cdr C.A. Kingsley-Rowe, 24/05/39

Lt W.H. Crawford, 29/11/41
Lt Cdr W.H. Nowell, 01/01/43
Lt Cdr (A) S.P. Luke, 07/05/43
Lt Cdr (A) P.N. Medd, 24/01/43
Lt Cdr (A) D. Brooks, DSC, RNVR, 08/07/44
Lt Cdr (A) G.C. Edwards, RCNVR, 07/04/45
Lt Cdr (A) G. Bennett, DSC, RNVR, 28/06/45

770 Squadron Formed as a deck landing training squadron at Lee-on-Solent, 07/11/39, with a small, but mixed, complement which included a Moth and 2 each of Sea Gladiators, Skuas and Swordfish. Embarked in *Argus*, and operated from this ship and Hyeres la Palyvestre, near Toulon, until disbanded 01/05/40. Reformed at Donibristle, 01/01/41, as a fleet requirements unit out of 771's 'X' Flight, with just 4 Rocs, 2 for target towing and 2 for marking the fall of shot. Additional aircraft, Skuas, were received when the squadron moved to Crail on 01/06/41, Chesapeakes and Defiants followed in 1942. Target towing passed to Martinets in 1943, and after a move to Dunino on 29/01/44, Hurricanes replaced the Chesapeakes and Blenheims were also added, before moving to Drem on 25/07. During 1945, a wide assortment of aircraft was operated, including Beaufighters, Mosquitoes and Spitfires. Disbanded shortly after the war.

Identification markings: Individual letters 1939–41; Skuas, C8A+; Blenheims, B8A+, BR8A+, D8A+; Beaufighters, BR8A+; Seafires. D8A+.

Commanding officers:
Lt E.W. Lawson, 01/01/41
Lt H.E.R. Torin, 05/05/41
Lt Cdr (A) W.H.C. Blake, 29/10/41
Lt Cdr (A) H.T. Molyneaux, RNVR, 13/11/41

Lt Cdr (A) A.F.E. Payen, RNVR, 04/04/42
Lt Cdr (A) D.R.M. Manthorpe, RNVR, 05/04/44
Lt Cdr (A) J.M.L. Wilson, RNZNVR, 13/08/45

771 Squadron Formed out of an unnumbered fleet requirements unit, 24/05/39, Portland. Initially 14 Swordfish and some Walruses were operated, with the squadron having a northern 'X' flight and a southern 'Y' flight; the former becoming 772 Squadron, 28/09/39. The new 771 was then based at Hatston, operating Swordfish, with a detachment at Abbotsinch and a new 'X' Flight at Donibristle, which formed the basis of 770 Squadron. Henleys, Rocs and Skuas were soon added, followed by Blenheims and Marylands. First to discover that the *Bismarck* had put to sea from her Norwegian fjord on 22/05/41, spotted by one of her Marylands, operating in weather that had grounded RAF Coastal Command. Moved to Twatt, 01/07/42, after Skuas had been replaced by Defiant target tugs and Chesapeakes. Defiants and Chesapeakes replaced by Martinets in 08/43, while Bostons and Havocs were also added before the Rocs and Skuas were replaced by Hurricanes in 05/44. Corsairs were later added, and early in 1945, the squadron became one of the first to operate Hoverfly helicopters. After VE Day, the squadron moved south to Zeals on 25/07, following the fleet and started to operate Wildcats in support of the Fighter Direction School at Yeovil.
Identification markings: R5A+; individual letters; then T8A+.
Commanding officers:
Lt Cdr K.W. Beard, 24/05/39
Lt Cdr F.E.C. Judd, 13/09/40
Maj A.R. Burch, RM, 15/01/41
Lt Cdr (A) N.E. Goddard, DSC, RNVR, 15/10/41
Lt Cdr (A) H.T. Molyneaux, RNVR, 04/05/42

Lt Cdr (A) W. Dobson, 13/02/44
Lt Cdr (A) C.C. Burke, RNZNVR, 11/04/45

772 Squadron Formed out of 'Y' Flight of 771 Squadron, Lee-on-Solent, 28/09/39. A fleet requirements unit operating 4 Swordfish seaplanes from Portland, until moving to Cambeltown on 14/07/40. Move to nearby Machrihanish, 15/06/41, saw the Swordfish replaced by Rocs, while Walruses were also added for search and rescue duties. The following year saw the Swordfish return, accompanied by Chesapeakes, Defiants and Fulmars. Martinets were added in 1943 and Blenheims and Hurricanes in early 1944. Duties included SAR, target-towing, radar calibration, height finding and photography, in addition, on 27/05/44, squadron carried out a dummy attack on the fleet in an exercise to prepare for the Normandy landings. Became the Fleet Requirements Unit School on moving to Ayr on 02/07/44. Late 1944, Bostons, Fireflies and Corsairs were obtained, but greater standardisation on fewer types took place throughout 1945, concentrating on Mosquitoes and Wildcats as well as the original Martinets. Detachments were based at Ronaldsway in 1945.
Identification markings: R3A+ to K9A+, 1942; M8A+, 1943; then later, AR8A+, AR9A+, BR8A+, BR9A+.
Commanding officers:
Lt Cdr M.A. Everett, 28/09/39
Lt Cdr R.E.P. Miers, 16/11/39
Lt Cdr K.W. Beard, 06/09/40
Lt Cdr C.L. Hill, 25/05/42
Lt Cdr (A) A.C. Mills RNVR, 04/08/42
Lt Cdr P.J. Connolly, 25/08/43
Lt Cdr C.R. Holman, RNR, 11/09/44
Lt Cdr P. Snow, 16/06/44

773 Squadron Formed 03/06/40, as a fleet requirements unit in Bermuda for ships on the West Indies Station. Initial equipment consisted of just 2 Walruses and 1 Swordfish floatplane, but joined by Seafoxes and land and floatplane versions of the Roc. Disbanded, at Bermuda, 25/04/44. Reformed, 01/06/45, still as a fleet requirements unit, at Lee-on-Solent. Moved to Brawdy after the war.

Identification markings: R4A+, 1940–44.
Commanding officers:
Lt Cdr H. Wright, 28/06/40
Lt Cdr G.C.W. Fowler, 09/41
Lt Cdr K.W. Beard, 06/08/43
Lt Cdr (E) W.P.T. Croome, 01/06/45

774 Squadron Formed at Worthy Down, 10/11/39, as an armament training squadron for observers and telegraphist air gunners, with a mixed strength of 3 Rocs, 3 Skuas, 4 Swordfish and 4 Shark target tugs. Six days later, it moved to Aldergrove, as part of No. 3 Bombing and Gunnery School. Moved twice in 1940, on 03/07 to Evanton, and on 17/09, to St Merryn, when it received Albacores. In 1941, the Rocs and Skuas were withdrawn, followed by the Sharks in 1942 and the Albacores and Swordfish in 1943, replaced by Barracudas, some Defiant target tugs and Sea Hurricanes. On 24/10/44, 774 moved to Rattray. Disbanded there, 01/08/45.

Identification markings: O4A+; then single letters, and S6A+.
Commanding officers:
Lt Cdr S. Borrett, 16/11/39
Lt Cdr W.G.C. Stokes, 24/11/39
Lt Cdr P.L. Mortimer, 30/08/40
Lt Cdr (A) J.H. Gibbons, 15/03/41
Lt Cdr L. Gilbert, RNVR, 10/42
Lt Cdr P.P. Pardoe-Matthews, RNR, 16/08/43
Lt (A) J.O. Sparke, RNVR, 07/10/44

775 Squadron Formed Dekheila, 11/40, as a fleet requirements unit for the Mediterranean Fleet at Alexandria. Initial complement of 4 Rocs was joined by Fulmars, Sea Gladiators, Swordfish, a few Albacores and Queen Bees in 1941. The squadron included the RN Fighter Flight's Fulmars from 10/41 until 13/03/42, when this became 889 Squadron. Detachment was deployed to Haifa in late 1942, and on 04/07/43, absorbed 728 Squadron. Defiants introduced in 1943, and after moving to Gibraltar on 01/02/44, Martinets followed, with a few Beaufighters, Hurricanes and Seafires, before moving back to Dekheila on 05/08/45. Disbanded after the war.

Identification markings: Single letters.
Commanding officers:
Not known, 11/40
Lt A.H. Abrams, 27/07/41
Lt Cdr (A) H.L. McCulloch, 27/10/41
Lt Cdr (A) J.W.G. Wellham, DSO, 29/11/42
Lt Cdr (A) J.M. Waddell, RNVR, 08/12/42
Lt Cdr (A) J.L. Wordsworth, RNVR, 24/03/45

776 Squadron Fleet requirements unit formed Lee-on-Solent, 01/01/41. Initially operated 3 Blenheims and several Rocs, some of which were detached to Speke, 22/03/41, while a second detachment went to Woodvale on 16/05/42. Chesapeakes and Skuas were introduced in 1942. The squadron moved to Speke, 18/10/42, and the following year, detachments were deployed at Llanbedr, Millom, Usworth and Waltham. Early in 1944, a major influx of new aircraft included 12 Defiant target tugs, replaced by Martinets the following year, as well as 14 Hurricanes, 8 Blenheims and 1 Swordfish. On 07/04/45, the Woodvale detachment was reabsorbed when the squadron moved there. 10 Seafires joined in 05/45. Disbanded, Burscough, 10/45.

Identification markings: Single letters initially; R7A+ and R8A+ in 1942.
Commanding officers:
Lt Cdr E.J.E. Burt, 10/01/41

Lt Cdr (A) N.E. Goddard, DSC, RNVR, 07/05/42
Lt Cdr (A) J. Goodyear, RNVR, 19 /08/42
Lt Cdr (A) B.A.G. Meads, MBE, RNVR, 24/07/43
Lt Cdr (A) R.M.B. Ward, RNVR, 10/04/44
Lt Cdr (A) N.G. Maclean, RNVR, 24/01/45

777 Squadron Originally planned as a reserve fighter pool squadron 12/39, eventually formed at Hastings, Sierra Leone, 01/08/41, as a fleet requirements unit, with a small number of Rocs and Swordfish. Defiants and Walruses added in 1942. Throughout most of 1943, the squadron was responsible for the air defence of Sierra Leone. It disbanded at Hastings on 25/12/44. Reformed on 23/05/45, from 'B' Flight of 778 Squadron, as a trials unit operating aboard *Pretoria Castle*, using a number of different aircraft, while shore bases used included Gosport, Ford and Ayr. Reabsorbed into 778 after the war.
Identification markings: Single letters initially; Defiants, SA+; single letters after reforming,1945.
Commanding officers:
Lt Cdr C.E. Fenwick, 01/08/41
Lt Cdr H.J. Gibbs, 05/08/41
Lt Cdr (A) F.C. Muir, RNVR, 22/07/42
Lt Cdr (A) C. Draper, RNVR, 27/09/43
Lt Cdr (A) M.N. Stewart, 15/03/44
Lt Cdr (A) D.R. Carter, RNVR, 23/05/45
Lt Cdr (A) J.R.N. Gardner, 04 /06/45

778 Squadron Formed Lee-on-Solent, 28/09/39, as a Service Trials Unit Squadron, testing and evaluating tactics, aircraft types, armament and equipment, such as flame floats and aerial mines. Operated Rocs, Skuas, Swordfish and Walruses, to which Albacores and Fulmars were soon added. Moved to Arbroath, 06/07/40, and then received Martlets and Sea Hurricanes, which were followed in 1941/42 by Barracudas, Chesapeakes, Kingfishers and Seafires. After moving to Crail, 05/03/43, 'B' Flight was formed 26/07/43, for deck trials aboard *Pretoria Castle* and this became 777 Squadron in 1945. The squadron next moved to Arbroath, 15/08/44, when it received Avenger, Corsair, Firebrand and Firefly aircraft. 'C' Flight was formed on 07/03/45, from the disbanded 739 Squadron, engaged in blind approach trials, but this was soon absorbed into the main body of 778. The squadron moved to Gosport in 08/45, and in the immediate postwar period absorbed several other squadrons.
Identification letters: CO from 03/43.
Commanding officers:
Lt Cdr R.A. Kilroy, 28/09/39
Lt Cdr J.P.G. Bryant, 22/04/40
Lt Cdr A.J. Tillard, 06/01/41
Lt Cdr H.P. Bramwell, DSO, DSC, 21/07/41
Lt Cdr H.J.F. Lane, 01/03/43
Lt Cdr P.B. Schofield, 25 /04/44
Lt Cdr E.M. Britton, 05/02/45

779 Squadron Formed as a fleet requirements unit, 01/10/41, Gibraltar. Initially operated just 2 Skuas for target towing and coastal defence. Original aircraft replaced by Defiants in 04/43, by which time Fulmars, Sea Hurricanes and Swordfish had also been introduced in small numbers. Later in 1943, Beaufighter IIs also joined the unit, while from 08–09/43, a detachment of these aircraft deployed to Taranto, after which they also saw service in North Africa. Starting in 06/44, the Defiants were replaced by 9 Martinets, operating with the 3 Beaufighters, 2 Hurricanes and 2 Swordfish. Disbanded, 05/08/45, at Gibraltar.
Identification markings: On some aircraft consisted of single letters.
Commanding officers:
Lt Cdr (A) B.F. Cox, RNVR, 01/10/41

Lt Cdr (A) L. Gilbert, RNVR, 17/01/42
Lt Cdr (A) J.M. Keene-Miller, RNVR, 22/06/42
Lt Cdr (A) C.R. Holman, RNR, 01/05/43
Lt Cdr (A) E.L. Meicklejohn, RNVR, 14/09/43

780 Squadron Conversion course unit formed at Eastleigh, 02/10/39, to train experienced civilian pilots in naval flying, for which it operated a variety of aircraft, including Hart Trainer, Nimrod, Shark, Gipsy Moth, Hornet Moth, Tiger Moth, Proctor, Shark, Swordfish and Vega Gull. Moved to Lee-on-Solent, 07/10/40, and by 08/43, its role had changed to converting Swordfish and Albacore pilots to the monoplane Barracuda, although this task soon passed to 798 Squadron. On 09/10/43, it moved to Charlton Horethorne, returning Lee-on-Solent on 28/11/44. Disbanded, 02/01/45.
Identification markings: Initially individual numbers; then L1A+, 1942; BY1A+, 1943; L1A+, late 1944.
Commanding officers:
Lt Cdr H.S. Cooper, 02/10/39
Lt Cdr (A) J. Goodyear, RNVR, 07/10/40
Lt Cdr (A) T.G. Stubley, RNVR, 17/08/42

781 Squadron Formed, 20/03/40, as a communications unit at Lee-on-Solent. Initially operated the Hornet Moth, Fulmar, Swordfish and Walrus, which were later joined by the Anson, Dominie, Hudson, Oxford, Proctor, Tiger Moth and Vega Gull. Remit expanded briefly 06/43, when Beaufighters arrived and a conversion course was provided, but this task soon passed to 798 Squadron, although soon refresher flying became part of the squadron's duties. Detachments provided from 02/44, when 'B' Flight, with Swordfish and a Proctor, based at Heathrow, then Fairey's factory aerodrome, for Admiralty

use. After the Normandy landings, an Anson was based at Rochester for the Commander-in-Chief, The Nore: 'X' Flight, operating Dominies, sent to the continent on 03/05/45. Disbanded, Lee-on-Solent, 31/07/45, into 782 and 799 Squadrons.
Identification markings from 1942 included: L8A+, L9A+ and L0A+.
Commanding officers:
Lt Cdr E.J.E. Burt, 20/03/40
Lt Cdr (A) A.C.S. Irwin, RNVR, 07/09/40
Lt Cdr (A) J.M. Keene-Miller, RNVR, 15/02/41
Lt Cdr (A) Sir G.J.E. Lewis, Bt, RNVR, 07/11/41
Lt Cdr (A) W.B. Caldwell, RNVR, 01/12/44

782 Squadron Although existing briefly at Ford for almost 3 weeks in late autumn 1939, with the intention of becoming an armament training squadron, 782 finally established 01/12/40, as the Northern Communications Squadron. Origins lay in an unnumbered communications flight at Donibristle, formed 07/40, using former Jersey Airways crews commissioned into the Royal Navy. Initial equipment included ex-airline de Havilland Flamingos and Dragon Expresses, as well as Proctors. Operated for the most part almost as an airline, linking isolated naval air stations in Scotland, Northern Ireland and the Northern Isles and also flying from these to Lee-on-Solent. Aircraft soon included Expeditors, Oxfords, Travellers and 'Sparrow' Harrows, which had been modified to carry engines and spares. On 31/07/45, 782 absorbed the work of 781, detaching flights of Dominies to Lee-on-Solent, Eglinton and Inverness. The squadron survived for some years after the war.
Identification markings: *Merlin* 1+.
Commanding officers:
Lt Cdr (A) A. Goodfellow, RNVR, 01/12/40
Lt Cdr (A) W.T.D. Gardner, RNVR, 21/03/41

Lt Cdr (A) G.H.G.S. Rayer, 07/12/44
Lt Cdr (A) J.K.N. Evans, RNVR, 27/07/45

783 Squadron An air-to-surface vessel radar training squadron formed Arbroath, 09/01/41. Operated Swordfish, Albacores and Walruses, joined several Ansons. A Dragon Express was equipped as a flying classroom until it had to be replaced by a Wellington after being damaged by 'friendly' fire from a minesweeper. Operated in conjunction with the Naval Air Signals School, from 03/43, when Barracudas, Fireflies and Avengers introduced. The squadron survived for some years after the war.
Identification markings: A6A+ and A0A+.
Commanding officers:
Lt Cdr (A) J.M. Waddell, RNVR, 09/01/41
Lt Cdr (A) J.M. Kene-Miller, RNVR, 07/11/41
Lt Cdr (A) D.M. Brown, RNVR, 15/06/42
Lt Cdr (A) R.P. Mason, RNVR, 29/12/42
Lt Cdr (A) T.B. Horsley, RNVR, 30/08/44

784 Squadron A night fighter training squadron formed at Lee-on-Solent, 01/06/42, using 2 Chesapeakes and 6 Fulmars, with additional Fulmars and Ansons following as the squadron moved to Drem, 18/10/42. Personnel were also detached to the Naval Air Radio Installation Unit at Christchurch in 1943 and from 10/43, a number of crews were attached to RAF night fighter squadrons, serving with 29 Squadron among others, 2 officers gained DFCs while on attachment. The squadron continued to take a combatant role in 1944, when flights each of 3 Fulmars were attached for service to 813 Squadron for service aboard *Campania*, 825 aboard *Vindex*, and 835 aboard *Nairana*, to provide fighter cover on convoy protection duties. Firefly 1NF night fighters were introduced from 09/44. Disbanded 1946, at Dale.

Identification markings: A0A+, October, 1942; with D1A+ to D3A+ and D5A+ in 1945.
Commanding officers:
Capt L.A. Harris, DSC, RM, 01/06/42
Lt Cdr P.N. Humphreys, GC, 01/12/42
Lt Cdr (A) J.E.M. Hoare, RCNVR, 10/09/43
Lt Cdr R.O. Davies, 18/01/44
Lt Cdr (A) P.R.V. Wheeler, RNVR, 03/09/44
Lt Cdr (A) G.E. Fenner, RNVR, 09/04/45

785 Squadron Formed as a TBR training squadron, Crail, 04/11/40. Initial equipment comprised 13 Sharks and 5 Swordfish, although the Sharks were replaced, 08/41, by Albacores and Barracudas were introduced in 12/42. The squadron became part of No. 1 Naval Operational Training Unit in late 1944. Avengers were introduced on 31/07/45, when 763 Squadron was absorbed. Disbanded early 1946.
Identification markings: Swordfish, individual letters and numbers, including A-Q, AA-EE; Albacores, individual letters and numbers, including R-Z, RR-ZZ; later types included C1A+ to C5A+.
Commanding officers:
Lt Cdr P.G.O. Sydney-Turner, 04/11/40
Capt O. Patch, DSO, DSC, RM, 22/08/41
Lt R.W. Thorne, 01/01/42
Lt A.H. Abrams, DSC, 07/09/42
Lt J.H. Stenning, 22/10/42
Lt Cdr (A) K.G. Sharp, 02/12/42
Lt Cdr (A) M. Thorpe, 01/07/43
Lt Cdr (A) R.B. Lunberg, 31/01/44
Lt Cdr (A) M.W. Rudorf, DSC, 05/12/44
Lt Cdr L.C. Watson, DSC, 13/06/45
Lt Cdr (A) N.G. Haigh, RNVR, 31/07/45

786 Squadron Also formed, Crail, 04/11/40, as a TBR squadron with 9 Albacores initially, which were joined early the following year by Chesapeakes and Swordfish. Aircraft were almost entirely replaced by Barracudas in 12/42 and in 1944, Ansons introduced. Disbanded into 785, late 1945.

Identification markings: individual letters initially; later C1A+ to C5A+.
Commanding officers:
unknown on formation
Capt F.W. Brown, RM, 06/12/40
Lt (A) S. Keane, 28/07/41
Lt R.W. Little, 11/41
Lt R.C.B. Stallard-Peyre, 23/02/42
Lt Cdr B.E. Boulding, DSC, 15/10/42
Lt Cdr D. Norcock, 10/08/43
Lt Cdr (A) R.J. Fisher, RNZNVR, 30/06/44
Lt Cdr (A) F.H. Franklin, RNVR, 30/10/44
Lt Cdr L.C. Watson, DSC, 13/06/45

787 Squadron Formed on 05/03/41, Yeovilton, out of 804 Squadron as a Fleet Fighter Development Unit. Almost every type of fighter was received by the squadron for testing and evaluation for naval use. An interesting aspect of the role was the comparative testing of captured aircraft, pitching a Fulmar II against a Fiat CR.42 and a Martlett I against a Messerschmitt Bf 109e. Moved to Duxford on 18/06/41, to become the Naval Air Fighting Development Unit, attached to the RAF's Air Fighting Development Unit. Early work on the use of rocket projectiles by naval aircraft followed in 01/43, with a special unit, 'Z' Flight, deployed to St Merryn in February for trials at the Treligga Range and then later to train operational squadrons in the use of these weapons.

Moved with the RAF AFDU to Wittering on 26/03/43, receiving Corsairs, Fireflies and Hellcats, as well as Barracudas and Avengers. 'Y' Flight was formed in 06/44, at Arbroath as a fighter affiliation unit equipped with Seafires, visiting operational squadrons to brief them on developments in fighter tactics, and help TBR squadrons in evading fighter attack. 'Z' Flight was disbanded, 01/07/44. 'Y' was successively based at Burscough, Ballyhalbert and Machrihanish, where it disbanded,

01/03/45. AFDU became the Air Fighting Development Squadron of the Central Fighter Establishment on 17/01/45, with a move to Tangmere, while 787 became the Air Support Development Section of the Naval Air Fighting Development Unit. Further flights included 'X' Flight at Odiham with 3 Hellcats and an Anson for Rebecca radar trials, while 5 Fireflies were detached to Ford on 29/04/45, for trials with ASH, US-built air-to-surface vessel radar. The squadron would have moved to the Far East as a new 'Z' Flight had VJ Day not intervened. Moved to Westhampnett 07/45 and survived for some years after the war.
Identification markings: Y⊖A+ starting in 1943.
Commanding officer:
Cdr B.H.M. Kendall, OBE, 05/03/41

788 Squadron Formed at China Bay in Ceylon, 18/01/42, as British Eastern Fleet's TBR pool, with an initial strength of just 6 Swordfish. All aircraft were shot down during the heavy raids by Japanese carrier-borne aircraft on 05/04 and surviving personnel were sent to East Africa, regrouping at Tanga on 20/05, then becoming a fleet requirements unit at Mombasa on 24/06. Equipment shortages and the difficulty of resupply meant that a variety of aircraft were operated, including a captured Italian SM79, in addition to the more usual Albacores, Fulmars, Sea Hurricanes, Skuas and Swordfish. A detachment operated from Nairobi's Eastleigh air station 05/42–11/42. Re-equipment took place during 1944, of 2 Beaufighter IIs, 4 Defiant target tugs and 1 Walrus, while a Beaufort was introduced in mid-1945, shortly before the squadron disbanded on 11/06.
Commanding officers:
Lt Cdr C.A. Kingsley-Rowe, 16/02/42

Maj V.B.G. Cheesman, RM, 01/05/42
Lt E.M. Britton, 07/08/42
Lt W.N. Waller, 25/08/42
Lt Cdr (A) E.H. Horn, RNVR, 12/08/43
Lt Cdr (A) J.A. Ansell, RNVR, 25/10/43
Lt Cdr (A) F.G. Hood, SANF(V), 15/08/44

789 Squadron Formed as a fleet requirements unit, Wingfield, South Africa, 01/07/42. Initial equipment consisted of 1 Walrus, but other aircraft were 'borrowed', including Albacores, Fulmars, Sea Hurricanes and Swordfish. 2 Skuas were obtained in 09/43, while further relief to the aircraft famine came when the squadron acquired a limited role as a pool squadron, holding Kingfishers for ships' catapult flights and for 726 Squadron, as well as sharing 799's aircraft. It was not until the following year that the squadron obtained an appreciable number of aircraft of its own, with the arrival of 4 Defiant target tugs early in the year, joined later by Ansons, Beaufighters, Harvards and Martinets. Disbanded, 11/45.
Identification markings: Single letters.
Commanding officers:
Lt Cdr (A) K.C. Johnson, RNVR, 01/07/42
Lt Cdr (A) W.T.E. White, SANF (V), 11/06/43
Lt (A) B. Sinclair, MBE, 10/09/43
Lt Cdr W.T.E. White, SANF (V), 20/06/44

790 Squadron Originally formed at Machrihanish, 15/06/41, as an air target towing squadron out of elements of 768 and 772 Squadrons, operating Swordfish and Rocs until being disbanded into 772 Squadron on 30/09. Reformed, 27/07/42, at Charlton Horethorne, attached to the Fighter Direction School, for which the squadron's Oxfords acted as bombers and its Fulmars as fighters, training fighter direction officers. Fireflies replaced the Fulmars in 06/44, while the squadron was moved briefly to Culmhead during August and September.

A move to Zeals in early 04/45, coincided with the introduction of Seafires. Remained operational until late 1949.
Identification markings: Y0A+, BY0A+, Z8A+, Z0A+.
Commanding officers:
Lt Cdr (A) C.R. Hodgson, RNVR, 27/07/42
Lt Cdr (A) R.P. Demuth, RNVR, 26/06/44
Lt Cdr (A) G.K. Pridham, RNVR, 13/11/44
Lt Cdr (A) R. Williamson, RNVR, 24/04/45

791 Squadron Formed as an air target towing squadron, Arbroath, 15/10/40, initially operating two Rocs, but soon joined by Defiants, Swordfish and Skuas. Disbanded on 10/12/44, although it was reformed briefly after the war.
Identification markings: A8A+.
Commanding officers:
Lt Cdr (A) L. Gilbert, RNVR, 15/10/40
Lt Cdr (A) K.B. Brotchie, RNVR, 06/12/41
Lt J.C.M. Harman, 10/09/42
Lt Cdr (A) C.A. Crighton, RNVR, 12/05/43
Lt Cdr (A) A.P.T. Pierssene, RNVR, 07/04/44

792 Squadron Formed as an air target towing unit, St Merryn, 15/08/40, initially operated a small number of Masters, Rocs and Skuas, although later these were replaced by Defiants and Martinets. Disbanded, 02/01/45, into 794 Squadron.
Identification markings: S8A+.
Commanding officers:
Lt H.E.R. Torin, DSC, 15/08/40
Lt (A) H.R. Dimock, RNVR, 09/12/40
Lt E.W. Lawson, 05/05/41
Lt Cdr (A) T.J. Archer, RNVR, 30/09/41
Lt Cdr (A) G.V. Oddy, RNVR, 08/12/44
No CO, 02–06/44
Lt Cdr (A) N.G. Maclean, RNVR, 12/06/44

793 Squadron Formed as an air target towing squadron, Ford, 25/10/39, equipped with Rocs. Detachment sent to Warmwell,

07/40, to tow targets for fighters based at Exeter, the only part of the squadron to escape destruction in the Luftwaffe raid on Ford on 18/08. Reassembled on 18/11/40, at Piarco, Trinidad, attached to No. 1 Observer School, initially using Rocs, with Albacores and Fulmars added in 1943. The Rocs replaced by Martinets in 06/44. Disbanded shortly after the war.

Identification markings: W6A+ to W8A+.

Commanding officers:

Lt (A) J.M. Gladish, RNVR, 25/10/39

No CO, 08–11/40

Lt Cdr (A) K.D.R. Davis, RNVR, 08/11/40

Lt Cdr (A) F.C. Booth, RNVR, 08/06/44

Lt Cdr (A) F.B. Gardner, RNVR, 07/12/44

794 Squadron Formed as an air target towing squadron, Yeovilton, 01/08/40, operating Rocs and Swordfish, joined by Blenheims, Tiger Moths, Defiants, Skuas and Spitfires. On 10/04/43, a detachment acted as an air firing unit at Warmwell, then on 01/07/43, the entire squadron became the Naval Air Firing Unit at Angle, operating 16 Sea Hurricanes, 4 Defiants, 4 Masters and 8 Martinets, operating alongside the Fighter School at Yeovilton. Further moves followed in quick succession, to Dale, 10/09, Henstridge, 22/11 and Charlton Horethorne on 01/12/43, by which time the unit was known as 1 Naval Air Firing Unit. Disbanded at Charlton Horethorne, 30/06/44. Reformed at St Merryn, 02/01/45, out of 719, 780 and 792 Squadrons as the School of Air Firing, using Harvards, Martinets, Corsairs, Fireflies, Seafires and Wildcats. Role expanded in 06/45 to support the newly-formed Ground Attack School. When it moved to Eglinton, 09/08, its 3 flights offered courses in air combat, ground attack and photo-reconnaissance. The squadron did not disband until 1947.

Identification markings: P8A+ to Y8A+ in 1943; S1A+ in 1945.

Commanding officers:

Lt (A) R.W.H. Everett, RNVR, 03/08/40

Lt Cdr (A) F.C. Muir, RNVR, 22/07/42

Lt (A) W.H. Stevens, 16/11/42

Lt Cdr (A) A.L. Hill, RNVR; 10/04/43

Lt Cdr (A) J.L. Appleby, 02/01/45

Lt Cdr R.A. Bird, DSC, 03/07/45

795 Squadron Originally formed as the Eastern Fleet Fighter Pool, Tanga, Tanganyika, 24/06/42, early equipment consisted of Martlets and Fulmars. Gained an operational role, with 'A' Flight's 6 Fulmars embarked in *Illustrious* to support the invasion of Madagascar, before being detached ashore at Majunga on 11/09 to maintain anti-submarine patrols as part of the RAF's 207 Group. Disbanded, 11/08/43.

Commanding officers:

Lt O.N. Bailey, 24/06/42

Lt Cdr (A) G.W. Parish, DSC, RNVR, 07/06/43

796 Squadron Formed as the Eastern Fleet TBR Pool, Port Reitz, Mombasa, 25/07/42, with Albacores and Swordfish. Detachment embarked in *Indomitable* on 29/08 to support the invasion of Madagascar. This unit also disembarked to Majunga on 10/09 to join the RAF's 207 Group. Reassembled at Tanga on 17/11. Although retaining its pool status, the squadron then became an operational training unit until disbanding on 28/04/44.

Identification markings: single letters.

Commanding officers:

Lt (A) H.E. Shilbach, RNVR, 25/07/42

Lt N.T. O'Neil, 19/08/42

Lt (A) A.J.I. Temple-West, 12/01/43

Lt Cdr (A) M.W. Rudorf, DSC, 14/07/43

797 Squadron A fleet requirements unit formed at Katukurunda, Ceylon, with 2 Skuas in 07/42, Sea Gladiators and Swordfish were soon added, with Albacores following in 1943. The squadron moved to

Colombo on 01/10/43, and Defiants replaced Skuas. On 01/07/44, 'X' Flight was detached to Juhu. Substantial numbers of new aircraft were introduced in 1944, including Harvards, Avengers, Barracudas and Beaufighters, followed by 6 Mosquitoes, which put in a brief appearance in 07/45. Disbanded, 24/10/45.

Identification markings: Defiants, R8A+; Beaufighters, L9A+.

Commanding officers:

Lt (A) F.L. Page, RNVR, 07/42

Lt (A) K.C. Winstanley, RNVR, 09/12/43

798 Squadron Formed at Lee-on-Solent, 11/10/43, to provide advanced conversion courses, with Barracudas, Beaufighters, Beauforts, Blenheims, Fulmars, Masters, Oxfords and Tiger Moths. Twin-engined aircraft broke away to become 762 Squadron in 03/44. After 20/04/44, a detachment at Stretton handled operational training for new Barracuda squadrons, but returned to Lee at the beginning of August. Fireflies and Harvards introduced in 1944. Role changed slightly during 1945, providing refresher training, including Fleet Air Arm ex-PoWs.

Identification markings: L1A+ to L4A+.

Commanding officers:

Lt Cdr (A) I.J. Wallace, OBE, RNVR, 11/10/43

Lt Cdr (A) S.W. Birse, DSC, RNR, 08/08/45

799 Squadron Formed as a pool squadron at Wingfield, 10/09/43, equipped with Albacores, shared with the hard-pressed 789 Squadron. Disbanded on 20/06/44. Reformed, 30/07/45, Lee-on-Solent, as a flying check and conversion refresher squadron operating Seafires. Aircraft were uncoded in 1943–44:1945, L8A+ and L9A+.

Commanding officers:

Lt Cdr (A) W.T.E. White, SANF (V), 10/09/43

Lt Cdr T.E. Sargent, RNR, 30/07/45

800 Squadron Dating from 1933, it was operating Skuas and Rocs aboard *Ark Royal*. Fighter and anti-submarine patrols were carried out before the carrier patrolled the South Atlantic hunting German shipping. Based ashore at Hatston when Germany invaded Norway in 1940. Squadron took part in the successful raid sinking the cruiser *Konigsberg* at Bergen, and later shot down 6 He111 bombers. Attack on *Scharnhorst* resulted in the loss of 4 aircraft and CO becoming a PoW. In 07/40, the squadron provided fighter cover for the attack on the French fleet at Oran, and later shot down 2 SM79 bombers off Sardinia.

Transferred to *Furious* at Gibraltar in 04/41, re-equipping with 9 Fulmars. Later 3 went to *Argus* as 'Y' Flight and the remainder became 'Z' Flight aboard *Victorious*, during the search for the German battleship *Bismarck*. By absorbing 801 Squadron as 800X Flight in 05/41, 9 Fulmars were added, sailing in *Furious* on a 6 month deployment to Malta.

Regrouped 06/41, at St Merryn and the following month embarked in *Furious* for the abortive raid on Petsamo, losing 2 aircraft to German fighters. Transferring to *Indomitable* for operations in the West Indies, it took part in the invasion of Madagascar. In 06/42, Sea Hurricanes replaced the Fulmars and with these the squadron embarked in the escort carrier *Biter* for the North African landings, Operation Torch, in 11/42. The squadron was the first to receive the Hellcat, and became part of 7 Naval Fighter Wing, embarking in *Emperor*. It provided the escort for an attack on the battleship *Tirpitz* on 03/04/44, lying in a Norwegian fjord. The squadron's strength doubled to 20 Hellcats on 18/06/44, when 804 Squadron disbanded. The squadron was present at the invasion of the South of France in 08/44. Updating its Hellcats, it took part in the

A Blackburn Skua, believed to be of 800 Squadron, aboard *Ark Royal*. (*via S.H. Wragg*)

liberation of territory in the Far East, being present at Rangoon and attacking Japanese shipping, with 8 aircraft detached aboard *Shah*. Disbanded, 12/45.

Battle honours: Norway, 1940, 1944; Mediterranean, 1940–41; Spartivento, 1940; Malta Convoys, 1941–42; *Bismarck*, 1941; Diego Suarez, 1942; North Africa, 1942; Normandy, 1944; South of France, 1944; Aegean, 1944; Burma, 1945.

Identification markings: Skua, single letters then A6A+; Fulmars single letters then 6A+; single letters for Sea Hurricanes and Hellcats, then E:A+ for Hellcats.

Commanding officers:
Lt Cdr G.N. Torry, 21/11/38
Capt R.T. Partridge, RM, 03/04/40
Lt E.G.D. Finch-Noyes (temp), 05/05/40
Lt R.M. Smeeton, 16/06/40
Lt Cdr J.A.D. Wroughton, DSC, 12/05/41
Lt Cdr J.M. Bruen, DSC, 16/03/42
Lt Cdr H. Muir-Mackenzie, DSC, 01/12/42
Lt Cdr S.J. Hall, DSC, 07/07/43
Lt Cdr M.F. Fell, DSC, 24/09/44
Lt Cdr (A) D.B. Law, DSC, RNVR, 12/12/44
Lt Cdr H. de Wit, RNethN, 20/05/45

801 Squadron On the outbreak of war, squadron was in abeyance. Reformed at Donibristle, 15/01/40, with 6 Skuas and in April was operating against German forces in Norway from *Ark Royal*. Afterwards, transferred to *Furious*, receiving 6 Rocs, later replaced by Skuas. Stationed ashore before disbanding into 800X Flight.

Reforming at Yeovilton on 01/08/41, the squadron operated 12 Sea Hurricanes and moved to Hatston to defend Scapa Flow. Embarking in *Argus* in 05/42, it sailed to the Mediterranean and transferred to *Eagle* to cover Malta convoys. Still with the ship when she was torpedoed on 11/08/42, her aircrew were absorbed into other squadrons.

Reformed at Stretton, 07/09/42, with 12 Spitfires which were replaced by Seafire Ibs and some IIcs. Embarked in *Furious* in October, for the North African landings, afterwards using Hatston as a shore base while operating from the carrier with the Home Fleet. Between 04–05/44, the squadron provided fighter escorts for attacks on the *Tirpitz*, re-equipping 05/44 with Seafire L.IIIs. In October, the squadron became part of the 30th Naval Fighter Wing. It embarked in *Implacable*; the strength was increased to 24 aircraft ready to became part of the British Pacific Fleet in May, escorting attacks on Truk and then targets on and around the Japanese home islands. Peak strength of 48 aircraft was reached after VJ Day when 880 Squadron was absorbed. Disbanded 1946.

Battle honours: Norway, 1940, 1944; Dunkirk, 1940; Atlantic, 1940; Malta Convoys, 1942; North Africa, 1942–43; Japan, 1945.

Identification markings: Skuas, uncoded operation, then U6A+ and A7A+; Sea Hurricanes, single letters then 7A+; single letters for Spitfires and Seafires.

Commanding officers:

Lt Cdr H.P. Bramwell, 15/01/40
Lt C.P. Campbell-Horsfall, 17/04/40
Lt I.R. Sarel, 28/06/40
Lt Cdr (A) R.A. Brabner, MP, RNVR, 11/08/41
Lt Cdr F.R.A. Turnbull, DSC, (temp), 07/09/42
Lt Cdr (A) R. McD Hall, 10/09/42
Lt Cdr (A) H.F. Bromwich, 03/11/43
Lt Cdr (A) S. Jewers, RNVR, 18/07/44

802 Squadron Formed April, 1933, by the outbreak of war, it was operating from *Glorious* with Sea Gladiators. The squadron was lost when the ship was sunk on 08/06 by the German battlecruisers, *Scharnhorst* and *Gneisenau*. Reformed on 21/11/40, out of part of 804 Squadron at Hatston, with 12 Martlets. Aircraft detached to operate from *Audacity* and *Argus* 07–08/41: The latter detachment, 802B Flight, soon transferred to *Victorious*. Reassembled aboard *Audacity* to provide fighter cover for Gibraltar convoys, shooting down 4 Fw200 maritime reconnaissance aircraft, although her CO was shot down on 08/11. The squadron went down with a carrier for the second time when *Audacity* was sunk by *U-741* on 21/12/41.

Reformed, Yeovilton 01/02/42, with 6 Sea Hurricanes and in September embarked aboard *Avenger* with 883 Squadron to provide fighter escorts for the Arctic convoy, PQ18, the first to be accompanied by an escort carrier. The 2 squadrons shot down 5 enemy aircraft and damaged another 17. On returning to the UK, the squadron equipped with 9 Sea Hurricane IIbs in September and re-embarked in *Avenger* to provide cover for part of the North African invasion force, but again the squadron was lost with the ship when she was torpedoed by *U-155* on 15/11/42. Did not reform again until 01/05/45, at Arbroath, with 24 Seafire L.IIIs, replaced by 12 Seafire XVs in August. The squadron remained operational for some years after the war.

Battle honours: Norway, 1940; Atlantic, 1941; Arctic, 1942; North Africa, 1942.

Identification markings: Sea Gladiator, G6A+: Martlet, single letters; no details for Sea Hurricane; Seafires, single letters.

Commanding officers included:

Lt Cdr J.P.G. Bryant, 11/01/38
Lt J.F. Marmont, 01/03/40
Lt Cdr J.M. Wintour, 21/11/40
Lt D.C.E.F. Gibson, 08/11/41
Lt Cdr E.W.T. Taylour, DSC, 07/04/42
Lt D.P.Z. Cox, 26/09/42
Lt Cdr R.E. Hargreaves, DSC, 01/05/45

803 Squadron Formed 03/04/33. By the outbreak of war, embarked in *Ark Royal*, operating Skuas and Rocs. Initial wartime task was to patrol off Norway, operating from Scapa Flow, which led to 803 scoring the first 'kill' of any British fighter squadron when its aircraft shot down a Do18 on 26/09. The squadron spent the winter ashore, mainly at Hatston, replacing Rocs with additional Skuas. Although operating from *Glorious* on occasion, the squadron joined 800, flying from Hatston, for the successful raid on the cruiser *Konigsberg*

Fairey Fulmar caught up in *Ark Royal*'s net, although without any apparent damage. (*via S.H. Wragg*)

during the Norwegian campaign in 04/40. Operating again from *Ark Royal* when it lost all but 2 of its aircraft in an attack on the battlecruiser *Scharnhorst* 06/06/40.

Re-equipped with 12 Fulmars 10/40, before embarking in *Formidable* to cover Malta convoys. At the Battle of Cape Matapan on 28/03/41, 2 enemy aircraft were shot down and another 2 damaged. After the carrier was damaged by the Luftwaffe, during the withdrawal from Crete, the squadron moved ashore to Dekheila in Egypt, equipped with Hurricanes, which were later replaced with Sea Hurricanes. Moving to Palestine 06/41 for operations against Syria, it returned 08/41 to become the RN Fighter Squadron operating over the Western Desert. The squadron received Fulmar IIs in 03/42, flew these to Ceylon, and re-embarked the following month in *Formidable*, carrying out long-range reconnaissance in the Indian Ocean.

Disembarked in East Africa and absorbed 806 Squadron 18/01/43. Operated on Army cooperation before disbanding at Tanga 12/08/43.

Reformed at Arbroath on 15/06/45, equipped with 25 Seafire L.IIIs, which were replaced by 12 Seafire XVs 08/45. Transferred to the Royal Canadian Navy after the war.

Battle honours: North Sea, 1939; Norway, 1940; Libya, 1940–41; Matapan, 1941; Mediterranean, 1941.

Identification markings: Skua, A7A+, A8A+ and S6A+; Fulmar, 6A+, then single letters, which were also used for the Hurricanes and Seafires.

Commanding officers:
Lt Cdr D.R.F. Cambell, 02/03/39
Lt W.P. Lucy, 08/02/40
Lt Cdr J. Casson, 23/05/40
Lt J.M. Bruen, 16/06/40
Lt Cdr J.M. Wintour, 16/10/40
Lt J.M. Bruen, 04/11/40

Lt D.C.E.F. Gibson, 20 /07/41
Lt B.S. McEwen, 09/41
Lt Cdr (A) B.F. Cox, RNVR, 07/10/42
Lt Cdr (A) L.D. Wilkinson, DSC, RNVR,
15/06/45

804 Squadron Formed 30/11/39, Hatston, as a fighter squadron with 4 Sea Gladiators from 769 Squadron. Embarked in *Glorious* 04/40, providing fighter cover while the ship ferried RAF Gladiators to Norway, while from 05/40, detachments operated from *Furious*. Re-equipped with Martlet Is 10/40, losing some to 802 Squadron 11/40, before re-equipping with a mixture of Fulmars and Sea Hurricanes 02/41. Assigned to operating Sea Hurricanes from catapult-armed merchant ships 05/41, although this was later given to the RAF's Merchant Ship Fighter Unit, but on 03/08/41, a Sea Hurricane from *Maplin* shot down a FW200 Condor.

The squadron became shore-based from 05/42, before embarking in *Argus* for a Gibraltar convoy 07/42, disembarking at Gibraltar before returning in *Furious*. In 10/42, it joined *Dasher* with 6 (later 9) Sea Hurricanes to provide air cover for the North African landings. The Sea Hurricanes were passed on to 835 Squadron in 06/43, replaced by 10 Hellcats in 08/43. The squadron became part of 7 Naval Fighter Wing 10/43, embarking in *Emperor* 12/43, providing fighter cover for North Atlantic convoys and for raids on the battleship *Tirpitz*. The squadron disbanded into 800 Squadron 18/06/44.

It reformed at Wingfield, 24/09/44, equipped with 24 Hellcats to embark in *Ameer* 01/45, to provide air cover for the landings on Ramree Island. After this, fighter cover, reconnaissance and spotting duties were undertaken over Malaya and Sumatra, with aircraft embarked on *Empress* and *Shah* for attacks on the Andaman Islands and the coast of Burma, before returning to *Ameer*, 06/45, for attacks on Sumatra and Phuket. Disbanded 11/45.

Battle honours: Norway, 1940–41; Atlantic, 1941; North Africa, 1942; Normandy, 1944; Burma, 1945.

Identification markings: Sea Gladiators, none; Martlets, S7A+; Fulmars, single letters: Sea Hurricanes, S7A+; Hellcat, single letters, then 1A+ and 2A+.

Commanding officers:
Capt R.T. Partridge, RM, 30/11/39
Lt Cdr J.C. Cockburn, 11/12/39
Lt Cdr B.H.M. Kendall, 18/11/40
Lt Cdr P.H. Havers, 05/03/41
Capt A.E. Marsh, RM, 09/02/42
Lt Cdr (A) A.J. Sewell, DSC, RNVR, 18/10/42
Lt O.R. Oakes, RM (temp), 13/07/43
Lt Cdr (A) J.W. Hedges, RNVR, 29/07/43
Lt Cdr S.G. Orr, DSC, RNVR, 10/08/43
Lt Cdr (A) G.B.C. Sangster, RNVR, 01/09/44
Lt Cdr (A) D.B. Law, RNVR, 20/05/45

Crest of 804 Squadron.

805 Squadron Formed at Donibristle, 04/05/40, as a Roc seaplane fighter squadron for operations in Norway, but the plan was abandoned and the squadron disbanded on 13 May. Reformed, 01/01/41, at Akrotiri in Cyprus, with a detachment at Aboukir in North Africa, using 12 aircraft, mainly Fulmars but with some Buffaloes. Detachments embarked in *Illustrious* and *Eagle*, before operations over Crete, operating from the airfield at Maleme, with the addition of some Sea Gladiators. The squadron then operated from Dekheila, with some Hurricanes, before re-equipping in 07/41, with 12 Martlets, operating with the RAF as a joint unit over the Western Desert. After this disbanded, the squadron moved to the Suez Canal Zone in 08/42, providing air cover for shipping. Disbanded, 10/01/43, after a move to Kenya.

Reformed at Machrihanish, 01/07/45, with 25 Seafire L.IIIs, soon replaced by Seafire XVs. Remained operational at reduced strength postwar, before disbanding in 1948.

Battle honours: Crete, 1941; Libya, 1941–42.
Identification markings: Fulmars, Buffalo and Martlet, single letters; Sea Gladiators, 6A+; Seafires, 5A+.
Commanding officers:
Maj R.C. Hay, RM, 04/05/40
Lt Cdr A.F. Black, 01/01/41
Capt L.A. Harris, RM, 27/07/41
Lt E.A. Shaw, 31/08/41
Lt Cdr T.P. Coode, DSC, 05/05/42
Lt Cdr (A) M.F. Fell, 27/08/42
Lt Cdr (A) P.J. Hutton, DSC, RNVR, 01/07/45

806 Squadron Formed 01/02/40, as a fighter squadron at Worthy Down, with 8 Skuas and 4 Rocs. Moved to Hatston 28/03, and took part in attacks on shipping and shore installations at Bergen, before returning south to cover the evacuation from Dunkirk with a detachment based at Detling.

Crest of 806 Squadron.

The Rocs were replaced by Fulmars and the squadron embarked in *Illustrious* in 06/40, while the Skuas were also replaced by Fulmars and augmented by Sea Gladiators before the ship sailed for the Mediterranean. In the Mediterranean, Dekheila was used as a shore base, in operations from there and from the carrier, the squadron accounted for more than 20 enemy aircraft. After providing air cover for the withdrawal from Crete, it embarked in *Formidable* from 03–05/41. Hurricanes were flown throughout the summer of 1941, operating as part of the RN Fighter Squadron in North Africa, before starting to re-equip with Fulmars in November, before deploying to Ceylon in late 03/42.

The squadron was divided into two flights, 'A' with Martlets for operations from *Indomitable*, and 'B' with Fulmars for operations from *Illustrious*, in 05/42. The former disbanded after *Indomitable* was damaged during Operation Pedestal on 12/08/42, leaving 806B as 806 Squadron, before disbanding into 803 Squadron while in East Africa on 18/01/43.

Reformed at Machrihanish, 01/08/45, with 12 Seafire IIIs, which were replaced by XVs. Disbanded, 1947.

Battle honours: Norway, 1940; Dunkirk, 1940; Mediterranean, 1940–41; Libya, 1940–41; Matapan, 1941; Diego Suarez, 1942; Malta Convoys, 1942.

Identification markings: Skua and Roc, L6A+; Fulmar and Sea Gladiator, 6A+; Hurricane, single letters.

Commanding officers:
Lt Cdr C.L.G. Evans, DSC, 01/02/40
Lt Cdr J.N. Garnett, 24/06/41
Lt R.L. Johnston, 12/08/42
Lt A.C. Lindsay, DSC, 01/08/45

807 Squadron Formed, 15/09/40, as a fighter squadron at Worthy Down, with 9 (later 12) Fulmar Is. In 12/40, 3 aircraft detached to *Pegasus* for fighter catapult operations. Entire squadron embarked in *Furious*, 02/41, to provide air cover for convoys. It re-equipped with Fulmar IIs in April before embarking in *Ark Royal* with 806 Squadron to cover Malta convoys. The 2 squadrons accounted for 15 enemy aircraft, as well as a number of probables and aircraft damaged. On 13/11/41, the carrier was torpedoed, but 4 aircraft survived and reached Gibraltar.

Re-equipped with Fulmars and Sea Hurricanes, it embarked in *Argus*, providing cover for convoys, and by 06/42 2 flights of 4 aircraft were embarked in *Argus* and *Eagle* for Operation Harpoon, a Malta convoy; accounting for 4 enemy aircraft, with the loss of 5 Fulmars. The first squadron to receive Seafires, joining *Furious* in time for the North African landings, 11/42, for Operation Torch. With a newer mark of Seafire, the LIIc, embarked in *Indomitable* at the end of 05/43, to provide air cover for the landings on Sicily. The squadron transferred to *Battler*, after *Indomitable* was damaged by an air-launched torpedo,

providing air cover for the Salerno landings. Returning to the UK in *Hunter*, the squadron became part of the 4th Naval Fighter Wing, absorbing part of 808 Squadron to reach a strength of 20 aircraft 02/44. Returned to the Mediterranean in 04/44, where some of its aircraft were detached to operate with the Desert Air Force in Italy, before regrouping aboard *Hunter* for the invasion of the South of France in 08/44, in Operation Dragoon. Later, support was provided for Army units in the Aegean. Re-embarking in *Hunter*, 03/45, for the Far East, it provided fighter support for the liberation of Rangoon 04–05/45 followed by air cover for anti-shipping strikes.

Battle honours: Atlantic, 1940; Malta Convoys, 1941–42; North Africa, 1942–43; Sicily, 1943; Salerno, 1943; South of France, 1944; Aegean, 1944; Burma, 1945.

Identification markings: Fulmars, uncoded, then 6A+; Seafire, single letters, but 8A+ on Battler and H:A+ on Hunter, then D5A+.

Commanding officers:
Lt Cdr (A) J. Sholto Douglas, 15/09/40
Lt A.B. Fraser Harris, DSC, 15/11/41
Lt Cdr (A) K. Firth, RNVR, 01/03/43
Lt Cdr (A) G.C. Baldwin, DSC, 25/10/43
Lt Cdr (A) L.G.C. Reece, RNZNVR, 02/06/44
Lt Cdr (A) E.J. Clark, RNVR, 10/11/44

808 Squadron Formed as a fleet fighter squadron, Worthy Down, 01/07/40, with Fulmar Is, but these were soon replaced by Fulmar IIs. Moved to Castletown, 09/40 patrolling the Irish Sea and Western Approaches. The following month, embarked in *Ark Royal*, joining Force H in the Western Mediterranean. With 807 Squadron, 808 accounted for 19 enemy aircraft over a period of 10 months in operations against Sicily and in defence of Malta convoys. Absorbed into 807 Squadron when *Ark Royal* sank on 13/11/41.

An aerial shot of *Ark Royal.* (*via S.H. Wragg*)

Reformed at Donibristle on 01/01/42, with 6 Fulmar IIs, moving in rapid succession to St Merryn, Yeovilton and Belfast before embarking in the escort carrier *Biter* in September and disembarked at Stretton. In 12/42 9 Seafire LIIcs were introduced, followed by a series of moves to shore bases, including Charlton Horethorne, Peterhead, Machrihanish and St Merryn, before operating briefly from *Battler* 04/43. In 05/43–06/43, while the squadron was based at Yeovilton and then Turnhouse, a detachment of 4 aircraft was embarked in *Battler* as 'A' Flight to cover a Gibraltar convoy, shooting down an Fw200 on the homeward passage. The entire squadron was embarked in the carrier for operations in the Mediterranean, 07/43, covering the Salerno landings. Returning home in *Hunter*, the squadron became part of the 3rd Naval Fighter Wing, training in close support operations at Burscough. Equipped with 20 Seafire LIIIs, 05/44, operated from Lee-on-Solent with the 2nd

Tactical Air Force before, during and after the Normandy landings.

Re-equipped with 24 Hellcats at Ballyhalbert, 10/44. Embarked in the escort carrier *Khedive*, 01/45, to join the British East Indies Fleet 04/45. Operated off Malaya and Sumatra maintaining air patrols and anti-shipping strikes, with 6 aircraft detached to *Emperor*, it provided air cover for the liberation of Rangoon, before returning to anti-shipping strikes off the Andaman Islands. It struck against airfields on Sumatra and was present for the Japanese surrender in Malaya. Disbanded, 12/45.

Battle honours: Spartivento, 1940; *Bismarck*, 1941; Malta Convoys, 1941; Atlantic, 1943; Salerno, 1943; Normandy, 1944; Burma, 1945.

Identification markings: Fulmar; 7A+; Seafire, 3A+; Hellcat, K6A+, C7A+.

Commanding officers:

Lt H.E.R. Torin, 01/07/40

Lt Cdr R.C. Tillard, 20/07/40

Lt Cdr E.D.G. Lewin, 31/05/41

Lt C.P. Campbell-Horsfall, 01/01/42
Lt Cdr (A) A.C. Wallace, RNVR, 17/03/43
Lt Cdr (A) J.F. Rankin, DSC, 25/10/43
Lt Cdr (A) C.F. Wheatley, RNVR, 20/05/45
Lt Cdr (A), R.F. Bryant, 25/06/45

809 Squadron Formed Lee-on-Solent, 15/01/41, as a fleet fighter squadron with Fulmar IIs, it embarked in *Victorious* 07/41 for the abortive raid on Kirkenes, shooting down 4 Bf109s and Me110s with the loss of 3 aircraft. While embarked in the carrier, it used Twatt as a shore station. On 09/03/42, operating from the carrier, the squadron provided fighter escorts for Albacores of 817 and 832 Squadrons for an attack on the German battleship *Tirpitz*. It then took part in the Malta convoy, Operation Pedestal, shooting down 2 Axis aircraft, but losing 3 Fulmars. Moved to Sawbridgeworth 08/42 for Army co-operation training, and was divided in two with 'B' Flight becoming 879 Squadron, leaving just 6 aircraft when it re-embarked in *Victorious* in 10/42. After tactical reconnaissance for Operation Torch, the North African landings, it re-equipped with Seafires. It embarked in *Unicorn* to provide air cover for the Salerno landings in 08/43.

Late in 1943, it became part of the 4th Naval Fighter Wing at Andover, embarking in *Stalker* for work up before disembarking at Dale, 02/44. In 03/44, strength was brought up to 20 aircraft. In 05/44, the squadron re-embarked in *Stalker* for operations in North Africa and Italy, including detachments operating ashore with the Desert Air Force, before returning to the ship to cover the landings in the South of France in 08/44. After operating in the Aegean, it returned to the UK 11/44, re-equipped with Seafire LIIIs and embarked in *Attacker* for operations in North Africa, with the squadron based ashore at Dekheila. Embarking in *Stalker*,

03/45, for operations with the British East Indies Fleet, fighter cover was provided for the liberation of Rangoon and reconnaissance over Malaya and Sumatra. It was present for the surrender of Japanese forces in Malaya. Disbanded early 1946.

Battle honours: Arctic, 1941; Malta Convoys, 1942; North Africa, 1942; Salerno, 1943; South of France, 1944; Aegean, 1944; Burma, 1945.

Identification markings: Fulmar 6A+; Seafire S: A+, D6A+.

Commanding officers:
Lt Cdr S.W.D. Colls, 15/01/41
Lt Cdr V.C. Grenfell, DSO, 03/07/41
Lt Cdr E.G. Savage, DSC, 16/10/41
Capt R.C. Hay, DSC, RM, 24/08/42
Maj A.J. Wright, RM, 01/06/43
Lt Cdr (A) H.D.B. Eadon, RNVR, 20/04/44
Lt Cdr (A) N.H. Lester, RNVR, 10 /11/44
Lt A.W. Bloomer, 17/04/45

810 Squadron Formed, 03/04/33, as a torpedo bomber squadron. At the outbreak of war it was operating Swordfish from *Ark Royal*, making one of the first attacks on a U-boat on 14/09/39. Continuing to operate from the carrier, it used several shore bases, including Hatston, Wingfield, Lee-on-Solent and Gosport, before *Ark Royal* joined the Mediterranean Fleet, then the squadron used Dekheila in Egypt as a shore base. Recalled for the Norwegian Campaign in 04/40, where it attacked the airfield at Vaernes. Operations against the French Fleet at Oran followed, joining an attack on the battleship *Strasbourg* on 03/07 and then on 07/07 against the battleship *Dunkerque* that beached after suffering heavy gunfire. Operations in the Mediterrean followed, bombing Cagliari, interrupted by renewed attacks on the French Fleet, this time at Dakar in West Africa, 09/40, with an attack on the battleship *Richelieu*, which was, as with all three attacks on the French battle fleet, unsuccessful. Returning to Mediterranean,

Swordfish of 810, 818 and 820 Squadrons ranged ready for take-off from *Ark Royal*. (*via S.H. Wragg*)

the squadron supported convoys and took part in action against the Italian Fleet at Cape Spartivento. Bombed the Tirso Dam in Sardinia, 02/02/41, causing little damage and then operated against the naval bases at Leghorn and La Spezia.

Still embarked in *Ark Royal* in 05/41, 810 joined her other squadrons in the search for the German battleship *Bismarck*, which was crippled in a torpedo attack by Swordfish from the carrier. Support for Malta and attacks on Sardinia followed, before being reduced to 6 aircraft, 09/41 and embarking in *Furious* to escort a Jamaica-bound convoy. After being based ashore in Jamaica and the USA and embarking first in *Illustrious* and then *Formidable*, the squadron returned to the UK, disembarking to Lee-on-Solent 12/41. Brought back up to strength in 01/42, 810 was based at Campbeltown and nearby Machrihanish, before re-embarking in *Illustrious* for the Madagascar operation 05/42. Afterwards, it disembarked at Cape Town and absorbed 829 Squadron, reaching

a strength of 15 aircraft, before returning to the UK 02/43.

Re-equipped with 12 Barracudas at Lee-on-Solent, 04/43, it became a TBR squadron, re-embarking in *Illustrious* for operations off Norway, 07/43, returning to the Mediterranean for the Salerno landings. It joined the 21st Naval TBR Wing 10/43, and in 11/43, embarked in *Illustrious* to join the British East Indies Fleet. In addition to reconnaissance sweeps in the Bay of Bengal, the squadron bombed the oil facilities and docks at Sabang in Sumatra and raided the Andaman Islands. 847 Squadron was absorbed 06/44, giving a peak strength of 21 aircraft, before disembarking at Cape Town while the carrier refitted, returning home in *Activity*.

Barracuda IIs continued in service while at Burscough in the winter of 1944/45, but these were replaced by radar-equipped Barracuda IIIs at Stretton in 02/45. Anti-shipping operations followed, first on the south coast and then off the east coast, operating with

RAF Coastal Command. The squadron was disbanded at the end of the war.

Battle honours: Norway, 1940; Mediterranean, 1940–41; Spartivento, 1940; Atlantic, 1941; *Bismarck*, 1941; Diego Suarez, 1942; Salerno, 1943.

Identification markings: Swordfish, A2A+; Barracuda, 2A+; 2A+, N6A+.

Commanding officers:
Capt N.R.M. Skene, RM, 09/12/38
Capt A.C. Newsom, RM, 16/06/40
Lt Cdr M. Johnstone, DSC, 16/07/40
Lt J.V. Hartley, 11/09/41
Lt Cdr R.N. Everett, 29/12/41
Lt Cdr W.E. Waters, 31/01/43
Lt Cdr (A) A.J.B. Forde, 18/03/43
Lt Cdr (A) A.G. McWilliam, RNVR, 27/02/44
Lt Cdr (A) A.J.B. Forde, DSC, 01/07/44
Lt Cdr (A) P.C. Heath, 16/12/44

811 Squadron The original 811 Squadron was redesignated 767, 24/05/39. A detachment, formed at Southampton just 9 days earlier as 811A, took over the designation. At the outbreak of war, the squadron embarked in *Courageous*, and lost its aircraft when the carrier was torpedoed on 17/09/39.

Reformed at Lee-on-Solent, 15/07/41, with 2 Chesapeakes and 2 Sea Hurricanes for operation from escort carriers, although this complement was soon changed to 6 Swordfish. After operations with RAF Coastal Command, the squadron absorbed 812 at Hatston, 12/42. With the addition of 3 Wildcats, the squadron finally embarked in *Biter*, 02/43, for convoy escort duties. On 25/04, *U-203* was attacked, followed by *U-89* on 12/05, with the Swordfish damaging both craft and leaving them to be destroyed

Pilots of 811 Squadron at Machrihanish, summer 1942. Left to right: Ian Whitelaw-Wilson, killed in action shortly afterwards; Jock Sayer; John Godley; Peter Bentley, PoW shortly afterwards; and Denis Fuller. (*via Lord Kilbracken*)

by surface vessels. Although some further attacks on U-boats were unsuccessful, the Wildcats accounted for a Ju290B, carrying a glider bomb on 16/02/44. Under Coastal Command control for most of 1944, in 09/44 it embarked in *Vindex*, with 12 Swordfish and 4 Wildcats, for an Arctic convoy. Disbanded 09/12/44.

Battle honours: English Channel, 1942; North Sea, 1942; Atlantic, 1943–44; Arctic, 1944.

Identification markings: Swordfish, single letters, then 1A+; Wildcats, single letters.

Commanding officers:
Lt Cdr S. Borrett, 01/07/39
Lt Cdr R.D. Wall, 15/07/39
Lt Cdr W.J. Lucas, 29/10/41
Lt Cdr H.S. Hayes, DSC; 27/02/42
Lt J.G. Baldwin, 28/01/43
Lt A.S. Kennard, DSC, 12/04/43
Lt Cdr E.B. Morgan, RANVR, 29/11/43
Lt Cdr (A) E.E.G. Emsley, RNVR, 27/07/44

812 Squadron Formed as a fleet torpedo bomber unit, 03/04/33, it was operating Swordfish from *Glorious*, on the outbreak of war. *Glorious* was sent to the Indian Ocean to hunt German merchant vessels and commerce raiders, but returned to the Mediterranean where the embarked squadrons used Dekheila and Hal Far as shore bases. *Glorious* was recalled to the Home Fleet on the German invasion of Norway, but 812 was assigned to Coastal Command for minelaying off the Dutch coast. In 03/41, 6 aircraft were detached to *Argus* for a convoy delivering aircraft to Malta. In 07/41, 9 aircraft were embarked in *Furious* for an attack on the Arctic port of Petsamo, before the carrier and her aircraft were once again sent on Malta convoys. Transferred to *Ark Royal*, it was fortunate to have sufficient aircraft airborne when the ship was torpedoed to be able to regroup at Gibraltar. Additional aircraft followed, all

were fitted with ASV air-to-surface anti-shipping radar, allowing it to score the first night sinking of a U-boat, *U-451*, on 21/12/41. It damaged another 5 U-boats operating from shore bases including Gibraltar. A number of aircraft were embarked in *Argus* for convoy protection duties. The squadron returned to the UK aboard the USS *Wasp* 04/42. At a reduced strength of just 6 aircraft, the squadron spent a further period with RAF Coastal Command, mainly on night operations over the English Channel, before amalgamating with 811 on 18/12/42.

Reformed at Stretton as a TBR squadron with 12, later 18, Barracudas, 01/06/44, 812 embarked in one of the new, light fleet carriers, *Vengeance*, 01/45, joining the British Pacific Fleet 07/45 after working up in the Mediterranean. It saw no action before the Japanese surrender and remained in the Far East after the war. Disbanded, Lee-on-Solent, 08/46.

Battle honours: North Sea, 1940; English Channel, 1940–42; Mediterranean, 1941; Malta Convoys, 1941.

Identification markings: Swordfish, G3A+, 3A+, A2A+, R2A+; Barracuda, N1A+.

Commanding officers:
Lt Cdr A.S. Bolt, 16 /06/39
Lt Cdr N.G.R. Crawford, 22/04/40
Lt Cdr W.E. Waters, DFC, 06/09/40
Lt Cdr G.A.L. Woods, 16/11/41
Lt Cdr B.J. Prendergast, 30/05/42
Lt Cdr (A) C.R.J. Coxon, 05/06/44

813 Squadron Formed 18/01/37, it was embarked in *Eagle* at Singapore with Seletar, as a shore base, operating Swordfish, on the outbreak of war. The carrier and her embarked squadrons searched for enemy shipping in the Indian Ocean. In spring 1940, the carrier sailed to the Mediterranean, where 813 acquired 4 Sea Gladiators. Operating from the ship and from shore bases, the squadron was involved in many successful operations, with the Sea Gladiators shooting down several Italian bombers, while the Swordfish sank merchant ships and a destroyer in a raid on Tobruk and another destroyer in a raid on Sicily. Four of its aircraft joined *Illustrious* for the successful attack on the Italian Fleet at Taranto on the night of 11–12/11/40. The Sea Gladiators were withdrawn 03/41, leaving the Swordfish to accompany the squadron to Port Sudan for Army cooperation duties. Operating from a shore base, the squadron accounted for 5 Italian destroyers, before re-embarking in *Eagle* and sailing via Cape Town for the Atlantic, where the U-boat support ship *Elbe* was sunk and a tanker forced to surrender. Returning home in late 10/41, the squadron settled briefly at Macrihanish before moving to Lee-on-Solent, where it received 9 new Swordfish and 2 (later 4) Sea Hurricanes, as well as briefly operating 2 Buffaloes.

The squadron re-embarked in *Eagle*, 01/42, operating with several Malta convoys. Reduced to 6 Swordfish, these were ashore at Gibraltar when the carrier was sunk 11/08/42, although the Sea Hurricanes were all lost. The squadron's strength was doubled within 10 days and it was able to support the North African landings, with a flight detached to Algeria. It continued to operate from Gibraltar and Algeria until taking passage to the UK, where it disbanded 18/10/43.

Reformed at Donibristle on 01/11/43, with 9 Swordfish II, it was joined, 03/44, by 3 of 784 Squadron's Fulmar night fighters and 4 of 1832's Wildcats for operations from *Campania*. Operating in the North Atlantic and on Arctic convoys, the Swordfish sank *U-921* on 30/09, and *U-365* on 13/12, while the Wildcats accounted for 4 German aircraft. In 01/45, part of the squadron re-embarked for anti-submarine operations off the Norwegian coast, while the replacement of its aircraft with Swordfish IIIs was completed by 03/45, by which time the Fulmars had been withdrawn and 8 new Wildcat Vs were in service. In 04/45, the squadron operated its final Arctic convoy aboard *Vindex*, and disbanded afterwards on 15/05/45.

Battle honours: Calabria, 1940; Mediterranean, 1940–41; Taranto, 1940; Libya, 1940–41; Malta Convoys, 1942; Atlantic, 1942–44; Arctic, 1944–45.

Identification markings: Swordfish, 4A+, then single letters; Sea Gladiator, 6A+; Wildcat Z:1-8, then single letters.

Commanding officers:
Lt Cdr N. Kennedy, DSC, 01/09/38
Lt Cdr D.H. Elles, 09 /01/41
Lt Cdr A.V. Lyle, 25/11/41
Lt Cdr C. Hutchinson, 25/03/42
Lt Cdr D.A.P. Weatherall, 02/43
Lt J.H. Ree, 27/06/43
Lt Cdr D.A.P. Weatherall, 01/08/43
Lt Cdr (A) J.R. Parish, DSC, RNVR, 01/11/43
Lt Cdr (A) C.A. Allen, RNVR, 02/09/44
Lt Cdr (A) S.G. Cooke, RNVR, 12/10/44

814 Squadron Formed as a TSR squadron at Southampton, 01/12/38, at the outbreak of war it was operating from *Hermes* with 9 Swordfish. In 10/39, *Hermes* was with the French, hunting German warships, in particular the battleship *Graf Spee*. With the fall of France, the squadron had to attack the French fleet, damaging the battleship *Richelieu* 08/07/40, at Dakar. *Hermes* sailed for the Indian Ocean in 12/40, protecting convoys and providing Army cooperation for British forces in East Africa, while hunting for enemy vessels. The squadron helped in the capture of 5 enemy merchant vessels by the cruiser, *Hawkins*, while a 6th was bombed. After operating with the RAF during 05/41, the squadron re-embarked in

Hermes and sailed for Ceylon, again operating convoy protection and anti-shipping duties, alternating between the carrier and a number of shore bases. It was ashore when *Hermes* was sunk by Japanese aircraft 09/04/42. Disbanded, 31/12/42, at Katukurunda.

Reformed at Stretton as a torpedo bomber reconnaissance unit, 01/07/44, with 16 (later 18) Barracuda IIs, the squadron embarked in the new, light fleet carrier *Venerable*, 03/44. The ship and her aircraft worked up in the Mediterranean on passage to the Far East, where it became part of the 15th Carrier Air Group 06/45, with 12 aircraft. The squadron saw no further action before the war ended.
Battle honours: Atlantic, 1940.
Identification markings: Swordfish, 701–710, then A3A+ to H3A+; Barracuda single letters, then B1A+ and R1A+.
Commanding officers:
Lt Cdr N.S. Luard, DSC, 01/12/38
Maj W.H.N. Martin, RM, 27/12/40
Lt A.F. Paterson, 25/09/42
Lt Cdr J.S.L. Crabbe, 01/07/44
Lt Cdr (A) G.R. Coy, DSC, 28/11/44

815 Squadron Formed, 09/10/39, Worthy Down, from the survivors of 811 and 820 Squadrons embarked in *Courageous* when she sank; it was equipped with 12 Swordfish as a TBR squadron. A planned move to Hatston in 11/39 was abandoned and it disbanded into 774 Squadron. Reformed on 23/11 with the same commanding officer, as a spare squadron with just 9 Swordfish. Moved, 02/40, to Cardiff and then, 04/40, to Bircham Newton on detachment to RAF Coastal Command, from where it provided cover for the Dunkirk evacuation at the end of 05/40. Embarked aboard *Illustrious* in 06/40, the squadron sailed with the ship to the Mediterranean, 08/40 and undertook torpedo, bombing and mine-laying operations over Benghazi, Rhodes and Tobruk. It formed the mainstay of the successful raid on Taranto on the night of 11–12/11/40, albeit with the loss of the CO's aircraft. The squadron also accounted for 2 ships in an Italian convoy off Sicily 12/40.

When *Illustrious* was badly damaged by bombing off Malta on 10/01/41, many of the aircraft were destroyed, but 5 in the air flew to Malta, where the squadron absorbed the survivors of another *Illustrious* squadron, 819 and 821X Flight, emerging with 12 Swordfish. The aircraft flew to Dekheila. At the end of 01/41, it moved to Crete for attacks on enemy shipping and mine-laying, with a flight detached to the Greek mainland. The squadron evacuated to Dekheila 04/41, and was then posted to Cyprus to attack Vichy French shipping in Syria, sinking a destroyer and damaging another. Returning to Dekheila 08/41, the squadron operated in support of the British 8th Army in the Western Desert, having re-equipped with 12 Albacores and 2 radar-equipped Swordfish, carrying out night attacks on enemy airfields and armoured formations, as well as anti-submarine patrols. A detachment was based in Cyprus for anti-submarine patrols. Equipped with additional ASV-fitted Swordfish, the squadron was able to support the 8th Army's advance into Libya in early 1942, sharing the sinking of a German U-boat with an RAF Blenheim. The squadron disbanded on 24/07/43, at Mersa Matruh.

Reformed as a TBR squadron at Lee-on-Solent, 01/10/43, with 12 Barracuda IIs, the squadron embarked in *Begum* 02/44, where it became part of the 12th Naval TBR Wing. It embarked aboard *Indomitable* 07/44, to become part of the British Eastern Fleet. In 08/44, it joined an attack on the port of Emmahaven in Summatra, followed by attacks on Sigli and on the Nicobar Islands.

By this time it had been decided that Avengers would replace the Barracudas in the Far East, so the squadron returned to the UK in *Activity* 11/44.

Re-equipped with new Barracuda IIs at Machrihanish, 11/44, before these were replaced by the newer Barracuda IIIs, 01/45. The addition of 825X Flight's Wildcats, 04/45, was followed by deck landing training aboard *Campania*. Supposed to return to the Far East, it set sail in *Smiter* without its aircraft, but the war ended before it could re-equip with Avengers. The personnel returned to the UK aboard *Fencer*. Disbanded Rattray, 01/46. Battle honours: Mediterranean, 1940–41; Taranto, 1940; Libya, 1940–41; Matapan, 1941; Burma, 1944.

Identification markings: Swordfish,U3A+ to L4A+, as well as single letters; Albacore, S7A+; Barracuda, 4A+ to I7A+.

Commanding officers:
Lt Cdr S. Borrett, 09/10/39
Lt Cdr R.A. Kilroy, DFC, 17/04/40
Lt Cdr K. Williamson, 03/08/40
Lt Cdr J. de F. Jago, 16/11/40
Lt Cdr F.M.A. Torrens-Spence, 15/03/41
Lt Cdr T.P. Coode, 27/10/41
Lt Cdr P.D. Gick, 14/12/41
Lt Cdr A.R. Hallett, 29/09/42
Lt Cdr (A) J.W.G. Wellham, DSC, 07/12/42
Lt Cdr (A) R.G. Lawson, RNVR, 01/10/43
Lt Cdr D. Norcock, 23/12/44
Lt Cdr (A) J.S. Bailey, OBE, 05/01/45
Lt Cdr (A) M.H. Meredith, DSC, RNVR, 18/04/45

816 Squadron Formed 03/10/39, aboard *Furious*, with 9 Swordfish to provide anti-submarine and strike support for North Atlantic convoys. It made the first aerial torpedo attack of the war during the Norwegian Campaign 04/40. A planned conversion to floats was abandoned with the fall of France. In 06/40 it re-embarked in the carrier. An attack was attempted on the German battlecruiser *Scharnhorst*, 09/40 and on 22/09/40, 5 aircraft were lost during an attack on shipping at Trondheim. The squadron joined RAF Coastal Command 03/41, for operations off the Dutch and French coasts. In 04/41 3 aircraft were detached to Detling, as 816X Flight, which formed the basis of 821 Squadron. The squadron re-embarked in *Furious* 06/41 to provide anti-submarine cover, while RAF aircraft were ferried to Malta. On the return voyage, it transferred to *Ark Royal* and remained with her until she was sunk on 13/11/41, when it was merged into 812 Squadron.

Reformed 01/02/42, at Palisadoes, Jamaica, as a TBR squadron, with 4 Swordfish which embarked in *Avenger* to cover a convoy from the USA to the UK. On arrival, aircraft were found to replace 2 lost aboard the carrier, then operations were undertaken under Coastal Command control. It joined *Dasher*, 02/43, for Arctic convoy escort duties, but suffered severe casualties when the ship blew up on 27/03/43, while exercising in the Firth of Clyde. Regrouped at Machrihanish with new aircraft and by 05/43 was able to operate against German shipping in the English Channel. Moving north to Fearn, 06/43, a fighter flight of Seafire LIIcs was formed from aircraft of 895 Squadron, although these were transferred just 2 months later into 897 Squadron. Later, 6 Seafire Ibs were received and the Swordfish strength increased from 6 to 9, then the squadron embarked in *Tracker* for North Atlantic convoys. Wildcat IVs replaced the Seafires 01/44, and the squadron transferred to *Chaser* for service with the Arctic convoys. On 04/03, an aircraft helped the destroyer *Onslaught* sink a German U-boat, and then over the following days, *U-366* and *U-973* were sunk by the squadron's aircraft. When the Wildcats were used 06/44 to form 833 Squadron,

Swordfish strength was increased to 12 and the squadron returned to operations over the English Channel in support of the Normandy landings. Disbanded at Perranporth, 01/08/44. Reformed at Lee-on-Solent on 01/02/45, with 18 Barracuda IIs for torpedo bomber reconnaissance duties, aboard a light fleet carrier, but in 07/45, it re-equipped with Firefly FR1s. It remained operational until 1948.

Battle honours: Norway, 1940; Malta Convoys, 1941; Mediterranean, 1941; Atlantic, 1943; Arctic, 1944; Normandy, 1944.

Identification markings: Swordfish, single letters, then U4A+, 4A+, 5A+; single letters for Barracuda, Wildcat and Firefly.

Commanding officers:
Lt J. Dalyell-Stead, (temp), 13/10/39
Lt Cdr H.H. Gardner, 19/10/39
Lt Cdr T.G.C. Jameson, 06/05/40
Capt O. Patch, RM, 01/02/42
Lt R.C.B. Stallard-Peyre, 15/10/42
Lt P.F. Pryor, (temp), 22/04/43
Lt Cdr (A) F.C. Nottingham, DSC, RNVR, 12/07/43
Lt Cdr P. Snow, 03/05/44
Lt Cdr The Hon W.A.C. Keppel, DSC, 01/02/45
Lt Cdr J.S.L. Crabbe, 26/06/45

817 Squadron Formed at Crail, 15/03/41, as a TSR squadron with 9 Albacores, it embarked in *Furious*, 07/41 for the attack on Petsamo, before transferring to *Victorious*, 08/41, for operations in the Barents Sea. Attacks were mounted on shipping off Norway in the autumn, remaining with the carrier and using Hatston as a shore base. A torpedo attack on the German battleship *Tirpitz*, 09/03/42, was unsuccessful. The squadron supported the North African landings, bombing fortifications, while on 21/11/42, one of its aircraft sank *U-517* in the North Atlantic.

Back in the UK, the squadron embarked in *Furious* at Scapa Flow, 12/02/43, before transferring to *Indomitable*, 03/43, and with a complement of 15 aircraft, 817 covered the landings at Sicily. After the ship was badly damaged in an aerial torpedo attack on 16/07/43, most of the squadron was put ashore at Gibraltar. It disbanded on 01/09/43.

Reformed at Lee-on-Solent, 01/12/43, with the same commanding officer and 12 new Barracuda IIs. It joined the 12th Naval TBR Wing 01/44, embarked in *Begum* for the voyage to Ceylon, where the Wing operated from shore bases before rejoining *Indomitable* on 23/07/43. Operations were carried out over Sumatra and the Nicobar Islands, before transferring to *Unicorn* on 07/11/43 for a visit to South Africa. The squadron returned to Sular in southern India on 13/01, losing its aircraft in a tropical storm. The crews returned home and the squadron disbanded, 21/02/45.

Reformed at Rattray on 01/04/45, with 18 Barracuda IIs, equipped with the US ASH radar, as a torpedo bomber reconnaissance squadron, the unit moved to Fearn later that month. As with 816, it was intended for service aboard a light fleet carrier, but disbanded, 23/08/45.

Battle honours: Norway, 1941; North Africa, 1942; Biscay, 1942; Sicily, 1943.

Identification markings: Albacore, 5A+; Barracuda, 3A+, 5A+, 7A+.

Commanding officers:
Lt Cdr D. Sanderson, DSC, 15/03/41
Lt Cdr P.G. Sugden, 23/02/42
Lt L.E.D. Walthall, DSC, (temp), 30/06/42
Lt Cdr N.R. Corbet-Milward, 15/07/42
Lt Cdr (A) T.W. May, SANF(V), 07/08/43
Lt Cdr (A) M.A. Lacayo, 01/04/45

818 Squadron Formed Evanton, 24/08/39, with 9 Swordfish for TSR duties and embarked on 25/08/39 in *Ark Royal* at

Scapa Flow. By 10/39, 3 aircraft were detached to *Furious*, the remainder based ashore, initially at Hatston and then at Abbotsinch. The Norwegian Campaign, 04/40, saw the entire squadron embarked in *Furious* and on 11/04, they attacked 2 German destroyers in Trondheim Fjord.

On 30/05 the squadron moved to Thorney Island to operate with Coastal Command, before joining *Ark Royal* for the Mediterranean. It took part in the attacks on the Vichy French Fleet at Oran, including the battleship *Strasbourg*, and then took part in operations against Sardinia and against the Italian Fleet, alternating between the ship and Gibraltar as a shore base, as well as providing anti-submarine protection for Malta convoys. In 04/41, the squadron joined the hunt for the battleship *Bismarck*; two of its aircraft scored the torpedo hits that disabled the ship and brought it within range of the fleet's guns.

The squadron moved to Arbroath, 12/07, aboard *Furious* and re-equipped with 9 Albacores on 01/11. After operations from *Argus*, the squadron embarked in *Formidable* on 04/02 to join the Eastern Fleet. Disembarking at Ceylon, 04/41 to provide reconnaissance and anti-shipping operations against the Japanese, it disbanded 24/06; its aircraft forming the new 796 Squadron.

Reformed at Lee-on-Solent, 19/10/42, with 6 Swordfish II for TBR duties, its strength was increased to 9 aircraft before joining *Unicorn* in 03/43, to support a Gibraltar convoy. 6 aircraft were disembarked at Gibraltar in 08/43, with part of the squadron forming the new 838 Squadron. The remainder sailed to Ceylon aboard *Unicorn*, arriving in 02/44. It disbanded at Cochin on 14/10/44.

Reforming, 01/05/45, at Rattray, for torpedo bomber reconnaissance duties and equipped with 18 Barracuda IIs, the squadron moved to Fearn in 06/45. It was one of those preparing to sail to the Far East aboard a Colossus-class carrier, but instead moved back to Rattray, to disband 15/08.

Battle honours: Norway, 1940; English Channel, 1940; Spartivento, 1940; Mediterranean, 1940–41; Atlantic, 1941; *Bismarck*, 1941.

Identification markings: Swordfish, U3A+ to A5A and 5A+, later 1A+; Albacore, 4A+; Barracuda, 8A+.

Commanding officers:
Lt Cdr J.E. Fenton, 30/08/39
Lt Cdr P.G.O. Sydney-Turner, 19/03/40
Lt Cdr T.P. Coode, 24/10/40
Lt Cdr T.W.B. Shaw, DSC, 28/07/41
Lt Cdr A.H. Abrams, DSC, 22/10/42
Lt Cdr (A) W.H. Lloyd, RNVR, 07/07/43
Lt Cdr (A) B.W. Vigrass, RNVR, 01/05/45

819 Squadron Originally formed at Ford, 15/01/40, with crews from *Ark Royal* and *Glorious* as a TSR squadron with 12 Swordfish. Part of the squadron detached to Coastal Command at Detling to protect the Dunkirk evacuation from U-boats. In 06/40, the squadron embarked in *Illustrious*, operating in the North Atlantic before joining the Mediterranean Fleet in August. Alternating between the carrier and Dekheila as a shore base, 819 became heavily involved in attacks on harbours and airfields in the Eastern Mediterranean. Aircraft from the squadron took part in the attack on Taranto on the night of 11–12/11/40. When *Illustrious* was attacked and badly damaged on 10/01/41, the squadron suffered heavy casualties in both men and aircraft; those aircraft in the air flew to Hal Far, where the squadron disbanded into 815 Squadron on 14/01/41.

Reformed at Lee-on-Solent, 01/10/41, with 9 Swordfish Is as a TBR squadron. Swordfish IIs were added before the squadron took part in trials in *Avenger* in 06/42. It was then seconded to Coastal Command for three months, minelaying in the North Sea and English Channel, using a number of bases. The squadron moved to Machrihanish on 16/04, prior to joining *Archer*, providing anti-submarine cover for North Atlantic convoys. On 23/05/43, one of the squadron's aircraft was the first to sink a U-boat, *U-752*, using rocket projectiles.

Three Wildcats were transferred from 892 Squadron during 08/43, before the squadron embarked in the escort carrier, *Activity* and the following month the Swordfish received anti-shipping ASV radar. Further Wildcats were received 03/44. On the next Arctic convoy, one of the squadron's Swordfish shared the destruction of *U-288* with an aircraft from 846 Squadron on 03/04/44, while the Wildcats shot down 4 enemy aircraft. After this, the Wildcats were taken away to form 833 Squadron and the Swordfish were based ashore with Coastal Command, operating from east coast airfields prior to the Normandy landings and then later with flights detached to airfields in Belgium. Returning to the UK, the squadron disbanded at Bircham Newton, 10/03/45.

Battle honours: Mediterranean, 1940–41; Libya, 1940; Taranto, 1940; English Channel, 1942; Atlantic, 1943; Arctic, 1944; Normandy, 1944.

Identification markings: Swordfish, L5A+ then single letters; Wildcats, single letters.

Commanding officers:

Lt Cdr J.W. Hale, DSO, 12/02/40
Lt Cdr D.G. Goodwin, DSC, 25/10/41
Lt H.S. McN Davenport, 10/04/42
Lt (A) O.A.G. Oxley, 23/01/43
Lt Cdr (A) P.D.T. Stevens, RNVR, 20/04/44

820 Squadron Formed 03/04/33, on the outbreak of the war, it was embarked in *Ark Royal* operating 9 Swordfish in the TSR role, having earlier that year been the first to land aboard the carrier. *Ark Royal* was sent to patrol the south Atlantic and then the Indian Ocean, searching for German shipping and after returning home briefly, moved to the Mediterranean, before being recalled for the Norwegian campaign. Off Norway, the squadron's aircraft maintained patrols and bombed targets ashore. Following the fall of France, *Ark Royal* was sent to North Africa, with 820 Squadron mining the French naval base at Oran and sending torpedo attacks against French warships. An attack on Cagliari followed, before the French naval base at Dakar in West Africa was attacked 09/40. Operations in the Mediterranean and North Atlantic throughout the winter months eventually saw 820's aircraft taking part in the successful operation against the German battleship *Bismarck*.

The squadron was transferred to *Victorious* on 17/06/41, for convoy protection duties, having already helped to protect a Malta convoy. It used a number of shore bases while embarked, including Lee-on-Solent, Crail and Hatston, and re-equipped with 12 Albacores. In 02/42 the squadron transferred to *Formidable* for the Indian Ocean, where it was present at the landings on Madagascar, returning to the UK in time for the landings in North Africa, Operation Torch. During this operation, a squadron aircraft sank *U-331*, already damaged by RAF Hudsons. The squadron supported the landings at Sicily and then at Salerno, before protecting a convoy to Iceland aboard *Formidable*. Disbanded at Donibristle, 13/11/43.

Reformed at Lee-on-Solent, 01/01/44, for the TBR role with 12 Barracuda IIs, embarking in *Indefatigable* on 10/06 for an attack on the German battleship *Tirpitz* in a Norwegian fjord. A detachment embarked briefly in *Formidable*. In 09/44, the squadron disembarked to re-equip with 21 Avenger Is, soon replaced by Avenger IIs, before

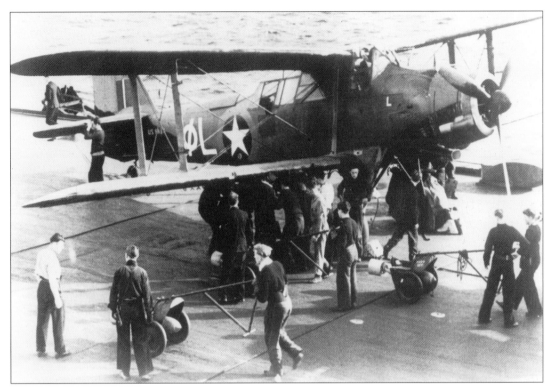

An Albacore of *Formidable*'s 820 Squadron loaded with six 250-lb bombs intended for Fort D'Estrees in Algiers, during Operation Torch. Note the unusual markings, and the star for this, the first Anglo-American operation. (*FAAM ALBACORE/10*)

re-embarking in *Indefatigable* on 21/11 for passage to Ceylon. As part of the 2nd Naval Strike Wing, during the first half of 1945, the squadron was involved in a successful series of raids, bombing the oil refineries at Palembang on Sumatra, followed by raids against the airfields of the Sakashima Gunto islands during 03–05/45. After becoming part of the 7th Carrier Air Group in 06/45, the squadron attacked targets in the Japanese home islands, including many in the Tokyo area, right up to VJ-Day. Disbanded, 03/46.
Battle honours: Norway, 1940–44; Spartivento, 1940; Mediterranean, 1940; *Bismarck*, 1941; Atlantic, 1941; Malta Convoys, 1941; North Africa, 1942–43; Sicily, 1943; Salerno, 1943; Palembang, 1945; Okinawa, 1945; Japan, 1945.

Identification markings: Swordfish, A4A+, then 4A+; Albacore, 5A+ and O/A+; Barracuda, 3A+ to 18A+; Avenger, 1A+.
Commanding officers:
Lt Cdr G.B. Hodgkinson, 07/01/39
Lt Cdr A. Yeoman, 29/08/40
Lt Cdr J.A. Stewart-Moore, 27/10/40
Lt Cdr W. Elliott, 18/07/41
Lt Cdr J.C.N. Shrubsole, 04/06/43
Lt Cdr (A) W.R. Well, 01/01/44
Lt Cdr (A) S.P. Luke, 23/10/44
Lt Cdr (A) F.L. Jones, DSC & Bar, RNVR, 18/05/45
Lt Cdr J.P. Camp, DSC & Bar, 14/06/45

821 Squadron Formed 03/04/33, at the outbreak of war it was operating 12 Swordfish from *Ark Royal*, with Hatston used as a shore base. Initially, the carrier operated in the North West Approaches, but was soon deployed in the South Atlantic, Indian Ocean and the Mediterranean, before being recalled in 04/40, for the Norwegian campaign. Off Norway, the squadron's aircraft maintained patrols and bombed targets ashore before disembarking to Hatston, to maintain anti-submarine patrols between Orkney and Norway. On 21/06 it was involved in the unsuccessful attack on the battlecruiser *Scharnhorst*. The squadron disbanded on 02/12/40, although 821X Flight embarked in *Argus* for Gibraltar, and continued to Malta aboard *Ark Royal*, to be absorbed into 815 Squadron.

Reforming at Detling on 01/07/41, from 'X' Flight of 816 Squadron, the squadron initially received 6 Swordfish for anti-submarine patrols north of Scotland, operating from Sumburgh and Hatston. Transferred to Egypt, it operated from Dekheila from 01/42, over the Western Desert. Re-equipped with 6 Albacores in 03/42, it briefly operated from Cyprus to attack enemy targets in Rhodes. In Dekheila, 09/42, the complement of Albacores was increased to 12, and returned to operations over the Western Desert and its coastal waters, including bombing and mine-laying. The squadron moved to Malta in 11/42 to attack enemy convoys from Italy to North Africa, with a flight detached to Castel Benito in North Africa in 03/43, to mark targets for the RAF. The entire squadron reassembled in North Africa in 06/43 for anti-submarine operations, before returning to the UK without its aircraft and disbanding on 10/10/43.

Reformed on 01/05/44, for the TBR role with 12 Barracuda IIs, it embarked in *Puncher* in 11/44, using Hatston as a shore base. It re-equipped with Barracuda IIIs in 01/45 and the following month began mine-laying off the Norwegian coast. While 6 Wildcats were transferred from 835 Squadron 04/45, these were soon withdrawn. The squadron embarked in *Trumpeter* on 03/07 for the Far East, reaching Cochin in southern India on 26/07, but returned home aboard *Fencer* without seeing further action. Disbanded early 1946.

Battle honours: Norway, 1940; Libya, 1942; Mediterranean, 1942–43.

Identification markings: Swordfish A5A+ then 5A+, later single letters; Albacore S5A+, then single letters; Barracuda N:A+, then single letters.

Commanding officers:
Lt Cdr G.M. Duncan, 24/05/39
Lt Cdr J.A.D. Wroughton, 14/09/39
Maj W.H.N. Martin, RM, 29/05/40
Lt Cdr R.R. Wood, 27/12/40
Lt C.W.B. Smith, 15/07/41
Maj A.C. Newsom, RM, 12/03/42
Lt Cdr C.H.C. O'Rorke, 24/03/43
Lt Cdr (A) M. Thorpe, 01/05/44
Lt Cdr (A) D. Brooks, DSC & Bar, RNVR, 14/06/45

822 Squadron Formed 03/04/33, after being absorbed into another unit before the outbreak of war, the squadron was regenerated from one of its flights, 822A, which became the new 822 Squadron on 01/07/39. At the outbreak of war, the squadron was operating Swordfish aboard *Courageous*, and ceased to exist after the carrier was torpedoed and sunk on 17/09/39.

Reformed at Lee-on-Solent, 15/10/41, for the TBR role with 9 Swordfish, which were replaced by Albacores in 03/42, before the squadron embarked aboard *Furious*, on 17/07, for convoy escort duty, followed by support for the North African landings. The squadron joined others in an attack on La Senia airfield on 10/11 in which 47 enemy aircraft were destroyed, although the squadron lost 4 aircraft including the CO's. The squadron disembarked to Gibraltar, rejoining *Furious* on 02/01/43 for Arctic convoys, using Hatston as a shore base. The squadron re-equipped with 12 Barracudas 07/43, at Lee-on-Solent, becoming part of the 45th Naval TBR Wing in 10/43. The squadron arrived at St Thomas Mount, an RAF base in southern India, 04/44, with personnel and aircraft travelling separately, and 07/44, absorbed 823 Squadron to bring the strength up to 21 aircraft. The enlarged squadron joined *Victorious* for dive bombing operations over Sumatra, but the aircraft proved ill-suited to tropical operations, so the squadron's personnel were shipped home in 10/44.

Regrouping at Lee-on-Solent on 18/11/44, the squadron was equipped with 12 Barracuda IIIs, commencing operations over the English Channel, under the control of RAF Coastal Command, using Thorney Island and then Manston. In 06/45, the aircraft were transferred to 860 Squadron, and 822 received Barracuda IIs fitted with the American ASH, ready to join a light fleet carrier for service in the Far East. These plans were cancelled following the end of the war. Disbanded 02/46.

Battle honours: Atlantic, 1942; North Africa, 1942–43; Arctic, 1943.

Identification markings: Swordfish, U5A+, single letters; Albacore, 4A+; Barracuda, single letters.

Commanding officers:
Lt Cdr P.W. Humphreys, 01/07/39
Maj A.R. Burch, DSC, RM, 15/10/41
Lt (A) J.G.A. McI Nares, 06/08/42
Lt H.A.L. Tibbets, RCNVR, 10/11/42
Lt J.W. Collett, 10/02/43
Lt Cdr (A) P.F. King, 03/03/43
Lt Cdr B.E. Boulding, DSC, 10/08/43
Lt Cdr (A) G.A. Woods, RNVR, 01/12/43
Lt Cdr (A) L.C. Watson, DSC, RNVR, 13/07/44

Lt Cdr (A) D.A. Davies, DSC, RNVR, 04/04/45

823 Squadron Formed 03/04/33, for the spotter reconnaissance role, at the outbreak of war the squadron was aboard *Glorious*, in the Mediterranean with Hal Far in Malta as a shore base, operating 12 Swordfish. The carrier was immediately sent to the Red Sea and Indian Ocean, both to protect British and French trade routes and to find German shipping. She returned to the Mediterranean 01/40, but was recalled to home waters on the invasion of Norway 04/40. Withdrawing from Norway, she was sunk by the German battlecruisers *Gneisenau* and *Scharnhorst* with heavy loss of life, and with half of 823's aircraft and personnel aboard. This left the squadron with just 9 aircraft based on Hatston. On 21/06/40, a combined force of 6 aircraft from 823 and 821 Squadrons mounted an unsuccessful attack on the *Scharnhorst*, with 823 losing one of its aircraft. Disbanded on Orkney, 03/12/40.

Reformed at Crail on 01/11/41, for the TBR role, with 9 Swordfish, although these were replaced in 04/42, by Albacores. It joined *Furious* 08/42 for convoy escort duty, disembarking 09/42 to operate with Coastal Command on English Channel anti-submarine patrols. It re-equipped 06/43, with 4, later 12, Barracudas and joined the 45th Naval TBR Wing. The aircraft reached India aboard *Atheling* and became part of the 11th Naval TBR Wing in April, 1945, but on 06/07 was merged into 822 Squadron.

Battle honour: Norway, 1940.

Identification markings: Swordfish, 4A+, then single letters; single letters for Albacore and Barracuda.

Commanding officers:
Lt Cdr R.D. Watkins, 24/05/39
Lt Cdr C.J.T. Stephens, 27/05/40
Lt Cdr D.H. Elles, 03/07/40

Lt Cdr (A) A.J.D. Harding, DSC, 01/11/41
Lt Cdr J.W. Collett, 01/08/42
Lt R.W. Sprackman, 24/11/42
Lt Cdr G. Douglas, 22/03/43
Lt Cdr (A) L.C. Watson, DSC, RNVR,
01/12/43

824 Squadron Formed on 03/04/33, at the outbreak of war it was on TSR duties aboard *Eagle* at Singapore, operating 9 Swordfish. The carrier was ordered to Trincomalee to conduct searches for German shipping in the Indian Ocean, then to the Mediterranean in 05/40. The squadron provided anti-submarine protection for Malta convoys and acted as gunnery spotters for the battleships. On 04/09, the squadron bombed the airfield at Maritza on Rhodes and two aircraft were detached to *Illustrious* for the raid on Taranto on 11–12/11/40. The squadron was divided in 01/41, between *Eagle* and Dekheila in Egypt, operating on anti-submarine patrols.

Reunited at Port Sudan in 03/41, 824 provided support for land forces in North-East Africa, sinking enemy destroyers off Eritrea on 03/04 and damaging 2 others so badly that they had to be beached. Rejoined *Eagle* on 19/04 to sail around the Cape of Good Hope to search for the battleship *Bismarck* in the South Atlantic, but instead sunk the U-boat support vessel *Elbe* on 06/06 and forced the tanker *Lothringen* to surrender on 15/06. While the carrier was refitted in the UK, the squadron was based ashore at Machrihanish, but re-embarked 01/42, to provide anti-submarine cover for a Gibraltar convoy and then for a Malta convoy. The squadron was 4 months ashore in Gibraltar although a flight was detached briefly aboard *Argus* for a Malta convoy ferrying aircraft to the island. Most of the aircraft were aboard *Eagle* when she sank on 11/08/42, while on a convoy to Malta; and the few aircraft ashore in Gibraltar merged into 813 Squadron.

Reformed, on 01/10/42, at Lee-on-Solent, although it had regrouped there 08/42 with 6 Swordfish Is, which were soon replaced by Swordfish IIs before the squadron embarked in *Unicorn* in 03/43. Swordfish numbers increased to 9 in 06/43, and 6 Sea Hurricanes provided a fighter element in 08/43, before the squadron transferred to *Striker* on 27/10, covering convoys across the Bay of Biscay and the North Atlantic. Another 3 Swordfish joined in 05/44, while ashore at Hatston, and Wildcats replaced the Sea Hurricanes in 06/44. Then the squadron returned to *Striker* to harry German convoys along the Norwegian coast, and then received 4 more Wildcats in 08/44, ready for Arctic convoy escort. While the squadron's Swordfish failed to sink any U-boats on the Arctic convoys, a Wildcat shot down a Bv138 flying-boat on 22/08. Disbanded, 16/10/44, at Abbotsinch.

Reformed at Katukurunda, Ceylon, 02/07/45, as a torpedo bomber reconnaissance unit with 12 Barracuda IIs, but the war ended and the personnel returned home. The squadron was eventually disbanded in 01/46.

Battle honours: Calabria, 1940; Mediterranean, 1940; Taranto, 1940; Libya, 1940–41; Malta Convoys, 1942; Atlantic, 1942; Arctic, 1944.

Identification markings: Swordfish, 5A+, 1A+, 2A+ and then single letters; single letters for Sea Hurricane, Wildcat and Barracuda.

Commanding officers:
Lt Cdr A.J. Debenham, DSC, 15/06/39
Capt F.W. Brown, RM, 11/08/41
Lt J.A. Ievers, 01/10/42
Lt Cdr (A) E.L. Russell, DSC, RNVR, 12/03/43
Lt Cdr (A) G.C. Edwards, RCNVR, 02/03/44
Lt (A) G.R. Clarke, RNVR, 02/07/45
Lt Cdr (A) S. Brilliant, RNVR, 10/07/45

825 Squadron Originally formed by renumbering 824 Squadron in 1934, at the outbreak of war the squadron was embarked in *Glorious*, in the Mediterranean with Hal Far as a shore base, operating 12 Swordfish. The carrier was deployed to the Red Sea and Indian Ocean, protecting British and French trade routes and seeking German shipping. She returned to the Mediterranean in 01/40, but was recalled to home waters on the invasion of Norway 04/40. The squadron disembarked to operate against enemy naval vessels and shore bases in the English Channel, during the evacuation from Dunkirk, with the loss of 8 aircraft. Deliveries of additional aircraft increased the strength to 9 aircraft when the squadron embarked in *Furious* in 07/40. During 09/40, 825 was involved in night bombing operations against Norwegian ports. A number of different shore stations were used during the winter of 1940/41, from Hatston to Lee-on-Solent, with flights detached to the carriers *Argus* and *Furious*, before it regrouped aboard *Victorious*, 19/05/41, to take part in the *Bismarck* operation. The squadron transferred to *Ark Royal* in 06/41 and provided anti-submarine cover for Malta convoys, as well as attacking targets in Pantellaria, Sardinia and Sicily. Some of its aircraft were airborne when the carrier was torpedoed on 13/11/41 and landed at Gibraltar to be absorbed by 812 Squadron.

Reformed on 01/01/42, at Lee-on-Solent as a TBR squadron with 9 Swordfish, 6 were detached to Manston ready for the break out of the German battlecruisers *Scharnhorst* and *Gneisenau*. On 12/02/42, amid great confusion at the Admiralty and Air Ministry, and without fighter cover, these aircraft pressed home an attack in poor weather and failing light. This action resulted in the loss of all 6 aircraft and 13 out of the 18 personnel aboard, for which the CO, Lt Cdr Esmonde, received a posthumous VC.

Regrouped on 02/03/42, still at Lee-on-Solent, with Swordfish IIs, later moving to Machrihanish. During the summer and autumn, 3 aircraft were detached to *Avenger* for Arctic convoys and during 09/42, they spotted 16 U-boats and attacked 6, sharing the sinking of one with the destroyer, *Onslow*. After this, the squadron worked under Coastal Command direction throughout the winter on operations over and around the English Channel. In 03/43, the squadron embarked in *Furious*, with Hatston as a shore base, and provided cover for Arctic convoys. In August, 6 Sea Hurricanes joined the squadron, and in December, it embarked in *Vindex* on convoy escort duties. Operating from the escort carrier with surface vessels, the squadron helped sink 2 U-boats.

The squadron was augmented with 3 Fulmar fighters briefly in 04/44 and in 06/44, Swordfish IIIs replaced the IIs. Returning to the Arctic convoys on 22/08/44, *U-354* was sunk, while a Sea Hurricane managed to damage a U-boat: over the next couple of weeks, 2 more U-boats were shared with surface vessels. The Sea Hurricanes were withdrawn 09/44, but replaced by 8 Wildcats 11/44. In 03/45, the squadron embarked in *Campania* for another Arctic convoy. The squadron disbanded into 815 Squadron on 03/04/45, although the Wildcats enjoyed a reprieve as 825X, before following the Swordfish into 815 on 23/04. Reformed with RCN personnel at Rattray, 01/07/45, with 12 Barracuda IIs, and formally transferred to the Royal Canadian Navy on 24/01/46.

Battle honours: Dunkirk, 1940; English Channel, 1940–42; Norway, 1940; *Bismarck*, 1941; Malta Convoys, 1941; Arctic, 1942–45; Atlantic, 1944.

Identification markings: Swordfish, G5A+, 5A+, then single letters; Sea Hurricane 2A+; Wildcat and Barracuda, single letters.

Commanding officers:
Lt Cdr J.W. Hale, 19/08/38
Lt Cdr J.B. Buckley, 22/01/40
Lt Cdr (A) E. Esmonde, DSO, 31/05/40
Lt Cdr (A) S. Keane, 23/02/42
Lt Cdr (A) S.G. Cooper, 15/12/42
Lt Cdr (A) A.H.D. Gough, 29/02/44
Lt Cdr (A) F.G.B. Sheffield, RNVR,
05/05/44
Lt Cdr P. Snow, 25/02/45
Lt Cdr (A) F. Stovin-Bradford, DSC,
01/07/45

826 Squadron Formed as a TSR squadron, 15/03/40, at Ford, with 12 Albacores. It helped to cover the Dunkirk evacuation, flying from Detling, bombing communications targets and E-boats off Zeebrugge. It operated as part of Coastal Command until 11/40, based at Bircham Newton and making 22 night attacks against coastal targets, dropping 7 tons of mines and 56 tons of bombs and was credited with the destruction of 5 enemy aircraft on the ground. In addition, more than 90 convoys were escorted, including 57 in 09/40. This effort was despite the temporary switch to Swordfish for 07/40, while modifications were made to the engines of the Albacores.

The squadron embarked in *Formidable*, 11/40 and in 12/40, the carrier escorted a convoy to Egypt, via the Cape and Suez Canal, before returning to the Red Sea in 02/41, attacking shore-based targets in Italian-held Eritrea and Somalia. Returning to the Mediterranean, 03/41, the squadron received 6 Swordfish to maintain its complement and remained with the carrier, using Dekheila as a shore station. Anti-submarine and reconnaissance cover was provided for a Malta convoy before the Battle of Matapan at the end 03/41, when the squadron's aircraft participated in a torpedo attack, damaging the battleship *Vittorio Veneto*. Raids followed on Axis bases in North Africa before the squadron covered the evacuation of Crete, following which *Formidable* was seriously damaged by bombing and was withdrawn to the USA for repairs.

Based ashore at Dekheila, the squadron operated over the Eastern Mediterranean and the Western Desert, before moving to Nicosia in Cyprus on 01/07/41, for attacks on Vichy French shipping at Beirut. Returning to Dekheila, detachments were deployed to other bases while Maaten Baagush was used as a satellite airfield. It provided flare illumination for both fleet gunnery attacks and the Eighth Army's artillery as well as the Desert Air Force. Half of the squadron was deployed to Hal Far in Malta in 12/42, to join 821 and 828 Squadrons in attacking convoys linking Europe with North Africa. Reunited at Dekheila in 01/43, before being deployed to Algeria for anti-shipping strikes, it returned to Malta, 06/43 to support the invasion of Sicily, Operation Husky. Disbanded at Ta Kali, 16/10/43.

Reformed at Lee-on-Solent, 01/12/43, with 12 Barracuda IIs as a torpedo bomber reconnaissance unit, becoming part of the 9th Naval TBR Wing. Embarking in *Indefatigable*, 06/44, it took part in an unsuccessful attack on the battleship *Tirpitz* in a Norwegian fjord and then conducted anti-submarine and anti-shipping patrols off Norway. A further attack on *Tirpitz* followed while embarked in *Formidable*. After anti-shipping operations, the squadron returned to the 9th Naval TBR and *Indefatigable*, before disbanding into 820 Squadron at Machrihanish on 23/10/44. Reformed at East Haven, 15/08/45, again as a Barracuda-equipped TBR squadron, manned by the Royal Canadian Navy. Disbanded 02/46.
Battle honours: Dunkirk, 1940; North Sea, 1940–44; Atlantic, 1940; Matapan, 1941; Mediterranean, 1941–43; Libya, 1941–42.

Identification markings: Albacore, L4A+, 4A+ and S4A+; 4A+ for Swordfish and Barracuda.

Commanding officers:
Lt F.H.E. Hopkins (temp), 15/03/40
Lt Cdr C.J.T. Stephens, 07/04/40
Lt Cdr W.H.G. Saunt, DSC, 27/05/40
Lt Cdr J.W.S. Corbett, 24/06/41
Lt C.W.B. Smith, DFC, 23/01/42
Lt P.W. Compton, 05/03/42
Lt V.G.H. Ramsey-Fairfax, 22/08/42
Lt Cdr (A) R.E. Bradshaw, DSC, 01/05/43
Lt Cdr (A) A.J.I. Temple-West, 01/12/43
Lt Cdr (A) S.P. Luke, 26/01/44
Lt Cdr E.S. Carver, DSC, 15/08/45

827 Squadron Formed with 12 Albacores as a TSR unit, 15/09/40, at Yeovilton. It worked up at Crail, before operating under Coastal Command on convoy protection and minelaying from Thorney Island and St Eval and then headed north to Machrihanish and Donibristle, 06/41, for attacks on the battlecruisers, *Scharnhorst* and *Gneisenau*. On 02/07, the squadron embarked in *Victorious* for the ill-fated raid on Kirkenes on 30/07, in which it lost half of its aircraft, although one Albacore shot down a Ju87.

Regrouped at Hatston 08/44, the squadron joined *Indomitable* 10/41, sailing to the USA and Jamaica and then via the Cape to Aden, where it arrived 01/42. Using the ship and various shore bases, 827 maintained anti-submarine patrols in the Red Sea and Indian Ocean. It joined the invasion of Madagascar, 05/42, although operating with just 9 aircraft. The ship sailed to Gibraltar ready for the Malta convoy, Operation Pedestal, 08/42, during which the squadron lost 5 of its officers during heavy aerial attack.

Re-equipping with 12 Barracuda IIs at Stretton in 01/43, and becoming a TSR unit, the squadron, with just 9 aircraft,

became part of the 8th Naval TBR Wing in October, aboard *Furious* with Hatston as a shore base. On 30/03, the squadron transferred for one of two temporary spells aboard *Victorious* and on 03/04 it shared ten hits with 830 Squadron during a dive bombing attack on the *Tirpitz* in Norway. Anti-shipping strikes off Norway followed from *Furious* in 04–05/43, despite exceptionally severe weather. Another attempt was made on *Tirpitz* in 07/43, from *Formidable*, when a smokescreen saved the ship, but two hits were made while flying from *Furious* in 08/43.

It absorbed 830 Squadron in 10/44, boosting the complement to 18 aircraft, before moving to Beccles and Langham to operate with Coastal Command's 16 Group over the Dutch coast. The squadron embarked in *Colossus*, 01/45, with the intention of becoming part of the British Pacific Fleet. En route, it reduced to 12 aircraft at Dekheila, and on arrival in Ceylon disembarked, becoming part of the 14th Carrier Air Group. It did not re-embark until after the war.

Battle honours: Diego Suarez, 1942; Malta Convoys, 1942; Norway, 1944.

Identification markings: 4A+ on *Victorious* and 5A+ on *Indomitable* for Albacores; 4A+ and U1A+ for Barracudas.

Commanding officers:
Lt W.G.C. Stokes, 15/09/40
Lt Cdr J.A. Stuart-Moore, 18/07/41
Lt Cdr P.G.O. Sydney-Turner, 22/08/41
Lt Cdr D.K. Buchanan-Dunlop, 15/05/42
Lt R.W. Little, 07/09/42
Lt Cdr (A) J.S. Bailey, 12/02/43
Lt Cdr (A) R.S. Baker-Faulkner, DSC, 12/08/43
Lt Cdr (A) K.H. Gibney, DSC, 25/10/43
Lt Cdr (A) G.R. Woolston, 30/06/44
Lt Cdr (A) G.R. Clarke, 06/07/45

828 Squadron Formed at Lee-on-Solent as a TSR squadron, 15/09/40, with 9 Albacores, it moved to St Merryn 10/40 and then to Campbeltown on 18/11, completing work up and then operating under Coastal Command. After visiting Hatston and Sumburgh, the squadron embarked in *Victorious*, 02/07/41, and took part in the raid on Kirkenes, losing 5 aircraft. Regrouping at Crail before embarking in *Argus* on 26/09, it provided anti-submarine cover for a Gibraltar convoy, before transferring to *Ark Royal* for a Malta convoy, flying off to Hal Far on 18/10. Operating from Malta, with 14 aircraft, the squadron attacked enemy convoys between Sicily and North Africa and targets at both ends of the route. In 03/42, the squadron operated jointly with 830 Squadron as the Naval Air Squadron Malta. Heavy aerial attack meant that the squadron spent long periods with just 2 aircraft operational, despite replacements being flown in. It subsequently absorbed aircraft from 830 Squadron and part of 826, before joining forces with 821 in 05/43, for further attacks on convoys and flare-dropping for a naval bombardment of the island of Pantellaria. Between them, these squadrons sank 30 ships and damaged another 50. The squadron moved to Monastir in Tunisia for anti-submarine duties, 28/06/43, returning to Hal Far to disband on 01/09/43.

Reformed as a torpedo bomber reconnaissance squadron at Lee-on-Solent, 01/03/44, with 12 Barracuda IIs, it became part of the 2nd Naval TBR Wing and embarked in *Implacable* in August. It was deployed to *Formidable* later that month to take part in Operation Goodwood, a strike against the battleship *Tirpitz*. Returning to *Implacable*, with Hatston as a shore base, it conducted anti-shipping operations off Norway, with its strength increased to 21 aircraft by absorbing 841 Squadron.

Avengers replaced the Barracudas, 01/45 and the squadron deployed a detachment of these aboard *Trumpeter* at the end of the month. On 13/03, the squadron re-embarked in *Implacable* to join the British Pacific Fleet. After reducing to 15 aircraft in 06/45, became part of the 8th Carrier Air Group. It undertook raids on Truk, in the Caroline Islands and later on the Japanese home islands. The carrier and its squadrons withdrew to Australia after the war, and was disbanded in 06/46.

Battle honours: Mediterranean, 1941–43; Norway, 1944; Japan, 1945.

Identification markings: Albacore, 5A+ and S5A+; single letters for Barracuda and Avenger.

Commanding officers:
Lt E.A. Greenwood, 15/09/40
Lt Cdr (A) L.A. Cubitt, 26/09/40
Lt Cdr D.E. Langmore, DSC, 06/05/41
Lt Cdr G.M. Haynes, RAN, 19/12/41
Lt Cdr M.E. Lashmore, DSC, 30/11/42
Lt H.H. Britton, 12/03/43
Lt Cdr (A) J.F. Turner, RNVR, 08/05/43
Lt Cdr (A) F.A. Swanton, DSC, 01/03/44

829 Squadron Formed at Ford, 15/06/40, as a TSR squadron with 9 Albacores, a detachment was sent to Campbeltown in 07/40, before regrouping there in late 09/40. On 07/10, it moved to St Eval, operating under Coastal Command on a series of raids on shipping off the French coast and the docks at Brest, losing its CO on 09/10. On 15/11, it embarked aboard *Formidable* from Crail and provided cover for a convoy to West Africa and Cape Town. In 01/41, the carrier sailed to the Red Sea, and the following month her aircraft were attacking targets in Mogadishu and Massawa, losing a number of aircraft, so that on arrival in the Mediterranean in 03/41, a number of Swordfish had to be added.

Still operating from *Formidable*, the squadron took part in the Battle of Matapan, when an Albacore scored a direct hit on the battleship *Vittorio Veneto*, but again losing her CO. Attacks followed against Vichy French targets in Syria, while Nicosia was used as a base for much of 07/41. After the carrier was damaged in an aerial attack, the squadron reduced to 6 Swordfish and sailed with her, providing anti-submarine cover on her passage from the Mediterranean to the United States, via Cape Town, for repairs.

The squadron was in Jamaica from 23/08 to 02/12 at Palisadoes, joining *Illustrious* for 6 days to sail to Norfolk, Virginia, to re-embark in *Formidable* on 10/12 for the voyage back to the UK. It used Eastleigh and then Lee-on-Solent as bases, re-equipping with 12 Swordfish IIs with ASV radar. The squadron next embarked in *Illustrious* on 07/03/42, taking part in the invasion of Madagascar, during which its aircraft attacked Diego Suarez. In a successful attack against 2 Vichy submarines and 2 escorts 5 aircraft were lost. Disbanded into 810 Squadron in South Africa 07/10/42.

Reformed as a TBR squadron at Lee-on-Solent, 01/10/43, with 12 Barracuda IIs, becoming part of the 52nd Naval TBR Wing. Embarking in *Victorious* on 12/02, the squadron took part in an attack on the battleship *Tirpitz* on 03/04/44, losing 2 aircraft. A further attempt in 05/44 was aborted, leaving the squadron on anti-shipping operations off the Norwegian coast. On 09/07, it merged into 831 Squadron, also aboard the carrier.

Battle honours: Atlantic, 1940; Matapan, 1941; Mediterranean, 1941; Diego Suarez, 1942; Norway, 1944.

Identification markings: Albacore, 4A+; Swordfish, 3A+; Barracuda., 4A+.

Commanding officers:
Lt Cdr O.S. Stevinson, 15/06/40
Lt Cdr J. Dalyell-Stead, 12 /10/40
Lt Cdr L.C.B. Ashburner, 29/03/41
Lt Cdr F.M. Griffiths, 24/12/41

Lt Cdr (A) G.P.C. Williams, DSC, 01/10/43
Lt Cdr (A) D.W. Phillips, 03/03/44

830 Squadron Formed out of 767 Squadron, Hal Far, 01/07/40, with 12 Swordfish, 830 carried out bombing raids against Sicily and Libya, including a dive-bombing raid on oil storage tanks in Sicily; on 19/07 it bombed a U-boat. In 1941, operations expanded to include minelaying and torpedo attacks, dropping TAGs in favour of additional fuel tanks. In 05/41, some of the aircraft were fitted with ASV radar. On a number of operations, the squadron operated with 828, combining in 03/42, as the Naval Air Squadron Malta. The squadron's aircraft later passed to 828, and on 31/03/43 it disbanded.

Reformed at Lee-on-Solent on 15/05/43, as a TBR unit with 12 Barracuda IIs, most of which were flown by members of the RNZNVR. It became part of the 8th Naval TBR Wing 10/43, joining *Furious* with a reduced strength of 9 aircraft, using Hatston as a shore base for operations off Norway. On 03/04/44, with 827 Squadron it shared ten hits during a dive bombing attack on the *Tirpitz* in Norway, in Operation Tungsten, losing one of its aircraft. Two further attacks were less successful: one in 05/44 was cancelled due to bad weather and Operation Goodwood, on 17/07, using *Formidable*, failed because the Germans had time to lay a thick smokescreen. On 03/10, the squadron was disbanded at Hatston into 827.

Battle honours: Mediterranean, 1940–42; Norway, 1944.

Identification markings: Swordfish, single letters; Barracuda, 5A+.

Commanding officers:
Lt Cdr F.D. Howie, DSO, 01/07/40
Lt H.E.H. Pain, 01/08/40
Lt Cdr J.G. Hunt, 01/09/41
Lt Cdr F.H.E. Hopkins, 06/12/41

Lt Cdr A.J.T. Roe, 07/06/42
Lt A. Gregory, 23/02/43
Lt Cdr (A) F.H. Fox, 24/05/43
Lt Cdr (A) R.D. Kingdom, DSC, RNVR,
21/01/44

831 Squadron Formed as a TSR squadron, 01/04/41, at Crail with 12 Albacores, it moved to Machrihanish in August before embarking in *Indomitable* in October for Jamaica. After a spell ashore at Norfolk, Virginia, the squadron re-embarked for the passage to Cape Town, arriving there at the end 12/41. Early in 1942, the carrier sailed first to Port Sudan, and then ferried 50 RAF Hurricanes to Java, with 831 providing anti-submarine cover. The squadron alternated between the ship and shore bases at Ratmalana and China Bay in Ceylon, before spending 3 weeks ashore on coastal patrols at the end of 02/42–03/42, at Khormaksar, the RAF base at Aden. The squadron re-embarked for the invasion of Madagascar, early 06/42, engaging in dive-bombing and anti-submarine patrols. *Indomitable* sailed to Gibraltar, via the Cape, and was severely damaged by aerial attack during Operation Pedestal, Malta convoy, 08/42, but got her squadrons back to the UK before sailing to the USA for repairs. The squadron was reduced to 9 aircraft at this time and its strength was augmented by a small number of Barracuda Is.

After spending time ashore at Crail, Lee-on-Solent, Hatston and Machrihanish, 831 re-embarked in *Indomitable*, 03/43, but returned to Lee-on-Solent, 05/43, to re-equip with Barracuda IIs, joining 52 Naval TBR Wing in 11/43. After deck landing training aboard *Victorious*, 02/44, the squadron transferred to *Furious*, 03/44, for an attack on the battleship *Tirpitz*. Further attempts were made using *Victorious* in 05/44, but bad weather intervened and instead attacks were made on convoys off

Norway. The squadron returned to the Far East aboard the carrier and on 09/07, absorbed 829 Squadron, increasing its strength to 21 aircraft, effectively disbanding the TBR Wing. The enlarged squadron attacked shore installations and oil storage facilities in Sabang Harbour on Sumatra and nearby airfields. Nevertheless, these and other operations showed the limitations of the Barracuda and the decision was taken to withdraw the aircraft and replace it with Avengers. The squadron abandoned its aircraft and returned home aboard *Battler* and *Thane* to disband at Lee-on-Solent on 06/12/44.

Battle honours: Diego Suarez, 1942; Malta Convoys, 1942; Norway, 1944; Sabang, 1944.
Identification markings: Albacore, 4A+; Barracuda., 5A+.
Commanding officers:
Lt Cdr P.L. Mortimer, 01/04/41
Lt Cdr A.G. Leatham, 01/07/42
Lt Cdr (A) D.E.C. Eyres, 08/05/43
Lt Cdr E.M. Britton, 15/09/43
Lt Cdr V. Rance, 04/01/44
Lt Cdr (A) D. Brooks, DSC, RNVR,
13/02/44
Lt Cdr (A) J.L. Fisher, RNVR, 06/05/44

832 Squadron Formed as a TSR unit at Lee-on-Solent on 01/04/41, with 12 Albacores, it embarked in *Victorious* 08/41, using Hatston as a shore base for operations off Norway. The squadron's officers are credited with 'inventing' the naval version of British battledress at their own expense, as a practical solution to the wear and tear on traditional uniform for the rough conditions of open cockpit flying. The carrier operated off Iceland in 11/41 and 02/42, 832 losing her CO later that month and on anti-shipping sorties off Norway. It then escorted Arctic convoys, 03/42–07/42 broken only by an unsuccessful raid on the battleship *Tirpitz*. The squadron came ashore at Crail,

21/08, after escorting the fast Malta convoy, Operation Pedestal. Operations were conducted from Crail and Machrihanish until 832 re-embarked in 10/42, for the North African landings, Operation Torch, leaving behind a flight for mine-laying and anti-shipping operations at Manston. The squadron carried out attacks on shore targets as well as maintaining anti-submarine patrols off the coast of North Africa.

Re-equipping with 12 ex-USN Avenger TBF-1s in 01/43, while on a visit to the USA aboard *Victorious*, the squadron passed through the Panama Canal to the Pacific. Operations were conducted from *Victorious* in the Coral Sea, 05/43, before transferring on 27/06 to the USS *Saratoga* to support landings in the Solomons. The squadron re-embarked in *Victorious* in 07/43, to return home via Pearl Harbor and the Panama Canal, to re-equip with Avenger Is at Hatston in September. It gained 4 Wildcat Vs from 1832 Squadron, 01/44, and in 02/44 embarked aboard *Athene* and *Engadine* for Ceylon, disembarking at Katukurunda on 15/04. Leaving the fighters behind, the squadron embarked in *Illustrious* on 03/05 for a bombing raid on Sourabaya on 17/05. Keeping Katukurunda as a shore base, the squadron then embarked in *Begum* on 26/05 for 6 months, providing cover for Allied shipping, before its complement was reduced to 9 aircraft in 10/44. It returned home aboard *Begum* early in 1945 and disbanded on 21/02/45.

Battle honours: Malta Convoys, 1942; North Africa, 1942; Arctic, 1942.

Identification markings: Albacore and Avenger, 4A+; single letters for Wildcat.

Commanding officers:
Lt Cdr A.J.P. Plugge, 01/04/41
Lt Cdr W.J. Lucas, 27/02/42
Lt Cdr (A) F.K.A. Low, 24/11/42
Lt Cdr (A) J. Randall, RNVR, 14/10/44

833 Squadron A TSR squadron formed with 9 Swordfish, 08/12/41, for *Dasher*. After the ship blew up it reduced to 6 aircraft, 05/42, and instead joined *Biter* in 09/42. Assigned to cover the North African landings, the squadron was split in 10/42, with 'A' Flight remaining aboard *Biter* and 'B' Flight aboard *Avenger*, with 3 Swordfish IIs apiece. Regrouping ashore at Gibraltar on 11/11/42, it embarked in *Argus* on 25/12 to return home to Stretton. On 01/02/43, the squadron moved to Thorney Island to operate with Coastal Command, taking over 825 Squadron's aircraft for mine-laying, anti-shipping and anti-submarine patrols over the English Channel. It moved to Scotland, 15/04, increasing its strength to 9 Swordfish at Machrihanish, before adding a flight of 6 Seafire LIICs, 06/43 at Ballykelly in Northern Ireland.

In 07/43 the Seafires and 6 Swordfish embarked in *Stalker* to cover a Gibraltar convoy, after which the Seafires transferred to 880 Squadron and the Swordfish became 833Z. Regrouped at Machrihanish with 9 aircraft, 10/43, with the intention of providing MAC-ship flights of 3 aircraft each, but disbanded into 836 Squadron on 07/01/44.

Reformed on 26/04/44, aboard the escort carrier *Activity*, taking 3 Swordfish IIs from 836 Squadron and 7 Wildcat Vs from 816 and 819. It provided cover for an Arctic convoy and afterwards for 2 North Atlantic convoys, before covering a Gibraltar convoy and then disbanding at Eglinton, in Northern Ireland, 13/09/44.

Battle honours: North Africa, 1942; Atlantic, 1944; Arctic, 1944.

Identification markings: initially single letters on Swordfish, but later 5A+; Seafire 5A+.

Commanding officers:
Lt Cdr R.J.H. Stephens, 08/12/41
Capt W.G.S. Aston, RM, 14/01/43
Lt Cdr J.R.C. Callander, 17/05/43
Lt Cdr (A) J.G. Large, RNVR, 26/04/44

834 Squadron Formed in Jamaica at Palisadoes, 10/12/41, as a TBR squadron, with just 4 Swordfish. It embarked in the first American-built escort carrier, *Archer*, 03/42, to sail to Cape Town via Freetown. Returned to the USA aboard the carrier 07/42, ready to provide anti-submarine cover for a convoy to the UK and then, with Swordfish IIs replacing the earlier aircraft, it covered a Gibraltar convoy. The squadron increased to 6 aircraft in 01/43, while at Crail, before operating under Coastal Command at Exeter as part of 19 Group.

Moving to Machrihanish in 04/43, the squadron acquired another 3 Swordfish, before moving to Eglinton and Ballykelly in Northern Ireland, returning to Machrihanish in 06/43, when 6 Seafire LIICs were added to form a fighter flight. On 08/07/43, the bulk of the squadron embarked in another escort carrier, *Hunter*, leaving 3 Swordfish behind to join 836 Squadron. The carrier escorted a Gibraltar convoy, and the squadron divided: the Swordfish moving ashore to become 834Z Squadron, while the Seafires were absorbed into 899 Squadron to provide fighter cover for the Salerno landings. The entire squadron of 9 Swordfish and 6 Seafires regrouped aboard *Battler* on 07/09/43 and sailed to Aden to provide anti-submarine patrols from a shore base. It rejoined *Battler* on 17/10/43 to sail for Bombay, where it provided convoy protection in the Indian Ocean. In 02/44, 3 more Swordfish were added, and the following month, one of the squadron's aircraft spotted the German tanker *Brake*, which was sunk by a destroyer. A U-boat may have been damaged in a rocket projectile attack.

A further fighter flight with 6 Wildcat Vs was formed at Puttalam in southern India 04/44, while the rest of the squadron was ashore at Durban. Embarked in *Battler*, the main body of the squadron and the new fighter flight regrouped in Ceylon 07/44, when the Seafires were withdrawn. The squadron provided shipping protection in the Indian Ocean, using the carrier and various shore bases until disembarking at Trincomalee, Ceylon, 07/10/44. The squadron left its aircraft and the personnel took passage back to the UK 11/44, disbanding 06/12/44.

Battle honours: Atlantic, 1942; Salerno, 1943.
Identification markings: Single letters for Seafire and Swordfish, although the latter also used 4A+.
Commanding officers included:
Lt Cdr L.C.B. Ashburner, 12/11/41
Lt L.G. Wilson, 20/11/41
Lt Cdr (A) E.D. Child, 21/01/43
Lt Cdr (A) D.W. Philips, DSC, 12/08/44

835 Squadron Formed at Palisadoes, Jamaica, 15/02/42, as a TBR squadron with 4 Swordfish, the squadron flew north to Norfolk, Virginia, reaching it on 22/03. The squadron embarked in *Furious* 03/04, disembarking to Lee-on-Solent 15/04, where it acquired another 2 aircraft the following month. Most of the following 12 months was spent in Scotland and Northern Ireland, where the squadron replaced its original Swordfish with Swordfish IIs, 11/42, between periods of deck landing training aboard the escort carrier *Activity*. The squadron embarked in *Battler* 10/04/43, for convoy escort duties, gaining another 3 Swordfish and a fighter flight of 6 Sea Hurricane IICs previously with 804 Squadron. Again, a number of shore stations in Scotland and Northern Ireland were used between spells aboard the carrier, but the squadron also spent some time aboard *Argus*, 09/43, while at the end of the month the fighter flight was detached to *Ravager*.

The squadron came together again in time to embark aboard *Chaser* on 06/11,

Lt John Godley lands his Swordfish of 836P Flight aboard the MAC-ship *Adula* in late 1944. Note the narrow flight deck, leaving little room for the batsman! (*via Lord Kilbracken*)

and then transfered to *Nairana* on 30/12, for further convoy duty. In 03/44 and 04/44, the fighter strength was increased briefly with the addition of 3 Fulmars from 784 Squadron, before the Swordfish increased to 12 in May. The squadron's fighters accounted for 2 Ju290s in 05/44 and 06/44. Swordfish IIIs replaced the original aircraft in 07/44, while the Sea Hurricanes were replaced by 4 Wildcat VIs in 09/44, before *Nairana* switched from Atlantic to Arctic convoys. The squadron's aircraft attacked 2 U-boats and shot down 4 enemy aircraft while on Arctic convoys. The squadron disbanded at Hatston on 31/03/45, its fighters passing to 821 Squadron.

Battle honours: Atlantic, 1943–44; Arctic, 1944–45.

Identification markings: Swordfish, single letters then 5A+, Y:A, Z:A; Sea Hurricane, 7A+; Wildcat, Y:A.

Commanding officers:
Lt Cdr M. Johnstone, DSC, 15/02/42
Lt Cdr J.R. Lang, 28/04/42
Lt Cdr W.N. Waller, 15/09/43
Lt Cdr (A) T.T. Miller, 02/12/43
Lt Cdr E.E. Barringer, RNVR, 17/02/44
Lt Cdr F.V. Jones, RNVR, 12/08/44
Lt Cdr (A) J.R. Godley, RNVR, 15/01/45

836 Squadron Formed at Palisadoes, Jamaica, 01/03/42, as a torpedo bomber reconnaissance squadron with 6 Swordfish Is. Moved to Floyd Bennett Field, New York, 18/05, before embarking in *Biter* 02/06 for the UK. The squadron operated from a number of Fleet Air Arm bases, mainly in

Scotland, until coming under the control of Coastal Command at Thorney Island on 30/12. On 16/03/43, re-equipped with Swordfish IIs, it moved to Machrihanish, becoming an operational pool of Swordfish assigned to the merchant aircraft carriers or MAC-ships. On 05/07, the squadron moved to Maydown, and by 13/08, its strength had grown to 27 Swordfish and 2 Walrus, largely through absorbing 838 and 840 Squadrons, 700W Flight, and flights from 833 and 834 Squadrons based at Machrihanish. The Walruses were discarded. The squadron became the parent squadron for MAC-ship flights. These consisted of 3 or 4 aircraft, depending on whether they were based aboard a tanker or grain carrier.

The remainder of 833 Squadron was absorbed in 01/44, and together with 860 Netherlands Squadron, a total of 83 aircraft were being operated from 19 MAC-ships, using Maydown, Belfast and Machrihanish at the eastern end of the Atlantic route, and Dartmouth, Nova Scotia, at the western. The squadron's strength was reduced with the decline of the U-boat menace and the growing use of escort carriers, so that it was down to 30 aircraft by 02/45. Although it survived long enough for Swordfish IIIs to be introduced, the squadron disbanded at Maydown on 29/07/45.

Battle honours: Atlantic, 1943–45.

Identification markings: Single letters, then flight letter/individual number, then M1–M4 plus flight letter.

Commanding officers:

Lt Cdr J.A. Crawford, 01/03/42

Lt Cdr R.W. Slater, OBE, DSC, 09/07/42

Lt Cdr J.R.C. Callander, 29/06/44

Lt Cdr (A) F.G.B. Sheffield, DSC, RNVR, 05/03/45

837 Squadron Formed 01/05/42, Palisadoes, as a TBR squadron with 4 Swordfish Is. Moved to New York's Floyd Bennett Field on 10/07, to embark in *Dasher* on 25/07, covering a North Atlantic convoy when the escort carrier sailed on 24/08. The squadron used several shore bases on arrival, while its strength also fluctuated, rising to 6 aircraft at Campbeltown shortly after arrival on 10/09, then reducing to 2 by the end of the month. Back to 6 aircraft at the end of the year, the squadron was divided into 2 flights in 01/43, with 837A Flight allocated to *Argus* to provide anti-submarine cover for a Gibraltar convoy, while 837D Flight embarked in *Dasher* again for a convoy to Iceland. When *Dasher* blew up in the Firth of Clyde on 27/03, 837D was ashore, and the squadron regrouped at Dunino 2 days later. After deck landing training aboard *Argus* in late 04/43, the squadron disbanded on 15/06, becoming 'Z' Flight of 886 Squadron at Machrihanish.

Reformed at Stretton, 01/08/44, still in the role of a TBR unit, officially with a complement of 16 Barracuda IIs, but did not receive the first of these aircraft until at Lee-on-Solent on 04/09. Moved to Fearn on 05/11, it had 18 aircraft in 12/44. It embarked in the new light fleet carrier *Glory* on 04/04/45, using Ayr as a shore base, sailing to join the British Pacific Fleet in 05/45, although the strength was halved until a visit to Dekheila in late 05/45 saw it increased to 12 before re-embarking to become part of the 16th Carrier Air Group. The war ended before the squadron could see action, but it remained with the ship using a number of shore bases in the Far East and Australia, and covered the Japanese surrender at Rabaul.

Battle honours: Atlantic, 1943.

Identification markings: Single letters for both Swordfish and Barracuda, although the latter also used Y1A+.

Commanding officers:

Lt Cdr A.S. Whitworth, DSC, 15/03/42

Lt Cdr (A) R.B. Martin, RNVR, 01/08/44

838 Squadron Formed Dartmouth, Nova Scotia, 15/05/42, as a TBR squadron with 4 Swordfish Is. Transferred to the US Naval Air Station at Alameda Island in California on 06/08, and did not embark aboard *Attacker* until 12/12. *Attacker* passed through the Panama Canal to Quonset Point, spending 2 months there from 01/01/43, before re-embarking on 02/03 to cover a convoy from the Caribbean to the UK. When it disembarked at Machrihanish on 02/04, it re-equipped with Swordfish IIs, and was assigned to MAC-ship duties, moving to Maydown on 13/06. After deck landing training in *Argus* and 2 weeks in the escort carrier *Activity*, the squadron was assigned to the MAC-ship MV *Rapana* on 02/08, before disbanding to become 'L' Flight of 836 Squadron on 13/08.

Reformed at Belfast on 01/11/43, from a flight of 818 Squadron as a TBR unit with 4 Swordfish IIs. After working up aboard *Nairana*, the squadron's strength was increased to 9 at Inskip in 02/44, and to 12 at Machrihanish on 01/04. On 20/04 the squadron moved to Harrowbeer, operating with Coastal Command's 156 GR Wing on anti-submarine duties in the English Channel, operating radar-equipped Swordfish II and IIIs in the period immediately before and during the Normandy Landings. Later, it moved north, first to Long Kesh in Northern Ireland and then to operate from Coastal Command's Scottish bases, including Benbecula and Fraserburgh. At Eglinton on 27/10, a fighter flight of 4 Wildcat VIs was formed, ready for escort carrier duty, but this was then transferred to 856 Squadron while 838 was moved to Thorney Island, disbanding on 03/02/45.

Battle honours: Atlantic, 1943; Normandy, 1944.

Identification markings: 2A+ then single letters for Swordfish; single letters for Wildcat.

Commanding officers:
Lt Cdr J.R.C. Callandar, 15/05/42
Lt Cdr (A) R.G. Large, RNVR, 07/06/43
Lt Cdr (A) J.M. Brown, DSC, RNVR, 01/11/43
Lt Cdr P. Snow, 19/08/44

840 Squadron After assembling at Eastleigh a month earlier, formed at Palisadoes on 01/06/42, as a TBR squadron with 6 Swordfish Is, which were replaced by Swordfish IIs before moving to Miami on 25/09. Joined *Battler* 12/12, disembarking at Quonset Point on 26/12. Later embarked in *Attacker* to provide anti-submarine cover for a UK-bound convoy, disembarking to Machrihanish, via Stretton, on 02/04/43. At Hatston in 05/43, the squadron was assigned to MAC-ship duties, initially aboard MV *Empire MacAndrew* from 12/07, but disbanded, 13/08/43, to become 'M' Flight of 836 Squadron.

Battle honours: Atlantic, 1943.

Identification markings: Single letters.

Commanding officers:
Lt (A) L.R. Tivy, 01/06/42
Lt (A) C.M.T. Hallewell, 21/04/43

841 Squadron An unusual unit, 842 formed at Lee-on-Solent, 01/07/42, as a special duty TBR unit with just 2 Albacores, although these were increased to 4 in August. Operated as part of the RAF, it moved to Middle Wallop on 17/08, then to Manston on 23/08, conducting a total of 99 night attacks against enemy shipping and E-boats. Early the following year, a series of detachments operated from Coltishall, Exeter and Tangmere, where it absorbed part of 823 Squadron on 31/05/43, eventually having 16 Albacore and 3 Swordfish. Disbanded at Manston, 01/12. Its duties and aircraft passed to the RCAF's 415 Squadron.

Reformed at Lee-on-Solent, 01/02/44, as a TBR unit with 12 Barracuda IIs, moving to

Fearn at the end of the month to work up. It was allocated to the 2nd Naval TBR Wing at Machrihanish in 06/44, joining *Formidable* for 6 days in 08/44, transferring via Grimsetter and Machrihanish at the end of the month to *Implacable*. Anti-submarine and anti-shipping strikes off Norway followed in 10/44, before disbanding into 828 Squadron at Haston, 28/11/44.

Battle honours: English Channel, 1943; Norway, 1944.

Identification markings: Albacores later allocated 5A+; single letters for Barracuda.

Commanding officers:
Lt R.L. Williamson, DSC, 01/07/42
Lt (A) L.J. Kiggell, DSC, 15/10/42
Lt Cdr (A) W.F.C. Garthwaite, DSC, RNVR, 28/12/42
Lt Cdr (A) S.M.P. Walsh, DSC, RNVR, 02/07/43
Lt Cdr (A) R.J. Fisher, RNZNVR, 01/02/44
Lt Cdr (A) E.F.L. Montgomery, RNZNVR, 01/06/44

842 Squadron Formed at Lee-on-Solent as a TBR unit, 01/03/43, with 6 Swordfish IIs, it moved to Machrihanish on 01/04 and to Hatston in 05/43; acquiring another 3 Swordfish and a fighter flight of 6 Seafire LIIcs from 895 Squadron. The Seafires were transferred to 897 Squadron and replaced by 6 Seafire Ibs. On 05/08, the squadron embarked in *Fencer*, and provided anti-submarine cover for the occupation of the Azores 10/43–11/43. Fighter strength was augmented by 4 Wildcat Vs, 'A' Flight of 1832 Squadron from 17/11, becoming 'Q' Flight, one of which shot down a German aircraft while covering a Gibraltar convoy on 01/12.

The Seafires were cut to 3 in 01/44, and replaced in 03/44 by a further 6 Wildcats from 1832 squadron. On 10/02, a Swordfish sank *U-666*. Swordfish strength increased to 12 on 01/05, for *Fencer* to escort an Arctic convoy, attacking 11 German U-boats and sinking 3, *U-277* on 01/05, and the next day, *U-674* and *U-959*.

The squadron was divided 07/44, with 6 Swordfish aboard *Indefatigable* and another three aboard *Furious*, while their aircraft attacked the battleship *Tirpitz*, leaving the remaining Swordfish and Wildcats with *Fencer* for a convoy to Gibraltar. While the Wildcats, down to four, remained with the carrier until transferred to *Campania* in 10/44, the Swordfish were reunited under Coastal Command in 09/44 for operations in Scotland. The Wildcats transferred to 813 Squadron in 11/44, and the Swordfish moved to Thorney Island, where the squadron disbanded, 15/01/45.

Battle honours: Atlantic, 1943–44; Norway, 1944; Arctic, 1944.

Identification markings: Swordfish, single letters, then F:A+ aboard Fencer; Seafires and Wildcats, single letters.

Commanding officers:
Lt Cdr (A) C.B. Lamb, DSO, DSC, 01/03/43
Lt Cdr (A) L.R. Tivy, 21/04/43
Lt Cdr (A) G.F.S. Hodson, RNR, 27/03/44
Lt Cdr (A) L.A. Edwards, 02/08/44

845 Squadron Formed at Quonset Point, 01/02/43, as a TBR squadron with 12 Avenger Is, after arriving in style aboard HMT *Queen Elizabeth*. During work up, the squadron remained at Quonset Point, using *Tracker* and USS *Charger* for deck landing training in late 04/43, before embarking aboard *Chaser* from Norfolk, Virginia, on 01/06, to provide anti-submarine cover for a convoy to the UK. Disembarking to Hatston on 06/07, the squadron briefly reduced to 9 aircraft 09/43–11/43. After a transfer to Machrihanish in 01/44, the squadron joined the 31st Naval TBR Wing, intended to join *Victorious*. In the event, boosted by the additional of a fighter flight of 4

Wildcats from 1832 Squadron, it was shipped aboard *Atheling*, *Engadine* and the SS *Strathnaver* to Katukurunda in Ceylon, arriving on 05/04. On arrival, the fighter flight transferred to 890 Squadron.

The squadron joined *Illustrious* in 05/44, and before the end of the month had mounted a dive bombing raid on the oil refinery and harbour at Sourabaya, Java. It transferred to the escort carrier *Ameer*, 07/44 for anti-submarine convoy protection in the Indian Ocean, gaining a fighter flight of 4 Wildcat Vs on 16/08. The Wildcats increased to 6, but after disembarking to Colombo Racecourse 10/44, the squadron lost 4 of its Avengers. In 02/45, the squadron lost its fighters, and after a day aboard *Begum*, embarked aboard *Empress* to provide anti-submarine cover during operations against Malaya and Sumatra, using Colombo Racecourse, and occasionally Trincomalee, as shore bases. Transferring to *Khedive* to return to Ceylon from one of these missions, a detachment of 4 Avengers joined *Shah*, and these were later joined by the rest of the squadron for a planned invasion of Sumatra, overtaken by the Japanese surrender. *Shah* brought the squadron's personnel back to the UK in 09/45. Disbanded, Gourock, 07/10/45. Identification markings: Avengers, single letters, then 5A+ and H1A+.
Commanding officers:
Lt Cdr W.H. Crawford, 01/02/43
Lt Cdr (A) J.F. Arnold, 25/10/43
Lt Cdr (A) D.S. Watts, RNVR, 15/05/45

846 Squadron Conveyed to the United States aboard HMT *Queen Elizabeth*, to form at Quonset Point as a TBR unit, 01/04/43, with 12 Avenger Is. After working up at Quonset Point, Norfolk and Brunswick, it joined *Ravager* on 02/07, providing anti-submarine cover for an eastbound convoy. Disembarking to Hatston on 28/07, after a

transit stop at Machrihanish, the squadron spent the rest of the year at various Scottish air stations, acquiring a fighter flight of 4 Wildcat Vs from 1832 Squadron on 20/12, before embarking aboard *Tracker* on 04/01/44, to provide cover for Gibraltar convoys, using Machrihanish and North Front as shore stations. In 03/44 and 04/44, the escort carrier covered Arctic convoys, and on one convoy the squadron's aircraft attacked 6 U-boats outward, and another 2 on the return.

After *Tracker* was damaged in a collision on 03/06/44, the squadron disembarked. Ashore, Wildcat strength briefly peaked at 10, but had fallen to 6 when the squadron embarked in *Trumpeter* on 05/07, using Hatston as a shore station, for anti-shipping and mine-laying operations off Norway. The Wildcat Vs were replaced by Wildcat VIs from 852 Squadron in 09/44. During early 12/44, 4 Avengers were detached to *Premier*. An Arctic convoy was escorted in 03/45. After VE-Day, the squadron lost its fighter flight and was based ashore at a number of Scottish bases. Plans to join the British Pacific Fleet were abandoned. It was renumbered as 751 Squadron, 22/09.
Battle honours: Atlantic, 1944; Arctic, 1944–45; Norway, 1944–45; Normandy, 1944.
Identification markings: Avengers, 4A+, J:A+; Wildcats, single letters, then J:A+.
Commanding officers:
Lt Cdr (A) R.D. Head, DSC, 01/03/43
Lt Cdr C.L.F. Webb, 07/10/44
Lt Cdr J.S.L. Crabbe, 09/05/45
Lt Cdr (A) D.J. Bunyan, RNVR, 16/06/45

847 Squadron Formed as a TBR unit at Lee-on-Solent on 01/06/43, with 12 Barracuda IIs, it worked up at Fearn and Machrihanish. Strength was reduced to 9 aircraft before joining the 21st Naval TBR Wing and embarking in *Illustrious* on 28/11, for the Indian Ocean. Apart from a brief detachment aboard *Unicorn*, the squadron alternated between *Illustrious* and China Bay or Katukurunda as shore bases. In 04/45, the squadron dive-bombed the oil storage tanks and harbour installations at Sabang, and later on the Andaman Islands. Strength was restored to 12 aircraft shortly before it was disbanded into 810 Squadron, Trincomalee, 30/06/44.

Identification markings: Barracuda, 3A+.

Commanding officers:

Lt Cdr (A) P.C. Whitfield, 01/06/43

Lt Cdr (A) J.L. Cullen, 20 /07/43

848 Squadron Formed, 01/06/43, as a TBR squadron with 12 Avenger Is at Quonset Point, after working up in the USA and Canada, with deck landing training aboard the USS *Charger*, 848 Squadron embarked in *Trumpeter* on 04/09, providing anti-submarine cover for an eastbound convoy. The squadron disembarked on 01/11, to Belfast, but within days passed through Ayr and Grimsetter before settling at Hatston on 24/11; moving to Gosport before the end of the year. Posted to Manston on 20/04/44, and then to Thorney Island, it operated as part of Coastal Command and provided anti-shipping and anti-submarine support for the Normandy landings.

It returned to Fleet Air Arm control to embark in *Formidable* with an enhanced strength of 21 aircraft, providing anti-submarine cover on the way to Gibraltar. As the carrier was delayed at Gibraltar with a propeller shaft problem, the squadron flew to Dekheila in Egypt, not re-embarking until 27/01/45. Arriving in the Far East after a visit to Australia, the squadron attacked airfields in the Sakishima Gunto during April, following this by attacks on Formosa. A number of aircraft were lost during kamikaze attacks on the carrier, which also suffered damage from a serious hangar fire.

Withdrawing to Australia in 06/44 with the ship, the squadron was reduced to 15 aircraft. Re-embarking for further strikes against the Japanese home islands, VJ-Day intervened and the carrier and her squadrons returned to Australia. The squadron left its aircraft in Australia and its personnel returned home aboard *Victorious*. Disbanded Devonport, 31/10/45.

Battle honours: Normandy, 1945; Okinawa, 1945; Japan, 1945.

Identification markings: 4A+.

Commanding officers:

Lt Cdr (A) R.G. Hunt, 0/06/43

Lt Cdr A.P. Boddam-Whetham, 09/05/44

Lt Cdr T.G.V. Percy, 21/08/44

Lt Cdr (A) A.W.R. Turney, 08/06/45

849 Squadron Formed at Quonset Point, 01/08/43, as a TBR squadron with 12 Avenger Is, it worked up at Quonset Point and Squantum, before joining *Khedive*, on 01/11. It disembarked to Speke on 17/11, before moving to Grimsetter on 25/11. After submarine training at Maydown and Eglinton from 14/02/44, it moved to Machrihanish on 25/03. The squadron was deployed to Perranporth on 20/04 to operate with 816 Swordfish and 850 Avenger Squadrons under Coastal Command for the period leading up to and during the Normandy landings.

Returning to Fleet Air Arm control, after several moves, the squadron embarked aboard the escort carrier *Rajah* on 09/09, sailing to Ceylon, where it gained an extra 9 aircraft, Avenger IIs. After detaching a flight to *Battler* in early 11/44, the squadron became part of the 2nd Naval Strike Wing on 10/12, with 820 Squadron, and embarked aboard *Victorious*, from which bombing raids were carried out against the oil refineries at Pangkalan Brandon and Palembang in Sumatra during 01/45. The squadron's strength was cut to 14 aircraft, and in 03/45 it mounted strikes against the Sakishima Gunto, attacking airfields and other shore targets. Later, Formosa was attacked, before the carrier withdrew to Australia, arriving early 06/45. Returning to the front line aboard *Victorious*, the squadron attacked the Japanese home islands, hitting targets in and around Tokyo, before returning to Australia in late 08/45. Aircraft left in Australia and personnel returned to the UK aboard Victorious. Disbanded, 31/10/45.

Battle honours: Normandy, 1944; Palembang, 1945; Okinawa, 1945; Japan, 1945.

Identification markings: Single letters, then P1A+.

Commanding officers:

Lt Cdr (A) K.G. Sharp, 01/08/43

Lt Cdr (A) D.R. Foster, DSO, DSC, RNVR, 05/09/44

Lt Cdr A.J. Griffith, DSC, RNVR, 14/06/45

850 Squadron Formed at Quonset Point on 01/01/43, to operate Seamews, but disbanding at the end of the month, it reformed as a TBR squadron, 01/09/43, at Squantum, with 12 Avenger Is. After deck landing training aboard USS *Charger*, the squadron embarked in *Empress*, 02/44, providing anti-submarine patrols for a UK convoy. Disembarking to Lee-on-Solent on 10/04, the squadron moved to Perranporth to operate under Coastal Command with 816 and 849 Squadrons for the Normandy landings, when the squadron sank one enemy merchant vessel and damaged another off the Channel Islands on 24/07. Moving to Limavady, in Northern Ireland, on 01/08, the squadron gained a fighter flight of 4 Wildcats, but disbanded on 24/12/44, after further operations with Coastal Command.

Battle honours: Normandy, 1944; Atlantic, 1944.

Identification markings: Avengers, single letters, later 4A+; Wildcats, single letters.

Commanding officers:

Lt J.H .Dundas, DSC, 01/01/43

Lt Cdr A.P. Boddam-Whetham, DSC, 01/09/43

Lt Cdr (A) B. White, DSC, RNVR, 28/05/44

Lt Cdr (A) F.S. Martin, RNVR, 18/12/44

851 Squadron A TBR unit formed at Squantum, 01/10/43, the squadron operated 12 Avenger Is, which after working up, including deck landing training on the USS *Charger*, embarked in *Shah* in 01/44, and sailed for the Indian Ocean. At Katukurunda in 04/44, a flight of 4 Wildcats was added, the squadron alternating between this and other shore bases and the carrier. During August 3 U-boats were attacked. Early in 1945, the Wildcat flight was disbanded. The squadron's aircraft raided targets in Burma 04/45–05/45 and attacked a Japanese cruiser and her escorts on 15/05 while embarked in *Emperor* for a week.

Postwar the squadron returned home aboard *Shah*. Disbanded, Gourock, 07/10/45.

Battle honours: Malaya, 1945; Burma, 1945.

Identification markings: Avengers, 1A+ to SA+; Wildcats, single letters.

Commanding officers:

Lt Cdr (A) A.M. Tuke, DSC, 01/10/43

Lt Cdr (A) M.T. Fuller, DSC, RNVR, 15/09/44

852 Squadron Formed as a TBR squadron at Squantum, 01/11/43, with 12 Avenger Is, it embarked in *Nabob* on 11/02/44, disembarking to Machrihanish on 06/04. A fighter flight of 4 Wildcat Vs was added in 05/44, and the squadron re-embarked for mine-laying and anti-shipping strikes off Norway. After *Nabob* was torpedoed by *U-354* in 08/44, limping back to Scapa Flow, the

squadron transferred to *Trumpeter* on 10/09. The fighter flight re-equipped with Wildcat VIs. Disbanded, 17/10/44.
Battle honours: Norway, 1944.
Identification markings: Avenger, 2A+; Wildcat, single letters, then 2A+.
Commanding officer:
Lt Cr (A) R.E. Bradshaw, DSC, 01/11/43

853 Squadron Another Squantum TBR squadron, 853 formed on 01/12/43 with 12 Avenger IIs, and after working up joined *Arbiter* on 31/05/44, and sailed for the UK. Meanwhile, a fighter flight of 4 Wildcat Vs had formed at Eglinton, although this disbanded after 10 days aboard *Formidable* in 06/44. A new fighter flight formed with 4 Wildcat VIs in 09/44, ready for the squadron to join *Tracker* on 12/09, to escort an Arctic convoy. The squadron transferred to *Queen* on 27/01/45, for operations off Norway, followed by further Arctic convoy duty, with Hatston as a shore base. Disbanded, 30/05/45.
Battle honours: Arctic, 1944–45; Norway, 1945.
Identification markings: Avenger, 3A+ to T:A+ ,Q:A+; Wildcat, T:A+, Q:A+.
Commanding officers:
Lt Cdr (A) N.G. Haigh, RNVR, 01/11/43
Lt Cdr (A) J.M. Glaser, 20/12/44

854 Squadron Formed at Squantum, 01/01/44, as a TBR squadron with 12 Avenger IIs, after working up it embarked in *Indomitable* on 10/04, disembarking to Machrihanish on 01/05/44. On 23/05, the squadron was assigned to Coastal Command as part of 157 Wing at Hawkinge and then at Thorney Island during the Normandy landings. Returning to the Fleet Air Arm at Lee-on-Solent on 27/08, the aircraft were left behind and personnel embarked in *Activity*, on 07/09, for Ceylon, where they worked up with Avenger Is on arrival at Katukurunda on 11/10.

Re-equipped with older aircraft, the squadron joined *Illustrious* on 01/12, bombing targets in Sumatra throughout 12/44–01/45, with attacks on the Sakishima Gunto 03/45–04/45. The following month, the squadron disembarked, losing its aircraft. It received Avenger IIIs at Nowra in 07/45. Although the squadron joined the 3rd Carrier Air Group, it lost its aircraft yet again in 09/45 and disbanded on its return to the UK on 08/12/45.
Battle honours: Normandy, 1944; Palembang, 1945; Okinawa, 1945.
Identification markings: 4A+, then J4A+, and finally Q4A+. Marking: Seafires, A:A+, D4A+.
Commanding officers:
Lt Cdr W.J. Mainprice, DSC, 01/01/44
Lt Cdr (A) F.C. Nottingham, DSC, RNVR, 30/01/45
Lt Cdr (A) R.E. Jess, DSC, RCNVR, 28/03/45
No CO for the final four months.

855 Squadron A very short history started on 01/02/44, when this TBR squadron formed at Squantum with 12 Avenger IIs, which embarked on 06/05 aboard *Queen* for the UK. Disembarking to Hawkinge, the squadron was immediately assigned to 157 Wing, Coastal Command, to cover the Normandy landings. Disbanded, 19/10/44, Machrihanish.
Battle honours: Normandy, 1944.
Identification markings: 5BA+, then 5A+.
Commanding officer:
Lt Cdr (A) J.B. Harrowar, RNR

856 Squadron Forming at Squantum as a TBR squadron on 01/03/44, with 12 Avenger IIs, it embarked in *Smiter* 06/44. On arrival, the squadron received anti-submarine training at Machrihanish, Maydown and Eglinton, while detachments were sent to Hatston, *Nabob* and *Trumpeter*, before regrouping aboard *Premier* on 13/09, for operations off Norway. A fighter flight of 4 Wildcat VIs had been formed 3 days earlier, and a further 4 were added later. During 04/45–05/45, *Premier* escorted Arctic convoys, returning after VE-Day. Disbanded Hatston, 15/06/45.

Battle honours: Norway, 1944–45; Arctic, 1945.

Identification markings: Avenger, 6A+ and P:A+; Wildcat, P:S+.

Commanding officers:

Lt Cdr (A) S.M.P. Walsh, 01/03/44

Lt (A) P.S. Foulds, RNVR, (temp), 31/12/44

Lt Cdr (A) H.C.K. Housser, RCNVR, 15/01/45

857 Squadron Formed at Squantum as a TBR squadron, 01/04/44, with 12 Avenger Is and IIs, which embarked aboard *Rajah* on 29/06. Disembarking to Belfast on 13/07, the squadron received another 9 Avengers, ready for anti-submarine training at Machrihanish. It re-embarked on 09/09 for Ceylon, where after a spell ashore at Coimbatore and Katukurunda, it embarked in *Indomitable* on 27/11. Through the rest of the winter, using the carrier and Nowra as a shore station, the squadron attacked targets in Sumatra, including Belawan Deli, Pangkalan Brandan and Palembang, before moving to targets in the Sakashima Gunto and Formosa in the spring. After this, the squadron reduced to 15 aircraft, but returned to the Far East after VJ-Day to operate against Japanese suicide boats off Hong Kong on 31/08 and 01/09. Leaving its aircraft in Australia, the squadron returned home. Disbanded 30/11/45.

Battle Honours: Palenbang, 1945; Okinawa, 1945.

Identification markings: 7A+, W7A+, W1A+, 370-386/W.

Commanding officer:

Lt Cdr (A) W. Stuart, DSC and 2 Bars; RNVR, 01/04/44

860 Squadron A Royal Netherlands Navy-manned squadron formed 15/06/43, at Donibristle for TBR duties with 6 Swordfish Is, although this number doubled during training at Machrihanish and Maydown. Squadron became part of the MAC-ship wing, alongside 836 Squadron. Divided into 'O' and 'S' flights, intially these operated from MV *Acavus* and *Gadila* respectively, although later 'O' transferred to the MV *Macoma*, being redesignated 'F' Flight.

VE-Day meant the end of the squadron's MAC-ship role. It received 822's 12 Barracuda IIIs on 30/06/45, although deck landing training did not follow until after the war. The squadron became an integral part of the Royal Netherlands Navy postwar.

Battle honours: Atlantic, 1944–45.

Identification markings: Swordfish, initially single letter, then flight/individual letter; Barracuda, single letters.

Commanding officer:

LTZ J. van der Tooren, RNethN, 15/06/43

877 Squadron Fleet fighter unit formed 01/04/43, at Tanga (then Tanganiyka, now Tanzania), the squadron initially operated 9 RAF long-range Hurricane IIBs. It moved to Port Reitz in Kenya in July, but plans to move it to Ceylon to augment the island's defence were abandoned and it disbanded on 30/12/43. Became an RCN squadron postwar.

Commanding officer:

Capt P.P. Nelson-Gracie, RM

878 Squadron Formed on 01/03/43, as a fleet fighter squadron with 12 Martlet IVs, it worked up at Hatston, Orkney, before embarking in *Illustrious* on 08/06. Squadron was operated from the carrier off Iceland, before providing fighter cover at Salerno. It re-equipped with 10 Martlet Vs while at Port Ellen in 10/43, only to disband at Eglinton on 25/01/44, its aircraft passing to 816 and 1832 Squadrons.

The other squadron providing MAC-ship flights was the Dutch-manned 860, one of whose Swordfish is seen here, armed with rocket projectiles for anti-submarine work. (*Royal Netherlands Navy Maritime Institute*)

Battle honours: Salerno, 1943.
Commanding officers:
Lt Cdr (A) M.F. Fell, 01/03/43
Lt Cdr (A) D.K. Evans, RNZNVR, 30/10/43

879 Squadron Formed out of 'B' Flight of 809 Squadron, St Merryn, 01/10/42, with 6 Fulmar Is as a fleet fighter squadron, it moved to Old Sarum on 18/11 to train in Army suppport. A move to Stretton on 22/03/43, was followed by re-equipment with 10 Seafire Ibs, before moving to Dundonald for a combined operations course, and then to Andover for Army cooperation training with 10 new Seafire LIICs. The squadron embarked in *Attacker* on 29/07, sailing to the Mediterranean where it flew 75 patrols covering the Salerno landings. It returned to the UK, dis-

embarking to Machrihanish on 06/10, and after 2 further spells at Andover, and at Burscough, became part of the 4th Naval Fighter Wing, and absorbed the aircraft of 886 Squadron on 24/02/44, raising its strength to 20 aircraft.

A number of Seafire LIIIs were introduced before the squadron underwent further Army cooperation training at Long Kesh 03/44–04/44, then re-embarking for a return to the Mediterranean. On arrival, the squadron split, providing detachments for Blida and Gibraltar, while other flights operated with the Desert Air Force in Italy. The squadron was reunited aboard *Attacker* on 23/07, to provide cover for the landings in the South of France, after which it undertook operations in the Aegean. On 11/12, it disembarked to Dekheila, where it re-equipped with 24 Seafire LIICs and LIIIs, before re-embarking on 14/04/45, for Ceylon.

At the end of the War in the Pacific, the squadron operated over Malaya and Singapore, before returning to disband at Nutts Corner, 07/01/46.

Battle honours: Salerno, 1943; South of France, 1944; Aegean, 1944.

Commanding officers:

Lt S.F.F. Shotton, RNR, 30/09/42

Lt Cdr (A) R.J.H. Grose, RNVR, 14/01/43

Lt Cdr P.E.I. Bailey, 09/11/44

Lt Cdr (A) B.H. Harris, 14/04/45

880 Squadron Formed as a fleet fighter unit, Arbroath, 15/01/41, with 3 Martlet Is, it borrowed 3 Sea Gladiators and then replaced these with 9 Sea Hurricane IAs, themselves replaced by IBs in 07/41 at Twatt. Meanwhile, a flight of 4 aircraft, 880A Squadron, had been detached to operate from *Furious*, providing air cover for the raid on Petsamo, when a Do18 was shot down. Reunited, the squadron joined *Indomitable* on 10/10/41, and sailed for the West Indies and then Cape Town, en route to join the British Eastern Fleet. In 05/42, operating from the carrier with Port Reitz as a shore base, the squadron supported the landings in Madagascar, attacking a Vichy French sloop and the airfield at Diego Suarez.

Sailing via the Cape to Gibraltar, air cover was provided for the major Malta convoy, Operation Pedestal, 08/42, when 8 enemy aircraft were shot down and 3 others damaged for the loss of 3 Sea Hurricanes. *Indomitable* herself was badly damaged on 12/08, after which the squadron disembarked to Gibraltar, before returning to the ship and then disembarking to Machrihanish on 27/08. At Stretton, the squadron re-equipped with 12 Seafire IICs in 09/42, before joining *Argus* on 16/10, to provide support for the North African landings 11/42. The squadron fulfilled a similar role for the landings in

Sicily in 07/43, and for the Salerno landings in 09/43, but operating from the repaired *Indomitable*.

The squadron transferred to *Furious* in 02/44, for operations off Norway, and then re-equipped the following month with 12 Seafire FIIIs, for further operations off Norway, including attacks on the battleship *Tirpitz*. 06/44, 4 aircraft were detached, to operate with 4 from 801 to operate as a composite squadron under RAF Fighter Command, before returning to their respective squadrons in 08/44.

Reunited, the squadron became part of the 30th Naval Fighter Wing in 10/44, providing fighter cover for an anti-shipping operation off Norway after embarking in *Implacable* on 08/11. With 24 aircraft by 01/45, the squadron returned to *Implacable* on 15/03 to join the British Pacific Fleet. In the Far East, it provided patrols and fighter escorts for attacks on the island of Truk, and dive-bombed oil storage tanks, before the 30th NF Wing was merged into the 8th Carrier Air Group. As the war came to an end, the squadron attacked the Japanese home islands, inflicting heavy losses on Japanese aircraft. After the war, the squadron disembarked in Australia, disbanding into 801 Squadron at Schofields, 11/09/45.

Battle honours: Diego Suarez, 1942; North Africa, 1942; Sicily, 1943; Salerno, 1943; Norway, 1944; Japan, 1945. Sea Hurricanes, 7A+ in October, 1941; Seafire, 7A+ to P7A+.

Commanding officers:

Lt Cdr F.E.C. Judd, 15/01/41

Lt Cdr R.J. Cork, DSO, DFC, 12 /08/42

Lt Cdr (A) W.H. Martyn, DSC, RNVR, 07/09/42

Lt Cdr (A) R.M. Crosley, DSC & Bar, RNVR, 05/08/44

881 Squadron Formed as a fleet fighter unit with 6 Martlet Is and IIs at Lee-on-Solent on 01/06/41, the squadron was earmarked for

Ark Royal, but the ship was torpedoed on 13/11, sinking the following day. With 9 aircraft, the squadron moved to Machrihanish on 13/02/42, and embarked in *Illustrious* on 15/03 for the Indian Ocean to take part in the invasion of Madagascar in 05/42. During the operation, it built up to a strength of 12 aircraft, and operated with 882 Squadron on fighter cover and reconnaissance, shooting down 7 enemy aircraft between them. A detachment went to Port Reitz. On 19/05, it was absorbed into 882 Squadron, remaining with the carrier, using shore bases in East Africa until it returned to the UK on 04/02/43. It was preceded by 'B' Flight, which had reached Scotland the previous October and disbanded into 890 Squadron, 08/01.

Operating out of Lee-on-Solent and then Hatston, a flight embarked aboard *Furious* for a few days in 07/43 for operations off Norway, accounting for 1 German aircraft. Re-equipping with 12 Wildcat Vs in 08/43 while at Eglinton, the squadron moved to Stretton in 09/43, and then joined *Formidable* briefly in 11/43, refreshing deck landing skills, before becoming part of the 7th Naval Fighter Wing and joining *Pursuer* on 26/11. Joining a Gibraltar convoy during 02/44, its aircraft shot down 2 enemy aircraft and damaged another. Fighter cover was provided for attacks on the German battleship *Tirpitz* in 04/44–06/44, accounting for another German aircraft. The squadron re-equipped with 20 Wildcat VIs, some of which from the disbanding 896 Squadron, and spent 3 days aboard *Fencer* covering an anti-shipping operation off Norway.

The squadron re-embarked in *Pursuer* on 04/07 for the Mediterranean, and flew almost 200 sorties during the landings in the South of France in 08/44, before moving to the Aegean in 09/44. Returning to the UK, the squadron spent the winter months operating from a number of carriers, including *Trumpeter*, *Puncher* and *Premier*, as well as *Pursuer*, and a detachment operated from *Implacable* in early 12/44. Re-embarking in *Pursuer* for Cape Town on 23/03/45, on reaching there the squadron re-equipped with 30 Hellcat IIs, intending to join the 12th Carrier Air Group and the British Pacific Fleet, but VJ-Day intervened. The squadron personnel took passage to the UK disbanding on arrival, 27/10/45.

Battle honours: Diego Suarez, 1942; Norway, 1944; Aegean, 1944; South of France, 1944; Normandy, 1944; Atlantic, 1944.

Identification markings: Martlet, single letters, later B:A+; Wildcat, 5A+ to U:A+; Hellcat 2A+ and 3A+.

Commanding officers:

Lt Cdr J.C. Cockburn, 01/06/41

Lt Cdr R.A. Bird, 01/03/43

Lt Cdr (A) D.R.B. Cosh, RCNVR, 27/11/43

Lt Cdr (A) L.A. Hordern, DSC, RNVR, 25/06/44

Lt Cdr (A) C. Ballard, RNVR, 23/10/44

882 Squadron Formed at Donibristle, 15/09/41, as a fleet fighter unit with 9 Martlet Is, the squadron also briefly operated a small number of Sea Hurricanes. After ground attack training at Turnhouse in 02/42, the squadron joined *Illustrious* on 22/03 to support the landings in Madagascar, when it operated with 881 Squadron, with the 2 squadrons shooting down 7 enemy aircraft between them. On 19/05, the 2 squadrons were merged, although a detachment that had joined *Archer* in 04/42 remained, switching to Swordfish and not disbanding until 30/09/42.

Reformed at Donibristle with 12 Martlet IVs on 07/09/42, it joined *Victorious* on 06/10 for the North African landings the following month. The squadron remained with the carrier, returning to the UK, then sailing to the United States, and then to the Pacific using the Panama Canal. Operations in the

Coral Sea in 05/43, were followed by support for the American landings in the Solomon Islands in 06/43, when the squadron flew USN F4F-4 Wildcats. The carrier returned to the UK and the squadron disembarked to Eglinton on 26/09, re-equipping with 10 Martlet Vs and joining the 7th Naval Fighter Wing. In December, it joined *Searcher*, covering a convoy to the United States, and after returning, the carrier joined the Home Fleet in 02/44, and the squadron covered attacks on the *Tirpitz*.

On 05/07/44, 898 Squadron was absorbed, making 24 aircraft. Re-embarked in *Searcher*, it covered the landings in the South of France, during which 167 sorties were flown, operating in the fighter-bomber role and providing reconnaissance in support of US Army units. The ship and the squadron then moved to the Aegean. Operating from Long Kesh and Ballyhalbert in Northern Ireland from October, the squadron re-equipped with 20 Wildcat VIs and re-embarked 09/02/45, augmented by 2 Firefly night-fighters from 746 Squadron, for operations off Norway, including a successful attack on the U-boat base at Kilbotn. *Searcher* sailed for Ceylon 06/45, but on arrival the war had ended and she returned home, the squadron disbanding on 09/10.

Battle honours: Diego Suarez, 1942; North Africa, 1942; Atlantic, 1943–44; South of France, 1944; Aegean, 1944; Norway, 1944–45; Arctic, 1945.

Identification markings: Initially individual letters, then 7A+, 6A+ and finally, S:A+.

Commanding officers:
Lt Cdr O.N. Bailey, 15/07/41
Lt (A) F.C. Furlong, RNVR, (temp) 10/08/41
Lt Cdr H.J.F. Lane, 09/09/41
Lt Cdr (A) I.L.F. Lowe, DSC, 07/09/42
Lt Cdr E.A. Shaw, 03/12/42
Lt Cdr (A) J. Cooper, DSC, RNVR, 25/10/43
Lt Cdr (A) G.R. Henderson, DSC, RNVR, 05/07/44

Lt Cdr R.A. Bird, 18/11/44
Lt Cdr (A) G.A.M. Flood, RNVR, 05/06/45

883 Squadron Formed as a fleet fighter squadron, 10/10/41, at Yeovilton, 883 was initially equipped with 6 Sea Hurricane Ibs, on 28/01/42, the squadron moved to Scotland to operate as part of RAF Fighter Command's 14 Group, initially from Fraserburgh and then from Peterhead. After returning to Fleet Air Arm control at Machrihanish, 11/05, the squadron embarked in *Avenger* on 16/06, for Arctic convoy duties, using Hatston as a shore base. The squadron was present when *Avenger* provided the first escort carrier for an Arctic convoy, PQ18, 09/42, and with 802 shot down 5 German aircraft, damaging another 17. The carrier was present during the North African landings, during which she was torpedoed, 15/11, and blew up, with the squadron aboard. Battle honours: Arctic, 1942; North Africa, 1942.

Commanding officers:
Capt W.H.C. Manson, RM, 10/10/41
Lt (A) P.W.V. Massey, DSC, 10/04/42

884 Squadron Formed as a fleet fighter squadron at Donibristle, 01/11/41, with 6 Fulmar IIs, which were replaced by hooked Spitfire Vs, 09/41. After working up the squadron joined Fighter Command's 13 Group on 22/03/42, initially at Turnhouse and then at Peterhead, before returning to Turnhouse. Rejoining the Fleet Air Arm at Hatston on 21/07, the squadron joined *Victorious* 2 days later, giving fighter cover to the Malta convoy, Operation Pedestal. After returning to the UK, and spending more time with the RAF at Skeabrae, the squadron re-embarked to provide fighter cover during Operation Torch, the landings in North Africa. It returned to Fighter Command, operating with 13 and 14 Groups from several Scottish bases before disbanding on 20/07/43, at Machrihanish.

Operation Pedestal, the convoy that marked the beginning of the end of the siege of Malta. Here two Sea Hurricanes of 885 Squadron are ranged aft on *Victorious* while an Albacore of 827 Squadron takes off from *Indomitable*. *Eagle* is next in line, with *Furious* just visible astern. (*IWM A15961*)

Battle honours: Malta Convoys, 1942; North Africa, 1942.
Identification markings not known.
Commanding officers:
Lt Cdr N.G. Hallett, 01/11/41
Lt Cdr R.T.B. Winstanley, 20/03/43

885 Squadron Formed at Dekheila as a fleet fighter unit on 01/03/41, with 6 Sea Gladiators and 3 Buffaloes, it embarked in *Eagle* on 03/03 for a week, returning as a shore-based squadron. It disbanded on 01/05. The squadron number was allocated to 775 10/41, but withdrawn almost immediately when it became the Royal Naval Fighter Flight, later 889 Squadron.

Reformed on 01/12/41, at Yeovilton as a fleet fighter unit, with 6 Sea Hurricane Ibs,

it eventually joined *Victorious* on 29/06/42, from Hatston, and provided distant fighter cover for 2 Arctic convoys, PQ17 and QP13, the following month. Afterwards, the squadron took part in Operation Pedestal, the Malta convoy of 08/42. On returning, it moved to Machrihanish, 09/42, training on Spitfire Vs until its own Seafire Ibs and IICs arrived. Still with just 6 aircraft, it joined *Formidable* on 28/10, providing fighter cover for the North African landings. Remaining with *Formidable* in the Mediterranean for the invasion of Sicily and the Salerno landings, the squadron returned to the UK on 18/10/43, when it disembarked to Lee-on-Solent, disbanding 15/11/43.

Reformed at Lee-on-Solent on 15/02/44, with 12 Seafire FIIIs and LIIIs, as part of the 3rd Naval Fighter Wing, it operated as part of the Air Spotting Pool of 34 Reconnaissance Wing, 2nd Tactical Air Force, after D-Day, having 20 Seafire LIIIs. In 07/44, while still at Lee-on-Solent, the squadron absorbed 886 and 887 Squadrons, before replacing its Seafires in 11/44 with 24 Hellcat Is and IIs. The squadron embarked in *Ruler* on 16/12, and early in 1945, sailed to join the British Pacific Fleet, initially to provide fighter cover over the fleet replenishment area. Time was spent ashore at Ponam, a USN airstrip at Manus in the Admiralty Islands, during which the strength was augmented first by a number of Corsairs, and then by Avengers to form a TBR flight. Although the Hellcats were equipped to carry rocket projectiles in 07/45, the war ended before these could be used, and the squadron disbanded while at Schofields, 27/09.

Battle honours: Malta Convoys, 1942; North Africa, 1942; Sicily, 1942; Normandy, 1944; Okinawa, 1945.

Identification markings: Sea Hurricane, single letters, eventually 7A+; Seafire, Ø6A+, D6A+ and 2A+; Hellcat, single letters then K8A+; Corsair single letters.

Commanding officers:
Lt Cdr J.N. Garnett, 01/03/41
Lt E.D.G. Lewin, 01/12/41
Lt Cdr (A) R.H.P. Carver, DSC, 02/02/42
Lt Cdr (A) S.L. Devonald, 15/02/44
Lt Cdr (A) J.R. Routley, RNVR, 07/11/44

886 Squadron A fleet fighter unit with 6 Fulmar IIs formed at Donibristle, 15/03/42, the squadron joined Fighter Command on 11/08, initially with 13 Group at Turnhouse, before moving to 14 Group at Peterhead 2 days later. Returned to the Fleet Air Arm on 07/10 at Stretton, spending the next 9 months at various shore stations in Scotland and Northern Ireland, during which it re-equipped with 9 Seafire LIICs, 03/43, and acquired a Swordfish flight of 6 aircraft in 06/43. The squadron embarked in *Attacker* on 19/06, sailing to the Mediterranean, providing fighter

and anti-submarine cover for the Salerno landings, with Swordfish detachments based ashore at Gibraltar and Paestum.

Returning to the UK at Burscough on 07/10, the squadron lost its Swordfish and joined the 3rd Naval Fighter Wing, receiving training in spotting and reconnaissance at Lee-on-Solent from 02/44, using Spitfires until 10 Seafire LIIIs could be delivered 03/44. After D-Day, it joined the Air Spotting Pool operated by 34 Reconnaissance Wing, 2nd Tactical Air Force, but also making offensive patrols and fighter sweeps. On 19/07, it was disbanded into 885 Squadron.

Battle honours: Salerno, 1943; Normandy, 1944.

Identification markings: Seafire, single letters, then 2A+; Swordfish, single letters; Spitfire 3A+.

Commanding officers:
Lt J.C.M. Harman, 15/03/42
Lt Cdr (A) R.H.H.L. Oliphant, 27/07/42
Lt Cdr P.E.I. Bailey, 28/10/43

887 Squadron Fleet fighter squadron formed at Lee-on-Solent, 01/05/42, with 6 Fulmar IIs, it re-equipped in December with Spitfire Vs while awaiting Seafire Ibs, in turn replaced by 9 Seafire IICs 03/43. The squadron embarked aboard *Unicorn* on 19/04, and 05/43 covered a Malta convoy. Disembarking to Belfast, the squadron re-embarked on 11/07/43 to return to the Mediterranean, providing fighter cover for the Salerno landings 09/43, with some aircraft detached ashore for a short period. The squadron joined the 24th Naval Fighter Wing 10/43, and on 06/07/44, embarked in *Indefatigable* and saw action off Norway, covering strikes against the battleship *Tirpitz*.

The squadron joined *Implacable* for the second half of 10/44, before returning to *Indefatigable* from Lee-on-Solent 21/11, and sailing to Ceylon to join the British Pacific Fleet. In 01/45, it covered attacks on

Sumatra, followed by the Sakishima Gunto 03/45–04/45, and then on Formosa, seeing action over the Japanese home islands shortly before the war ended. Disbanded postwar.

Battle honours: Atlantic, 1943; Salerno, 1943; Norway, 1944; Palembang, 1945; Okinawa, 1945; Japan, 1945.

Identification markings: Seafire, 1A+ 2A+, later P5A+, H5A+ and 111/S+.

Commanding officers:

Lt G.R. Callingham, 01/05/42

Lt Cdr D.W. Kirke, 29/08/42

Lt Cdr (A) B.F. Wiggington, DSC, RNVR, 19/01/44

Lt Cdr (A) A.J. Thomson, DSC, RNVR, 19/08/44

Lt Cdr N.G. Hallett, DSC & Bar, 14/05/45

888 Squadron Fleet fighter squadron formed at Lee-on-Solent, 01/11/41, with 6 Martlet Is, it re-equipped with 12 Martlet IIs before the end of the year. From Machrihanish, it embarked in *Formidable* on 04/02/42, sailing to the Indian Ocean for the invasion of Madagascar, during which detachments were sent ashore, mainly to Port Reitz. Returned home to Donibristle, 21/09, receiving Martlet IVs the following month. On 20/10, the squadron re-embarked for the North African landings, when it accounted for 2 enemy aircraft. Remaining in the Mediterranean for most of 1943, 888 covered the landings in Sicily and at Salerno, using shore bases, including Gibraltar and Ta Kali, as well as the carrier. Returning to Machrihanish on 18/10, the squadron disbanded at Yeovilton on 16/11.

Reformed at Burscough with 6 Hellcat II(PR)s on 10/06/44. On 09/09, the squadron joined *Rajah* for Ceylon, to be based ashore as a PR squadron. Joining *Indefatigable* on 24/12, it started 1945 operating over Sumatra, moving to *Empress* on 07/02 for PR operations at altitudes of up to 42,000 feet over the Kra Isthmus, Penang,

Phuket and Sumatra. Between this time and the end of the war, the squadron conducted similar duties operating from other carriers, including *Khedive*, *Emperor*, *Shah* and *Ameer*, as well as a further spell aboard *Empress*, with airfields in Ceylon, mainly Colombo Racecourse, as shore stations. Postwar, the squadron engaged in aerial surveys. Returning home to disband in 08/46.

Battle honours: North Africa, 1942; Sicily, 1943; Salerno, 1943.

Identification markings: Martlet, single letters, then Ø7A+; later 7A+.

Commanding officers:

Capt F.D.G. Bird, RM

Lt Cdr M. Hordern, 22/10/43

Lt Cdr (A) L. Mann, RNVR, 10/06/44

Lt Cdr (A) B.A. MacCaw, DSC, RNVR, 20/03/45

889 Squadron Formed out of the RN Fighter Flight 16/03/42, with 12 Fulmar IIs for the fighter defence of the Suez Canal, with early night fighter operations as part of the RAF's 234 and 252 Wings, and then, in Syria, 250 Wing. By the end of the year, the squadron returned to Egypt, and partially re-equipped with 7 Hawker Hurricane IIbs for operations over the Western Desert. The squadron disbanded on 28/02/43.

Reformed at Colombo Racecourse on 01/04/44, with 10 Seafire LIICs and FIIIs, joining *Atheling* on 13/05 for operations over the Bay of Bengal. Heavy losses due to accidents, including the loss of the CO, saw the squadron disband at Puttalam 11/07/44.

Reforming again on 01/06/45, at Woodvale with 6 Hellcat Is and II (PR)s, the squadron was intended for the British Pacific Fleet, but disbanded on 11/09, the day after embarking.

Identification markings: Single letters for Seafire; and possibly also for Hellcat.

Commanding officers:

Lt Cdr (A) A.R. Ramsey, DSC, RNVR, 16/03/42

Lt Cdr (A) R.E. Gardner, DSC, RNVR, 18/07/42
Lt Cdr (A) F.A.J. Pennington, RNZNVR, 01/04/44
Lt Cdr J.B. Edmundson, 24/04/44
Lt Cdr D.A.E. Holbrook, 11/06/44
Lt (A) N.D. Fisher, RNVR, 01/06/45

890 Squadron Formed on 15/06/42, Dartmouth, Nova Scotia, as a fighter squadron, no aircraft were received until it reached Norfolk, Virginia, on 26/06, when ex-USN F4F-3 Wildcats were obtained. After deck landing training aboard the USS *Charger* in late 08/42, the squadron received 6 Martlet IVs in 09/42, and joined *Battler* on 8/12 for the UK. Disembarking to Machrihanish on 08/01/43, and then to Donibristle, the squadron enlarged by absorbing 'A' Flight of 881 Squadron. It joined *Illustrious* on 14/06 for operations off Iceland and Norway, before joining Force H in the Mediterranean, and providing support for the Salerno landings in

Crest of 890 Squadron.

09/43. On returning to the UK, the squadron received 10 Wildcat Vs, and its personnel embarked in *London* to take passage to Ceylon, where the squadron disbanded at Puttalam on 01/08/44.
Battle honours: Salerno, 1943.
Identification markings: Individual letters.
Commanding officers:
Lt Cdr J.W. Sleigh, DSC, 15/06/42
Lt Cdr N.A. Bartlett, 04/11/43

891 Squadron Formed, 01/07/42, at Lee-on-Solent as a single seat fighter squadron with 6 Sea Hurricane Ibs. After working up at Charlton Horethorne and St Merryn, embarked aboard the *Dasher* on 15/10, re-equipped with 6 Sea Hurricane IIBs, and sailed to provide fighter cover over the North African invasion beaches. In December, 3 additional aircraft were received, by which time the ship was with the Home Fleet in northern waters, and the squadron was using Machrihanish and Hatston as shore bases. The squadron joined the ship to provide fighter cover for a convoy to Iceland, and a detachment of 3 aircraft was aboard when she blew up in the Firth of Clyde on 27/03/43, with heavy loss of life. The squadron disbanded 05/04/43.

Reformed on 01/06/45, at Eglinton, as a night fighter squadron, with 16 Hellcat II(NF)s, but disbanded at Nutts Corner 24/09.
Battle honours: North Africa, 1942.
Commanding officer:
Lt (A) M.J.S. Newman, 01/07/42
Lt (A) B.H.StA.H. Hurle-Hobbs, 12/03/43
Lt O.N. Bailey, 19/03/43
Lt Cdr N. Perrett, RNZNVR, 01/06/45

892 Squadron Formed on 15/07/42, as a fighter squadron at Norfolk, Virginia, with 6 Martlet IVs, it embarked in *Battler* on 08/12, sailing to the UK and disembarking to Machrihanish. On 19/02/43, the squadron joined *Archer* to provide fighter cover for Atlantic convoys, but in 06/43 its strength was reduced to 3 aircraft, and it disbanded aboard the ship 11/08, its remaining aircraft being transferred to 819 Squadron.

Reforming as a night fighter squadron with 16 Hellcat II(NF)s at Eglinton on 01/04/45, the squadron worked up at Drem before embarking in *Ocean* at the end of the year, and disbanding in spring 1946.
Battle honours: Atlantic, 1943.
Identification markings: Martlet, single letters; Hellcat, 05A+.
Commanding officers:
Lt (A) R.G. French, RNVR
Lt (A) K. Firth, RNVR, 13/12/42
Lt (A) J.G. Large, RNVR, 01/03/43
Maj J.O. Armour, RM, 01/04/45

893 Squadron Formed as a fighter squadron, Donibristle, 15/06/42, with 6 Martlet Is augmented by some Fulmars, the squadron was operating 10 Martlet IVs when it joined *Formidable* on 21/10. It provided fighter cover for the North African landings, Operation Torch, and then remained in the Mediterranean, using the carrier and a number of shore bases. It was at the invasion of Sicily 07/42, and the Salerno landings in 09/43. Returning home to Machrihanish on 18/10, the squadron re-embarked to cover an Arctic convoy, disbanding on 16/11, shortly after its return.
Battle honours: North Africa, 1942–43; Sicily, 1943; Salerno, 1943; Arctic, 1943.
Identification markings: Ø9A+, then 9A+.
Commanding officers:
Lt(A) R.G. French, RNVR, 15/06/42
Lt Cdr (A) R.B. Pearson, 12/09/43
Lt Cdr D.R.B. Cosh, RCNVR, 11/11/43

894 Squadron Officially formed at Norfolk, Virginia, on 15/08/42, as a fighter squadron with 6 Martlet IVs, it was one of the few FAA units to use USS *Wolverine*, a converted paddle steamer, for deck landing training. On 08/12, the squadron joined *Battler* for the UK, disembarking to Machrihanish on 08/01/43, before moving to Hatston on 18/02, where it re-equipped with 9 Seafire IICs. A detachment joined *Illustrious* on 02/07, to be followed by the rest of the squadron on 24/07, sailing with the ship to Malta 08/43. The squadron provided fighter cover for the Salerno landings 09/43, mainly operating from shore bases, including a captured airstrip. The squadron returned home to Henstridge in late 10/43, re-equipping with 12 Seafire FIIIs the following month as part of the 24th Naval Fighter Wing. After deck landing training aboard *Indefatigable* on 23/05, the squadron embarked in the ship on 24/07, covering operations over and off Norway, including 2 attacks on the battleship *Tirpitz*, and shooting down 2 German aircraft on 22/08.

In 11/43, ashore at Lee-on-Solent, the squadron re-equipped with 24 Seafire LIIIs, before joining *Implacable* for Ceylon on 21/11. Re-embarking in *Indefatigable*, it covered attacks on Sumatra 01/45, and the Sakishima Gunto 03–04/45, with Schofields as a shore station. The squadron was active over the Japanese home islands in the closing stages of the war. Disbanded, Gosport, 15/03/46.
Battle honours: Salerno, 1943; Norway, 1944; Palembang, 1945; Okinawa, 1945.
Identification markings: Seafires, single letters, later 1A+, P6A+, H6A+.
Commanding officers:
Lt Cdr (A) D.A. van Epps, RNVR, 15/08/42
Lt Cdr F.R.A. Turnbull, DSC, 17/06/43
Lt Cdr (A) C. Walker, 17/01/44
Lt Cdr (A) J. Crossman, DSO, RNVR, 22/11/44

895 Squadron Formed at Stretton as a fighter squadron on 15/11/42, with 6 Sea Hurricane Ibs, later replaced by 9 Seafire

IICs before disbanding at Turnhouse, on 30/06/43, providing fighter flights for 816 and 842 Squadrons.
Commanding officer:
Lt Cdr (A) J.W. Hedges, RNVR, 15/11/42

896 Squadron Formed as a fighter squadron, 15/09/42, at Norfolk, Virginia, with 6 Martlet IVs, working up included deck landing training on the USS *Charger*, before joining *Victorious* en route to the Pacific on 01/02/43. In 05/43, fighter operations were carried out over the Coral Sea, before helping to provide air cover for landings by the US Marines in the Solomons during 06/43, during which time Tontouta was used as a shore station. Returning to the UK at Eglinton on 26/09, the squadron re-equipped with 10 Wildcat Vs and then joined the 7th Naval Fighter Wing 11/43. It embarked in *Pursuer* on 26/11, and sailed to provide air cover for a Gibraltar convoy 02/44. In 04/44, the squadron provided air cover for an attack on the battleship *Tirpitz*, before being disbanded aboard *Pursuer* into 881 Squadron on 12/06/44.

Reformed on 09/01/45, at Wingfield, as a fighter squadron, with 24 Hellcat FB.IIs, it joined *Ameer* 24/04 for Ceylon. Fighter-bomber sorties were mounted over the Nicobar Islands in 07/45, before transferring to *Empress* on 17/07 to cover minesweeping operations off Phuket. The squadron returned home to disband on 19/12/45.
Battle honours: Norway, 1944; Atlantic, 1944; Normandy, 1944; Burma, 1945.
Identification markings: Martlet, single letters, then 8A+; Hellcat, 2A+, then B7+ and B8+.
Commanding officers:
Lt (A) S.G. Orr, DSC, RNVR, 15/09/42
Lt Cdr (A) B.H.C. Nation, 28/03/43
Lt Cdr (A) L.A. Hordern, DSC, RNVR, 25/10/43
Lt Cdr (A) R. Morris, RNVR, 09/01/45

LTZ G.J. Zegers de Beijil, DSC, RNethN, 14/07/45

897 Squadron Formed as a fighter squadron with 3 Seafire IICs and 3 Fulmar IIs, at Stretton, 01/08/42, the squadron disbanded into 801 and 880 Squadrons on 03/09.

Reformed at Stretton as a fighter squadron, 01/12/42, with 6 Sea Hurricane Ibs; these were replaced by 10 Seafire Ibs 03/43, which were replaced by Seafire LIICs 08/43. On 04/08, the squadron joined *Unicorn*, and sailed for the Mediterranean, providing fighter cover for the Salerno landings 09/43. On moving to Burscough 10/10, the squadron became part of the 3rd Naval Fighter Wing, training in tactical reconnaissance and bombardment spotting. In 03/44, it re-equipped with Spitfire LVBs, providing cover for the Normandy landings, during which it accounted for a Bf 109 and damaged a midget submarine. On 15/07/44, the squadron disbanded into 885 Squadron while at Lee-on-Solent.
Battle honours: Salerno, 1943; Normandy, 1944.
Identification markings: Seafires, 4A+.
Commanding officers:
Capt R.C. Hay, DSC, RM, 01/08/42
Lt Cdr (A) W.C. Simpson, DSC, 01/12/42

898 Squadron Officially formed at Norfolk, Virginia, on 15/10/42, as a fighter squadron with 6 Martlet IVs, it practised deck landing aboard USS *Charger* at Brunswick in 01/43, joining *Victorious* on 03/02, on her way to the Pacific. Reaching the Pacific via the Panama Canal, the squadron operated over the Coral Sea 05/43, and 06/43 helped cover the US Marines landing on the Solomons. On its return to the UK, disembarking to Eglinton 26/09, the squadron re-equipped with 10 Wildcat Vs and became part of the 7th Naval Fighter Wing. On 09/12, it embarked in *Searcher* to cover for North Atlantic convoys, mainly using Hatston as a shore station.

Maintainers with a Seafire of 897 Squadron aboard *Stalker*. The author's father is crouching. (*via S.H. Wragg*)

In 04/44, fighter cover was provided for an attack on the battleship *Tirpitz*, and then for anti-shipping strikes off Norway 05/44–06/44, accounting for 4 Bv138s and a Fw200. In 06/44, the squadron provided cover for a Gibraltar convoy, before disbanding into 882 on 05/07/44.

Reformed at Wingfield, near Cape Town, as a fighter squadron with 24 Hellcat IIs on 01/01/45. Joining *Attacker* 23/06, it sailed for Ceylon, where its aircraft were fitted with rocket projectiles in 07/45. Too late for further action, the squadron left its aircraft in Ceylon and returned home in *Pursuer*, disbanding 12/12/45.
Battle honours: Norway, 1944; Atlantic, 1944.
Identification markings: Martlets/Wildcats, 7A+; Hellcats, 3A+, B9A+ and B0A+.
Commanding officers:

Capt A.J. Wright, RM, 15/10/42
Lt Cdr (A) I.L.F. Lowe, DSC, 24/11/42
Lt Cdr (A) G.R. Henderson, DSC, RNVR, 20/10/43
Lt Cdr (A) R.W. Kearsley, 01/01/45

899 Squadron Formed out of surplus aircraft and personnel from 880 Squadron at Hatston 15/12/42, with 12 Seafire IICs as a fighter squadron, it moved to Machrihanish in 02/43, before joining *Indomitable* in 11/03. The carrier sailed to the Mediterranean in 06/43. The squadron covered the invasion of Sicily, but had to disembark at Gibraltar as *Indomitable* was damaged by an aerial torpedo. The squadron covered the landings at Salerno from *Hunter*, with some of its aircraft deployed ashore. On returning to the UK to Ballyhalbert 13/10, the squadron re-equipped twice, first with 20 Spitfire VBs, 12/43, and then with Seafire LIIIs in 02/44.

After deck landing training using *Argus*, the squadron joined *Khedive* on 01/04, and 07/44 sailed for the Mediterranean, to cover the Allied landings in the South of France 08/44, when more than 200 sorties were flown. Shore targets and shipping were attacked at Crete and Rhodes, 09/44, before returning to the UK, initially to Long Kesh 12/10, and then Ayr 23/11. At Ayr, the squadron was given a bombardment course, and increased its strength to 24 aircraft before embarking in *Chaser*, 25/01/45, and sailing to Ceylon in 02/45. The squadron saw no further action, becoming a Seafire pool at Schofields in 04/45, and gradually losing its pilots as replacements to other squadrons. Eventually, after service as an Operational Training Unit for RAAF personnel who had volunteered to transfer to become the nucleus of an Australian Fleet Air Arm, it disbanded 18/09/45.
Battle honours: Sicily, 1943; Salerno, 1943; South of France, 1944; Aegean, 1944.
Identification markings: 6A+, then 2A+, and later K:A+ and C:A+.
Commanding officers:
Lt Cdr (A) R.F. Walker, RNVR, 15/12/42
Lt Cdr (A) R.B. Howarth, RNVR, 02/08/43
Lt Cdr (A) G. Dennison, RNVR, 01/11/44

1700 Squadron Formed as an amphibian bomber reconnaissance squadron on 01/11/44, at Lee-on-Solent, with 6 Sea Otters, it joined *Khedive*, 08/01/45, sailing to southern India. Disembarking to Sulur 08/02, the squadron added some Walruses, since the Sea Otter had still to be cleared for deck landing. After moving to Ceylon, the squadron's aircraft embarked in a number of escort carriers for mine sweeping and search and rescue duties, including *Stalker, Hunter, Emperor, Ameer, Attacker* and *Shah*, as well as *Khedive*. The squadron moved ashore once the war ended, but

continued to operate from Ceylon until disbanded into 733 Squadron on 03/06/46.
Battle honours: Burma, 1945.
Commanding officer:
Lt (A) A.B. Edgar, RNVR, 01/11/44

1701 Squadron Amphibian bomber reconnaissance squadron formed at Lee-on-Solent, 01/02/45, with 6 Sea Otters. It joined *Begum* 17/04 for the Far East, becoming the mother squadron for search and rescue units attached to Mobile Naval Air Bases, or MONABs. On the cessation of hostilities, the squadron regrouped at Kai Tak 11/45, and disbanded in 1946.
Commanding officer:
Lt (A) L.F. Plant, RNVR, 01/02/45

1702 Squadron A special service squadron with 6 Sea Otters formed at Lee-on-Solent, 01/06/45, originally for service in the Pacific. Postwar, deployed to the Mediterranean, eventually disbanding in late 1946.
Commanding officer:
Lt (A) O.G.W. Hutchinson, RNVR, 01/06/45

1703 Squadron Formed on 01/08/45, just before the war ended, with 6 Sea Otters at Lee-on-Solent, it suffered considerable difficulty with its aircraft and their engines, and was disbanded 18/09.
Commanding officer:
Lt (A) K.A. Chare, RNVR, 01/08/45

1770 Squadron Fighter squadron formed at Yeovilton, 10/09/43, with 12 Firefly Is, it moved to Grimsetter 14/12, and then to nearby Hatston 15/02/44. Joining *Indefatigable* on 18/05, it took part in operations against the battleship *Tirpitz* in 07/44, attacking auxiliary vessels and shore-based gun positions. Further operations off Norway, including another attack on *Tirpitz*, were covered by the squadron before *Indefatigable* sailed to the Far East. The squadron joined attacks on the oil and port installations on Sumatra 04/45. It also operated over the Sakishima Gunto 03/45–05/45, and later against Formosa. Disembarking to Schofields 05/06, the squadron joined the 7th Carrier Air Group, but disbanded shortly after the war ended, 30/09/45.

Battle honours: Norway, 1944; Palembang, 1945; Okinawa, 1945.

Identification markings: 4A+.

Commanding officers:

Lt Cdr (A) I.P. Godfrey, RNVR, 10/09/43

Maj V.B.G. Cheesman, DSO, MBE, DSC, RM, 05/02/44

Lt Cdr (A) D.J. Holmes, 22/06/45

1771 Squadron Fighter squadron with 12 Firefly Is formed at Yeovilton, 01/02/44, and operated from Burscough and Machrihanish, with deck landing training on *Trumpeter* and *Ravager* before joining *Implacable* on 22/09. In 10/44, the squadron flew reconnaissance over Norway, including the *Tirpitz* anchorage, followed by strike sorties in 11/44, sinking a troopship and damaging four other ships. *Implacable* sailed for the Far East in 03/45, joining the British Pacific Fleet, with the squadron joining attacks on Truk, in the Caroline Islands, 06/45. As part of the 8th Carrier Air Group, it operated against the Japanese home islands shortly before the war ended. Disbanded at Nowra, near Sydney, 16/10/45.

Battle honours: Norway, 1944; Japan, 1945.

Identification markings: 4A+, then 270–281/N.

Commanding officers:

Lt Cdr (A) H.M. Ellis, DFC, DSC, 01/02/44

Lt Cdr (A) W.J.R. MacWhirter, DSC, 09/03/45

1772 Squadron Formed at Burscough as a fighter squadron with 12 Firefly Is, 01/05/44. Deck landing training was carried out using *Empress* 11/44. The squadron's aircraft were re-allocated to 766 Squadron, and new Fireflies with long-range tanks replaced them, ready for the squadron to join *Ruler* 20/01/45. Disembarking to Schofields, 18/03, the squadron embarked in *Indefatigable* 07/07, joining the British Pacific Fleet in time for attacks against the Japanese home islands. The squadron dropped supplies on PoW camps once the war ended. Disbanded, Portsmouth, 10/03/46.

Battle honours: Japan, 1945.

Identification markings: Single letters, then 4A+, 270–281/S.

Commanding officers included:

Lt Cdr (A) A.H.D. Gough, 01/05/44

Lt Cdr (A) L.C. Wort, DSC, RNVR, 03/11/45

1790 Squadron Formed as a night fighter squadron at Burscough, 01/01/45, with 12 Firefly Is, replaced 05/45 by Firefly INFs fitted with ASH, the US air-to-surface vessel radar. Joined *Vindex* 24/06 for Australia, arriving as the war ended. Disbanded at Devonport, 03/06/46.

Identification markings: 4A+.

Commanding officer:

Lt Cdr (A) J.H. Kneale, RNVR, 01/01/45

1791 Squadron Formed, 15/03/45, as a night fighter squadron with 12 Firefly INFs at Lee-on-Solent, and joined *Puncher* for deck landing training 11/06, but VJ-Day intervened. The squadron disbanded at Burscough 23/09/45.

Identification markings: Single letters.

Commanding officer:

Lt Cdr H.J. Hunter, RCNVR

1792 Squadron Night fighter squadron formed at Lee-on-Solent, 15/05/45, with 12 Firefly INFs, it worked in Scotland and joined *Ocean* postwar for the Mediterranean.

Identification markings: Single letters.

Commanding officer:

Lt Cdr (A) S. Dixon-Child, RNVR

1820 Squadron Formed 01/04/44, at Brunswick as a dive bomber squadron with 9 Helldivers, the squadron worked up at Squantum before joining *Arbiter* for passage to the UK 05/07. The aircraft type failed to meet expectations, and the squadron lost several aircraft with their crews in accidents, with no less than 3 aircraft failing to pull out of vertical dives. Disbanded at Burscough, 16/12/44.

Identification markings: 4A+.
Commanding officer:
Lt Cdr (A) H.I.A. Swayne, DSC

1830 Squadron Formed at Quonset Point, 01/06/43, as a fighter squadron with 10 Corsair Is for work up, but replaced by Corsair IIs 08/43. On 09/10, the squadron embarked in *Slinger* for passage to the UK, disembarking to Belfast 01/11, moving to Stretton 2 days later. Squadron strength was increased to 14 aircraft in early 12/43 by absorbing aircraft from 1831 Squadron, becoming part of the 15th Naval Fighter Wing. Embarked in *Illustrious* on 09/12, working up on the Firth of Clyde while using Machrihanish as a shore station. In early 01/44, the ship sailed for Ceylon to join the Eastern Fleet, where initially the squadron used China Bay as a shore station, disembarking there 28/01. Fighter sweeps over the Bay of Bengal were followed by attacks on shore installations and shipping at Sabang 04/44, and 05/44 at Sourabaya, and the Andaman Islands 06/44, before returning to Sabang 07/44.

Illustrious refitted at Durban from mid-08–mid-10/44, and the squadron increased to 18 aircraft while based ashore at Wingfield. Returning to Ceylon on 02/11, it covered attacks on oil refineries and harbours on Sumatra in 12/44, and 01/45, before the carrier joined the British Pacific Fleet. In 03/45–04/45 operations were carried out against airfields in the Sakishima Gunto. Serious damage to *Illustrious* by a near miss by a Kamikaze, resulted in her withdrawal 14/04, and return to the UK via Australia. The squadron disbanded, 28/07/45, on arrival in the UK.

Battle honours: Sabang, 1944; Palembang, 1945; Okinawa, 1945.
Identification markings: 7A+, then A7A+, then 111–128/Q.
Commanding officers:
Lt Cdr D.B. M Fiddes, DSO, 01/06/43
Lt Cdr (A) A.M. Tritton, DSC, RNVR, 18/12/43

1831 Squadron Formed Quonset Point, 01/07/43, as a fighter squadron with 10 Corsair Is, after working up at Quonset and Brunswick, the squadron embarked in *Trumpeter* 06/10, disembarking to Belfast 01/11, reaching Stretton 2 days later. It disbanded 10/12, after becoming part of the 15th Naval Fighter Wing, and its personnel and aircraft were divided between the other 2 squadrons in the wing, 1830 and 1833.

Reformed at Brunswick with 18 Corsair IVs 01/11/44, 1831 worked up at Brunswick and Norfolk before joining *Pursuer* 01/02/45. The squadron disembarked to Eglinton 18/02. Its strength was increased to 21 aircraft in 05/45 before it joined the light fleet carrier *Glory* in 11/05. The ship sailed to the Far East to become part of the British Pacific Fleet's 16th Carrier Air Group, disembarking to Katukurunda 15/07. The squadron saw no action before the war ended. Disbanded, 1946.

Identification markings: 1V7+, then Y8A+, then 112/Y+.
Commanding officers:
Lt Cdr H.P. Allingham, RNR, 01/07/43
Lt Cdr R.W.M. Walsh, 01/11/44
Lt (A) R.W.H. Boyns, RNVR, 02/08/45

1832 Squadron Formed 15/08/43, at Eglinton with 10 Wildcat V fighters, it moved first to Speke, near Liverpool, 20/09.

A Corsair is unhooked aboard a carrier. (*Vought Aircraft*)

Its role was the creation of 4 aircraft fighter flights that could be attached to TBR squadrons embarked in escort carriers. The first of 10 such flights embarked in *Fencer* 20/11, and a pattern emerged of the flights being absorbed into TBR squadrons to which they were attached. The squadron moved to Stretton 09/12, and returned to Eglinton 02/02/44, where it absorbed the remaining aircraft and personnel of 878 Squadron, before disbanding 01/06/44.
Battle honours: Norway, 1944; Atlantic, 1944; Arctic, 1944.
Identification markings: Single letters.
Commanding officers:
Lt Cdr (A) T.W. Harrington, 15/08/43
Lt Cdr M. Hordern, 15/12/43

1833 Squadron Fighter squadron formed at Quonset Point with 10 Corsair Is, 15/06/43.

These aircraft were replaced by Corsair IIs during work up at Brunswick. On 17/10, it embarked in *Trumpeter*, reaching Belfast 01/11, before moving on to Stretton 03/11. The transfer of aircraft from 1831 Squadron raised the strength to 14, and after deck landing training using *Ravager*, the squadron became part of the 15th Naval Fighter Wing and joined *Illustrious* 22/12. Sailing to join the Eastern Fleet, the squadron initially used China Bay as a shore station, disembarking there for the first time on 28/01/44. Fighter sweeps over the Bay of Bengal were followed by attacks on shore installations and shipping at Sabang 04/44, and 05/44 at Sourabaya, and the Andaman Islands 06/44, before returning to Sabang in 07/44.

While the carrier refitted at Durban from mid-08–mid-10/44, the squadron grew to 18 aircraft while based ashore at Wingfield. Returning to Ceylon 02/11, the squadron covered attacks on oil refineries and harbours on Sumatra in 12/44, and 01/45, before the carrier joined the British Pacific Fleet. During 03–04/45, operations were carried out against airfields in the Sakishima Gunto, but serious damage to *Illustrious* from a near miss by a Kamikaze resulted in her withdrawal 14/04. Reaching Australia, the squadron left its aircraft ashore and its personnel re-embarked to return to the UK, where the squadron disbanded on 28/07/45, on arrival.

Battle honours: Sabang, 1944; Palembang, 1945; Okinawa, 1945.

Identification markings: 6A+, then A6A+, then 129–147/Q.

Commanding officers:
Lt Cdr (A) H.A. Monk, DSM and Bar, 15/07/43
Lt Cdr: N.S. Hanson, DSC, RNVR, 20/03/44

1834 Squadron Fighter squadron formed 15/07/43, at Quonset Point, with 10 Corsair Is while it worked up, including deck landing training on the USS *Charger*. The aircraft were replaced by Corsair IIs before joining *Khedive*, 01/11, for the UK, disembarking to Maydown 16/11, and quickly moved on to Speke, back to Maydown 22/11, before finally settling at Stretton 20/12. It joined the 47th Naval Fighter Wing with 14 aircraft in 01/44, and 01/02 moved to Machrihanish ready for deck landing training on *Ravager*, before joining *Victorious* 12/02. After providing fighter cover for attacks on the battleship *Tirpitz*, the squadron sailed with the carrier to the Far East in 06/44, disembarking to Colombo Racecourse 07/07. Between 07/44 and 01/45, the squadron covered attacks against Sumatra, before joining the British Pacific Fleet and becoming involved in operations against the Sakishima Gunto 03/45–05/45.

As part of the 1st Carrier Air Group, with 18 Corsair IVs, the squadron flew against targets in the Tokyo area, with the ship sailing to Australia after the war ended. Postwar, the squadron left its aircraft at Nowra, near Sydney, returning home aboard the carrier to disband on arrival, 31/10.

Battle honours: Norway, 1944; Sabang, 1944; Palembang, 1945; Okinawa, 1945; Japan, 1945.

Identification markings: 9A+, then 7A+, and eventually 111–128/P.

Commanding officers:
Lt Cdr (A) A.M. Tritton, DSC, RNVR
Lt Cdr (A) P.N. Charlton, DFC, 23/12/43
Lt Cdr (A) R.D.B. Hopkins, 10/10/44
Lt Cdr J.G. Baldwin, DSC, 26/04/45

1835 Squadron Fighter squadron formed Quonset Point, 15/08/43, with 10 Corsair Is, soon replaced by Corsair IIs. Instead of returning to the UK and becoming part of the 47th Naval Fighter Wing, it disbanded on 23/11 at Brunswick, Maine.

Reformed at Brunswick 01/12/44, with 18 Corsair IVs, although these remained in the United States. On arriving at Eglinton 21/04, the squadron was equipped with 18 Corsair IIIs, which passed to 1837 in 06/44 when the squadron reverted to the Corsair IV. The squadron was earmarked for the 17th Carrier Air Group of the British Pacific Fleet, but the war ended before this could happen. Disbanded, Nutts Corner, 03/09/45.

Identification markings: 5A+, 1V11+, and finally single letters.

Commanding officers:
Lt Cdr (A) M.S. Godson, 15/08/43
Lt Cdr (A) T.J.A. King-Joyce, 01/12/44

1836 Squadron Fighter squadron formed Quonset Point, 15/08/43, with 10 Corsair Is, which were replaced with 18 Corsair IIs at Brunswick in 11/43. Joined *Atheling* 18/12, arriving in Belfast 09/01/44, before moving

The FAA often hit hard at the Japanese. Here aircraft from 1833 Squadron, from *Illustrious*, attack an oil refinery on Palembang. (*FAAM CAMP/66*)

to Burscough the following day. Joining the 47th Naval Fighter Wing, it reduced to 14 aircraft and joined *Victorious* 08/03. After providing fighter cover for attacks on the battleship *Tirpitz* 04/44, the squadron sailed with the carrier to the Far East 06/44, disembarking to Colombo Racecourse 07/07. Between 07/44, and 01/45, the squadron covered attacks against Sumatra, before joining the British Pacific Fleet and becoming involved in operations against the Sakishima Gunto 03/45–05/45. Part of the 1st Carrier Air Group, with 18 Corsair IVs, the squadron joined operations against targets in the Tokyo area, with the ship sailing to Australia after the war. Postwar, the squadron left its aircraft at Nowra, near Sydney, and returned home aboard the carrier, disbanding on arrival 31/10/45.

Battle honours: Norway, 1944; Sabang, 1944; Palembang, 1945; Okinawa, 1945; Japan, 1945.

Identification markings: 3A+, 8A+, T8A+, then 131–150/P.

Commanding officers included:

Lt Cdr (A) C.C. Tomkinson, RNVR, 18/08/43

Lt Cdr J.B. Edmundson, DSC, 27/03/45

Lt Cdr (A) D.K. Evans, RNZNVR, 14/06/45

1837 Squadron Fighter squadron formed with 10 Corsair Is at Quonset Point, 01/09/43: the aircraft were replaced by 14 Corsair IIs at Brunswick from 01/10. Squadron embarked in *Begum* on 19/01/44, disembarking to Burscough, 01/02, then moved to Stretton 12/02. Becoming the sole squadron in the 6th Naval Fighter Wing, it joined *Atheling* on 26/02, sailing for Ceylon, where it went ashore to the RAF station at Minneriya 13/04. After deck landing training using *Unicorn* on 05/06, the squadron embarked in *Illustrious* on 19/06, from which it saw action over the Andaman Islands and then in 07/44 provided fighter cover for for

a raid on Sabang. On 14/08, the squadron transferred to *Victorious*, but disbanded into 1834 and 1836 Squadrons 09/09.

Reformed 01/07/45, at Eglinton with 22 Corsairs IIIs, mainly from 1835 Squadron. Disbanded 18/08, Nutts Corner.

Battle honours: Sabang, 1945.

Identification markings: 7A+, but single letters once reformed.

Commanding officers:

Lt Cdr (A) A.J. Sewell, DSC, RNVR, 01/09/43

Lt Cdr R. Pridham-Wippell, 17/10/43

Lt Cdr (A) R. Tebble, RNVR, 01/07/45

1838 Squadron Formed as a fighter squadron at Brunswick, 01/10/43, with 10 Corsair Is, replaced with 14 Corsair IIs before joining1837 aboard *Begum* on 19/01. The squadron disembarked to Burscough, via Machrihanish, on 01/02/44, it remained with 1837 and embarked in *Atheling* 26/02 for Ceylon, disembarking to Minneriya on 13/04. *Unicorn* provided deck landing training on 06/06. Joined *Victorious* on 23/07 for the raid on Sabang, returning ashore 27/07 to Colombo Racecourse. The squadron re-embarked in *Atheling* 25/08, sailing to South Africa, disembarking to Wingfield, disbanding into 1830 and 1833 Squadrons, 13/09.

Battle honours: Sabang, 1945.

Commanding officers:

Lt Cdr (A) F.B.P. Sanderson, RNVR, 01/10/43

Lt Cdr (A) M.S. Godson, 28/06/44

1839 Squadron Formed as a fighter squadron at Eglinton, 15/11/43, with 10 Hellcat Is, it joined the 5th Naval Fighter Wing and embarked in *Begum* on 26/02/44, and sailed for southern India, disembarking to Ulunderpet on 07/04. Moved to Colombo Racecourse 23/06, and 25/07 embarked in *Indomitable*, using China Bay and Nowra as shore stations. During July, the squadron covered attacks on Sumatra, and also undertook photographic recon-naissance. It returned to operations over Sumatra in 12/44, and 01/45, before the carrier joined the British Pacific Fleet, when the squadron was in action over the Sakashima Gunto. Absorbed 1840 Squadron on 27/04/45, raising its strength to 18 aircraft and 06/45, the 5th NFW was absorbed into the 11th Carrier Air Group. As the war ended, the squadron was aboard the carrier ready to resume operations, but instead the ship was diverted to Hong Kong. Disbanded postwar, 30/11/45, on returning to the UK.

Battle honours: Palembang, 1945; Okinawa, 1945.

Identification markings: Single letters, then 5A+ and R5A+, before becoming 111–126/W.

Commanding officers:

Lt Cdr (A) D.M. Jerram, 15/11/43

Lt Cdr S.F.F. Shotton, DSC, RNR, 08/09/44

Lt Cdr (A) B.H.C. Nation, 26/04/45

1840 Squadron Formed at Burscough, 01/03/44, with 10 Hellcat I fighters, the squadron worked up at Stretton and in Northern Ireland, with deck landing training aboard *Trumpeter* 06/44, before joining *Indefatigable* on 25/06 with 20 aircraft. Disembarking to Machrihanish 02/07, the squadron moved to Hatston 06/07, which became its shore station while it operated in turn from *Furious* on 09/07, *Formidable* on 31/07, and *Indefatigable* on 07/08 and 15/08. While aboard *Furious*, the squadron covered an attack on the battleship *Tirpitz*, and repeated this while in *Indefatigable*, by which time it also included a number of Hellcat IIs. While at Eglinton in 09/44 and 10/44, the squadron joined the 3rd Naval Fighter Wing, before joining *Speaker* on 16/12. It re-equipped at Ayr on 31/12 with Hellcat IIs, before re-embarking and sailing to provide cover for the British Pacific Fleet's auxiliaries. Disbanded into 1839 Squadron, 27/04/45.

Battle honours: Norway, 1944; Okinawa, 1945.

Identification markings: Single letters, then K7A+.

Commanding officers:

Lt Cdr (A) A.R. Richardson, RNZNVR, 01/03/44

Lt Cdr (A) B.H.C. Nation, 12/09/44

1841 Squadron Formed as a fighter squadron at Brunswick, 01/03/44, with a mixture of 18 Corsairs Is, IIs and IIIs, but later standardising on Corsair IIs before joining *Smiter* 05/06. The squadron reached the UK 21/06, with a detachment at Speke while the rest of the squadron was at Ayr, before regrouping aboard *Formidable* on 26/06, with Hatston as the main shore station. During 07/44 and 08/44, the squadron was part of the fighter escort for attacks on the battleship *Tirpitz*. Becoming part of the 6th Naval Fighter Wing in 09/44, it sailed with the carrier to the Far East, being based ashore briefly at Gibraltar and Dekheila before arriving to disembark to Puttalam, Ceylon, 08/02/45.

Re-equipped with Corsair IVs, the squadron saw action over the Sakashima Gunto in 04/45 and 05/45, before the wing merged into the 2nd Carrier Air Group 06/45. Towards the end of the war, the squadron saw action around Tokyo, with 1 of its pilots, Lt R.H. Gray, DSC, RCNVR, being killed while attacking a Japanese destroyer under heavy fire, for which he was awarded a posthumous Victoria Cross. After VJ-Day, the squadron lost its aircraft and its personnel returned to the UK aboard *Victorious*, disbanding on arrival on 31/10/45.

Battle honours: Norway, 1944; Okinawa, 1945; Japan, 1945.

Identification markings: 7A+, then 111–128/X.

Commanding officer:

Lt Cdr (A) R.L. Bigg-Wither, DSC & Bar

1842 Squadron Fighter squadron formed at Brunswick, 01/04/44, with 18 Corsair IIIs, which were replaced with Corsair IIs on arrival in the UK aboard *Rajah* 13/07. The squadron was based ashore at Stretton and then Eglinton, before joining the 6th Naval Fighter Wing and embarking in *Formidable* 07/08. Covering attacks on the *Tirpitz* in 08/44, the squadron lost several aircraft. The ship sailed to the Far East, and en route the squadron had detachments at Gibraltar and Dekheila for some time in late 1944 through to mid-01/45.

After arriving in the Far East, the squadron re-equipped with Corsair IVs in 03/45, and used these on operations over the Sakishima Gunto. Becoming part of the 2nd Carrier Air Group in 06/45, it took part in operations in the Tokyo area, with 2 pilots shot down inside a Japanese harbour who were rescued by an American destroyer. After the war ended, the squadron left its aircraft in Australia and its personnel embarked for the UK in *Victorious*, disbanding on arrival 31/10/45.
Battle honours: Norway, 1944; Okinawa, 1945; Japan, 1945.
Identification markings: Single letters, single numbers, then 129–146X.
Commanding officers:
Lt Cdr (A) A.McD Garland, RNVR, 01/04/44
Lt Cdr (A) D.G. Parker, DSC, RNVR, 27/04/45

1843 Squadron Formed at Brunswick, 01/05/44, with 18 Corsair III fighters, which were replaced with Corsair IIs on arrival in the UK aboard *Trouncer* on 24/08. Based at Eglinton and Ayr, the squadron had deck landing training aboard *Patroller* 21–23/12, before joining *Arbiter* on 14/02/45, with 24 aircraft as part of the 10th Naval Fighter Wing. Sailing to Australia, the squadron became part of the 3rd Carrier Air Group, but saw no action before the war ended.

Leaving its aircraft in Australia, the personnel returned home in a merchant vessel. Disbanded on arrival, 10/12/45.
Identification markings: 1V11+.
Commanding officers:
Lt Cdr (A) D.K. Evans, RNZNVR, 01/05/44
Lt Cdr (A) D.F.V. Davis, RCNVR, (temp), 20/09/44
Maj P.P. Nelson-Gracie, RM, 14/10/44
Lt Cdr (A) P.C.S. Chilton, 11/02/45

1844 Squadron Formed at Eglinton, 15/12/43; with 10 Hellcat I fighters, the squadron embarked in *Begum* on 26/02/44, for the Far East, disembarking to Ulunderpet in southern India 07/04. It moved to Colombo Racecourse on 07/06, then to China Bay 5 days later, with deck landing training on *Unicorn* mid-06/44. It joined *Indomitable* on 25/07, and 08/44 provided fighter cover for attacks on Indaroeng and Emmahaven in Sumatra, as well as photographic reconnaissance. The same roles were carried out during attacks on Sigli in 09/44 and the Nicobar Islands in 10/44. Returning to China Bay on 21/10, the squadron re-embarked on

Crest of 1844 Squadron.

01/12 for operations over Sumatra, attacking oil installations at Belawan Deli. During 01/45, the squadron was involved in attacks on airfields at Pangkalan Brandan, and oil refineries at Palembang.

At Nowra 02/45, the squadron re-equipped with 18 Hellcat IIs, before re-embarking on 27/02 for raids on the Sakashima Gunto and Formosa. Plans for attacks on the Japanese home islands were abandoned as the war ended. Aircraft were left behind at Nowra while the squadron's personnel returned home on the carrier, so that it disbanded on arrival on 30/11/45.

Battle honours: Palembang, 1945; Okinawa, 1945.

Identification markings: 6A+, then R6A+, then 131-146, 162-163/W.

Commanding officers:

Lt Cdr (A) T.W. Harrington, 15/12/43

Lt Cdr (A) M.S. Godson, 09/09/44

Lt Cdr P.J.P. Leckie, 12/05/45

1845 Squadron Formed at Brunswick, 01/06/44, with 18 Corsair III fighters. It joined *Puncher* on 30/08, disembarking to Eglinton on 18/09, and joining the 10th Naval Fighter Wing. After moving to Ayr on 23/10, it returned to Eglinton on 06/11 to re-equip with 24 Corsair IVs, and joined *Slinger* on 19/12. Sailing to join the British Pacific Fleet, the squadron was disbanded on 05/04/45, and its aircraft and personnel absorbed into squadrons aboard *Formidable* and *Victorious*.

Identification markings: 1V7+, then 7A+, and then 139+.

Commanding officer:

Lt Cdr (A) D.G. Parker, RNVR

1846 Squadron Formed at Brunswick, 01/07/44, with 18 Corsair III fighters. It joined *Ranee* on 18/10, disembarking to Eglinton 02/11, when it expanded to 24 aircraft by absorbing part of the disbanded

1848 Squadron. In 02/45, it re-equipped with Corsair IVs, having joined *Colossus* 02/01/45. The carrier sailed to the Far East in 02/45, and its aircraft became part of the 14th Carrier Air Group when this formed in 06/45 at Tambaram. The squadron was too late for action, and eventually disbanded at Gosport 23/07/46.

Identification markings: 1V4+, then 111-131/D:C.

Commanding officers:

Lt Cdr (A) D.G. Brooker, RNVR, 01/07/44

Lt Cdr (A) S.L. Devonald, DFC, 04/04/45

1847 Squadron Formed, 01/02/44, at Eglinton as a fighter squadron with 8 of its 12 pilots from the Royal Netherlands Navy, and 10 Hellcats. It was absorbed into 1840 Squadron while still at Eglinton 20/05.

Identification markings: Single letters.

Commanding officer:

Lt Cdr (A) H. Colville-Stewart, RNVR

1848 Squadron Formed at Brunswick, 01/07/44, with 12 (later 18) Corsair I and II fighters, and joining *Ranee* on 18/10 for the UK. Disembarking to Machrihanish on 03/11, the squadron disbanded on 21/11, with its aircraft and pilots being shared between 1843, 1845 and 1846 Squadrons.

Identification markings: 1V9+.

Commanding officer:

Lt Cdr (A) E.J. Clarke, RNVR

1849 Squadron Formed at Brunswick, 01/08/44, with 18 Corsair III fighters, which were replaced by Corsair IVs before joining *Reaper* on 22/11. The squadron suffered from a high accident rate and disbanded on arrival in the UK on 06/12, with its aircraft and personnel being shared between 1845 and 1850 Squadrons.

Identification markings: 1V11+.

Commanding Officer:

Lt Cdr (A) P.C.S. Chilton

1850 Squadron Formed at Brunswick, 01/08/44, with 18 Corsair III fighters, replaced with Corsair IVs before joining *Reaper* on 23/11. On arrival in the UK it expanded to 24 aircraft with the addition of part of the disbanded 1849. After working up at Belfast, Eglinton and Ayr, the squadron undertook deck landing training on the new light fleet carrier, *Venerable* on 10/02/45, before joining her sister ship, *Vengeance* on 25/02/45. Sailing for the Far East to join the British Pacific Fleet, the squadron went ashore to Tambaram and Coimbatore in southern India on 11/06 for weapon training and dive bombing practice, becoming part of the 13th Carrier Air Group. Too late for the war, it disbanded at Gosport, 12/08/46.

Identification markings: Single letters, then N5A+.

Commanding officer:

Lt Cdr (A) M. Hordern

1851 Squadron Formed at Brunswick, 01/09/44, with 18 Corsair III fighters, replaced with Corsair IVs after deck landing training on USS *Charger* and before joining *Thane* on 28/12. Disembarking to Belfast 14/01/45, the squadron missed her being torpedoed by *U-482* in the Clyde the next day, although the ship was saved. Joining *Venerable* on 06/03, it spent some time in the Mediterranean using Hal Far as a shore station from 20/03. Eventually reaching Tambaram in southern India on 07/07, the squadron became part of the 15th Carrier Air Group, but too late to see action. Disbanded postwar.

Identification markings: 1V7+ , R6A+.

Commanding officers:

Lt Cdr (A) D.J. McDonald, 01/09/44
Lt (A) C. Malins, RNVR, (temp), 12/02/45
Lt Cdr (A) D.J. McDonald, 29/04/45
Lt (A) M.B. Gerrish, (temp), 30/05/45
Lt Cdr (A) K. Stilliard, RNVR, 29/06/45

1852 Squadron Formed at Brunswick, 01/02/45, with 18 Corsair IV fighters, it joined *Patroller* on 04/05 for the UK. It disembarked to Belfast on 25/05, and moved to Eglinton the following day, while continuing to work up, and convert from normal reflector gunsights to gyro gunsights. After VJ-Day, the squadron disbanded at Nutts Corner, 29/08/45.

Identification markings: 1V10+, then single letters.

Commanding officer:

Lt Cdr (A) I.F. Voller, RNVR

1853 Squadron Formed at Brunswick, 01/04/45, with 18 Corsair IV fighters, after deck landing training aboard USS *Charger*, it joined *Rajah* for the UK on 24/07. Disembarking to Machrihanish on 06/08, only to disband there on 15/08, VJ-Day.

Identification markings: 1V11+.

Commanding officer:

LTZ J.R. Schuiling, RNethN

NAVAL WINGS

2nd Naval TBR Wing

828 and 841 Squadrons, formed 24/01/44, allocated to *Implacable* 11/03. The wing's aircraft, Barracudas, embarked in 08/44, although some were detached briefly to *Formidable*. Wing disbanded when 828 absorbed 841, 28/11/44.

Wing Leaders: Lt Cdr E.M. Britton, 24/01/44; unidentified, 23/07.

3rd Naval Fighter Wing

808, 886 and 897 Squadrons, formed 25/10/43, Burscough. Squadrons embarked in *Hunter, Attacker* and *Stalker* respectively. On 25/02/44, moved to Lee-on-Solent, expanding with 885 Squadron. Role changed to air spotting pool for the 2nd Tactical Air

Force for the Normandy landings. The wing changed afterwards, with 808 absorbing 886, and 885 absorbing 897, before moving to Ballyhalbert on 04/08. Further changes occurred in the autumn, with the 2 squadrons re-equipping with Hellcats, and then joined by the 2 Hellcat squadrons, 800 and 1840. In 10/44, there was a further, but temporary, increase in strength through the addition of the Wildcats of 881 and 882 Squadrons for three weeks.

Wing sailed for the East early in 1945, using the escort carriers *Emperor* (800), *Khedive* (808), *Ruler* (885) and *Speaker* (1840), seeing active service, before disbanding on 09/12/45.

Wing leaders: Lt Cdr (A) S.J. Hall, RNVR, 25/10/43
Lt Cdr (A) R. McD Hill, RNVR, 13/03/44
Lt Cdr N.G. Hallett, DSC, 22/05/44
Lt Cdr R.H.P. Carver, DSC, 30/09/44
Lt Cdr (A) B.H.C. Nation, 16/11/44
Maj P.P. Nelson-Gracie, RM, 11/02/45
Lt Cdr R.H.P. Carver, DSC, 08/04/45

4th Naval Fighter Wing
807, 809 and 879 Seafire Squadrons, formed 25/10/43, Burscough. Operating from escort carriers, the wing's squadrons supported operations in Italy mid-1944, the invasion of the South of France in August, and Army support operations in the Aegean, before moving to Egypt. Re-embarking for Ceylon, the wing saw service. Postwar, it disbanded 25/01/46, at Nutts Corner.

Wing leaders: Lt Cdr (A) A.C. Wallace, RNVR, 25/10/43
Lt Cdr (A) G.C. Baldwin, DSC, 03/06/44–16/11/45

5th Naval Fighter Wing
1839 and 1844 Hellcat Squadrons, formed in late 1943, Eglinton. Squadrons joined

Begum, 02/44, sailing to join the Eastern Fleet, transferring to *Indomitable* 07/44. Saw action with the British Pacific Fleet, staying with the ship to disband in the UK, 30/11/45.

Wing leaders: Cdr H.P. Sears (also 5, 6, 12 and 45 Wings), 28/02/44
Cdr T.G.C. Jameson (Senior Officer Air), 07/04/44
Lt Cdr (A) T.W. Harrington, 09/09/44
an unidentified officer from 04/45

6th Naval Fighter Wing
1837 Corsair Squadron, formed 28/02/44, Burscough. Joined *Atheling* for Ceylon to work up. Transferred to *Illustrious* 06/44, but disbanded on 14/08, into 47th Wing aboard *Victorious*.

Reformed in the UK, 14/08/44, with 1841 and 1842 Corsair Squadrons, joining *Formidable*. The wing's squadrons provided cover for attacks on the *Tirpitz*, and then with the British Pacific Fleet, before disbanding into the 2nd Carrier Air Group on 30/06/45.

Wing leaders: Cdr H.P. Sears, Wing, 28/02/44
Maj R.C. Hay, DSO and Bar, DSC, RM, 24/05/44
Lt Cdr (A) R.L. Bigg-Wither, 14/08/44

7th Naval Fighter Wing
800 and 804 Hellcat Squadrons for *Emperor*; 881 and 896 Wildcat squadrons for *Pursuer*; 882 and 898 Wildcat Squadrons for *Searcher*; formed 30/10/43, Eglinton. Operating two squadrons in the confines of escort carriers proved difficult, and in 06/44, 804, 896 and 898 disbanded into their companion squadrons. After taking part in the landings in the South of France, and then in the Aegean, the wing returned to the UK and its squadrons were re-allocated to other wings. Disbanded 16/12/44.
Wing leader: Lt Cdr (A) M.F. Fell, 30/10/43

8th Naval TBR Wing

827 and 830 Barracuda Squadrons, formed 25/10/43, for *Furious*. Wing's squadrons operated mainly in Norwegian waters and on strikes against the battleship *Tirpitz*. Disbanded when 830 merged into 827, 03/10/44.

Wing leader: Lt Cdr R.S. Baker-Faulkner, DSC, 25/10/43; unidentified, 18/07/44.

9th Naval TBR Wing

820 and 826 Barracuda Squadrons, formed 11/02/44, for *Indefatigable*. The wing undertook operations off Norway and againgst *Tirpitz*. Disbanded on 23/10/44, when 820 absorbed its companion squadron.

Wing leaders: Lt Cdr (A) A.J.I. Temple-West, 11/02/44
Lt Cdr (A) W.R. Well, 01/08/44

10th Naval Fighter Wing

1843 and 1845 Corsair Squadrons, formed 14/10/44, Eglinton for the British Pacific Fleet. 1845 joined *Slinger* 12/44; 1843 joined *Arbiter*, 02/45. Never saw action as a wing: 1845 disbanded 05/04/45, to reinforce squadrons on *Formidable*; 1843 absorbed 30/06/45, into the 3rd Carrier Air Group.

Wing leader: Maj P.P. Nelson-Gracie, RM

11th Naval TBR Wing

822 and 823 Barracuda Squadrons, formed 21/04/44, Ulunderpet, by renumbering 45th Naval TBR Wing. It disbanded when 822 absorbed its companion, 06/07/44.

12th Naval TBR Wing

815 and 817 Barracuda Squadrons, formed 24/01/44, for the British Pacific Fleet, joining *Begum* the following month. Embarked in *Indomitable*, 07/44, seeing operational service before disbanding, 28/12/44.

Wing leader: Lt Cdr E.M. Britton

15th Naval Fighter Wing

1830, 1831 and 1833 Corsair Squadrons, formed 08/11/43, Stretton. 1831 was disbanded into the other 2 squadrons before joining *Illustrious*. Wing operated from the carrier with both the Eastern Fleet and then the British Pacific Fleet, disbanding on return to the UK, 28/07/45.

Wing leaders: Lt Cdr J.W. Sleigh, DSC, 08/11/43
Ltd Cdr (A) R.J. Cork, DSO, DSC, 02/12/43
Lt Cdr (A) A.M. Tritton, DSC & 2 Bars, RNVR, 04/04/44

21st Naval TBR Wing

810 and 847 Barracuda Squadrons, formed, 25/10/43, Machrihanish. Joined *Illustrious*, 11/43, sailed to join the Eastern Fleet. Disbanded after 810 absorbed 847, 30/06/44.

Wing leaders: Lt Cdr N.R. Corbet-Milward, 25/10/43
Lt Cdr B.E. Boulding, DSC, 18/11/43
Lt Cdr (A) A.J.B. Forde, 27/02/44

24th Naval Fighter Wing

887 and 894 Seafire Squadrons, formed 25/10/43, Henstridge. Joined *Indefatigable*, 05/44, for operations off Norway. Carrier sailed to join Eastern Fleet 11/44, then joined British Pacific Fleet. Wing saw operations against Japanese forces before absorbed into 7th Carrier Air Group, 30/06/45.

Wing leaders: Lt Cdr N.G. Hallett, DSC, 31/12/43; vacancy, 22/05/44
Lt Cdr (A) A.J. Thomson, DSC, RNVR, 01/11/44
Lt Cdr N.G. Hallett, DSC, 12/03/45

30th Naval Fighter Wing

810 and 880 Seafire Squadrons, formed 10/10/44, Machrihanish. Joined *Implacable* 11/44, for British Pacific Fleet, but disbanded into the 8th Carrier Air Group, 30/06/45, before seeing action.

Wing leader: Lt Cdr C.P. Campbell-Horsfall, 10/10/44

45th Naval TBR Wing

822 and 823 Barracuda Squadrons, formed 25/10/43, but squadrons did not combine until ready to sail in *Atheling* to join the Eastern Fleet, 02/44. On arrival, wing renumbered as 11th Naval TBR Wing, 21/04/44.

Wing leaders: Lt Cdr B.E. Boulding, DSC, 25/10/43
Lt Cdr G. Douglas, DFC, 01/12/43
unidentified, 31/01/44

47th Naval Fighter Wing

1834 and 1836 Corsair Squadrons, formed 17/01/44, Stretton. Joined *Victorious* 03/44 to cover attacks on the *Tirpitz*. In 06/44, it sailed to Ceylon, briefly augmented by 1837 Squadron 08/44, until this disbanded into the other 2 squadrons. In action against Japanese before absorbed into 1st Carrier Air Group, 30/06/45.

Wing leaders: Lt Cdr F.R.A. Turnbull, DSC, 17/01/44
Lt Col R.C. Hay, DSO & Bar, RM, 14/08/44

52nd Naval TBR Wing

False start, 26/11/43, with squadrons re-allocated to 12th Naval TBR Wing. 829 and 831 Barracuda Squadrons, formed 05/01/44, for *Victorious*. Augmented by 827 Squadron for attack on *Tirpitz*. Disbanded when 831 absorbed 827, 09/07/44.

Wing leaders: Lt Cdr J.C.N. Shrubsole, 26/11/43
Lt Cdr E.M. Britton, 05/01/44
Lt Cdr (A) F.H. Fox, 24/03/44
Lt Cdr V. Rance, DSO, 15/02/44

CARRIER AIR GROUPS

The first 6 air groups were allocated to the 3 Illustrious-class ships, with each having 2 squadrons of Corsairs and 1 of Avengers, with squadron strengths standardised on 15 aircraft. The next 4 were allocated to the 2 Implacable-class ships, with 4 squadrons per group, 2 each with 24 Seafires, and 1 each of 15 Avengers and 15 Fireflies, reflecting the greater capacity from the extra hangar deck on these ships. *Indomitable* was to have 2 air groups, each having 4 squadrons, comprising 2 with 24 Hellcats apiece, 1 with 15 Avengers and 1 with 12 Fireflies.

For the 4 light fleet carriers of the Colossus-class, 6 air groups, numbered 13 to 18, were to each have a squadron of 21 Corsairs and one of 12 Barracudas. Another 2 Colossus-class carriers were to have air groups, 19 to 22 inclusive, each with a squadron of 21 Seafires and one of 12 Barracudas, with CAG 19 earmarked to be manned by the Royal Canadian Navy. Later, a similar arrangement was planned for the Royal Australian Navy.

When the air groups came into being on 30/06/45, squadrons were immediately available for Nos 1, 2, 7, 8, 11, 13, 14, 15 and 16. Few of the remainder could be activated in the period of less than seven weeks before the war ended. Although a number of air groups were reactivated postwar, generally the organisation was far too large for peacetime requirements.

1st Carrier Air Group

1834, 1836 Corsair, 849 Avenger Squadrons, formed 30/06/45, for *Victorious*. Disbanded when the carrier returned to the UK, 08/09/45.

Air group commander:
Cdr J.C.N. Shrubsole.

2nd Carrier Air Group:
1841, 1842 Corsair, 848 Avenger Squadrons, formed 30/06/45, for *Formidable*. Disbanded on the ship's return to the UK, 31/10/45.
Air group commander:
Lt Col P.P. Nelson-Gracie, RM

3rd Carrier Air Group
1843, 1845 Corsair, 854 Avenger Squadrons, formed 02/08/45, Nowra, as a spare group. Too late to embark. Disbanded, 20/10/45. Personnel returned to the UK on a merchant vessel.
Air group commanders:
Cdr N.S. Luaard (temp), 02/08/45
Cdr J.C.N. Shrubsole, 08/09/45.

4th, 5th, 6th Carrier Air Groups
Planned, but failed to materialise before the war ended.

7th Carrier Air Group
887, 894 Seafire, 820 Avenger, 1770 Firefly Squadrons, formed 30/06/45, Schofields, for *Indefatigable*. Disbanded 03/46.
Air group commander:
Lt Cdr N.G. Hallett, DSC and Bar

8th Carrier Air Group
801, 880 Seafire, 828 Avenger, 1771 Firefly squadrons, formed 30/06/45, for *Implacable*. Disbanded 04/46, although some squadrons disbanded earlier.
No air group commander appointed.

9th and 10th Carrier Air Groups
Planned, but war ended.

11th Carrier Air Group
1839,1844 Hellcat, 857 Avenger Squadrons, formed 30/06/45, for *Indomitable*. Disbanded 30/11/45.
No air group commander appointed.

12th Carrier Air Group
Planned, but war ended.

13th Carrier Air Group
812 Barracuda, 1850 Corsair Squadrons, formed 30/06/45, for *Vengeance*. Disbanded 08/46.
Air group commander appointed postwar.

14th Carrier Air Group
827 Barracuda, 1846 Corsair Squadrons, 30/06/46, for *Colossus*. Disbanded 23/07/46.
No air group commander appointed.

15th Carrier Air Group
814 Barracuda, 1851 Corsair Squadrons, formed 30/06/46, for *Venerable*. Disbanded 1947, although composition changed postwar.
Air group commander: Lt Cdr P.D. Gick

16th Carrier Air Group
837 Barracuda, 1831 Corsair Squadrons, formed 30/06/46, for *Glory*. Disbanded 1947, although composition changed postwar.
Air group commander:
Maj A.J. Wright, RM

17th, 18th, 20th, 21st Carrier Air Group
Formed postwar.

19th Carrier Air Group
Formed postwar as part of the Royal Canadian Navy.

22nd Carrier Air Group
Planned, but abandoned after VJ-Day.

CHAPTER 11

WARTIME NAVAL AIRCRAFT

When the batsman gives 'Lower', I always go higher;
I drift off to starboard and prang my Seafire,
The chaps up in goofers all think I am green,
But I get my commission from Supermarine!
Cracking show! I'm alive!
But I've still got to render my A25!

The Fleet Air Arm Songbook

The outbreak of the Second World War found the Fleet Air Arm with an inadequate range of aircraft. The Fairey Swordfish was out-dated. Its successor, the Albacore, was, amazingly enough, yet another biplane, and one with an engine so troublesome that the Swordfish soldiered on. The Gloster Sea Gladiator fighter was based on the last biplane fighter built for the RAF, and it is amazing that production of this antique continued for so long. The Fairey Fulmar looked modern, but the need to carry a two-man crew made the aircraft too heavy and its performance was barely adequate to counter a bomber, and it was vulnerable to enemy fighters. An oddity was the Blackburn Skua, officially fighter/dive-bomber-reconnaissance, but to those who had to cope with it, it was 'more dive-bomber than fighter'. All of this was partly the neglect of the Fleet Air Arm's aircraft procurement needs while under RAF stewardship, but also partly because many believed that high performance aircraft could not operate safely from aircraft carriers.

War soon changed all of this. In fact, it is impossible in a book of this size and scope to include details of all of the aircraft operated by the Fleet Air Arm during the war years. These included many transport types on communications and training duties, and many of the aircraft were not unique to naval aviation. While the aircraft available to the Fleet Air Arm improved as the war progressed, the newcomers were not without their failings. Apart from the Albacore's problems, the Fairey Barracuda was a maintenance nightmare and while it did useful work in the European theatre, it was badly outclassed in the Far East and was soon withdrawn. The Sea Hurricane was an interim measure, lacking folding wings. The Seafire was too delicate for carrier work and lacked range. The Corsair was a tough, fast, fighter-bomber with a good range, but would bounce on landing and, having a long nose, could topple forwards.

One newcomer was the helicopter, although these machines were not deployed operationally by the Royal Navy during the war. Nevertheless, the Fleet Air Arm was involved with the helicopter's early years.

Lots of struts in all directions,
Curved and cut-out centre-sections—
Stringbag the Sailor's had his day,
But in his own inimitable way
He's left his mark on history's page,
The champion of the biplane age!

Ode to *Stringbag the Sailor*. (*via Lord Kilbracken*)

Personnel were trained in the United States by the United States Coast Guard, which had been given responsibility for helicopter trials in 1943, primarily to assess the scope for ASW. The USCG used a merchant vessel, SS *Daghestan*, and a joint trials unit was set up with the Royal Navy using Sikorsky HNS-1 and HOS-1 helicopters. The early machines were too small to make an impact on the war at sea, but this was the beginning of a development that would revolutionise naval air power, and change the shape of escort vessels in the years to come.

The large numbers of aircraft put into service reflected not only losses to enemy action or accident, but the intense wear and tear of carrier operations, and the constant need to up-date equipment.

THE AIRCRAFT

Blackburn Skua
Role: Fighter/DBR. First Flight: 02/37. Service: late 38–08/41. Wingspan: 46 ft 2 in. Length: 35 ft 7 in. Height: 14 ft 2 in. Max

weight: 8,320 lb. 620 hp (830 hp take-off) Bristol Perseus II. Max speed: 196 kts. Range: 760 nm. Crew: 2. Armament: 4 × 0.303 Vickers, 1 × 0.303 Lewis; 1 × 500-lb bombs, or 6 × 60 lb rockets. 192 built.

Fairey Swordfish

Role: TBR. First Flight: 04/34. Service: 07/36–07/45. Wingspan: 45 ft 5 in. Length: 36 ft 3 in. Height: 12 ft 10 in. Max weight: 9,250- lb. 690 hp Bristol Pegasus III; 750 hp Pegasus XXX in late Mk II and Mk III versions. Max speed: 100 kts. Range: 450 nm; 896 nm with 93 gallon tank in observer's cockpit. Crew: 2/3. Armament: 2 × 0.303 Vickers GO; 1 × 18 in Mk XIIB 1,620-lb torpedo, or 1 × 1,610-lb mine, or 4 × 250-lb depth charges, or 3 × 500-lb bombs, or 6 × 60-lb rockets. 2,392 built.

Fairey Albacore

Role: TBR. First flight: 12/38. Service: 03/40–12/43. Wingspan: 50 ft; Length: 39 ft 10 in; Height: 15 ft 3 in; Max weight: 11,186-lb. 1,085 hp Bristol Taurus II or XII. Max speed: 150 kts. Range: 550 nm; 900 miles with 120 gallon extra tank. Crew 3. Armament: 2 × 0.303 Vickers GO; 1 × 18 in Mk XII 1,620-lb torpedo, or 1 × 1,610-lb mine, or 6 × 250-lb depth charges, or 4 × 500-lb bombs. 800 built.

Fairey Barracuda

Role: TBR. First Flight: 12/40. Service: 01/43. Wingspan: 49 ft 2 in. Length: 39 ft 9 in. Height: 15 ft 1 in. Max weight: 18,200 lb. 1,640 hp Rolls-Royce Merlin XXXII; Max speed: 150 kts. Range: 596 nm; 1,000 nm with 116 gallon extra tank. Crew: 2. Armament: 2 × 0.303 Vickers K; 1 × 18 in Mk XII 1,620-lb torpedo, or 1 × 1,610-lb mine, or 4 × 450-lb depth charges, either 3 × 500-lb or 6 × 250-lb, bombs. 2,572 built.

Fairey Fulmar

Role: Fighter. First Flight: 01/37. Service: 06/40–03/45. Wingspan: 46 ft. Length: 40 ft 2 in. Height: 11 ft 6in. Max weight: 10,350 lb. 1,260 hp Rolls-Royce Merlin XXX. Max speed: 231 kts. Range: 691 nm. Crew: 2. Armament: 8 × 0.303 Browning; 2 × 250-lb bombs. 600 built.

Fairey Firefly

Role: Fighter. First Flight: 22/12/41. Service: 05/43. Wingspan: 44 ft 5 in. Length: 37 ft. Height: 13 ft 7 in. Max weight: 12,131 lb. 1,495 hp Rolls-Royce Griffon II. Max speed: 277 kts. Range: 671 nm. Crew: 2. Armament: 4 × 20mm cannon; 2 × 1,000-lb bombs or 8 × 60-lb rocket projectiles. 1,515 built.

Grumman Martlet/Wildcat

Role: Fighter. First Flight: 09/37. Service: 09/40. Wingspan: 38 ft. Length: 29 ft. Height: 10 ft 6 in. Max weight: 7975 lb. 1,100 hp (1,200 hp take-off) Pratt & Whitney R-1830-86 Twin Wasp. Max speed: 278 kts. Range: 722 nm, 1,109 with 2 × 48 gallon drop tanks. Crew: 1. Armament: 4 or 6 × 0.50; 2 × 100-lb bombs. Approx 900 delivered.

Grumman Hellcat

Role: Fighter. First Flight: 26/06/42. Service: 07/43–08/45. Wingspan: 42 ft 10 in. Length: 33 ft 7 in. Height: 14 ft 5 in. Max weight: 13,797 lb. 1,675 hp Pratt & Whitney P-2800-10W. Max speed: 330 kts. Range: 950 nm, 1,340 with 125 gallon drop tank. Crew: 1. Armament: 4 × 0.50; 2 × 20 mm cannon; 2 × 1000-lb bombs. 1,182 delivered.

Grumman Avenger

Role: TBR. First Flight: 08/41. Service: 04/43.Wingspan: 54 ft 2 in. Length: 41 ft. Height: 15 ft 8 in. Max weight: 16,761 lb. 1,600 hp (1,800 hp take-off) Wright GR-2600-8 Cyclone; Max speed: 232 kts. Range: 983 nm; 2,200 nm with 2 × 83 gallon

A more robust aircraft was the Grumman Wildcat, known initially to the Fleet Air Arm as the Martlet, until aircraft names had to be standardised between the British and American forces later in the war. It did have an unusual fuselage mounted undercarriage, which could result in 'dancing' from one wheel to the other if a carrier was rolling heavily. (*Northrop Grumman*)

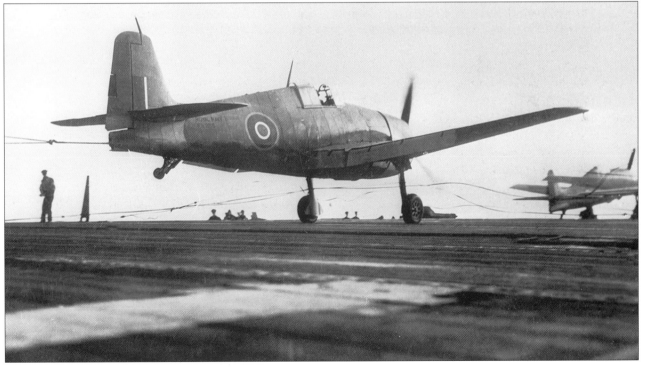

Better still was the Hellcat, with speed and range. This one has just caught the arrester wire aboard *Ravager*. (*Northrop Grumman*)

A Grumman Hellcat comes to grief aboard one of the fast armoured carriers. Piston-engined aircraft could, and did, suddenly explode into flames if fuel pipes were ruptured, hence the fire crews dashing to the rescue. (*FAAM HELLCAT/105*)

When it appeared, the Grumman Avenger gave the FAA what it really needed, a substantial and powerful carrier-borne bomber. (*Northrop Grumman*)

The first high performance fighter was the Sea Hurricane, which lacked folding wings. To increase accommodation on cramped flight decks, many carriers had outriggers for the tailwheel of fighter aircraft. This is aboard *Vindex*. (*FAAM HURRICANE/57*)

The Vought Corsair was described variously as 'the best fighter aircraft of the war', the 'bent wing bastard from Connecticut', and, by the Japanese, as the 'whispering death', because the position of its exhaust manifolds left those visited by this aircraft unaware of its presence until it was too late. (*Vought Aircraft*)

drop tanks. Crew: 3. Armament: 5 × 0.50 Browning; 1 × 22 in Mk XII 1,620-lb torpedo, or 1 × 2,000-lb, or 2 × 1,000-lb, bombs. 958 delivered.

Hawker Sea Hurricane

Role: Fighter. First Flight: 1935, Hurricane. Service: 07/41. Wingspan: 40 ft. Length: 32 ft 3 in. Height: 13 ft 1½ in. Max weight: 7,015 lb. 1,030 hp Rolls-Royce Merlin III, Merlin XX, Mk 1C and IIC. Max speed: 268 kts. Range: 482 nm. Crew: 1. Armament: 8 × 0.303 Browning, on 4 × 20 mm cannon Mk1C/IIC; 2 × 250-lb bombs. 800 converted from RAF standard.

Supermarine Seafire

Role: Fighter. First Flight: 03/36, Spitfire. Service: 06/42. Wingspan: 36 ft 11 in, clipped wing: 32 ft 7 in. Length: 32 ft 3 in. Height: 13 ft 6 in. Max weight: 706 lb. 1,415 hp Rolls-Royce Merlin XLVI. Max speed: 352 kts. Range: 440 nm, 600 with 1 × 45 gallon drop tank. Crew: 1. Armament: 4 × 0.303 Browning, 2 × 20 mm cannon; 3 × 500-lb bombs. Approximately 1,700 built.

Vought Corsair

Role: Fighter-bomber. First Flight: 29/05/40. Service: 06/43. Wingspan: 41 ft. Length: 33 ft 8 in. Height: 15 ft 1 in. Max weight: 13,597 lb. 1,700 hp Pratt & Whitney P-2800-18W. Max speed: 393 kts. Range: 1,005 nm, 1,300 with 2 × 125 gallon drop tank. Crew: 1. Armament: 6 × 0.50; 2 × 1,000-lb bombs. 2,012 delivered.

CHAPTER 12

WARTIME BRITISH AIRCRAFT CARRIERS

Priest: 'Bless our ship.'
Men: 'May God the Father Bless her.'
P: 'Bless our ship.'
M: 'May Jesus Christ bless her.'
P: 'Bless our ship.'
M: 'May the Holy Spirit Bless her.'
P: What do you fear, seeing that God the Father is with you?'
M: 'We fear nothing.'
P: What do you fear, seeing that God the Son is with you?'
M: 'We fear nothing.'
P: What do you fear, seeing that God the Holy Spirit is with you?'
M: 'We fear nothing.'
From the dedication ceremony for HMS *Vindex* by the Bishop of Newcastle,
20 November 1943

Despite having kept ships intended for disposal in service, and having new fast armoured carriers on order, losses and the demands placed on the carrier force meant that additional ships were needed. The solution lay in cheap conversions of merchant ships. A reluctant Admiralty allowed the captured German banana boat *Hanover* to be converted, becoming *Audacity*. Completed in June 1941, she operated Martlets of 802 Squadron to provide air cover for a convoy to Gibraltar. Eventually, wholesale conversion of merchant vessels was permitted, with orders divided between British and American yards. The Admiralty

preferred liners, because of their size and speed, and the experience of having converted *Argus*. The Ministry of War Transport objected, not wanting to loose fast troop transports. Only *Pretoria Castle*, already an armed merchant cruiser, was converted. The Americans converted cargo vessels, and had the advantage of converting ships from a small number of standardised designs.

To the Royal Navy, the escort carriers were known officially as 'auxiliary aircraft carriers', an appropriate name since they did more than escort convoys. Unofficially, they were known as 'Woolworth carriers',

A young 'Harry' Wragg aboard *Ark Royal*, by the two-pounder multiple pom-pom, which was one of the best AA weapons of the war against low-flying aircraft. (*via S.H. Wragg*)

because they were cheap and cheerful. The United States Navy had invented the escort carrier designation, or CVE, and to its personnel, this was interpreted as 'combustible, vulnerable, expendable', all too appropriately since several of these ships did blow up. While for the most part, the Royal Navy relied on standardised US-built escort carriers, a small number of British-built ships were also provided as the Admiralty felt that their rivetted construction was better suited to Arctic conditions than the welded construction of the American ships.

An interim solution was to modify merchant vessels, the merchant aircraft carriers or MAC-ships. There were two types, converted tankers, able to carry three Swordfish, and converted grain ships, able to carry four Swordfish, with the added advantage of a converted hold aft as a hangar.

AIRCRAFT CARRIERS

In each case, pennant numbers are given, while for ships in service at the end of the war, mainly with the British Pacific Fleet, parent ship letters are also given. While these originated in the parent ship letter prefixes carried by the aircraft of many squadrons, they were not painted on carrier flight decks until April 1945, and wartime security considerations meant that they were changed from time to time. They were also to be found on the tailfins of the ship's aircraft.

In contrast to the more standardised armaments of today, during wartime, even within ships of the same class, defensive armament often varied, reflecting either the intended role or, more often, availablity of weaponry under wartime supply problems. There could also be small differences in tonnages and dimensions. Where a date is given, this reflects post-construction modifications.

The first true 'flat top', *Argus* alternated between deck landing training and operations, but by 1944 was in such poor state that she was relegated to harbour duties.

Activity D94 escort carrier

Built: Caledon Shipbuilding & Engineering Co, Dundee; laid down: 01/02/40, as refrigerated cargo vessel *Telemachus* for Ocean Steamship, converted on slipway; launched: 30/05/42; completed: 14/10/42; LOA: 512 ft; beam: 66.5 ft; displacement: 11,800 tons standard, 14,250 tons deep load; armament: 1 twin 4 in, 6 twin 20-mm Oerlikon, 8 single 20-mm Oerlikon; endurance: 4,500 miles @ 18 kts; complement: 700; aircraft: 15; lifts: 1 aft; no catapult; sold as merchantman, 25/04/46.

Archer D78 escort carrier

Built: Sun Shipbuilding & Drydock Corp, Chester, USA; converted by Newport News Shipbuilding & Dry Dock Co, Newport News, USA; laid down: 07/06/39; launched: 14/12/39; completed: 24/04/40 as US merchant vessel *Morcamacland*; converted: 17/05/41; displacement: 10,220 tons standard, 12,860 tons deep load; LOA: 492 ft; beam: 111.25 ft; armament: 3 single 4 in, 6 twin 20-mm Oerlikon, 7 single 20-mm Oerlikon; endurance: 7,000 miles @ 10 kts; complement: 555; Aircraft: 12–15; lifts: 1 aft; catapults 1; purchased, not lend/lease. Technical problems led to withdrawal

06/05/43. Accommodation hulk then aircraft ferry *Empire Lagan*, 15/03/45.

Argus I49 fleet carrier

Built: William Beardmore & Co, Dalmuir, Scotland; laid down: 06/14, passenger liner for Italy, converted on slipway; launched: 02/12/17; completed: 16/09/18; displacement: 14,000 tons standard, 16,500 tons deep load; LOA: 560 ft; beam: 79.5 ft; armament: 6 single 4 in, 4 single 3 pdr, 4 single MG; 1943 13 single 20-mm Oerlikon added; endurance: 5,200 miles @ 12 kts; complement: 760; aircraft: originally 20, 15 in 1941; lifts: 2, but aft lift removed, 1941; Catapults: 1, 1936; 09/42, DLT carrier, then Operation Torch and escort duties. DLT, 04/43. Accommodation ship, Chatham, 08/44.

Ark Royal D91 fleet carrier

Built: Cammell Laird & Co, Birkenhead, England; laid down: 16/09/35; launched: 13/04/37; completed: 16/05/38; displacement: 22,000 tons standard, 27,720 tons deep load; LOA: 800 ft; beam: 112 ft; armament: 8 twin 4.5, 4 oct 2 pdr pompom, 4 single 3 pdr, 8 single MG; endurance: 11,200 miles @ 10 kts; complement: 1,580;

Blackburn Skuas of 800 Squadron, ranged ready for take-off from *Ark Royal*. (*via S.H. Wragg*)

The ship's crest of *Ark Royal*.

tons deep load; LOA: 491.5 ft; beam: 105 ft; armament: 2 single 4 in, 4 twin 40 mm Bofors, 8 twin 20-mm Oerlikon, 4 single 20-mm Oerlikon; endurance: 27,300 miles @ 11 kts; complement: 646; aircraft: 20 op, 90 ferry; lifts: 2 catapults: 1; returned to USN, 05/01/46, sold as merchantman.
Similar:

Battler D18 escort carrier
Built: Ingalls Shipbuilding Corp, Pascagoula; laid down: 15/04/41; launched: 04/04/42; completed: 15/05/42; returned to USN, 12/02/46.

Chaser D32 escort carrier
Built: as *Battler*, laid down: 28/06/41; launched: 15/01/42; completed: 09/04/43; returned USN, 12/05/46, sold as merchantman.

Fencer D64 escort carrier
Built: As *Attacker*; laid down: 05/09/42; launched: 04/04/42; completed: 20/02/43; returned USN, 21/05/46, sold as merchantman.

Hunter D80 escort carrier
Built: as *Battler*; laid down: 15/05/41; launched: 22/05/42; completed: 11/01/43; returned USN, 29 12/45, sold as merchantman.

Pursuer D73 fighter carrier
Built: as *Battler*; laid down: 31/07/41, merchant vessel *Mormacland*; launched:

aircraft: originally 60, 54 in 1941; lifts: 3; catapults: 2; torpedoed 13/05/41; sank 14/05/41; 1 crew member lost.

Attacker D02 Attacker-class assault carrier
Built: Western Pipe & Steel Corp, San Francisco; laid down: 17/04/41; Launched: 27/09/41; completed: 10/10/42; displacement: 10,200 tons standard, 14,400

Attacker shows her merchant ship origins. (*FAAM CARRIER A/216*)

18/07/42; completed: 14/06/43, after conversion as USS *St George* CVE-17; returned USN, 12/02/46 and scrapped.

Stalker D91 assault carrier

Built: as *Attacker*; laid down: 06/10/41; launched: 05/03/42, as USS *Hamlin* CVE-15; completed: 30/12/42; laid down as merchantman, converted to Bogue-class escort carrier before launch; returned USN, 29/12/45; sold as merchantman.

Striker D12: escort carrier

Built: as *Attacker*; laid down: 16/12/41, as USS *Prince William* CVE-19 (not to be confused with the later CVE-31 Prince William/Ruler-class leadship); launched: 07/05/42; completed: 29/04/43; returned USN, 12/02/46

Tracker D24 Improved Attacker-class escort carrier

Built: Seattle-Tacoma Shipbuilding Corp, Seattle; laid down: 03/05/41; Launched: 07/03/42; completed: 31/01/43; LOA: 492 ft; beam: 102 ft; armament: 2 single 4 in, 4 twin 40-mm Bofors, 8 twin 20-mm Oerlikon, 10 single 20-mm Oerlikon; lifts: 2; catapults: 1; returned USN, 29/05/45; sold as merchantman.

Audacity D10 escort carrier

Built: Vulkan, Bremen, as cargo liner *Hanover*; converted after capture, 20/06/41; displacement: 10,200 tons standard, 11,000 tons deep load; LOA: 497.25 ft; beam: 56.25 ft; armament: 1 single 4 in, 1 6 pdr, 4 single 2 pdr, 4 single 20-mm Oerlikon; endurance: 12,000 miles @ 14 kts; complement: 210; Aircraft: 8; no lifts or catapults; first escort carrier to prove the concept, hence the limited features; torpedoed, 21/12/41.

Avenger D14 Avenger-class escort carrier

Built: Sun Shipbuilding & Drydock Corp, Chester, USA; completed Bethlehem Steel Co.; laid down: 28/05/39; launched: 17/05/40; completed: 01/03/42; displacement: 12,150 tons standard, 15,700 tons deep load; LOA: 492 ft; beam: 70 ft; armament: 3 single 4 in, 10 single 20-mm Oerlikon, 6 single 0.5 Browning MG; endurance: 14,550 miles @ 10 kts; complement: 545; aircraft: 15; lifts: 1 aft; catapults: 1; torpedoed 15/05/42, causing bomb room to explode leaving just 17 survivors.

Campania was one of the small number of British-built escort carriers. (*FAAM CARS C/213*)

Similar:

Biter D97 escort carrier

Completed by Atlantic Basin Iron Works, Brooklyn; laid down: 28/12/39, as merchant ship *Rio Parana*; launched: 18/12/40; completed: 01/05/42; major fire damage, Greenock, 24/08/44. Laid up due to shortage of dockyard capacity. Returned USN, 09/04/45, refitted, loaned to France as *Dixmude*.

Dasher D37 escort carrier

Laid down: 14/03/40; launched: 12/04/41; completed: 01/07/42; blew up 27/03/43, Clyde Estuary, probably fuel vapour explosion, leaving 149 survivors.

Campania R48 escort carrier

Built: Harland & Wolff, Belfast; laid down: 12/08/41; launched: 17/06/43; completed: 07/03/44; displacement: 13,000 tons standard, 15,970 tons deep load; LOA: 540 ft; beam: 70 ft; armament: 1 twin 4-in, 4 quad 2-pdr pompom, 8 twin 20-mm Oerlikon; endurance: 17,000 miles @ 17 kts; complement: 639; aircraft: 20; lifts: 1 aft; no catapults; converted from merchantman for Arctic convoys because rivetted hull considered less prone to cracking than welded hulls of US CVEs. Postwar served as troopship until 12/45, when put into reserve.

Colossus R15 Colossus-class light fleet carrier

Built: Vickers-Armstrong, Newcastle-upon-Tyne; laid down: 01/06/42; launched: 30/09/43; completed: 16/12/44; displacement: 13,190 tons standard, 18,040 tons deep load; LOA: 695 ft; beam: 112.5 ft; armament: 6 quad 2-pdr pompoms, 11 twin 20-mm Oerlikon, 10 single 20-mm Oerlikon, 4 single 3-pdr saluting; endurance: 8,300 miles @ 20 kts; complement: 1,300; aircraft: 42 lifts: 2; catapults: 1; built to merchant standards to permit construction in yards not familiar with warship work. One hangar deck. Loaned to French Navy as *Arromanches*, 06/08/46, purchased 1951.

Entering service just before the end of the war, *Colossus* and her sister ships were destined for long postwar careers, but often with many other navies. This cutaway shows the layout of the ship. (*FAAM*)

The hangar deck of *Colossus*, ready to bring home British PoWs from the Far East. (*FAAM CARS C/88*)

Similar:

Glory R62 (R)

Built: Harland & Wolff, Belfast; laid down: 27/08/42; launched: 27/05/43; completed: 02/04/45; maintained reserve: 1956; scrapped: 1961.

Ocean R68 (O)

Built: Alexander Stephen & Sons, Govan; laid down: 08/05/42; launched: 08/07/44; completed: 08/08/45. Despite her small size, on 03/12/45, the first pure jet deck landing on a carrier was made aboard this ship by Lt Cdr Eric 'Winkle' Brown using a modified DH Vampire. Into reserve, 05/12/57; scrapped: 1962.

Pioneer R76 ferry carrier

Built: Vickers-Armstrong, Barrow-in-Furness laid down: 02/12/42; launched: 20/05/43; completed: 08/02/45; complement: 1,076, 60 aircraft could be ferried; paid off early 1946; designated ferry carrier 06/53; sold for breaking, 09/54.

Venerable R04 (B)

Built: Cammell Laird & Co, Birkenhead; laid down: 03/12/42; launched: 30/12/43; completed: 17/01/45; launched some of the last sorties againgst the Japanese, including operations against suicide boats. Present at the Japanese surrender in Hong Kong. Sold to RNethNavy, 01/04/48, becoming the new *Karel Doorman*, 28/05/48. Sold to Argentina as *25 de Mayo*, 01/09/69.

Vengeance R71 (A)

Built: Swan Hunter & Wigham Richardson, Wallsend-on-Tyne; laid down: 16/05/42; launched: 23/02/44; completed: 15/01/45; loaned RAN 13/05/52; reserve RN 13/08/55; sold to Brazilian Navy as *Minas Gerais*, 13/12/56.

Courageous D50 Courageous-class fleet carrier

Built: Armstrong Whitworth & Co, Newcastle-upon-Tyne; laid down: 28/03/15; launched: 05/02/16; completed: 04/05/16 as battlecruiser, converted 05/05/28, Devonport Dockyard; displacement: 22,500 tons standard, 27,560 tons deep load; LOA: 786.5 ft; beam: 110 ft; armament: 16 single 4.7-in, 4 single 3-pdr, 10 single .303 mg; endurance: 2,920 miles @ 24 kts; complement: 1,260; aircraft: 48; lifts: 2 catapults: 2, 1936; torpedoed 17/09/39 by *U-29* in S-W Approaches, with loss of 518 lives.

Similar:

Glorious D77

Built: Harland & Wolff, Belfast; laid down: 01/05/15; launched: 20/04/16; completed: 14/10/16 as battlecruiser; converted: 07/01/30, Devonport Dockyard; sunk by gunfire from German battlecruisers *Scharnhorst* and *Gneisenau*, 08/06/40, withdrawing from Norway. Lost most of her crew.

Eagle D94 fleet carrier

Built: Armstrong Whitworth & Co, Newcastle-upon-Tyne; completed Portsmouth Dockyard; laid down: 20/02/13 as battleship *Almirante Cochrane* for Chile; launched: 08/06/18;

The ship's crest of *Glorious*.

Less fortunate was the first carrier to be designed as such, *Hermes*. By 1939, she was too small and too slow, but she could have made a useful escort carrier on the North Atlantic, had she not been sent east, where she was sunk. (*FAAM CARRIER H/130*)

completed: 20/02/24; displacement: 22,600 tons standard, 27,500 tons deep load; LOA: 667.5 ft; beam: 115 ft; armament: 9 single 6-in, 5 single 4-in, 2 octuple 2-pdr (1937), 12 single 20-mm Oerlikon (1942), 4 single 3-pdr; 2 twin 0.303 mg; endurance: 3,000 miles @ 17 kts; complement: 988; aircraft: 22 in 1942; lifts: 2; no catapults; work suspended during the First World War. Ship evaluated concept of starboard island. Hit by 4 torpedoes from *U73*, 11/08/42, while on Malta convoy, sank with loss of 160 lives.

Furious D47 fleet carrier

Built: Armstrong Whitworth & Co, Newcastle-on-Tyne; laid down: 08/06/15; launched: 15/08/16; completed: 04/07/17 as battlecruiser, sister of *Courageous* and *Glorious*. Converted in stages as first aircraft carrier, with final flush deck at Devonport 01/08/25; displacement: 22,450 tons standard, 27,165

tons deep load; LOA: 786.5 ft; beam: 90 ft; armament: 6 twin 4-in, 4 octuple 2-pdr pompom, 4 twin 20-mm Oerlikon, 7 single 20-mm Oerlikon; endurance: 3,700 miles @ 20 kts; complement: 1,218; aircraft: 33 in 1939; lifts: 2; no catapults; reserve, 15/09/44, poor mechanical condition, then target ship; sold for scrap 1948.

Hermes D95 fleet carrier

Built: Armstrong Whitworth & Co, Newcastle-upon-Tyne, completed Devonport Dockyard; laid down: 15/01/18; launched: 11/09/19; completed: 18/02/24; displacement: 10,850 tons standard, 13,700 tons deep load; LOA: 600 ft; beam: 90 ft; armament: 6 single 5.5-in, 3 single 4-in, 2 quad 0.5-in; endurance: 2,930 miles @ 18 kts; complement: 700; aircraft: 12 in 1939; lifts: 2; no catapults; completion delayed while design finalised. Sunk, 09/04/42, by Japanese aircraft off Ceylon.

The ship's crest of *Illustrious*.

Illustrious 87 (L, Q, 1945) Illustrious-class fleet carrier

Built: Vickers-Armstrong, Barrow-in-Furness; laid down: 27/04/37; launched: 05/04/39; completed: 25/05/40 displacement: 23,207 tons standard, 28, 619 tons deep load; LOA: 740 ft; beam: 106.75 ft; armament: 8 twin 4.5-in, 5 oct 2-pdr pompom, 3 single 40-mm Bofors, 19 twin 20-mm Oerlikon, 14 single 20-mm Oerlikon; endurance: 11,000 miles @ 12 kts; complement: 1,997; aircraft: 54; lifts: 2; catapults: 1; refitted, 06/46, trials and training carrier; reserve until returned to trials and training 1949–54; then reserve. Scrapped 1957. Similar:

Formidable 67 (R, X, 1945)

Built: Harland & Wolff, Belfast; laid down: 17/06/36; launched: 17/08/39; completed: 24/05/40; 05/49 to reserve, unmaintained; scrapped 1953.

Victorious 38 (P, S, V, X, 1945)

Built: Vickers-Armstrong, Newcastle-upon-Tyne; laid down: 04/05/37; launched: 14/09/39; completed: 15/05/41; extensively rebuilt 1950–58 to emerge as one of the world's most advanced carriers; scrapped: 07/69.

Even a carrier could ship a green sea, as *Victorious* shows while off the Scottish coast. (*FAAM CARS V/86*)

Implacable 86 (M) Modified Illustrious-class fleet carrier

Built: Fairfield Shipbuilding & Engineering. Co; Clydeside; laid down: 21/02/39; launched: 10/12/42; completed: 28/08/44; displacement: 23,450 tons standard, 32,110 tons deep load; LOA: 766 ft; beam: 131.25 ft; armament: 8 twin 4.5-in, 5 oct 2-pdr pompom, 3 quad 2-pdr pompom, 21 twin 20-mm Oerlikon, 19 single 20-mm Oerlikon; endurance: 12,000 miles @ 10 kts; complement: 2,300; aircraft: 81; lifts: 2; catapults: 1; modifications included upper and lower hangars, although forward lift only served upper hangar; four propeller shafts instead of three; reserve: 01/09/54; scrapped: 03/05/55.

Similar:

Indefatigable 10 (D)

Built: John Brown & Co, Clydebank; laid down: 03/05/38; launched: 08/12/42; completed: 03/05/44; reserve 12/46; training ship 1949, with classrooms and accommodation in hangar spaces; reserve 1954; scrapped: 1956.

Indomitable 92 (N/O/W) Illustrious-class fleet carrier

As for *Illustrious*, but:

Built: Vickers-Armstrong, Barrow-in-Furness; laid down: 10/05/37; launched: 26/03/40; completed: 10/10/41; armament: 8 twin 4.5-in plus 6 oct 2-pdr pompom, 2quad 40-mm Bofors, 2 twin 40-mm Bofors, 21 twin 20-mm Oerlikon, 18 single 20-mm Oerlikon; complement: 2,100; aircraft: 56; lifts: 2 (as for modified Illustrious-class); catapults 1; design modified to incorporate a lower hangar. Upper hangar was fitted with rails to increase capacity to 3 squadrons of Seafires and reduce handling damage to the aircraft, but this had to be abandoned as the system proved cumbersome under intensive combat conditions. Many regard

The ship's crest of *Indomitable*.

her as the most successful ship of the entire class. Extensive operational use postwar, including flagship, Home Fleet, in 1951, the first time an aircraft carrier had this role. Reserve: 05/10/53; scrapped: 1955.

Nairana D05 escort carrier

Built: John Brown & Co, Clydebank; laid down: 06/41; launched: 20/05/43; completed: 12/12/43; displacement: 13,825 tons standard, 17,210 tons deep load; LOA: 524 ft; beam: 68 ft; armament: 1 twin 4-in, 4 quad 2-pdr pompom, 8 twin 20-mm Oerlikon; endurance: 13,000 miles @ 16 kts; complement: 554; aircraft: 20; lifts: 1 aft; no catapults; built for the Russian convoys, loaned to RNethN as *Karel Doorman*, 23/03/46. Returned, 28/05/48; sold as merchantman.

Pretoria Castle F61 trials/training carrier

Built: Harland & Wolff, Belfast, as Union Castle passenger liner, 1938. Purchased by Admiralty as armed merchant cruiser, then converted Swan Hunter & Wigham Richardson, Wallsend-on-Tyne, 09/04/43;

Even escort carriers had their own crests, here is that of *Nairana*.

displacement: 19,650 tons standard, 23,450 tons deep load, LOA 592 ft; beam: 74.3 ft; armament: 2 twin 4-in, 10 twin 20-mm Oerlikon, 2 quad pompom; endurance: 16,000 miles @ 16 kts; complement: 580; aircraft: 21; lifts: 1 fwd; catapults: 1. Sold back to Union Castle, 26/01/46.

Ruler D72 Ruler-class escort carrier

Built: Seattle-Tacoma Shipbuilding Corp, Seattle; laid down: 25/03/43, as USS *St Joseph*, CVE-50; launched: 21/08/43; completed: 22/12/43; displacement: 11,400 tons standard, 15,390 tons deep load; LOA: 492 ft; beam: 108.5 ft; armament: 2 single 5-in, 8 twin 40-mm Bofors, 14 twin 20-mm Oerlikon, 7 single 20-mm Oerlikon; endurance: 27,500 miles @ 11 kts; complement: 646; aircraft: 30 operational, 90 ferry; lifts: 2; catapults: 1. One of 23 vessels of the US Prince William-class transferred to RN under Lend/Lease programme, laid down as carriers using the US C3 merchant hull. Only *Prince William*

remained in USN service. Returned USN, 29/01/46; scrapped: 1946.

Similar:

Ameer D01

Laid down: 18/07/42; launched 18/10/42; completed: 20/07/43; returned USN: 17/01/46, converted to merchantman.

Arbiter D31

Laid Down: 26/04/43; launched: 09/09/43 as USS *St Simon* (CVE-51); completed: 31/12/43; returned USN, 03/03/46, converted to merchantman.

Atheling D51

Laid down: 09/06/42; launched: 07/09/42; completed: 01/08/43; returned USN, 13/12/46.

Begum D38

Laid down: 03/08/42; launched: 11/05/42; completed: 03/08/43; returned to USN, 05/01/46, converted to merchantman.

Emperor D98 (E)

Laid down: 23/06/42; launched: 07/10/42; completed: 06/08/43; returned USN, 12/02/46, then scrapped.

Empress D43

Laid down: 09/09/42; launched: 30/12/42; completed: 13/08/43; returned USN, 04/02/46, then scrapped.

Khedive D62 (K)

Laid down: 22/09/42, as USS *Cordova* (CVE-39); launched: 20/01/43; completed: 23/08/43; returned USN, 26/01/46, sold as merchantman.

Nabob D77

Laid down: 20/10/42; launched: 09/03/43, as USS *Edisto* (CVE-41); completed: 07/09/43; torpedoed by *U-354*, 22/08/44, but saved by her mainly RCN crew. Paid off unrepaired 30/09/44. Returned to USN 16/03/45, while still on mud bank on Firth of Forth.

Patroller D07

Laid down: 27/05/42, as USS *Keweenam* (CVE-44); launched: 06/05/43; completed: 25/10/43; returned USN, 13/12/46; sold as merchantman.

Premier **D23**

Laid down: 31/10/42, as USS *Estero* (CVE-42); launched: 22/03/43; completed: 03/05/43; returned to USN 12/04/46, sold as merchantman.

Puncher **D79 (N)**

Laid down: 21/05/43, as USS *Willapa* CVE-53; completed: 05/02/44; displacement: 11,400 tons standard, 15,390 tons deep load; returned USN, 16/01/46, sold as merchantman.

Queen **D19**

Laid down: 12/03/43, as USS *St Andrews* (CVE-49); launched: 02/08/43; completed: 07/12/43; returned to USN, 31/10/46, sold as merchantman.

Rajah **D10 ferry carrier**

Laid down: 17/12/42, as USS *Prince*, but renamed USS *McClure* (CVE-45); launched: 18/05/43; completed: 17/01/44; refitted as troopship, 05/08/45; returned USN, 13/12/46, sold as merchantman.

Ranee **D03 ferry carrier**

Laid down: 05/01/43, as USS *Niantic* (CVE-46); launched: 02/06/43; completed: 08/05/43; refitted as troopship, 04/06/45; returned USN, 08/05/46, sold as merchantman.

Ravager **D70 (V) training/ferry carrier**

Laid down: 30/04/42; launched: 16/07/42; completed: 26/04/43; originally to have been named *Charger*; returned USN 27/02/46; sold as merchantman.

Reaper **D82 ferry carrier**

Laid down: 05/06/43; launched: 22/05/43; completed: 21/02/44; returned USN, 20/05/46; sold as merchantman.

Searcher **D40**

Laid down: 20/02/42; launched: 20/06/42; completed: 08/04/43; returned USN, 29/05/45; sold as merchantman.

Shah **D21**

Laid down: 13/05/42, as USS *Jamaica* (CVE-43); launched: 21/04/43; completed: 27/09/43; returned USN, 06/12/45; sold as merchantman.

Slinger **D26 ferry/replenishment carrier**

Laid down: 25/05/42, as USS *Chatham* (CVE-32); launched: 15/12/42; completed: 11/08/43; returned USN, 27/02/46; sold as merchantman.

Smiter **D55**

Laid down: 10/05/43, as USS *Vermillion* (CVE-52); launched: 27/09/43; completed: 20/01/44; returned USN, 06/04/46; sold as merchantman.

Speaker **D90**

Laid down: 09/10/42, as USS *Delgada* (CVE-40); launched: 20/02/43; completed: 20/05/43. The highlight of this ship's service came on 03/09/45, sailing from Tokyo Bay to Sydney with almost 500 POWs aboard. Capt 'Jimmy' James sailed around the BPF ships in harbour so that their crews could pay their respects to the POWs! Returned USN, 17/07/46; sold as merchantman.

Thane **D48 ferry carrier**

Laid down: 23/02/43, as USS *Sunset* (CVE-48); launched: 15/07/43; completed: 19/05/43; torpedoed 15/01/45 by *U-482* in Firth of Clyde and towed to Faslane. Could not be repaired due to pressure on dockyard capacity. Returned to USN 'as lies', 05/12/45, then scrapped.

Trouncer **D85 ferry carrier**

Laid down: 01/02/43, as USS *Perdido* (CVE-47); launched: 16/07/43; completed: 31/01/44; returned USN, 03/03/46; sold as merchantman.

Trumpeter **D09**

Laid down: 25/08/42, as USS *Bastian* (CVE-37); launched: 15/12/42; completed: 04/08/43; returned USN, 06/04/46; sold as merchantman.

Unicorn **I72 (X) aircraft repair ship**

Built: Harland & Wolff, Belfast; laid down: 29/06/39; launched: 20/05/41; completed: 12/03/43; displacement: 14,750 tons standard; 20,300 tons deep load; LOA: 640 ft;

beam: 90 ft; armament: 4 twin 4-in, 4 quad 2-pdr pompom, 5 twin 20-mm Oerlikon, 6 single 20-mm Oerlikon, 4 single 3-pdr; endurance 7,500 miles @ 20 kts; complement: 1,200; aircraft: 20 under repair, or 35 as operational carrier; lifts: 2; catapults: 1; 2 hangar decks: upper open aft for aircraft engine runs, and the extended flight deck aft had a self-propelled aircraft lighter suspended beneath it so that aircraft could be loaded directly from the upper hangar. Spent time as an operational carrier. In 1953, redesignated A195 as a ferry carrier. Reserve: 05/53; scrapped: 06/59.

Vindex **D15 escort carrier**

Built: Swan Hunter & Wigham Richardson, Wallsend-on-Tyne; laid down: 01/07/42; launched: 04/05/43; completed: 03/12/43; displacement: 14,500 tons standard, 17,200 tons deep load; LOA: 525.5 ft; beam: 68 ft; armament: 1 twin 4-in, 4 quad 2-pdr pompom, 8 twin 20-mm Oerlikon; endurance 13,000 miles @ 16 kts; complement: 639; aircraft: 20; lifts: 1 aft; no catapult; converted on slipway. A one-off converted merchantman with rivetted hull for Arctic convoys. After trooping duties postwar, sold 02/10/47 to original owners, Port Line, and reconverted.

Admiralty doubts about the suitability of welded hulls for the Arctic resulted in a small number of British-built escort carriers, such as *Vindex*. (*FAAM CARRIER V/25*)

MERCHANT AIRCRAFT CARRIERS

Two main types: Modified tankers with flight deck only, while grain carriers provided a limited small hangar with hoist rather than lift. Tanker-MAC ships carried 80 per cent of their original cargo, with the remainder AVGAS for the aircraft, usually 3 Swordfish.

Acavus – converted 10/43. Anglo-Saxon Petroleum Co.

Similar: *Adula* – modified 02/44, sister of above.

Alexia – modified 10/43.

Amastra – modified 09/43.

Ancylus – modified 10/43.

Empire MacAlpine – modified grain ship, 04/43, and able to carry 4 Swordfish using small hangar below decks.

Similar:

Empire MacAndrew – modified 07/43.

Empire MacCallum – modified 10/43.

Empire MacCabe – modified tanker, 12/43.

Empire MacColl – modified tanker, 05/43.

Empire MacDermott – modified grain ship, 03/44.

Empire MacKay – modified tanker, 10/43.

Empire MacKendrick – modified grain ship, 12/43.

Empire MacMahon – modified tanker 12/43.

Empire MacRae – modified grain ship, 09/43.

Gadila – modified tanker, 03/44.

Macoma – modified tanker, 05/44.

Miralda – modified tanker, 01/44.

Rapana – first modified tanker, 07/43.

SEAPLANE CARRIERS

Albatross D22

Built: Cockatoo Island Dockyard, Sydney; laid down: 05/05/26; launched: 23/02/28 completed: 01/29; displacement: 4,800 tons standard, 6,350 tons deep load; LOA: 443.75 ft; beam: 68 ft; armament: 4 single 4.7-in, 4 quad 2-pdr, 6 single 20-mm Oerlikon;

MAC-ships were a welcome addition to the carrier force, giving highly cost-effective protection against U-boats on the North Atlantic convoys. This is the Dutch-operated *Macoma*, a converted tanker. (*Royal Netherlands Navy Maritime Institute*)

The ideal way of getting an aircraft aboard a carrier was to fly it on, but often aircraft had to be loaded in port, usually from barges. This is one of 860 Squadron's Swordfish being 'craned' aboard. (*Royal Netherlands Navy Maritime Institute*)

endurance 9,500 miles @ 10 kts; complement: 450; aircraft: 6 usually, but up to 9 could be carried; lifts: hatch with crane; catapults 1; built for an Australian squadron as a cheaper alternative to an aircraft carrier, she was transferred to the RN in 1938 in exchange for a cruiser. Operated as a trials ship for the new Sea Otter amphibian in 10/43, before refitting as landing craft repair ship. Reserve 1945. Sold for conversion into passenger ship by Greek shipping line.

Athene D25

Completed 10/41 – seaplane carrier and aircraft transport, converted from fast cargo liner, 9,435 tons standard displacement. Could take up to 10 seaplanes or 40 crated aircraft.

Similar:

Engadine D71

Postwar, both sold back to Clan Line.

Pegasus D35

Built: Blyth Shipbuilding & Dry Dock Co, Blyth; laid down: 07/05/13; launched:

05/09/14; completed: 10/12/14, as HMS *Ark Royal*; displacement: 7,080 tons standard; 7,450 tons deep load; dimensions: 366 ft LOA; beam: 50.5 ft; armament: 4 single 12-pdr, 2 single .303 Maxim; endurance: 3,030 miles @ 10 kts; complement: 180; catapult: 1; aircraft: up to 10 seaplanes/amphibians.

Laid down as a collier, but purchased by the Admiralty and converted on the slipway, serving initially as *Ark Royal* until renamed in 1931 to release the name for the new fleet carrier. At the start of the Second World War, she was used as an aircraft transport, then as a fighter catapult ship with 3 Fulmars to provide air cover against Luftwaffe aircraft based in France for Gibraltar-bound convoys. After several unsuccessful launches, she was assigned to training duties on the Clyde and Irish Sea for Walrus crews assigned to battleships and cruisers. Reserve 02/44, sold for conversion to merchant vessel 1946, but work not completed. Scrapped 1950.

WARSHIPS FITTED WITH CATAPULTS

The importance of aircraft in the fleet spotter role was recognised as early as the First World War, so it became general practice for battleships and cruisers to be able to carry at least one aircraft. These were catapulted off and were seaplanes or amphibians that could be recovered using a crane after each flight. These aircraft were also used for communications duties and search and rescue. The growing use of radar and the availability of substantial numbers of aircraft carriers as the war progressed, meant that eventually most ships lost their aircraft, freeing space for additional anti-aircraft guns.

Some armed merchant cruisers were also fitted with catapults. Generally, with one exception, SS *Michael E*, with an FAA fighter, the famous CAM-ships used RAF fighters.

Armed merchant cruisers fitted with catapults were: *Alcantara*, *Asturias*, *Carnarvon Castle*, *Canton*, *Cilicia*, *Corfu*, *Fidelity*, *Maora**, *Pretoria Castle*, *Queen of Bermuda*, *Ranpura*, *Westralia**. (* HMAS)

Flights embarked on these ships initially were drawn from squadrons assigned to the various fleets, but from 01/40, all major warships had flights drawn from 700 Squadron. A second squadron, 703, was formed in mid-1942, to provide catapult flights with longer range aircraft, mainly for operations from armed merchant cruisers, and occasionally from other warships.

HMNZS *Achilles*: Cruiser; single Walrus. Catapult removed 04/43.

***Ajax*:** Cruiser; 2 Seafox until 05/40, then single Walrus. Catapult removed mid-1941.

***Anson*:** Battleship; 2 Walrus 04/42–08/43. Catapult removed late 1944.

***Arethusa*:** Cruiser; 2 Seafox. Catapult removed early 1941.

***Australia*:** Cruiser; 1 Seagull V during 1940.

***Barham*:** Battleship; 1 Swordfish to 01/40, then 1 Walrus. Sunk 25/11/41.

***Belfast*:** Cruiser; 1 Walrus, increased to two, 09/42. Catapult removed late 1944.

***Bermuda*:** Cruiser; 2 Walrus until 08/43. Catapult removed 04/44.

***Berwick*:** Cruiser; 2 Walrus until 06/42. Catapult removed mid-1942.

***Birmingham*:** Cruiser; 1 Walrus. Catapult removed mid-1943.

HMAS *Canberra*: Cruiser; 1 Walrus or Seagull V. Sunk 09/08/42.

***Ceylon*:** Cruiser; ship's flight formed but never embarked.

***Cornwall*:** Cruiser; 1 Walrus. Sunk 05/04/42.

***Cumberland*:** Cruiser; 1 Walrus.

***Devonshire*:** Cruiser; 1 Walrus. Catapult removed mid-1943.

***Dorsetshire*:** Cruiser; 1 Seafox or Kingfisher. Catapult removed 04/44.

Duke of York: Battleship; 2 Walrus. Catapult removed late 1944.

Edinburgh: Cruiser; 1 Walrus. Sunk 02/05/42.

Effingham: Cruiser; 2 Walrus. Sunk 17/05/40.

Emerald: Cruiser; 1 Seafox or Kingfisher. Catapult removed 04/44.

Enterprise: Cruiser; 1 Seafox or Kingfisher. Catapult removed 02/44.

Exeter: Cruiser; 2 Walrus. Sunk 01/03/42.

Fiji: Cruiser; 1 Walrus. Sunk 22/05/41.

Galatea: Cruiser; 1 Seafox. Sunk 15/12/41.

Gambia: Cruiser; 1 Walrus. Catapult removed mid-1943.

Glasgow: Cruiser; 2 Walrus. Catapult removed mid-1944.

Gloucester: Cruiser; 2 Walrus. Sunk 22/05/41.

HMAS *Hobart*: Cruiser; 2 Walrus. Catapult removed 1941–42.

Howe: Battleship; 2 Walrus. Catapult removed 1944.

Jamaica: Cruiser; 1 Walrus.

Kent: Cruiser; 1 Walrus. Catapult removed mid-1942.

Kenya: Cruiser; 2 Walrus.

King George V: Battleship; 2 Walrus. Catapult removed early 1944

HMNZS *Leander*: Cruiser, 1 Walrus. Catapult removed mid-1941, replaced, finally removed 1943.

Liverpool: Cruiser; 2 Walrus. Catapult removed late 1942.

London: Cruiser; 2 Walrus. Catapult removed early 1943.

Malaya: Battleship; 2 Swordfish, then 2 Walrus, 11/41. Catapult removed late 1942.

Manchester: Cruiser; 2 Walrus. Sunk 13/08/42.

Mauritius: Cruiser; 2 Walrus. Catapult removed 06/42.

Neptune: Cruiser; 2 Seafox. Sunk 19/12/41.

Newcastle: Cruiser; 2 Walrus. Catapult removed late 1942.

Newfoundland: Cruiser; 2 Walrus. Catapult removed mid-1944.

Nigeria: Cruiser; 2 Walrus. Catapult removed 01/44.

Norfolk: Cruiser; 1 Walrus. Catapult removed spring 1943.

Orion: Cruiser; 2 Seafox. Catapult removed mid-1941.

Penelope: Cruiser; 1 Seafox. Catapult removed 1940/41.

HMAS *Perth*: Cruiser; 1 Walrus or Seagull V. Sunk 01/03/42.

Prince of Wales: Battleship; 2 Walrus. Catapult, removed summer, 1941; sunk 10/12/41.

Queen Elizabeth: Battleship; 2 Walrus. Catapult removed late 1942.

Renown: Battlecruiser; 1 Walrus. Catapult removed 02/43.

Repulse: Battlecruiser; 2 Swordfish, then 1 Walrus, 08/41. Sunk 10/12/41.

Resolution: Battleship; 1 Swordfish or Walrus 08/41. Catapult removed late 1942.

Rodney: Battleship; 1 Swordfish, then Walrus, 01/40. Catapult removed early 1943.

Sheffield: Cruiser; 2 Walrus. Catapult removed 02/44.

Shropshire: Cruiser; 1 Walrus. Catapult removed late 1942.

Southampton: Cruiser; 2 Walrus. Sunk 11/01/41.

Suffolk: Cruiser; 2 Walrus. Catapult removed early 1943.

Sussex: Cruiser; 1 Walrus. Catapult removed late 1943.

HMAS *Sydney*: Cruiser; 1 Walrus or Seagull V. Sunk 19/11/41.

Trinidad: Cruiser; 2 Walrus. Sunk 15/05/42.

Uganda: Cruiser; 2 Walrus. Catapult removed late 1944.

Valiant: Battleship; 2 Swordfish, then 2 Walrus, 03/42. Catapult removed early 1943.

Warspite: Battleship; 1 Swordfish, then Walrus, 05/42. Catapult removed mid-1943.

York: Cruiser; 1 Walrus. Sunk 22/05/41.

CHAPTER 13

SHORE BASES AND NAVAL AIR STATIONS

To Lee-on-Solent and Arbroath
and Machrihanish we may pass,
We have searched the pubs and brothels far and wide,
Oh we've flown until we've grown
A pair of wings upon our arse,
But we'll never find the Archer *on the Clyde.*

From *Bring Back My Stringbag*, by Lord Kilbracken

The Fleet Air Arm's air stations complied with the tradition of having both a place name and an accompanying ship's name; for example, the Royal Naval Air Station, or more usually RNAS Lee-on-Solent, was also HMS *Daedalus*. A handful of bases were transferred from the RAF to the Royal Navy, but then many more had to be built. With a few notable exceptions, such as *Daedalus*, the Admiralty favoured bird names for shore stations, keeping the heroic and traditional ships' names for the fleet and light fleet carriers. A single name could, for administrative and command purposes, cover more than one site, especially if some of the others were RAF bases providing lodging facilities for the FAA.

Many bases were close to the coast and especially to naval ports, so that aircraft could be flown ashore before the carrier entered harbour, remaining operational. This was important, since aircraft aboard a carrier in port were vulnerable.

The number of RNAS grew from five in 1939 to forty-five active stations in 1945. Many were in exposed positions, often little more than muddy building sites. Many naval airmen endured a Scottish winter under canvas, and even when buildings were provided, it was the utilitarian nissen hut, with few creature comforts. Despite the hazards and hardships, including cramped conditions with wartime ships' complements, many were only too keen to get away to sea. One base for which little love was lost was Machrihanish, known as Machri-bloody-hanish, the ideal jumping off point for carriers arriving and departing the Clyde. Hatston, the main air station for the Home Fleet while in northern waters, had a significant combat role itself, sending its squadrons to account for the German cruiser *Konigsberg* during the Norwegian campaign of 1940.

Aircraft operating from shore stations carried identification letters, and the number of them meant that often two-letter combinations had to be used. Two systems were used, the initial one of May 1942, being adapted in January 1943, as the number of stations and squadrons built up. Where known, these are given after the name of the shore station. It was usual for satellite airfields to use the letter(s) of their parent station. As the focus of the war changed, letters were transferred from a station running down to one that was more active.

NAVAL AIR STATIONS IN THE UK

Numbers relate to the map opposite.

1) Abbotsinch (X), HMS *Sanderling*
Commissioned: 20/09/43. Previously, FAA had lodger facilities here. Transferred and used for aircraft storage and as maintenance yard.

2) Angle, HMS *Goldcrest*
Commissioned: 15/05/43. Moved to Dale, 05/09/43.

3) Anthorn (AN), HMS *Nuthatch*
Commissioned: 07/09/44. Housed No. 1 Aircraft Receipt and Despatch Unit.

4) Arbroath (A), HMS *Condor.* Arbroath, also known as Aberbrothock.
Commissioned: 19/06/40. Capacity: 200 aircraft. Initially No. 2 Observers School, also a deck landing school, and, later, a naval air signals school. Survived postwar, passing to RM, 1971.

5) Ayr (AR), HMS *Wagtail*
Commissioned: 20/10/44. Capacity: 110 aircraft. Originally a lodger station. It accommodated disembarked squadrons, FRU, communications squadron, a calibration flight, and the Bombardment Training School. Decommissioned: 10/03/46.

6) Ballyhalbert (BH), HMS *Corncrake*
Commissioned 17/07/45. Capacity: 100 aircraft. Originally lodger facilities from the RAF, but transferred for No. 4 Naval Air Fighter School. Paid off 13/11/45. Kirkistown commissioned 17/07/45, as a satellite having previously been lodger facilities on RAF station, and paid off 15/01/46.

7) Burscough (O, AH), HMS *Ringtail*
Commissioned: 01/09/43. At one time a satellite of Inskip, it received disembarking squadrons as well as those working up. Radar training also provided. Operated Woodvale as a satellite. Decommissioned: 15/06/46.

8) Campbeltown (P, then AN), HMS *Landrail/Landrail II*
Commissioned: 01/04/41. Capacity: 85 aircraft. Civil aerodrome, initially a satellite of Donibristle, became *Landrail II* when Machrihanish became the parent station, 15/06/41. Mainly used for carriers using the Clyde. Decommissioned: 06/45.

9) Charlton Horethorne (BY), HMS *Heron II*
Commissioned: 01/01/43. Satellite for Yeovilton. Decommissioned: 17/04/45. Exchanged with RAF in return for Zeals.

10) Crail (C), HMS *Jackdaw*
Commissioned: 01/10/40. Used for air torpedo training. Decommissioned: 04/47.

11) Culham (CM), HMS *Hornbill*
Commissioned: 01/11/44. No. 2 Aircraft Receipt and Despatch Unit.

12) Dale (P), HMS *Goldcrest*
Commissioned: 07 /09/43. Airfield for RN Aircraft Direction Centre at Kete, and twin-engined aircraft conversion courses provided.

13) Donibristle (D, then B), HMS *Merlin*
Commissioned: 24/05/39. Capacity: 220 aircraft. Originally RNAS station in 1917. Housed a communications squadron and an aircraft repair yard, as well as accommodating many visiting units and, towards the end of the war, Flag Officer, Carrier Training. Lodger facilities at Drem, satellites at Campeltown, Evanton and Fearn.

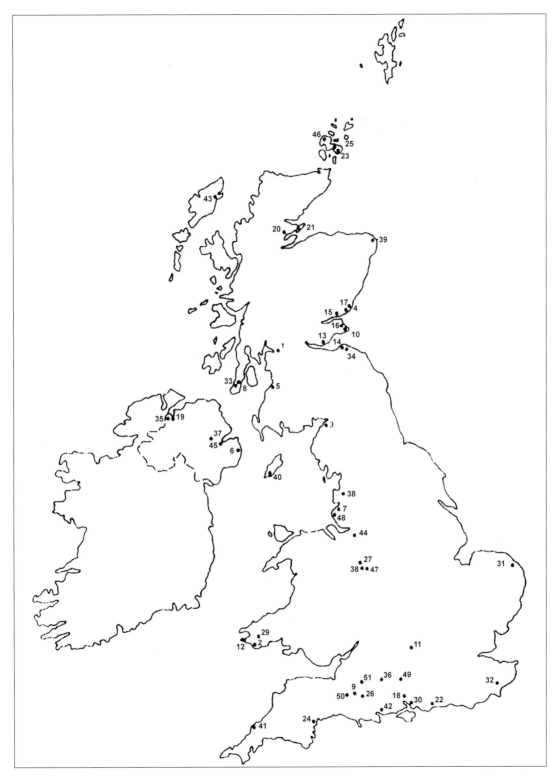

A map of the British Isles showing the Naval Air Stations. The numbers show the situation of the stations.

14) Drem (D), HMS *Nighthawk*
Commissioned: 01/06/45. Originally lodger facilities, then a satellite of Donibristle from 21/04/45. Housed Night Fighter School and FRU.

15) Dundee (A, then AA), HMS *Condor II*
Commissioned: 15/07/41. Satellite seaplane base for Condor. Paid off 15/06/44.

16) Dunino (D, then DO), HMS *Jackdaw II*
Commissioned: 15/12/42. Capacity: 180 aircraft. Satellite of Crail, providing reserve aircraft storage. Decommissioned: 02/04/46.

17) East Haven (B, then E), HMS *Peewit*
Commissioned: 01/05/943. TBR Deck Landing School, providing Part II TBR Training, Deck Landing Control Officer training and aircraft handling training. Decommissioned: 08/46.

18) Eastleigh (E, then I, EL), HMS *Raven*
Commissioned: 01/07/39. Shore base for carrier squadrons; housed the Safety Equipment School, School of Air Medicine and Naval Air Radio Installation Unit, as well as firefighting training. Lodger facilities at RAF Christchurch. Decommissioned: 04/47.

19) Eglinton (J), HMS *Gannet*
Commissioned: 15/05/43. Squadrons working up, or preparing for squadrons North Atlantic convoy escort duties.

20) Evanton (V, then EV), HMS *Fieldfare*
Comissioned: 09/10/44: Capacity: 500 aircraft. Used by FAA pre-war and lodger facilities in wartime. After commissioning became aircraft maintenance yard. Decommissioned postwar.

21) Fearn (F), HMS *Owl*
Commissioned: 11/10/42. Capacity: 96 aircraft. Previously a satellite of Donibristle. Used by TBR squadrons when working up. Decommissioned: 02/07/46.

22) Ford (FD), HMS *Peregrine*
Commissioned: 24/05/39. Immediate reserve storage unit housing Albacores and Swordfish, and accommodating No. 1 Observer School. Returned to RAF,

30/09/40, but School of Naval Photography remained as lodgers from *Daedalus*. Returned to FAA and recommissioned 15/08/45.

23) Grimsetter (Z, then GM), HMS *Robin*
Commissioned: 15/08/43. Capacity: 48 aircraft. Initially a satellite of Hatston. Decommissioned: 31/07/45.

24) Haldon (AY), HMS *Heron II*
Commissioned: 18/08/41. Satellite of Yeovilton. Reduced to care and maintenance basis, 05/43, and name transferred to Charlton Horethorne.

25) Hatston (H), HMS *Sparrowhawk*
Commissioned: 02/10/39. Shore base for units embarked with the Home Fleet at Scapa Flow. Decommissioned: 01/08/45,

26) Henstridge (G, then N), HMS *Dipper*
Commissioned: 01/04/43. Capacity: 120 aircraft. No. 2 Naval Air Fighter School. Decommissioned: 11/10/46.

27) Hinstock (U), HMS *Godwit*
Commissioned: 14/06/43. Capacity: 120 aircraft. Originally operated by the Ministry of Aircraft Production, transferred to FAA, 23/07/42, as a beam approach school under control of Stretton. Home to the Naval Advanced Instrument Flying School. Decommissioned: 28/02/47.

28) Inskip (K), HMS *Nightjar*
Commissioned: 15/05/43. Capacity: 145 aircraft. Housed No. 1 Operational Training Unit and controlled Burscough at one stage. Decommissioned: 02/07/46.

29) Lawrenny Ferry (F), HMS *Daedalus II*
Commissioned: 01/02/42. Seaplane base under the control of *Daedalus*; became care and maintenance only, 24/10/43.

30) Lee-on-Solent (L), HMS *Daedalus*
Commissioned: 24/05/39. Capacity 100 aircraft. Founded as a seaplane training station, 1917, and expanded to include an aerodrome in 1934. Many squadrons formed while others assembled for passage overseas. Wartime office of the Admiral

Seafires of 897 Squadron lined up at Henstridge. (*via S.H. Wragg*)

(Air) and was the main depot for naval air ratings. Portland used occasionally during the war for seaplanes. Satellite airfields and lodging arrangements included Cowdray Park, private airfield for storing withdrawn aircraft; Tangmere until transferred to *Heron*; plus Defford, Ford, Gosport, Heston, Manston and Thorney Island.

31) Ludham, HMS *Flycatcher*

Commissioned: 04/09/44. Transferred from RAF as headquarters for the Mobile Naval Airfield organisation, until this moved to Middle Wallop in 02/45. Returned to the RAF, 16/02/45.

32) Lympe, HMS *Daedalus II*

Commissioned: 01/07/39, as *Buzzard*, reduced to care and maintenance on 25/09. Reopened as *Daedalus II* later, but handed back to the RAF on 23/05/40. Accommodated RN Aircraft Training Establishment, providing technical training for air apprentices, air fitters and air mechanics, and W/T training, until this transferred to Newcastle-under-Lyme, 05/40, with the *Daedalus II* name.

33) Machrihanish (K, then M), HMS *Landrail*

Commissioned: 15/06/41. Capacity: 85 aircraft. Originally known as Strabane. Transferred from Campbeltown. Mainly used for carriers using the Clyde. Decommissioned 16/04/46.

34) MacMerry, HMS *Nighthawk*

Commissioned: 01/06/45. Satellite of Drem. Decommissioned: 15/03/46.

35) Maydown (N), HMS *Shrike*

Commissioned: 01/01/44. Capacity: 105 aircraft. Previously satellite of Eglinton. Became HQ for MAC-ship flights and housed Anti-U-Boat School, plus refresher and operational training. Decommissioned: 13/09/45.

36) Middle Wallop, HMS *Flycatcher*

Commissioned: 16/02/45. Former RAF airfield taken over as MONAB HQ and Maintenance Test Pilots School. Decommissioned: 10/04/46.

37) Nutts Corner, HMS *Pintail*

Commissioned: 11/07/45. Capacity: 60 aircraft. Used by fighter squadrons. Decommissioned: 31/03/46.

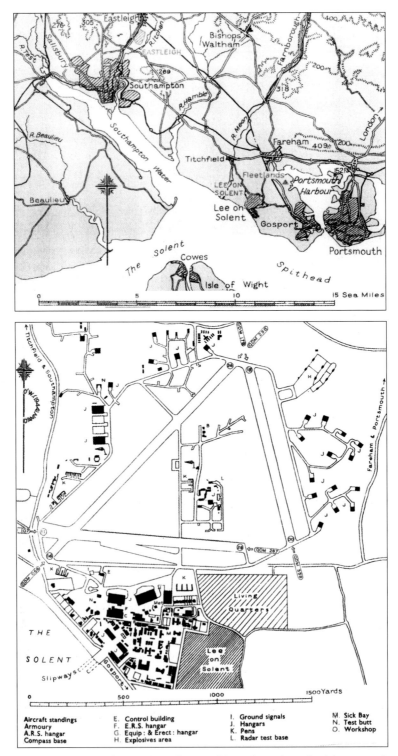

Aircraft standings
Armoury
A.R.S. hangar
Compass base

E. Control building
F. E.R.S. hangar
G. Equip: & Erect: hangar
H. Explosives area

I. Ground signals
J. Hangars
K. Pens
L. Radar test base

M. Sick Bay
N. Test butt
O. Workshop

HMS *Daedalus*, RNAS Lee-on-Solent, offered everything that aircraft ships entering Portsmouth needed, including a slipway for seaplanes, which was much appreciated by hovercraft postwar. (*FAAM*)

38) Peplow, HMS *Godwit II*
Commissioned: 28/02/45. Satellite of Hinstock.

39) Rattray Head/Crimond (AT, then I), HMS *Merganser*
Commissioned: 31/10/44. Capacity: 130 aircraft. Known as Crimond until 01/07/45. Provided TBR Training Part II. Decommissioned: 30/09/46.

40) Ronaldsway (R, AR), HMS *Urley*
Commissioned: 21/06/44. Capacity: 120 aircraft. Provided TBR training and Naval Operational Training Part III. Decommissioned: 14/01/46.

41) St Merryn (M), HMS *Vulture*
Commissioned: 10/08/40. Capacity: 145 aircraft. Housed School of Naval Air Warfare. Used by many squadrons. Decommissioned postwar. Responsible for *Vulture II*, bombing and gunnery range, with an emergency landing strip.

42) Sandbanks (S), HMS *Daedalus II*
Commissioned: 15/05/40. Satellite of Daedalus for seaplanes. Decommissioned: 09/10/43.

43) Stornoway, HMS *Mentor II*
Commissioned: 11/40. Seaplane base for *Mentor*, RN Stornoway. Decommissioned: 06/41. Transferred to RAF, who granted lodging facilities 1943–44.

44) Stretton (R, then ST), HMS *Blackcap*
Commissioned: 01/06/42. Capacity: 180 aircraft. Operational use plus RN Aircraft Maintenance Yard. Postwar, used by RNVR.

45) Sydenham (Belfast) (Q), HMS *Gadwall*
Commissioned: 21/06/43. Previously part of HMS *Caroline*. Used for disembarked squadrons, especially those moving from the US and Canada. Housed aircraft maintenance yard. Responsible for the shipment of aircraft overseas with escort carrier berth. Decommissioned: 30/04/46.

46) Twatt (T), HMS *Tern*
Commissioned: 01/01/41. Capacity: 50 aircraft. Originally a satellite of Hatston. Decommissioned: 30/09/46.

47) Weston Park, HMS *Godwit II*
Satellite landing strip for Hinstock during 1945.

48) Woodvale (V), HMS *Ringtail II*
Commissioned: 07/04/45. Originally lodger facilities at an RAF station, transferred to FAA as satellite of Burscough. Accommodated visiting squadrons. Own FRU. Decommissioned: 28/01/46.

49) Worthy Down (W), HMS *Kestrel*
Commissoned: 24/05/39. Capacity: 150 aircraft. Housed No. 1 Air Gunners School, the School of Aircraft Maintenance and the Engine Handling Unit.

50) Yeovilton (Y), HMS *Heron*
Commissioned: 01/06/40. Used earlier. Home to No. 1 Naval Air Fighter School and the Aircraft Direction Centre, and then the Naval Air Fighting Development Unit. Lodger facilities at RAF Duxford, Tangemere and Wittering.

51) Zeals (Z), HMS *Humming Bird*
Commissioned: 18/05/45. Ex-RAF, initially a satellite of Yeovilton. Accommodated FRU and provided fighter conversion. Decommissioned: 01/01/46.

MOBILE NAVAL AIR BASES

As the war progressed in the Far East, it became clear that improvised air stations would be needed ashore. It was important for the Royal Navy to be self-reliant because of the political sensitivity in its relations with the United States Navy that would make reliance on USN/USMC bases unacceptable. Mobile naval air bases, or MONABs, were the answer, able to provide the full range of facilities to support squadrons embarked with the fleet.

The headquarters for this new organisation was HMS *Flycatcher*, at Ludham, which later moved to Middle Wallop. There were ten MONABs, although the tenth formed too late and did not leave the UK,

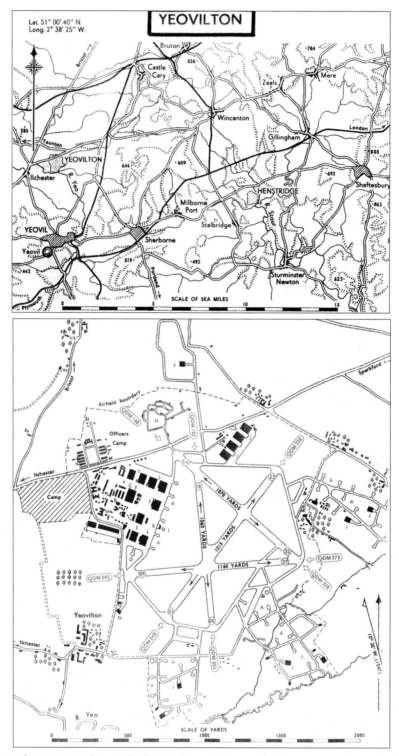

Yeovilton was under construction at the beginning of the war, but became so important that satellite airfields, including Henstridge, were soon needed. (*FAAM*)

and a Transportable Aircraft Yard, or TAMY. All received ship's names, started with 'Nab'.

MONAB 1, HMS *Nabbington*

Commissioned: Ludham, 28/10/44. Disembarked, Sydney, 20/12. Took over RAAF Nowra, 02/01/45, able to support Corsairs and Avengers. During 03–04/45, problems with the runways at Nowra meant the temporary use of the satellite base of Jervis Bay. Decommissioned: 15/11/45.

MONAB 2, HMS *Nabberley*

Commissioned: Ludham, 11/11/44. Took over RAAF Bankstown, becoming operational on 29/01/45. Able to support every aircraft type in FAA service, including Sea Otters and Expeditors. Decommissioned: 31/03/46.

MONAB 3, HMS *Nabthorpe*

Commissioned: Ludham, 04/12/44. Reached Sydney, 27/01/45. Took over RAAF Schofields, 07/02/45, where it supported Seafires and Fireflies. Decommissioned: 15/11.

MONAB 4, HMS *Nabaron*

Commissioned: Ludham, 01/01/45. Reached Manus in the Admiralty Islands via Sydney, taking over the USN base at Pityilu on 02/04. Decommissioned: 10/11/45, in Australia.

MONAB 5, HMS *Nabswick*

Commissioned: Ludham, 01/02/45. Disembarking Sydney, 29/03. Took over RAAF Jervis Bay, 01/05. Postwar, it moved from Jervis Bay on 15/11 and took over Nowra from MONAB 1. Decommissioned: 03/46.

HMS *Nabberly*, or MONAB 2, at Bankstown at the end of the war, with aircraft awaiting disposal, mainly scrapping or return to the USN under Lend/Lease. (*FAAM*)

MONAB 6, HMS *Nabstock*
Commissioned: Middle Wallop, 01/04/45.
Reached Sydney, 23/05. Lodged at RAAF
Maryborough, 01/06. Took over Schofields
from MONAB 3, 15 /11. Decommissioned:
06/46.

MONAB 7, HMS *Nabreekie*
Commissioned: Middle Wallop, 01/06/45.
Receipt and despatch unit, it reached the
former USN See Bee camp at Meendale,
near Brisbane, on 09/08. It shared the
airfield at Archerfield with TAMY 1.
Decommissioned: 05/11/45.

MONAB 8, HMS *Nabcatcher*
Commissioned: Middle Wallop, 01/07/45.
Receipt and despatch unit, reaching
Kai Tak, via Australia, in September. Decom-
missioned: 08/46. Kai Tak then came
under the control of the shore station,
Tamar.

MONAB 9, HMS *Nabrock*
Commissioned: Middle Wallop, 01/08/45.
Reached Singapore via Sydney.
Decommissioned at Sembawang, 15/12/45.

MONAB 10, HMS *Nabhurst*
Commissioned: Middle Wallop, 01/09/45.
Decommissioned: 12/10/45.

TAMY 1, HMS *Nabsford*
Commissioned: Ludham, 01/02/45. Took
over a number of installations near Brisbane,
including the civil airfield at Archerfield and
an Army camp at Focklea. Its role included
assembly of aircraft shipped out from the
USA and UK, including Corsairs and
Seafires. Decommissioned: 31/03/46.

OVERSEAS NAVAL AIR STATIONS

Addu Atoll (now Gan) (A)
HMS *Haitan*
Capacity: 24 aircraft. Secret refuelling base
for the Eastern Fleet. Airstrip part of shore
base, but operated as a secondary base to
China Bay/Trincomalee. Renamed HMS
Moraga: 01/02/44.

Aden
Khormaksar, HMS *Sheba*
Shore base with a naval air section at RAF
Khormaksar.

Australia
Bankstown (B), HMS *Nabberley*
Loaned from RAAF as base for MONAB 2,
29/01/45.

Jervis Bay (J), HMS *Nabwick*: RAAF airstrip
and satellite to Nowra, taken over
01/05/45, by MONAB 5.

Nowra (N), HMS *Nabbington, Nabswick*: RAAF
station loaned on 02/01/45, for MONAB 1,
until taken over by MONAB 5 postwar.

Canada
Dartmouth/Yarmouth, HMS *Seaborn*
Capacity 32 aircraft. RCAF Dartmouth
provided lodger facilities from 09/40, for
disembarked Swordfish and Walruses,
operated as part of *Seaborn*. Responsibility
was transferred to HMS *Saker* on 01/10/41,
then to HMS *Canada*, which was renamed
Seaborn on 01/07/44, by which time it was
looking after Swordfish disembarked from
MAC-ships bound for Halifax. RCAF
Yarmouth, transferred 01/01/43, for No. 2
Telegraphist Air Gunners School (No. 1
Telegraphist Air Gunners School to the
RCN), also controlled by *Canada* until
01/07/44. The school paid off 30/03/45.
Seaborn paid off 28/01/46, and Dartmouth
returned to the RCAF.

Halifax/Dartmouth/Yarmouth, HMS *Canada*
Overall ship's name for shore stations in
Canada, 1942–43.

Ceylon
Colombo Racecourse (L), HMS *Bherunda*
Commissioned: 01/10/43. Capacity: 90
aircraft. Accommodation for visiting
squadrons, plus FRU and a communications squadron, assembly of aircraft
shipped to the Far East and recovery of

crashed and damaged aircraft. Local garage acquired to repair engines. Decommissioned: 30/11/45.

Katukurunda (K), HMS *Ukussa*
Commissioned: 15/10/42. Capacity: 144 aircraft. Used by visiting squadrons, and included RN Aircraft Repair Yard with aircraft storage. Decommissioned: 27/09/46.

Maharagama, HMS *Monara*
Commissioned: 01/12/44. Housed RN Aircraft Training Establishment training Singalese recruits.

Puttalam (P), HMS *Rajaliya*
Commissioned: 01/02/43. Capacity 104 aircraft. Previously under control of HMS *Lanka* since 05/42. Facilities for visiting squadrons from the Eastern Fleet and reserve aircraft storage. Decommissioned: 31/10/45.

Trincomalee/Clappenburg Bay C), HMS *Bambara*
Commissioned: 01/01/44. Originally RAF China Bay, with lodger facilities, and 08/40–04/42, part of shore station, Lanka, then part of HMS *Highflyer*. Responsible for Addu Atoll. It later included RN Aircraft Maintenance Yard at Clappenburg Bay. Decommissioned: 31/12/47.

East Africa
Kilindini and Port Reitz, HMS *Kipanga*
Shore base at Mombasa, Kenya, also responsible for FAA units ashore in East Africa.

Mackinnon Road/Port Reitz (Mombasa)/Voi (R), HMS *Kipanga II*
Capacity: 64 aircraft, Mackinnon Road; 2 squadrons, Port Reitz. Under control of *Kipanga*, for units using the lodging facilities at the RAF base at Mackinnon Road, used by visiting squadrons and for fighter combat training. Eastern Fleet TBR pool and aircraft erection facilities at Port Reitz, a joint RAF/SAAF station.

Voi provided accommodation for disembarked squadrons under the same control. Decommissioned postwar.

Nairobi, HMS *Korongo*
Commissioned: 01/09/42. Capacity: 160 aircraft. RAF base with naval presence, known as Eastleigh locally, but to avoid confusion referred to as Nairobi by the armed forces. Aircraft repair yard and storage facility. Decommissioned: 15/10/44.

Tanga, HMS *Kilele*
Commissioned: 01/10/42. Capacity: 96 aircraft. Accommodated squadrons visiting Tanganyika. Also assembled crated aircraft. Decommissioned: 31/05/44.

Egypt
Dekheila (D), HMS *Grebe*
Commissioned: 16/09/40. Capacity: 72 aircraft. Loaned by Egypt, initially as HMS *Nile II*, it remained under the control of the shore base, *Nile* until 01/04/41. Used by squadrons from Mediterranean Fleet carriers or in transit to and from the Far East, and for Western Desert operations. Accommodated FRU. Came under control of *Nile* again on 01/04/43, but retained own ship's name. Decommissioned: 31/01/46.

Fayid, HMS *Phoenix*
Commissioned: 15/05/41. Storage for 130 aircraft. Airfield in the Suez Canal Zone, with RN Aircraft Repair Yard. Decommissioned: 28/02/46.

Gibraltar
North Front (G), HMS *Cormorant II*
Commissioned: 26/09/40. Capacity: 24 aircraft. Built on racecourse site. Initially landing strip operated by RAF, but RNAS developed and transferred to the FAA, under the control of the local naval base, *Cormorant*. Returned to RAF, 01/08/41, although lodger facilities remained. Recommissioned: 01/01/44. FRU. Returned to RAF postwar.

Gibraltar was an important base. Here Royal Marines process German naval PoWs. The blue RM uniform was worn more frequently than today. (*via S.H. Wragg*)

Gold Coast (now Ghana)
Komenda, HMS *Wara*
Commissioned: 01/10/42. Capacity:104 aircraft. At Takoradi, uncrated and assembled aircraft to be flown across sub-Saharan Africa as reinforcements. Decommissioned: 07/12/43.

Iceland
Huitanes/Kaldadarnes, HMS *Baidur*
Shore stations in Iceland, part of local naval base, *Baidur*. Facilities for aircraft disembarked from visiting carriers, mainly on Arctic convoys.

India
Cochin (H), HMS *Kaluga*
Commissioned: 01/02/45. Lodger facilities on RAF station, but remained under the control of *Garuda* until early 1946. Aircraft erection depot main activity, but limited facilities for disembarked squadrons. Decommissionmed: 08/46.

Coimbatore (Q), HMS *Garuda*
Commissioned: 01/10/42. Capacity: 250 aircraft in storage. RN Aircraft Repair Yard, assembling aircraft shipped from UK and USA. Decommissioned: 01/04/46.

Sulur (R), HMS *Vairi*
Commissioned: 01/02/45. Sometimes spelt Sollur. Ex-RAF base. Under the control of *Garuda*. Planned aircraft storage never fully realised, but would have been 300 aircraft. Decommissioned: 01/04/46.

Tambaram (T), HMS *Valluru*
Commissioned: 01/07/44. FRU and aircraft maintenance yard, and accommodation for visiting squadrons. Plans for aircraft repair yard abandoned after VJ-Day. Decommissioned: 01/12/45.

Malta
Ta Kali (M), HMS *Goldfinch*
Commissioned: 01/04/45. Previously, FAA had lodger facilities at RAF Ta Kali, under control of shore base, *St Angelo*. Housed FRU. Returned to the RAF postwar. Lodger facilities also at RAF Hal Far, transferred to FAA postwar.

Sierra Leone
Hastings (H), HMS *Spurwing*
Commissioned: 22/03/43. Capacity: 84 aircraft. Civil aerodrome at Freetown, operated by the RAF. Initially under the control of the local headquarters ship, *Edinburgh Castle*. Decommissioned: 31/12/44.

South Africa
Simonstown/Wingfield/Wynberg (W), HMS *Afrikander*
RN shore base at Simonstown, was responsible for naval units using SAAF Wingfield and Wynberg, although the latter was sometimes known as *Afrikander III*.
Stamford Hill, HMS *Kongoni*
Commissioned: 31/03/44. Previously SAAF station near Durban with lodger facilties, including an FRU. Decommissioned: 31/01/46.
Wingfield (W), HMS *Malagas*
Commissioned: 15/03/42. SAAF base with lodger facilities, originally under *Afrikander* at Simonstown. Air station and aircraft repair yard for Eastern Fleet and ships on passage from the Atlantic to the Eastern Mediterranean via the Cape. Later absorbed air section from Wynberg, and worked up Hellcat squadrons. Decommissioned: 31/05/46.

United States
Lewiston/Quonset Point/Dartmouth, HMS *Saker II*
Commissioned: 01/10/42. Lewiston, Maine, a loaned USN base, relieved pressure on *Saker*, but reabsorbed pressure on *Saker*, but reabsorbed 01/11/42. Quonset Point, Rhode Island, became Saker II when Asbury decommissioned, 31/03/44.
Quonset Point, Rhode Island, HMS *Asbury*
Commissioned: 01/10/42. Accommodated FAA squadrons working up after taking delivering of US-built aircraft and escort carriers. Decommissioned: 31/03/44, to become *Saker II* (see below).
Washington/Halifax/Lewiston/Brunswick, Maine/Squantum/NewYork, HMS *Saker*
Commissioned: 01/10/41. Accounting and administrative base in Washington for FAA throughout North America. Halifax was the RN base at Halifax, Nova Scotia, under the control of *Saker*, passing to *Canada*, 01/08/42. Lewiston, Maine, USN base, part of *Saker* 1943–45. Brunswick, Maine, USN base loaned in 08/43, part of *Saker* for the next 2 years, for Corsair squadrons to work up. Pressure on runway and airspace meant that ADDLs, used satellite USN stations at Rockland and Sanford. Decommissioned: 29/02/48.

West Indies
Bermuda, HMS *Malabar II* and *Malabar III*
Capacity: 12 aircraft. Pre-war seaplane base was used by ships of the America and West Indies Station for their catapult aircraft. Used the ships' names at different times after a landing strip was added. Care and maintenance, 1944.
Palisadoes, HMS *Buzzard*
Commissioned: 01/08/41. Capacity: 60 aircraft. Name originally used when Lympne transferred from RAF in 1939. Air station in Jamaica operated as part of *Malabar* from 21/12/40. Accommodated disembarked squadrons and provided reserve aircraft storage. Decommissioned: 15/07/43, but remained as part of *Moga* until 31/12/44.
Piarco, HMS *Goshawk*
Comissioned: 06/11/40. Capacity: 162 aircraft. Housed No. 1 Observer School. Decommissioned: 28/02/46.

LODGING FACILITIES AT AIR FORCE BASES AND CIVIL AIRFIELDS

Operational necessity often meant that Fleet Air Arm squadrons had to make use of other airfields from time to time, mainly RAF bases, and, to a lesser extent, RAAF, SAAF and RCAF bases and civil aerodromes. Although this was partly because the FAA was short of air stations at the start of the war, the main reason was that operational requirements were constantly changing. Lodger facilities were not usually accorded ships' names and did not have the prefix RNAS, but did have pre-arranged facilities available to naval air squadrons.

The main lodging facilities, with dates used, were:

Aboukir, Egypt: RAF station used throughout the war; during 1941 on the books of *Nile*, the RN shore base at Alexandria.

Aldergrove: RAF, 1939–40, with 774 Squadron attached to No. 3 RAF Bombing and Gunnery School.

Andraka, Diego Suarez, Madagascar: Airfield used after invasion, on books of shore station *Ironclad*.

Argentia, Newfoundland: RCAF used for disembarked flights and squadrons from MAC-ships and escort carriers.

Benbecula: RAF

Bircham Newton: RAF

Bratton: RAF, used mainly for training facilities for RNAS Hinstock, 1943–44.

Cholavarum, southern India: RAF, with resident RN Air Section.

Culmhead (also known as Church Stanton): RAF, used occasionally.

Detling: RAF 1940–41.

Docking: RAF 1942–44.

Dundonald: RAF, used mainly during 1944 by 3rd Naval Fighter Wing.

Duxford: RAF, used mainly during 1941–43 as part of the Air Fighting Development Unit, and on the books of *Raven*.

Fraserburgh: RAF, used occasionally.

Hal Far, Malta: RAF, used extensively by disembarked squadrons throughout the war and transferred postwar.

Harrowbeer: RAF, 1944.

Heath Row: Fairey Aviation's airfield, 1944–45.

Heston: also a civilian airfield, used from 04/45, until after the war.

Hyeres de la Palyvestre, France: French naval air station near Toulon, used before the fall of France, 1939–40.

Jersey: a civil airport used from 11/03/40, until it was evacuated on 31/05/40.

Kalafrana, Malta: RAF, used by disembarked seaplanes.

Lands End (also known as St Just): civil aerodrome used briefly during 1940.

Langham: RAF, 1942–44.

Limavady: RAF, 1944.

Long Kesh: RAF, 1944–45.

Manston: RAF, used occasionally.

Merston: RAF, used occasionally during 1945.

Minneriya, Ceylon: RAF, with resident RN Air Section.

Mullaghmore: RAF, 1944–45.

Norfolk, Virginia: USN, used by disembarked squadrons and those working up with US-built aircraft, transferred to Quonset Point, 11/42.

North Coates: 1940–41.

Pembroke Dock: RAF, 1940–41.

Perranporth: RAF, 1944, under control of St Merryn.

Peterhead: RAF, 1942–44.

Port Ellen: RAF, 1943.

Prestwick: RAF, 1940–41.

St Eval: RAF, 1940–44.

St Thomas Mount, Madras, southern India: Extensive lodger facilities for up to 7 FAA squadrons, plus resident RN Air Section.

Gala Opening Dance

at the

Royal Naval Air Station

Palisadoes

Friday November 28, 1941

Music by

Hugh Coxe and his Orchestra

Dancing 8.30 pm - 1 am   *Admission 2/-*
                                   Refreshments Inclusive

Overseas bases included Palisadoes in Jamaica, initially administered by the local naval base, HMS *Malabar*, before having an independent existence as HMS *Buzzard*, when, of course, they held a dance to celebrate! (*via S.H. Wragg*)

Santa Cruz, southern India: Extensive lodger facilities for up to 4 FAA squadrons, plus resident RN Air Section.

Sigriya, Ceylon: RAF, with resident RN Air Section.

Skitten: RAF, 1940–41.

Speke: RAF, 1942–45, with a resident RN Air Section which eventually moved to *Ringtail II* 04/45.

Squantum: USN, TBR Avenger squadrons working up, 1943–44.

Sullom Voe: RAF, RN Air Section under control of *Sparrowhawk*, resident from mid-1940 to mid-1941 for disembarked seaplanes.

Sumburgh: RAF, 1941–42.

Tain: RAF, 1942–44.

Thorney Island: RAF, used from 1940 onwards.

Turnhouse: RAF, 1942–44.

Vavuniya, Ceylon: RAF, with resident RN Air Section.

West Freugh: RAF, 1940–43.

Westhampnett: RAF, 1945.

West Raynham: RAF, 1945.

Wick: RAF, 1939–40.

APPENDIX I

BATTLE HONOURS 1939–1945

Thirty battle honours were awarded to naval air squadrons during the Second World War, with the Fleet Air Arm assuming the tradition of battle honours for ships.

The honours and squadrons involved were:

Aegean 1943–44
Engagements with the enemy in all waters of the Aegean Archipelago, between 35–42° N, 22–30° E, 07/09/43–28/11/43, and 01/44–12/44. Squadron Nos: 800, 807, 809, 879, 881, 899.

Arctic 1941–45
Covering forces employed as escorts or in support of convoys running to and from northern Russia within the Arctic Circle, 01/41–05/45. Squadron Nos: 802, 809, 811, 813, 816, 819, 822, 824, 825, 832, 833, 835, 842, 846, 853, 856, 882, 883, 893, 1832.

Atlantic 1939–45
Awarded both for convoy escort duty and for participation in any successful action between the Arctic Circle and the Equator. Squadron Nos: 700, 801, 802, 804, 807, 808, 810, 811, 813, 814, 816, 818, 820, 824, 825, 826, 833, 835, 836, 837, 838, 840, 842, 846, 850, 860, 881, 882, 896, 898, 1832.

Biscay 1940–45
Awarded for forces taking part in a successful action between Ushant and Cape Ortegal, from 12° W to the French coast, Squadron No.: 817.

Bismarck 1941
Pursuit and destruction of German battleship *Bismarck* in North Atlantic, 23–27/05/41. Squadron Nos: 800, 808, 810, 818, 820, 825.

Burma 1944–45
Operations over Burma, 10/44–04/45, and 05–08/45. Squadron Nos: 800, 804, 807, 808, 809, 815, 851, 896, 1700.

Calabria 1940
Action against Italian fleet off Calabria, Italy, 09/07/40; Squadron Nos: 813, 824.

Crete 1941
Awarded to No. 805 Squadron for action during the defence and evacuation of Crete, 20/05–01/06/41.

Diego Suarez 1942
Support of landings in Madagascar, Operation Ironclad, 5–7/05/42. Squadron Nos: 800, 806, 810, 827, 829, 831, 880, 881, 882.

Dunkirk 1940
Evacuation of British Expeditionary Force, Operation Dynamo, 26/05/40–04/06/40. Squadron Nos: 801, 806, 825, 826.

English Channel 1939–45
Awarded to coastal convoy escorts and for participation in any successful action in the English Channel and other waters between Southend and Bristol, east of a line between Ushant and the Isles of Scilly, and including the north coast of Cornwall. Squadron Nos: 811, 812, 818, 819, 825, 841.

Japan 1945
Operations against warships and mainland targets on the Japanese home islands, 16/07/45–11/08/45. Squadron Nos: 801, 820, 828, 848, 849, 880, 887, 1771, 1772, 1834, 1836, 1841, 1842.

Libya 1940–42

Inshore operations between Port Said and Benghazi, and in support of the Army in the Western Desert, 09/40–06/42. Squadron Nos: 803, 805, 806, 813, 819, 821, 824, 826.

Malaya 1942–45

Awarded to No. 851 Squadron for participation in successful actions in the Straits of Malacca and waters adjacent to the Malay Peninsula and Sumatra between 7° N and 7° S, and 95–108° E, between 01/42–08/45.

Malta Convoys 1941–42

Operations to resupply aircraft and stores to Malta, 01/41–12/42. Squadron Nos: 800, 801, 806, 807, 808, 809, 812, 813, 816, 820, 824, 825, 827, 831, 832, 884, 885.

Matapan 1941

Night action off Cape Matapan, Greece, against Italian fleet, 28–29/03/41. Squadron Nos: 700, 803, 806, 815, 826, 829.

Mediterranean 1940–45

Awarded for any operation in the Mediterranean not covered by a successful award of any other battle honour. Squadron Nos: 700, 767, 800, 803, 806, 810, 812, 813, 815, 816, 818, 819, 820, 821, 824, 826, 828, 829, 830.

Normandy 1944

Covering and support of forces in the English Channel, Dover to Ushant, for landings in France, 06/06/44–03/07/44, Operation Neptune. Squadron Nos: 800, 804, 808, 816, 819, 838, 846, 848, 849, 850, 854, 855, 881, 885, 886, 896, 897. No. 700 Squadron was also included, even though it had officially disbanded 03/44.

North Africa 1942–43

Support of landing forces and of Army ashore in Algeria and Tunisia, Operation Torch, 08/11/42–20/02/43. Squadron Nos: 700, 800, 801, 802, 804, 807, 809, 817, 820, 822, 832, 833, 880, 882, 883, 884, 885, 888, 891, 893.

North Sea 1939–45

Awarded to coastal convoy escorts and for participation in any successful action in the North Sea and other waters between Southend and Shetland, excepting coastal waters off Norway. Squadron Nos: 803, 811, 812, 826.

Norway 1940–45

Operations in coastal waters off Norway as far north as Tromso, initially 08/04/40–08/06/40, but later extended to successful actions in these waters up to VE-Day. Squadron Nos: 700, 701, 800, 801, 802, 803, 804, 806, 810, 816, 817, 818, 820, 821, 823, 825, 827, 828, 829, 830, 831, 841, 842, 846, 852, 853, 856, 880, 881, 882, 887, 894, 896, 898, 1770, 1771, 1832, 1834, 1836, 1840, 1841, 1842.

Okinawa 1945

Attacks on airfields in the Sakashima Gunto group of islands in the East China Sea, up to and including the assault on Okinawa, 26/03/45–25/03/45, Operation Iceberg. Squadron Nos: 820, 848, 849, 854, 857, 885, 887, 894, 1770, 1830, 1833, 1834, 1836, 1839, 1840, 1841, 1842, 1844, 1845.

Palembang 1945

Air strikes on oil refineries on Sumatra, 24/01/45, Operation Meridian I. Squadron Nos: 820, 849, 854, 857, 887, 894, 1770, 1830, 1833, 1834, 1836, 1839, 1844.

River Plate 1939

Pursuit and sinking of German battleship *Graf Spee*, 12/39, No. 700 Squadron.

Sabang 1944

Air strikes and bombardment on harbour and oil installations at Sabang, North Sumatra, 25/07/44, Operation Crimson. Squadron Nos: 831, 1830, 1833, 1836, 1837, 1838.

Salerno 1943

Support of landing forces at Salerno on the Italian mainland, 09/09/43–09/10/43, Operation Avalanche. Squadron Nos: 807, 808, 809, 810, 820, 834, 878, 879, 880, 886, 887, 888, 890, 893, 894, 897, 899.

Sicily 1943

Support of landing forces in Sicily, 10/07/43–17/08/43, Operation Husky. Squadron Nos: 807, 817, 820, 880, 885, 888, 893, 899.

South of France 1944
Support of landing forces on the south coast of France, 15–27/08/44, Operation Dragoon. Squadron Nos: 800, 807, 809, 879, 881, 882, 899.

Spartivento 1940
Action off Cape Spartivento, Sardinia, against Italian battleships and cruisers, 27/11/40. Squadron Nos 700, 800, 808, 810, 818, 820.

Taranto 1940
Night air strike on Italian fleet and harbour, 11–12/11/40. Squadron Nos: 813, 815, 819, 824.

APPENDIX II

FLEET AIR ARM FLAG OFFICERS 1939–1945

Flag Officer Home Air Command
Rear Adm R. Bell-Davis, VC, CB, DSO, AFC, 24/05/39
Rear Adm C. Moody, CB, 30/09/41
Rear Adm C.V. Robinson, CB, 12/05/43
Rear Adm Sir C. Robinson, KCB, 01/01/45
Vice Adm Sir D. Boyd KCB, CBE, DSC, 01/06/45

Flag Officer Carrier Training and Administration
Vice Adm Sir L. Lyster, KCB, CBE, CVO, DSO, 27/04/43 (knighted 02/06/45)

Flag Officer Home Fleet Aircraft Carriers
Rear Adm Sir L. Lyster, CVO, DSO, 11/07/42 (promoted to Vice Adm, 29/10/42)
Rear Adm C. Moody, CB, 21/05/43

Flag Officer Mediterranean Aircraft Carriers
Until 01/09/40, this post was known as Rear Adm/Vice Adm Aircraft Carriers.
Vice Adm L.V. Wells, CB, DSO, 31/07/39
Rear Adm Sir L. Lyster, CVO, DSO, 19/07/40
Rear Adm D. Boyd, CBE, DSC, 18/02/41

Flag Officer Force H
Vice Adm Sir N. Syfret KCB, 10/01/42 (acting VA until 08/09/42, when knighted)
Vice Adm Sir A. Willis, KCB, DSO, 24/02/43 (knighted 02/06/43)

Flag Officer Force V – Salerno
Rear Adm P. Vian, DSO, 09/42

Naval Commander Operation Torch
Cdre T.H. Troubridge, DSO, 11/42

Flag Officer Eastern Fleet Aircraft Carriers
Rear Adm D. Boyd, CBE, DSC, 02/42
Rear Adm C. Moody, CB, 01/12/43 (promoted to Vice Adm as Flag Officer (Air) East Indies, 13/12/44)

Flag Officer Naval Air Stations Indian Ocean
Rear Adm H.C. Rawlings, 30/04/43– 12/44

Flag Officer Naval Air Stations Australia and Pacific
Rear Adm R.H. Portal DSC, 1944–47

Flag Officer Aircraft Carriers British Pacific Fleet/ Flag Officer 1st Aircraft Carrier Squadron British Pacific Fleet (from 23/02/45)
Rear Adm Sir P. Vian, KCB, KBE, DSO, 15/11/44 (promoted to Vice Adm 08/05/45)

Flag Officer 11th Aircraft Carrier Squadron British Pacific Fleet
Rear Adm C.J.J.H. Harcourt, CB, CBE, 03/45–09/45

Commodore 30th Aircraft Carrier Squadron British Pacific Fleet
Cdre W.P. Carne, 03/45–09/45

Rear Admiral Escort Carriers British Pacific Fleet/Rear Admiral 21st Aircraft Carrier Squadron Eastern Fleet (from 23/02/45)
Rear Adm A.W. LaT. Bisset, 28/10/43
Cdre G.N. Oliver 07/44 (promoted to Rear Adm, 07/45)

APPENDIX III

MEDALS AND AWARDS

Those serving with the Fleet Air Arm were eligible for the Royal Navy's awards for gallantry and for a number of campaign medals. They were also eligible for many of the medals awarded to RAF personnel, including the Distinguished Flying Cross, to the dismay and sometimes outright hostility of many senior naval officers of the old school. It took nerve to wear the DFC ribbon, even if the wearer had earned it during the Battle of Britain.

As with all three services, the full medal and ribbon was only worn on ceremonial occasions, and miniature versions were available to wear with mess kit. On ordinary uniforms, the every day practice was to wear ribbons only.

In addition to medals, members of all three services were also eligible for the full range of honours, traditionally awarded on the king's birthday and at the New Year and, in theory, since there were no general elections until after the war in Europe, on the dissolution of Parliament. Several of these, including the Order of the Bath and the Order of the British Empire, had a military division, and holders would wear the ribbon of the order with their medal ribbons. Knighthoods – unless inherited – were usually reserved for senior officers.

Victoria Cross (VC).

AWARDS FOR GALLANTRY

Victoria Cross

The highest award for the British armed services, open to all services and all ranks. It has a crimson-maroon ribbon, with a bronze cross depicting a lion standing upon the Royal crown, below which a semi-circular scroll carries the inscription 'For Valour' on the obverse, and the date of the act of valour on the reverse. The recipient's details were recorded on the reverse of the suspender clasp.

Distinguished Service Order

Normally awarded for outstanding command and leadership under fire by officers in all three services. It has a red ribbon with dark blue edges,

Distinguished Service Order (DSO).

Distinguished Service Cross (DSC).

and a gold or silver gilt white enamelled cross with curved arms. The monarch's crown within a laurel wreath is on the obverse, while the reverse has the Royal cypher surmounted by a crown. The year of award appears on the reverse of the suspender clasp.

Distinguished Service Cross

Available to RN, Merchant Navy and RAF officers serving with the fleet, for 'meritorious or distinguished services in action'. The ribbon has equal widths of dark blue, white and dark blue, and a silver cross with curved arms. The obverse shows the monarch's cypher surmounted by a Royal crown within a circle, while the reverse shows the year of award in the lower arm of the cross.

Distinguished Flying Cross

Available only to commissioned officers of the RAF and RN. The ribbon has violet and white diagonal stripes with a silver cross *flory*, into which feathered wings, an aeroplane propeller and bombs are incorporated on the obverse, with the entwined cypher 'RAF' in the centre, while on the reverse there is the

Royal cypher. The year of award is engraved on the lower arm.

Distinguished Flying Cross (DFC).

249

Distinguished Conduct Medal (DCM).

Conspicuous Gallantry Medal (CGM).

Distinguished Conduct Medal

Available to personnel of the rank of warrant officer and below in all services for 'distinguished conduct in the field', and this stamped on the reverse side. The ribbon has equal widths of crimson, dark blue and crimson, while the round silver medal carries George VI's head.

Conspicuous Gallantry Medal

For Royal Navy and Royal Marines personnel of warrant officer rank and below who 'distinguish themselves by acts of conspicious gallantry in action with the enemy'. The ribbon is white with narrow blue edges with a round silver medal with the king's head and title on the obverse, and on the reverse, 'For Conspicuous Gallantry' surrounded by a wreath of two laurel branches, surmounted by a crown. A variation, the **Conspicuous Gallantry Medal (Flying)**, was created on 10/11/42, for personnel of warrant officer rank and below from any of the armed services flying in active operations against the enemy. The ribbon is pale blue with narrow dark blue edges.

Distinguished Service Medal

For Royal Navy and Royal Marines personnel of warrant officer rank and below who 'show themselves to the fore in action and set an example of bravery and resource under fire'. The ribbon is dark blue with two white central stripes. The round silver medal showed George VI's head on the obverse, while the reverse was similar to the style of the CGM above, but with the words 'For Distinguished Service'.

Distinguished Flying Medal

For Royal Navy and Royal Marines personnel of warrant officer rank and below who showed 'valour, courage or devotion to duty performed while flying in active operations against the enemy'. The ribbon has narrow violet and white diagonal stripes, with a silver opal medal carrying George VI's head on the obverse, while the reverse shows Athena Nike seated upon an aeroplane with a hawk rising from her hand and below this the words 'For Courage', as well as the date 1918.

Mention in Despatches Emblem

Available to all ranks and all services for those mention in despatches, but not receiving a

Distinguished Service Medal (DSM).

Distinguished Flying Medal (DFM).

higher award. For the Second World War, a bronze oak leaf emblem is worn on the War Medal ribbon at an angle of 60° from the inside edge of the ribbon, or as a smaller emblem worn horizontally when only the medal ribbon is worn.

CAMPAIGN MEDALS AND STARS

War Medal, 1939–45

All members of the armed forces received this providing they completed twenty-eight days' service between 03/09/39–02/09/45. The ribbon has five equal stripes of red, blue, white, blue, red, with a narrow red stripe in the centre of the white, with a single bronze oak leaf emblem if the wearer has been mentioned in despatches. The obverse of the medal has the crowned head of George VI, while the reverse shows a lion standing on a fallen dragon, with the dates '1939, 1945' at the top.

All stars were six-pointed, made of copper-zinc alloy, with the royal cypher, 'GRI', in script and with 'VI' below. The surrounding circlet, with a

crown at the top, carries the name of the star. The reverse is plain.

In the following, the qualifying time periods were ignored when service was ended by death, when the recipient was evacuated due to wounds or serious illness, or when the recipient was decorated or mentioned in despatches. Time spent as a PoW also counted. No more than five 'stars' could be held by any one recipient.

1939–1945 Star

Authorised in 1943 and originally known as the 1939–1943 Star, it was amended twice, first to 05/45, and then to 02/09/45. Awarded for six months' operational service to all services and all ranks. The ribbon has equal stripes of dark blue, red and pale blue (for RN, Army and RAF). A 'Battle of Britain' bar was authorised for fighter aircrew engaged in the battle, 10/07/40–31/10/40, and this was represented by a gilt heraldic rose when ribbons only were worn.

Atlantic Star

Commemorating the Battle of the Atlantic, and available to any one serving at sea, including

War Medal, 1939–1945, obverse and reverse.

1939–1945 Star

Merchant Navy, RAF and Army personnel. Unusual watered ribbon, so that the equal stripes are blue merging into white, merging into sea green.

Air Crew Europe Star

Awarded for two months' operational flying from UK bases over Europe up to 05/06/44, providing that the recipient had already qualified for the 1939–1945 Star. The ribbon has a pale blue centre bordered by narrow yellow stripes with slightly wider black edges for day and night operations. Two bars were authorised, 'Atlantic' and 'France and Germany', but only one could be worn, and the bar was represented by a silver heraldic rose when ribbons only were worn.

Africa Star

Awarded to anyone, including Merchant Navy, in the operational area between 10/06/40–12/05/43. The ribbon is pale buff, for the desert sand, with a central red stripe, with narrow dark blue left edge and light blue right edge stripes,

Campaign stars were six-pointed, made of copper-zinc alloy, with a plain reverse, while bars were represented by a silver heraldic rose when ribbons only were worn. From left to right: the Atlantic Star, the Air Crew Europe Star, the Africa Star. Below: the Pacific Star, the Burma Star, the Italy Star.

for the three services. Naval personnel have a bar, 'North Africa 1942–43', represented by a silver rose when ribbons only are worn.

Pacific Star

Awarded to anyone in the operational area, 08/12/41–02 /09/45, but RN and Merchant

Navy personnel had to have qualified for the 1939–45 Star first, even though this restriction was removed for the Army and RAF postwar. The ribbon has a dark green centre with a narrow yellow central stripe, for the forests and beaches of the Pacific, with red edges and narrower dark blue left and light blue right

The France and Germany Star (left). The Atlantic bar is shown (right).

stripes between the edges and the green. Because of the limitation on the number of stars that could be awarded, those who qualified for the Burma Star after first receiving the Pacific Star usually use the bar, 'Burma', which is represented by a silver heraldic rose when ribbons only are worn.

Burma Star

Awarded to anyone within the operational area, which included part of India, 11/12/41–02/09/45, the qualifying conditions were similar to those for the Pacific Star. The ribbon has a red centre with slightly wider edges of dark blue, orange-yellow and dark blue, equally divided. Again, there is a bar, 'Pacific', for those who qualified for the Pacific Star after first receiving a Burma Star.

Italy Star

Awarded to anyone in the operational area, 11/06/43–08/05/45, with no pre-conditions. The ribbon has five equal stripes, appropriately red, white, green, white, red.

France and Germany Star

Awarded for operational service on land, from 06/06/44, in France, the Low Countries and Germany, with no pre-conditions. The ribbon has five equal strips, blue, white, red, blue, white, for the colours of the Dutch and French flags. Those eligible for the Atlantic Star afterwards could wear the bar, 'Atlantic'.

In addition to the above, personnel from Canada, New Zealand, South Africa and Australia could qualify for their own national wartime medals, such as the New Zealand War Service Medal.

COMPARISON OF RANKS: ROYAL NAVY AND ARMY

OFFICERS

ROYAL NAVY		ARMY	
Admiral of the Fleet	(AF)	Field Marshal	(FM)
Admiral	(Adm)	General	(Gen)
Vice-Admiral	(Vice Adm)	Lieutenant-General	(Lt Gen)
Rear Admiral	(Rear Adm)	Major-General	(Maj Gen)
Commodore 2nd Class	(Cdre 2nd Cl)	Brigadier	(Brig)
Captain	(Capt)	Colonel	(Col)
Commander	(Cdr)	Lieutenant-Colonel	(Lt Col)
Lieutenant-Commander	(Lt Cdr)	Major	(Maj)
Lieutenant	(Lt)	Captain	(Capt)
Sub-Lieutenant	(Sub Lt)	First Lieutenant	(1/Lt)
Temporary Sub-Lieutenant	(Temp Sub Lt)	Second Lieutenant	(2/Lt)
Midshipman	(Mid)	no equivalent	
Warrant Officer	(WO)	no equivalent	
no equivalent		Sergeant Major (RSM and CSM)	(Sgt Maj)

Ratings (RN) and Non Commissioned Ranks

Chief Petty Officer	(CPO)	Colour Sergeant	(C/Sgt)
Petty Officer	(PO)	Sergeant	(Sgt)
Leading Airman	(LA)	Corporal	(Cpl)
Able Seaman	(AB)	no equivalent	
Ordinary Seaman	(OS)	Private	(Pte)

RM ranks were similar to those of the Army, but with a senior rank of Commandant General (Com Gen) and a lower rank of Marine, equivalent to Private.

(*Source: Imperial War Museum*)

APPENDIX V

THE FLEET AIR ARM MUSEUM

Founded in May, 1964, the Fleet Air Arm Museum has grown from its original collection of just six aircraft to more than forty, representing one of the largest collections devoted to naval aviation in the world. In addition to the aircraft, a wide range of displays deals with every aspect of naval air power, including one on the history of V/STOL, so vital to modern naval aviation. There are around 250 models of aircraft and ships.

The museum is based near Ilchester in Somerset, on the B3151, just off the A303. As the museum is constantly adding to its collection of restored aircraft and displays, and has some on loan to other collections, up-to-date information on the current collection can be found by accessing the museum's web-site, www.fleetairarm.com.

ABBREVIATIONS

(A)	Air Branch of the RN or RNVR
AA	Anti-aircraft
AB	Able seaman
ADDL	Aerodrome dummy deck landing
Adm	Admiral
AFC	Air Force Cross
ASH	Air-to-surface vessel radar (US built)
ASV	Air-to-surface vessel radar (British built)
BPF	British Pacific Fleet
CAG	Carrier Air Group
CAM-ship	Catapult-armed merchant vessel
Capt	Captain
CAP	Combat Air Patrol
CB	Commander of the Order of the Bath
CCA	Carrier controlled approach
Cdr	Commander
C-in-C	Commander-in-Chief
CMG	Companion of the Order of St Michael and St George
CO	Commanding Officer
CPO	Chief Petty Officer
CVE	Escort carrier, more usually known to the RN as auxiliary carriers
CVO	Commander of the Royal Victorian Order
DFC	Distinguished Flying Cross
DLCO	Deck Landing Control Officer, more usually known as the 'batsman'.
DLP	Deck landing practice
DLT	Deck landing training
DSO	Distinguished Service Order
DSC	Distinguished Service Cross
Dt	detachment
E-boat	German MTBs or MGBs
FAA	Fleet Air Arm
Flt	Flight
HMS	His Majesty's Ship
HMAS	His Majesty's Australian Ship
HMCS	His Majesty's Canadian Ship
KCB	Knight Commander of the Bath
Lt	Lieutenant
Lt Cdr	Lieutenant-Commander
MAC-ship	Merchant aircraft carrier (a merchant vessel with a flight deck)
MBE	Member of the British Empire
MONAB	Mobile Naval Air Base
MGB	Motor Gunboat
MTBs	Motor Torpedo Boat
MV	Motor Vessel
OBE	Officer of the British Empire
PO	Petty Officer
PR	Photo-Reconnaissance
RAAF	Royal Australian Air Force
RAF	Royal Air Force
RAN	Royal Australian Navy
RCAF	Royal Canadian Air Force
RCN	Royal Canadian Navy
RM	Royal Marines
RN	Royal Navy
RNethN	Royal Netherlands Navy
RANVR	Royal Australian Naval Volunteer Reserve
RCNVR	Royal Canadian Naval Volunteer Reserve
RNR	Royal Naval Reserve
RNVR	Royal Naval Volunteer Reserve
RNZNVR	Royal New Zealand Naval Volunteer Reserve
RP	rocket projectile
SANF(V)	South African Naval Force (Volunteer), equivalent of RNVR
SAAF	South African Air Force
TAG	Telegraphist Air Gunner
TBR	Torpedo Bomber Reconnaissance
TF	Task Force
TSR	Torpedo Spotter Reconnaissance
U-boat	German submarine
USN	United States Navy
USS	United States Ship
VC	Victoria Cross

BIBLIOGRAPHY

(Published in London unless otherwise stated)

Brooke, G., *Alarm Starboard: A Remarkable True Story of the War at Sea*, Cambridge, Patrick Stephens, 1982.

Clarke, J.D., *Gallantry Awards & Medals of the World*, Yeovil, Patrick Stephens, 1993.

Cunningham, Admiral of the Fleet Sir A., *A Sailor's Odyssey*, Hutchinson, 1951.

Gelb, N., *Desperate Venture*, Hodder & Stoughton, 1992.

Gould, R.W, *British Campaign Medals: Waterloo to the Falklands*, Arms & Armour, 1984.

Hanson, N., *Carrier Pilot*, Cambridge, Patrick Stephens, 1979.

Hickey, D. and Smith, G., *Operation Avalanche: Salerno Landings 1943*, Heinnemann, 1983.

Hobbs, C.D., *Aircraft Carriers of the Royal & Commonwealth Navies*, Greenhill Books, 1996.

Johnson, B., *Fly Navy*, Newton Abbot and London, David & Charles, 1981.

Kennedy, L., *Menace: The Life and Death of the Tirpitz*, Sidgwick & Jackson, 1979.

Kilbracken, Lord, *Bring Back My Stringbag: A Stringbag Pilot at War*, Pan Books, 1980.

Masters, A. O 'Cappy', *Memoirs of a Reluctant Batsman*, Janus, 1995.

Nichols, Cdr J.B., USN (Ret) and Pack, S.W.C., *Cunningham the Commander*, Batsford, London, 1974.

Poolman, K., *Escort Carrier: HMS Vindex at War*, Secker & Warburg, 1983.

Roskill, Capt., S.W., *The Navy at War, 1939–45*, HMSO, 1960.

——, *The War at Sea*, 1939–45, vols I–III, HMSO, 1976.

Sturtevant, R., and Balance, T., *The Squadrons of the Fleet Air Arm*, Tonbridge, Air Britain, 1994.

Thompson, J., *Imperial War Museum Book of the War at Sea, 1939–45: The Royal Navy in the Second World War*, IWM, 1996.

Vian, Adm Sir P., *Action This Day*, Muller, 1960.

Winton, J., *Air Power at Sea, 1939–45*, Sidgwick & Jackson, 1976.

——, *Carrier Glorious*, Leo Cooper, 1986.

——, *The Forgotten Fleet*, Michael Joseph, 1960.

Woodman, R., *Artic Convoys*, John Murray, 1974.

Woods, G.A, *Wings at Sea: A Fleet Air Arm Observer's War, 1940–45*, Conway Maritime, 1985.

Wragg, D., *Carrier Combat*, Stroud, Sutton, 1997.

——, *Wings Over The Sea: A History of Naval Aviation*, Newton Abbot and London, David & Charles, 1979.

INDEX

(Page numbers in *italics* refer to illustrations)